D1715867

Niles' Weekly
Register

HEZEKIAH NILES AS A YOUNG MAN

Niles' Weekly Register

News Magazine of the Nineteenth Century

By

NORVAL NEIL LUXON

GREENWOOD PRESS, PUBLISHERS
WESTPORT, CONNECTICUT

To the

American Newspaperman

Preface

AMERICAN newspapers and magazines and their editors deserve more attention than they have received from historians and biographers. Their influence, locally and nationally, has been felt in this country since Benjamin Harris published the first and only issue of *Publick Occurrences Both Forreign and Domestick* on September 26, 1690.

This work is a history of *Niles' Weekly Register* from 1811, when it was founded as the *Weekly Register,* to 1849, when the last number of *Niles' National Register* was printed. The extent of the influence of this one weekly publication on the American scene is examined and in some instances evaluated in the following pages. The book in its present form is a revision and condensation of a dissertation presented in partial fulfillment of the requirements for the degree of Doctor of Philosophy at the University of California at Los Angeles. The original study was an outgrowth of my interest in American journalism carried out upon the suggestion of and encouragement from the late John C. Parish of the University of California at Los Angeles, whose untimely death came before any of the chapters were in final shape although the outline of the work was practically completed.

In the absorbing task of examining each page of the seventy-six volumes of the *Register,* I found much of interest to myself and to many others which cannot be included here because of space limitations. If judgment has been faulty, blame for it is mine. As to spelling, punctuation, and capitalization in the numerous quotations from the *Register,* every passage has been reproduced exactly as printed in the periodical. An excessive use of *sic* has been avoided by not using it when the spelling of common or proper nouns and other words was merely an early-nineteenth-century variant of the accepted usage of today.

Preface

The manuscript in its original form was read and criticized by Louis Knott Koontz of the University of California at Los Angeles, to whom I hereby express my sincere appreciation. Joseph B. Lockey's criticism of form and style was invaluable. I am also indebted to Charles H. Titus and Brainerd Dyer of the University of California at Los Angeles and to Lawrence F. Hill of the Ohio State University for helpful suggestions.

To the officials and workers in the Library of Congress, the University of California at Los Angeles Library, the Los Angeles Public Library, the Henry E. Huntington Library, and the Ohio State University Library I express my appreciation for their assistance.

Finally, but by no means last in importance, acknowledgment, inadequate as it may be, must be made to the unflagging encouragement and steady assistance, in more ways than can here be detailed, of my wife, Ermina Munn Luxon.

NORVAL NEIL LUXON

Contents

Illustrations

Chapter 1

The Periodical

THE periodical customarily referred to as *Niles' Register* was published from September 7, 1811, to September 28, 1849. It had three names. The first two and one-half years it appeared each Saturday as the *Weekly Register;* the next twenty-three and one-half years it bore the title *Niles' Weekly Register;* and during the last twelve years this name was changed to *Niles' National Register,* descriptive of the scope rather than of the periodicity of the publication.

None of these names described the publication adequately in the light of present-day terminology, for none advertised its purpose as a magazine of current news as well as a formal record for future use. It may be stretching a point to call it a forerunner of the news magazine of today, except in priority, but a cursory reading of almost any of its hundreds of different issues will demonstrate that the *Register* differed markedly from the weekly newspapers and other weekly magazines of its day.

The *Register* was founded in Baltimore by Hezekiah Niles who edited it for twenty-five years and who hoped that it would remain in the possession of his descendants. In this desire however he was doomed to disappointment, for, six months after his death, it was sold by his heirs.

To Niles belongs the credit for the conception of the idea of such a periodical. He visualized the value of a publication with the dual purpose of printing significant news for contemporaries and of preserving for posterity speeches, documents, messages, and correspondence of public officials. Thus, he felt, he would mirror for the future a true picture of the period. That he succeeded is indicated by the widespread use made of the *Register* by historians and other students seeking a contemporary picture of the first half of the nineteenth century in America.

In the prospectus for the proposed work, which was printed on June 24, 1811, and reprinted in the first issue of the *Register*, Niles promised that each number would contain one-fourth more material than was carried in the largest of the newspapers and assured his readers that it promised "something interesting at the present moment, and, as a BOOK OF REFERENCE, a FUND OF READING always at hand, a work of much probable value." The title page of each volume described the publication as "Containing Political, Historical, Geographical, Scientific, Astronomical, Statistical and Biographical Documents, Essays and Facts; Together with the Notices of Arts and Manufactures, and a Record of the Events of the Times."

The motto by which the *Register* is known to historians and journalists, "The Past—The Present—For the Future," was not adopted until 1817. Niles apparently was the author of this slogan, which so succinctly described the purpose of the periodical. It replaced a quotation from Virgil which had been carried on the *Register*'s first page since 1812. This motto, *"Haec olim meminisse juvabit,"* also expressed Niles' feeling of responsibility to the future reader, as did the Shakespearean quotation from Henry VIII, carried in Volume I:

"———— I wish no other herald,
"No other speaker of *my living actions,*
"To keep mine honor from corruption
"But such an honest chronicler."

The nature of the *Register* made it virtually a one-man publication, and so it remained. Niles had an assistant for a time in 1816 and from 1827 to 1830 had his son, William Ogden Niles, as an associate, but much of the time the labor of collecting and compiling the news articles and of writing the editorials fell upon his shoulders alone. He had set his heart upon rounding out twenty-five years as editor of fifty volumes of the *Register,* and after an accident had incapacitated him, he advertised in April, 1836, for an assistant. Hezekiah Niles' name was carried at the head of the first page as editor and publisher through the fiftieth volume, but he was paralyzed on the right side during the last three months of this period, and his son edited the *Register,* although no announcement was made until

THE WEEKLY REGISTER.

Vol. I.]   BALTIMORE, SATURDAY, September 7, 1811.   [No 1.

" ————I wish no other herald,
" No other speaker of *my living actions,*
" To keep mine honor from corruption
" But such an honest chronicler."
Shakspeare—HENRY VIII.

Printed and published by H. NILES, Water-street, near the Merchants' Coffee-House, at $5 per an.

THE EDITOR TO THE PUBLIC.

Custom forms a *"common law"*—it is second nature. A first number without an address would outrage the law: as we propose to demean ourselves in the most peaceable manner, we submit to the law, and offer our thanks for the very liberal patronage our work has received in many parts of the Union.

The current of sentiment is evidently in *our* favor *(we* say *our,* for *printers* and *kings* have an unquestionable right, by the aforesaid law, to make *much* of themselves)—the unusual number of sub scribers already obtained, convinces the editor that his opinion was just as to the want of a work such as the WEEKLY REGISTER is intended to be ; but while so great success flatters his pride and provokes his exertion, it also alarms his fears, lest, in despite of all he can do, the public expectation may be disappointed, though to guard against this, he has made some extensive as well as expensive preparations.

In arranging his matter for the first number, the editor has compared himself to a young shop keeper (just commencing business) suddenly thrust into an immense warehouse of most valuable goods.— His eye is pleased with a great variety of articles, and his judgment convinced they would, in due season, answer his customers—but he cannot pur chase all; and, hurried by the quantities before him, perhaps, selects some things that, *for the present,* he had better leave untouched, though ultimately and unquestionably good. As time tempers his judg ment, and experience, the great teacher, enlightens his views, he enters the same warehouse without palpitation, and deliberately lays off such articles as are adapted to the wants of his neighbors. We hope thus to meet the wishes of our numerous friends ; and trust that, by a *single number,* they will not attempt to judge the merits of our work—as its utility (if any it shall have) will not become so manifest before several are joined together.

Some have feared we should "dabble too much in politics "—i. e. *party* politics ; and others have ap prehended "the work will not stand." It is in our power to remove the first cause of apprehension— but the latter depends on the public as well as ourselves. The first shall be removed, as the REGIS TER proceeds—it is not intended for *electioneering* purposes, of course *party* politics will be avoided ; yet, by the insertion of original and selected essays, on both sides of great national questions, we shall feel it our duty to preserve a history of the feelings of the times on men and things. If we have discovered the rock on which our predecessors have shipwrecked, the second cause of apprehension may, perhaps, be removed. We attribute the gene ral failure of periodical publications to too great a dependence on voluntary contributions from persons without an *interest* in the work, whose spirit flags when novelty ceases to charm. Though we

intend to pay the most grateful attention to communications of this kind, and hereby respectfully solicit them, still we have made no calculation upon them, except so far as they relate to the arts and sciences—to manufactures—and to agriculture, in which, from the public patriotism, we hope for considerable aid. We may sometimes do our work roughly, but for our own sakes (that is, the editor and those associated with him) will attend to it diligently ; and by close application strive to render it useful.

This number is to be regarded as a fair sample of the paper and manner in which the work will be *uniformly* printed. Further to manifest our views and intentions, the patrons of the REGISTER are informed, that the Editor proposes, among his selections, to insert the official reports of *Alexander Hamilton* and *Albert Gallatin,* Esquires, on the manufactures of the United States, also the report of the latter on *Roads* and *Canals;* likewise to publish *Mr. Jefferson's* celebrated report on weights and measures.—When the present secretaries of State and of the Treasury shall lay their respective reports before Congress on the population, manufactures, &c. of the United States, they shall be given to our readers as a single number, however voluminous they may be—and to the report of the former shall be prefixed the state of population as ascertained by the census of 1790 and 1800 and such other facts as can be collected relating to the same subject at more distant periods ; so that, by comparison, the rising importance of our country may be duly esteemed.* *Mr. John Quincy Adams'* letter to *Harrison Gray Otis,* Esq. as containing an admirable history of the causes which produced the *embargo,* and rendered necessary some other important acts of the government, shall have place in the Register. *Mr. Pickering's* political essays shall also be recorded in an *extra* number or numbers ; likewise *Mr Robert Smith's* address, with the " *Review* " of it, published in the *National Intelligencer. These things are particularised merely to shew our general design.*

In the original prospectus we promised only twenty six numbers to a volume—it is more than probable they will exceed thirty perhaps amount to thirty-two. For this extra expense, if incurred, we shall seek indemnification in the hope of pleas ing the public, and so increase our patronage ; with which we will try to keep pace.

As a proper close for this article we put on record the prospectus for the WEEKLY REGISTER, as first issued from the press—

* *The Editor respectfully gives notice* to the trade, *that he intends to print an extra number of these tracts for sale, with which he will supply booksellers and others on very liberal terms. Mr. P's essays will be printed in 18mo—the pocket size, on a beautiful better type, and fine paper.*

A

the first number of the fifty-first volume. The son edited the magazine from 1836 to 1839, at the end of which time it was taken over by Jeremiah Hughes, who was the editor and publisher through February, 1848, when it was temporarily suspended. When publication was resumed in July, 1848, George Beatty, the new editor and publisher, had moved the office to Philadelphia where the periodical ceased publication on September 28, 1849, after a series of ineffectual attempts to keep it alive.

The size of the *Register* invariably surprises the reader who thinks of it as a newspaper. For twenty-five years, during which the first fifty volumes appeared, it was medium octavo, and the bound volumes of 416 or more pages are no larger than the average book. The actual size was six and one-eighth by nine and five-eighths inches. The type page was five by eight and one-half inches, divided into two columns. When William Ogden Niles took over the publication, he enlarged it to quarto size, and the last twenty-six volumes retained this format. Actual size was eight and one-half by twelve and one-half inches, with a type page of seven and one-eighth by ten and three-fourths inches which was later altered to seven and three-eighths by ten and five-eighths inches. There were now three columns to a page.

The periodical was printed on good paper throughout its career as one can readily see by examining copies today, more than a century after publication. Hezekiah Niles had promised "fine super-royal paper" in his prospectus. Type size was small, compared with the modern trend to larger and more legible types. In the prospectus he had promised that the periodical would be printed in nonpareil or brevier, but in practice little brevier was used and fonts of agate and pearl were employed extensively, in spite of repeated protests by readers, whose eyesight must have been put to a severe strain.

Niles' long experience as a printer is reflected in the typographical appearance of the *Register*. He frequently bought new fonts of type and never permitted the type to become worn so as to mar its appearance and legibility. This typographical excellence was not generally maintained by his successors, although his son did away almost entirely with the use of the very small type, and Jeremiah Hughes in 1841 installed a new Baltimore-manufactured type. The last few volumes published by Hughes show very plainly the worn condition of the type.

There was little typographical display. The headline had not yet made its appearance in American journalism, and most of the items had captions of 10-point light capitals over them, if, indeed, any at all. Such standing captions as "Foreign News," "Foreign Items," "Proceedings of Congress," "The Nation's Guest" (used for months over accounts of Lafayette's trip), "A Chronicle" (used over a department of miscellaneous items for years), "Politics," "Postscript" (inserted over last-minute news of importance for which the press was often stopped), and "Events of the War" (used through the War of 1812), are typical. Sometimes the caption gave more of a hint of the contents of the article as "Free Negroes" and "New Tariff." Some of the main departmental captions were set in 14-point type, boldface being used at some periods and lightface at others.

The first page contained the nameplate in 18-point (later 24-point) bold caps, and the usual information about volume and number, editor, place of publication, date, and subscription price. More often than not the first-page articles had no captions, although no rule was followed. Variety marked the order of departments, except that "A Chronicle" usually appeared on the last page, or, at least, near the back of each issue.

Hezekiah Niles used italic type extensively to emphasize points in his editorials. Almost every issue published under his direction serves as an example of this practice. Much less common, but still seen frequently, was his use of capital letters for emphasis.

Illustrations were practically nonexistent in the *Register*. In an appendix to an early volume, a drawing of a steam engine was printed. In 1822 a one-column drawing of a new hay and grain rake adorned the columns, and during the Mexican War two thirds of the first page of an issue, which devoted fifteen of its sixteen pages to the war, was occupied by two maps.

The first use made by the *Register* of a striking typographical display was when it turned its column rules on all sixteen pages in the April 10, 1841, number carrying the news of the death of President Harrison. Seven years later, February 26, 1848, when the news of John Quincy Adams' death was printed, the four horizontal rules below the periodical's nameplate were turned, with the one-column cut-off rules above and below the caption on his obituary also reversed.

Each issue contained 16 pages, making a total of 416 pages for a volume of 26 numbers. However, Niles was prodigal in the issuance of free supplements, usually of a half-sheet, that is, 8 pages, and many volumes ran nearer 500 pages. After the change to quarto size, there was no deviation from the 16-page size.

Because his subscribers objected so strenuously to the use of small type, Niles, in the *Register* for December 4, 1813, suggested that they vote on increasing by half or doubling the size of the periodical, with a concurrent increase in the subscription price to $7.00. The change was to be made only if the majority approved and no reply would indicate opposition. The proposal was not approved.

In the early thirties, Niles printed many twenty-four-page numbers instead of issuing supplements. Undoubtedly, better press facilities enabled him to use this plan, and on at least three occasions he doubled the size of the *Register* and printed thirty-two pages. This plan of printing supplements and large issues was expensive and brought in no extra income, but it enabled him to give a more nearly complete coverage to his subscribers.

One typographical oddity which strikes the modern reader was the practice of running articles from the last page of an issue to the first page of the succeeding one without a break. In the early years of the *Register*, articles were frequently continued from one number to another with an intervening break of several pages, but later, Niles, thinking as always of his future readers, followed the plan of arranging his make-up so that there was no break. Thus, now and then the first page of a number presented, often without headline or other identification, the continuation of a document, letter, or court decision.

The *Register* carried no advertising. In consequence of that policy every line of the available space was devoted to its editorial contents, and Hezekiah Niles' promise that the periodical would print more news than the largest of the newspapers was fulfilled during much of its career. Most of the daily newspapers of the time consisted of only four pages, with much of the space occupied by advertisements.

Circulation figures, before the advent of publishers' sworn statements and co-operative bureaus which today have access to the office records of newspapers and periodicals, are open to question. The publisher's unsupported statement is the only evidence available in the case of the *Register,* but Niles' unimpeachable integrity gives these figures more weight than those of editors with less enviable reputations.

The *Register* started with 1,500 subscribers, a fact which may be explained by noting that they were invited to take the periodical for six months before remitting the $5.00 subscription for the first year. At the end of the fourth number, the list had grown to 1,893, and two weeks later the names of 2,144 were on the books. At the end of the first year of publication, 3,300 received the weekly, although the editor was compelled to observe in the August 29, 1812, issue that many subscribers were in arrears. By February 27, 1813, the list had grown to 3,700, but because of nonpayment of subscriptions Niles cut 500 names from the rolls, saying, "No man shall patronize me for two years by the use of his *name* only." At the close of this volume he noted that "if the REGISTER yields to no work in America as to the number of copies printed, it has equal high ground in regard to the respectability of its subscribers."

There apparently was a gradual increase in the circulation of the periodical over the next decade, for the editor took many opportunities to mention increases of one hundred within a month, "many" during a year, and two hundred within three months without "any extraordinary exertion" on his part. At the end of volumes and calendar years, Niles liked to take a retrospective glance at his circulation lists, and mention the increases, although in his New Year's editorial in 1821 he was forced to take solace in the thought that his list had not been diminished, something, he felt sure, "few others of his fellow publishers" could say. The next year, in the April 6, 1822, issue, in a discussion of the influence of power in industry, he incidentally mentioned the 4,500 copies of the *Register* printed each week by the "four able workmen" in his office. In 1827 and 1831 he wrote of the great increase in the demand for numbers,

NILES' WEEKLY REGISTER.

No. 1 of vol. VI.]   BALTIMORE, SATURDAY, March 5, 1814.   [whole no. 131.

Hæc olim meminisse juvabit.—Virgil.

Printed and published by H. Niles, South-st. next door to the Merchants' Coffee House, at $5 per annum.

CONDITIONS OF THE WEEKLY REGISTER.

The Weekly Register is published at *Baltimore* every Saturday, at *$5 per annum*, payable in advance; making two heavy volumes a year, of between 4 and 500 pages each. It is packed with great care and sent off by the mails of the day, safely, to the most distant post-offices in the United States. The work began September 7, 1811; the second volume, March 7, 1812; the third, September 5; the fourth, March 6, 1813; the fifth, September 4; the sixth commences this day. New subscribers may be furnished from the first number, or from any of the volumes, by paying for the volumes required, with the current year in advance. The safety of the mail is guaranteed, so as to preserve the files of subscribers (except in *Louisiana* and some parts of the *Mississippi* territory) and missing numbers are liberally furnished, without charge, in all cases, to a reasonable extent. A *supplement* will speedily be published for the fifth, or last volume, for which those desiring to have it will pay *one dollar extra. Subscribers must begin and end with a volume.* Letters to the editor should be post-paid; and *especially those of* gentlemen *who request favors.*

Editorial retrospect and remarks.

The editor looks back on his labors of the last six months, with a consciousness that he did all that his judgment or ability allowed, to requite the great patronage bestowed: this feeling of honest pride, acquired by patient industry, is amply supported by the continually increasing subscriptions of the most distinguished citizens of the United States, of either [American] party.

Two things designed to have been inserted in the last volume were postponed, not neglected: 1, an U. S. army and navy list; and 2, a collection of statistical facts and remarks to shew the *madness* of faction. Just at the time when the names of the officers in the army and navy *officially* appeared, so many promotions took place, and so many new dispositions were made, that we thought it best to suspend a publication of the list in the hope of obtaining one more perfect and settled. Towards the other, which promises to be a work of considerable labor, some progress was made; but the want of certain documents, which it was hoped would have appeared some months ago, has prevented a conclusion. We shall shew, so "that he who runs may read," that the *"commerce,"* about which some persons clamor so much, must needs be an insignificant thing, without an intercourse with those states, they (the *foolish* men of the east) are pleased to call *anti-commercial*.

It is, indeed, a painful duty to notice the late disgraceful proceedings and movements in the state of *Massachusetts.* We have not to reprehend a few factious printers, "writers," smugglers or *British* agents, only; but the *legislative* body of that important member of the confederacy. Live the constitution! is the first and the last article of my politics; the "alpha and omega" of the peace, liberty and safety of my country; and if, in exposing or

Vol. VI

condemning those that would destroy it, or weaken its bonds, I offend any,—let them be offended. I have no part, interest or feeling; nay, hardly *charity*, for the *British antifederal* faction alluded to.

Perhaps, it is one of the most serious misfortunes suffered by the people of the United States, *as politicians*, that rather than fairly disavow and abandon the party to which by accident, through interest, or even by reason and reflection they may have attached themselves, too many, indirectly, support and encourage others in a course of proceeding which they, as individuals, seriously deprecate and condemn. I do not pretend to say that either of our *two* great parties is clear of this censure; but there is a portion of one of them, under the comely garb of *federalism*, to whom it applies with full force.— Let me ask those who *really* are "federalists," who honestly and sincerely receive Washington's Farewell Address, as the rule and guide of their political faith, how it is possible they can act with the faction at *Boston*—a faction that daily flies in the face of the most solemn precepts of the illustrious dead? *Washington* charged us always to speak of the *union of the states* with reverence. He most pointedly directed us to "*frown indignantly upon the first dawnings of an attempt to alienate one portion of the union from the rest, or enfeeble the sacred ties that now link its various parts.*" He directed us to suppose a dissolution of the union as impossible as to avoid death;—with this view, that while a looking to the latter, as certainty, might excite us to the improvement of our lives in our duty to GOD—the former should lead us, by social, intellectual and commercial intercourse, by roads, bridges and canals and other permanent works, to "strengthen the bonds that made us one people," and quiet the haggard spirit of jealousy that a *foreign influence* might introduce to divert the resources and check the prosperity of the republic. Little did that great man believe that in ten or fifteen years after his death, men in *Boston*, the "cradle of the revolution," should coldly sit down and *calculate a separation of the states.* Less did he suppose that in the *legislature of Massachusetts*, the *expediency* of that diabolical measure should become a question of debate! Much less did he believe that the faction which proposed, supported and encouraged such notions, would fasten upon *his* name, and cloak *their* baseness with *his* virtues. Unmanly hypocrites! thus to abuse the memory of the dead; and, as far as in you lies, to ascribe to the deceased a depravity that he would have looked into annihilation! The best of you—the most exalted and distinguished of all the clan, would never have *dared*, hypothetically, to have spoken of a dissolution of the union, in the presence of *Washington*, no more than (if the comparison may be allowed, and with a feeling reverence it is offered) an *atheist* would have attempted to reason with him on the existence a Supreme Being. He would have said to you, *"That* is a subject on which I never converse; for I would not have it *supposed* to be *possible*,"* or he would have turned on

---

* I am fully warranted in ascribing those words to the supposed occasion, by every line of the *Farewell Address*—read it over carefully.

and on October 8, 1831, engaging in one of his editorial jousts with Thomas Ritchie of the *Richmond Enquirer,* boasted of an increase of 752 subscribers in nine months, saying that he now printed 4,104 copies, requiring 171 quires of paper for every number. These figures indicate that the circulation of the *Register* remained between 3,500 and 4,500 throughout at least the first two thirds of its life. In commenting on the purchase of a new press shortly after he took over the *Register's* management, William Ogden Niles wrote on December 3, 1836, that he published "within a fraction of 3,500 copies." Circulation figures are not mentioned specifically thereafter and one may assume that there probably was a gradual decline in the subscription list after the retirement of the founder.

Hezekiah Niles never let the fear of public disapproval of his policies alter his editorial course. His tariff fight and his strong opposition to the Congressional caucus, which are discussed in detail in later chapters, brought subscription cancellations, but in no way influenced him. A concerted campaign in the South to induce subscribers to cancel their subscriptions because of the *Register's* stand on the protective tariff caused a number to quit, but friends of the tariff and of fair play more than made up the loss, and in the first issue of 1829 he declared that new subscriptions during the past year had amounted to 646 with 320 discontinuances, making a net gain of 326. "At this rate, we shall not soon be broken down," he wrote. Reviewing other editorial battles which reduced his subscription lists in localities affected, he recalled the severe curtailment in the New England states which followed his fight against the Hartford Convention, and the attempts made by politicians to boycott the *Register* while he was campaigning against the caucus in the early twenties. He concluded by humorously inferring that many who quit were far in arrears in their payments, saying, "We would, however, respectfully suggest, that when individuals get angry with us, and order this paper stopped, they will recollect what is due from themselves as *gentlemen;* or become so *very angry* as to hurl a 5, 10 or 20 dollar bank note at us, as they may be indebted, without further trouble to themselves or us."

The *Register* cost the subscriber $5.00 per year plus postage, a rate which was maintained for thirty-seven years. It was not

until the seventy-fifth volume that this was lowered to $4.00.
A further cut to $3.00 was announced in the three issues of the
seventy-sixth volume, although it is unlikely that either offer
enticed many to subscribe.

The circulation was national in character. Less than three
months after the periodical was founded, the editor said in the
November 30, 1811, issue that it literally circulated from "Maine
to Georgia, and from the Atlantic beyond the Mississippi."
Twelve years later, on October 25, 1823, Niles asserted that it
was sent to from 700 to 800 post offices each week. He listed by
state and territory the 198 new subscribers he had received in
five months. Twenty-four states, the District of Columbia, and
Arkansas Territory were on the list, and he remarked that the
Territory of Michigan was the only district in the country that
was not represented by a new subscriber. There also was a considerable foreign circulation. Statesmen and politicians of the
day took and paid for the *Register*. John Adams wrote of the
receipt of eleven volumes; [1] Thomas Jefferson was a regular
subscriber; [2] Andrew Jackson had a complete file, at least for
the first dozen years; [3] and Madison [4] and Lafayette [5] had correspondence with Niles regarding their subscriptions. Congress
subscribed for ten copies for the use of members,[6] and the government supplied copies to its representatives in foreign countries.[7]

One circulation problem which added to the expense of publication and caused many editorial skirmishes was that of exchanges with newspapers. As this was before the day of co-
operative news-gathering agencies, newspapers and periodicals

[1] *Register*, XII, 161, May 10, 1817, where his letter is printed.

[2] Niles to Jefferson, September 11, 1816; Jefferson to Niles, August 22, 1817, and December 9, 1818, Jefferson MSS, Library of Congress. *Id.* to *id.*, May 6, 1826, printed in *Register*, LXVI, 146, May 4, 1844. This last letter was picked up in Paris in 1844 by an autograph hunter, and a copy sent to the Boston *Atlas* by its Paris correspondent.

[3] *Id.* to Jackson, July 23, 1823, thanking him for the receipt of $10, mailed on June 9. Jackson MSS, Library of Congress.

[4] *Id.* to Madison, March 6, 1818, apologizing for his office's error in not sending the *Register* for the past year. Madison MSS, Library of Congress.

[5] Lafayette to Niles, June 28, 1831, printed in *Register*, XLI, 39, September 17, 1831.

[6] *Register*, XXXIII, 265, December 22, 1827.

[7] *Register*, XII, 404, August 23, 1817.

freely copied items from each other's columns, and the *Register*
was in great demand among newspaper editors the country over.
Niles started with the policy of exchanging with those who
would pay him the difference between their subscription price
and his, but he found that many of his editorial brethren forgot
to remit this difference.[8] Within a decade after founding the
Register he wrote that he was receiving at least "an hundred
newspapers that are of little, if any, use to us—indeed perhaps
worse than useless, as the receipt of them imposes an obligation
to open and examine them. . . ." This obligation apparently
was a real one to Niles, who referred to it in discussions of his
exchange problem year after year.[9]

The irregularity of the mails and the inefficiency of postmasters troubled Niles constantly. He prided himself on the
way in which he met the deadline each week and in the care
which he took to have the *Register* carefully wrapped and addressed for mailing.[10] As a result, negligence on the part of the
post office department exasperated him, and he even went so
far at times as to express the suspicion that the slowness and
irregularity of the deliveries were not without an ulterior motive.[11] This failure of the post office to deliver the *Register*
expeditiously caused from fifty to a hundred subscribers to
cancel their subscriptions annually, he wrote in 1823, and ten
years later when the post office department was under criticism,
he said that he "could well afford to give the present incumbent
[William T. Barry] a 'retiring pension' of $200 a year, (for
our share), provided a competent man was put in his place." [12]

[8] *Register,* XVII, 385, February 5, 1820; XXI, 289, January 5, 1822; XXXI, 33,
September 16, 1826; XL, 417, August 17, 1831, are typical of dozens of editorials
on this subject.

[9] For typical comments see *Register,* XX, 193, May 26, 1821; XXXII, 305, July
7, 1827; XXXIII, 17, September 8, 1827; XXXVII, 289, January 2, 1830; XLIII, 39,
September 15, 1832.

[10] Descriptions of the pains taken to ensure delivery of the *Register* in good
condition may be found in *Register,* I, 449, February 22, 1812; II, 47, March 21,
1812; IV, 1, March 6, 1813; XXV, 122–23, October 25, 1823; XXXII, 161, May 5,
1827.

[11] Scores of citations on this point might be made; the following illustrate the
belief: *Register,* V, 121, October 23, 1813; VI, 41, March 19, 1814; IX, 389, February 3, 1816; XX, 97, April 14, 1821; XLIV, 49, March 23, 1833; XLVI, 1, March 1,
1834; XLVIII, 145, May 2, 1835.

[12] *Register,* XXV, 65, October 4, 1823; XLV, 147, November 2, 1833.

From the beginning he fought to get newspaper postage, which was cheaper than that for magazines or pamphlets, for the *Register*, and when Gideon Granger, postmaster general in 1812, ruled that the *Register* was a "newspaper and to be rated at News-paper postage," Niles used this as precedent and cited it as authority whenever a subscriber complained that a postmaster was charging the higher rate.[13]

In a period when the average life span of a magazine was two years or less and when publication of those that survived was none too regular, the record of the *Register* is truly phenomenal. It went into the mails Saturday after Saturday with clocklike regularity. The British attack on Baltimore in the War of 1812 caused the first interruption when all of the employees, "one small boy excepted," were engaged in military duties. Three issues were published in the five weeks from September 3 to October 1, 1814, but the missing ones were made up by two extra numbers in October and December.[14] Thus, the subscribers had their full quota of numbers for the volume.

Delays in publication after the war were infrequent during Hezekiah Niles' editorship. The lack of paper held up one issue, the death of his first wife another, the death of a son a third, and once he mailed an issue late in order to permit prior publication of a convention report in New York.[15] His son was less successful in meeting publication deadlines, and the first few numbers after the move to Washington, D. C., were late. After Hezekiah Niles' death, the periodical was temporarily suspended

[13] Letter to Niles, January 13, 1812, *Register*, I, 361, January 18, 1812; VII, 305, January 14, 1815; VII, 368, February 4, 1815; XXX, 137, April 22, 1826; in an editorial (XLIV, 82, April 6, 1833) Niles irately wrote: "The occasion is here apt to observe, that some blockheads, recently appointed postmasters, have undertaken to call the REGISTER a 'pamphlet,' and charge postage accordingly. That question was settled by the postmaster general, *Gideon Granger*, in 1812. The law no more prescribes the form of a *newspaper* than it establishes the color of a man's eyes, or the length of one's nose; and, as the REGISTER contains more *news* than any weekly newspaper published in the United States, the lowest rate of postage can only be legally charged upon it."

[14] *Register*, VI, 448, August 27, 1814. This was actually published on September 1, but carried the earlier date in order to preserve continuity (see VI, 443); VII, 49, October 6, 1814; 97, October 27, 1814; 113, October 29, 1814; 209–40, December 10, 1814. Two sixteen-page numbers were published on this last date.

[15] *Register*, VIII, 1, March 4, 1815; XXVI, 217, June 5, 1824; XLI, 1, September 3, 1831; 201, November 12, 1831.

for eleven weeks. Five of these missing numbers were made up by William Ogden Niles, and the other six by Jeremiah Hughes, who observed publication dates thereafter closely.[16] Following a four months' suspension in 1848, the magazine was sold. The last editor was late with many numbers and finally suspended publication through July, August, and early September, 1849, before publishing the last three issues.

Some subscribers had the *Register* sent to them in bound volumes at the end of each six months' period, and many who became subscribers after the periodical was well launched bought the preceding volumes in order to have a complete file. At the time of his retirement Niles had on hand 250 sets of the 50 volumes.[17]

Neither the regular subscriptions nor the complete sets were sold without hard work on the part of the editor and publisher. While the *Register* carried no advertising, it devoted space in many issues to circulation promotion. The prospectus printed in the first number outlined in detail the plan to be followed,[18] and often in the course of his ownership Niles called attention to the comprehensiveness of the coverage of the *Register,* and, in discussing coming events, suggested that excellent accounts of them could be obtained by reading the publication. He argued against the idea that the *Register* was expensive, writing that two volumes usually contained "about or more than 900 pages, or *four million five hundred thousand 'ems.'* . . . and a greater quantity of *reading* or *record* matter than any similar work, being without advertisements or other things 'that perish in the using.' " He also stressed its convenient size.[19]

Early volumes were dedicated to military and naval heroes and to the manufacturers of the nation, a proceeding designed to create good will. In 1816 he presented eight volumes to Commander John Rodgers, as a tribute, and printed his accompany-

---

[16] *Register,* LIII, 1, September 2, 1837; LVI, 145–320, May 4 to July 13, 1839. The casual reader probably would not suspect that these were printed several months after the dates on the respective first pages.

[17] *Register,* LI, 1, September 3, 1836. A 25 per cent discount was offered on 150 sets, the remaining ones to be retained to supply future wants.

[18] *Register,* I, 2, September 7, 1811.

[19] *Register,* XXVII, 401, February 26, 1825; XXXIX, 457, February 26, 1831; XLVI, 291, June 21, 1834; 393, August 9, 1834; XLVIII, 58, March 28, 1835.

ing letter and Rodgers' reply, which praised "the intrinsic merit of your work, and the public benefits which have resulted from it." [20]

In 1817 Niles wrote to Andrew Jackson, James Madison,[21] John Adams, Thomas Jefferson, and other public figures, asking their opinion of the *Register,* "to be spread before the people." He hoped that the influence of their replies would serve to counteract any ill effects his new policy of demanding cash in advance would have on the *Register*'s circulation, a policy, it may be parenthetically remarked, never carried out *in toto.* Jefferson's reply was prompt. He wrote: "I have found it very valuable as a Repository of documents, original papers and the facts of the day, and for the ease with which the index enables us to turn to them. . . . If payment for the paper in advance can save it, I think that no one should object to that. It is as reasonable and as safe for your readers to trust you, as you them." With this letter Jefferson sent a year's subscription in advance.[22] No evidence exists that the others replied, although it is probable that they did for they were subscribers and had correspondence with Niles on other matters. Niles apparently did not make use of Jefferson's letter in the *Register* itself, but may have included it and others in circulars inserted in the *Register,* few of which have survived.

Niles frequently urged his subscribers to show copies of the *Register* to their friends and neighbors, saying that was the best way to advertise it.[23] He printed prospectuses describing the

[20] *Register,* IV (reverse of title page) is dedicated to Zebulon Montgomery Pike and James Lawrence; Volume V (reverse of title page) to Brigadier General Leonard Covington, who died in Canada, and Lieutenant William Burrows of the Navy, killed in an engagement; Volume VIII (reverse of title page); X, 153, May 4, 1816.

[21] July 31, 1817. Jackson MSS, Library of Congress; July, 1817 (no day), Madison MSS, Library of Congress. These two letters are identical, except for several mistakes in writing; in each, he mentions that he is sending "exactly similar" letters to seven others, naming them.

[22] August 22, 1817. Jefferson MSS, Library of Congress.

[23] *Register,* XX, 385, August 18, 1821; XXXVII, 289, January 2, 1830; attention of subscribers was called to enclosed prospectuses in *Register,* XVII, 209, December 4, 1819; XXI, 33, September 15, 1821; XXVIII, 241, June 18, 1825. Few of these pieces of promotion have survived, but occasionally one is found bound in a volume. One dated May 9, 1835, was found by the author in Volume XLVIII, inserted between pp. 182–83 in the volume in the Library of the University of

periodical at intervals, enclosing one with each copy, asking that the recipient pass it on to a potential subscriber.

When William Ogden Niles moved the publication office to Washington he received editorial good wishes from nearly one hundred newspapers,[24] and later made good use of these kindly messages by including excerpts from twenty-nine of the most flattering in a prospectus, printed in September, 1838, and inserted in the September 15 number.[25] Prospectuses issued by Jeremiah Hughes outlined his policies, described the improvements he had made, and called attention to the value of the *Register* as a permanent record where "impartial truth" might be found.[26]

The promotion activities kept the circulation of the *Register* at a respectable level, but they did not bring cash into the counting room. Subscriptions to American magazines were seldom paid in advance, which undoubtedly contributed to their high mortality. English magazines, on the contrary, were distributed through dealers who paid the publisher monthly, a fact pointed out in the London *Monthly Magazine*.[27] From the conclusion of the first volume until the *Register* perished from financial famine, the ever-growing total of accounts receivable on its books was a source of constant worry to the four successive owners.

At the end of the first year of publication, a third of the *Register*'s subscribers were delinquent in their payments. Niles wrote in the November 7, 1812, issue that the arrearages to-

California at Los Angeles. It is an excellent piece of newspaper promotion literature.

[24] *Register*, LII, 385, August 19, 1837.

[25] This circular was found in Volume LV, inserted between pp. 40–41 in the volume at the University of California at Los Angeles. It is not bound in other copies of the volume examined by the author. Among the newspapers quoted are Charleston *Mercury*, Richmond *Enquirer*, St. Louis *Republican*, Zanesville *Gazette*, *United States Gazette* of New York, *Mercantile Advertiser*, Boston *Atlas*.

[26] Apparently Hughes mailed a prospectus with the title page and index to a volume. Those described were bound with the title pages to Volumes LIX and LX at the University of California at Los Angeles. Hughes also used the plan of mailing sample copies direct to prospective subscribers (*Register*, LVII, 113, October 19, 1839).

[27] The editorial comment of the London *Monthly Magazine* contrasting the English plan of sale of magazines by the month with the subscription plan in the United States is quoted in *Register*, XXIV, 51–52, March 29, 1823.

taled $5,000, which "greatly embarrassed the editor, as well as thwarting many favorite schemes for adding value to the work, in maps, plates, and supplements." On June 5, 1813, he wrote there was due the establishment "the enormous sum of from 10 to 12,000 dollars." This amount had grown to $25,000 by 1824, and at the time of Hezekiah Niles' retirement $40,000 was outstanding on his books.[28] Two years after he had taken over the periodical William Ogden Niles wrote that there was *"nearly thirty thousand dollars due upon our books! a tithe of which would free us from all difficulty and embarrassment."* [29]

The expense of publishing the *Register* amounted to $7,000 annually, Niles wrote in the September 6, 1823, issue, and it is probable that there was little change in this cost during his ownership, as paper, ink, and the wages of compositors formed the main items of his disbursements. The fact that the establishment's entire income was derived from subscriptions and that many fully able to pay their annual account with him neglected to do so because the amount seemed small was commented on by Niles time and again.

With an average weekly expenditure of between $100 and $150 and with a constantly mounting total of overdue subscription money, it is not surprising that Niles frequently reiterated appeals to his negligent readers to pay their accounts. This constant dunning through the columns of the *Register* was extremely distasteful to him, and he wrote that his time was wasted, his mind's equanimity destroyed, and the *Register* made a less valuable work because of the necessity of devoting so much time to the pecuniary affairs of the office.[30] It was with "mortification" that he felt compelled to refer so often to money

[28] *Register*, XXVI, 149, May 8, 1824; Register of Administrations, Baltimore County, X, 201, 202, quoted in Richard Gabriel Stone, *Hezekiah Niles As An Economist* (Baltimore, 1933), 55; also published in the Johns Hopkins University *Studies in Historical and Political Science* (Baltimore), LI, No. 5, 615.

[29] *Register*, LV, 99, October 13, 1838. Whether this applied only to the two-year period after he had purchased the establishment is not entirely clear. If so, very few of the 3,500 subscribers could have paid their subscriptions, as the entire income, had all subscriptions been paid, would have been $35,000.

[30] *Register*, II, 285, June 27, 1812; X, 349, June 15, 1816; XX, 97, April 14, 1821, offer examples of appeals for money. He wrote Dr. William Darlington on March 28, 1816, "I am endeavoring to collect the monies I have earned—& the labor of it is Herculean." Darlington MSS, Library of Congress.

matters, but he pointed out that a press to be independent must have adequate financial resources.[31]

A number of times he resolved to remove from the mailing lists subscribers who did not pay, but apparently never carried out the policy rigidly. His chief effort in attempting to put this plan into effect came at the start of the thirteenth volume in the fall of 1817, but various editorial remarks made shortly thereafter indicate that enforcement was not strict.[32] Receipts of the *Register* were a barometer of the general financial condition of the country and in periods of stringency they dropped to the vanishing point. Methods of collection, in addition to appeals through the columns of the *Register* and correspondence, included the employment of agents in many localities, payment through members of Congress, and business trips taken by Niles at infrequent intervals. Two of these methods increased the expense of collection considerably.

Postage was another item of not inconsiderable cost to the *Register*, for many of its subscribers, even those requesting favors, did not prepay postage on their letters. Niles offered to pay postage on letters containing remittances, especially when receipts were low. The great discount at which the notes of many banks circulated also seriously cut into the receipts of the office but Niles usually accepted notes on which he did not have to take more than a 20 per cent discount.

In the mid-twenties Niles had $37,500 worth of unbound *Register* sets on hand. The stock, of course, had not cost him that much, but it represented a potential book value of that amount. In order to turn this immense stock into cash, he obtained, after a period of negotiation, authority from the Maryland legislature to conduct a lottery. Three hundred sets of Volumes I–XXIV and five hundred sets of Volumes XIII–XXIV were the chief prizes. The plan, however, was not a financial

[31] *Register*, IX, 137, October 21, 1815; 437, February 24, 1816; X, 201, May 25, 1816; XI, 297, January 4, 1817; XV, 149, October 31, 1818; XVI, 433, August 28, 1819; XXIV, 1, March 8, 1823; 256, June 21, 1823.

[32] *Register*, XII, 369, August 9, 1817; XIII, 17, September 6, 1817; 65, September 27, 1817. On September 5 he wrote to Darlington, "My new arrangement will, I believe, succeed—if it does, it will relieve me of half my present labor, & save me great expence & loss." Darlington MSS, Library of Congress. *Register*, XIII, 298, January 3, 1818; XIV, 177, May 9, 1818; XVI, 113, April 10, 1819; XVIII, 57, March 25, 1820.

success, although he printed the list of winning numbers and awarded the prizes to winners.[33]

The main source of revenue of most his fellow publishers—advertising—was never tapped by Niles and two of his successors maintained his policy. The acceptance of advertising in the three issues of the seventy-sixth volume marked the only deviation from this procedure. It came too late to save the *Register* and deserves mention only to present a complete picture of the publication. The first two and last two of the sixteen pages of these three issues were unnumbered and were marked "Advertising Columns." No advertisements appeared on the first page, which carried statistical matter used as filler, as did much of the second page. Three advertisements on the second page were for *Horn's U. S. Railroad Gazette, American Tourist and Merchants' and Travellers' Guide, De Bow's Commercial Review,* and *The Plough, the Loom, and the Anvil.* The inside of the back cover contained advertisements of books and magazines, and the back cover advertisements for the following magazines: *Littell's Living Age, Holden's Dollar Magazine, The Southern Literary Messenger, The Southern Methodist Quarterly Review, The Southern Lady's Companion, The Literary World,* and *The African Repository and Colonial Journal.* An engraving of the first prayer delivered in Congress was also advertised on the back cover.[34] The advertising rates occupied a card in the lower right hand of the page.

Although William Ogden Niles and George Beatty failed to make a financial success of the *Register* and Jeremiah Hughes was disappointed in his pecuniary reward, Hezekiah Niles, in spite of the large sum owed him at the time of his death, undoubtedly made a good living from the periodical.

Having noted the physical form, the circulation, and the financial operation of the *Register,* it is not unfitting to turn to the man who conceived the idea of the periodical and who for twenty-five years labored to have it meet his high conception.

[33] Niles to Darlington, December 3, 1824, Darlington MSS, Library of Congress. *Register,* XXX, 16, March 4, 1826; 152, April 22, 1826; 248, June 3, 1826; 249, June 10, 1826; 291–92, June 17, 1826.

[34] *Register,* LXXVI, inside cover, advertising pages and unnumbered pages following pp. 14, 144, 156 in issues dated September 14, 21, 28, 1849.

NILES' NATIONAL REGISTER.

FIFTH SERIES. No. 1.—Vol. V.]   WASHINGTON CITY, SEPTEMBER 1, 1838.   [Vol. LV.—Whole No. 1,405

THE PAST—THE PRESENT—FOR THE FUTURE.

PRINTED AND PUBLISHED, EVERY SATURDAY, BY WILLIAM OGDEN NILES, EDITOR AND PROPRIETOR, AT $5 PER ANNUM, PAYABLE IN ADVANCE.

☞ We have seldom issued a sheet containing a greater variety of useful and valuable documents connected with the politics of the day, than the present, viz:

I. The address of the republican members of congress.

II. Gen. McDuffie's opinions of the sub-treasury scheme, &c.

III. Judge White's speech at the Knoxville dinner.

IV. Letter from Mr. Dickerson, late secretary of the navy, in reply to an invitation of the citizens of Newark, N. J., to partake of a public dinner.

V. Address of Mr. Briggs of Mass. to his constituents, on declining to be a candidate for re-election.

VI. Letter of Mr. Crockett of Tenn. in reply to an invitation to partake of a public dinner.

We have also on file a large number of important papers relating to this subject, which we will lay before our readers with all possible despatch.

NEAPOLITAN INDEMNITY—(Official.) Treasury department, 1st Sept. 1838. Notice is hereby given, that the whole of the fifth instalment of the Neapolitan indemnity has been received in this country, and that the nett proceeds thereof are $221,635 96. Claimants can obtain their due proportions of it on application to the Bank of America, in New York city. LEVI WOODBURY, Secretary of the treasury.

TREASURY NOTES—(Official.) Treasury department, September 1, 1838. The whole amount of treasury notes authorized by the act of October 12, 1837, having been issued, viz: $10,000,000 00

And there having been redeemed of them about 7,350,000 00

The new emissions made in place of those under the act of May 12, 1838, have been 5,547,310 01

There have been redeemed of these last about 100,000 00

This leaves a balance of all outstanding equal to only about $8,097,310 01

LEVI WOODBURY, Secretary of the treasury.

Treasury department, September 1, 1838. Notice is hereby given, that the outstanding treasury notes issued in pursuance of the acts of congress of the 12th October, 1837, and the act additional thereto, will be paid agreeably to their tenor upon presentment at the treasury of the United States whenever they fall due.

Each parcel of notes offered for payment should be accompanied by a schedule, showing the dates and sums of the several notes, with the rate of interest thereon.

Holders of treasury notes, to whom it may be more convenient to have the amount due upon the same made available at either of the ports of entry or land offices, are informed that all collectors and receivers of public money will continue to receive them, and allow the principal and interest due thereon, in payments for lands and customs.

Those who may not wish to use the notes in payments to the United States, nor find it convenient to take the amount due on them at the treasury, will be accommodated with drafts therefor, payable at their places of residence, whenever it is found to be practicable. LEVI WOODBURY, Secretary of the treasury.

NAVY DEPARTMENT, Sept. 1, 1838. The firm of Edward McCall and Co., of Lima, have been appointed special agents for supplying the United States squadron on the Pacific station.

TEXAS. Alarming rumor. The New Orleans Bulletin of the 25th ult. says, that an officer of the steamboat Teche, states that before that vessel left Natchitoches, a report reached there and was generally credited, that the Indians from the north had invaded Texas in a numerous and formidable body, and were driving the white population before
VOL. V—No. 1.

---

them in great consternation. The town of Nacogdoches had been pillaged and burnt, and all the inhabitants driven from their homes. [Doubtful.]

FROM HAVANA. There were three arrivals at New Orleans from Havana on the 23d ult. Papers from that city, as late as the 13th, were received, which state that Porto Rico was in possession of the insurgents, except the fort at St. Johns, in which the governor had taken refuge. The necessities of the queen of Spain have led to the imposition of additional burdens on the Island of Cuba. The good people have been called upon to contribute $2,500,000 towards paying the expenses incurred by the young queen, in her struggle with Don Carlos for the throne of Spain. The governor general and his counsellors, ever prompt to manifest their loyalty, have set about raising the sum required, by levying an additional duty on all articles of import, and an export duty on the agricultural products of their soil.

The yellow fever prevailed at Havana, among the non-acclimated population. Five or six vessels are reported to have arrived from the coast of Africa, and succeeded in landing their slaves.

FROM THE PACIFIC. The U. S. ship North Carolina, 74, was at Callao in all July. The Falmouth sloop of war had sailed with Mr. Pickett, who had the treaty of the Peru Bolivian confederation with the United States, to have it ratified by Santa Cruz. The Lexington sloop of war was at Callao in May.

The French squadron at Callao consisted of the Androneda, 56 guns; the Venus, 50 guns; and the Alcrita brig. The Chilian squadron, consisting of seven vessels, was off Callao. The blockade had not been carried into effect against Peru. The Peruvian squadron of four vessels was moored close to the town of Callao.

ELECTIONS. North Carolina. According to the "Raleigh Register" the whigs have a majority of fourteen in the legislature on joint ballot, viz: four in the senate, and ten in the house.

The returns for governor are complete, except nine counties. The vote stands:

Dudley,	35,366
Branch,	17,697
Majority for Dudley,	17,669
Dudley's majority in 1836 in the counties heard from,	5,768
Whig gain,	13,901

The nine counties, it is said, will increase Dudley's majority.

Illinois. The Illinoian of the 18th, published at Jacksonville, has the following:

"Below we give the returns of the members elect to the legislature, so far as heard from. There are 40 members of the senate, one half of whom are elected at each general election. There are 91 members in the lower house. In the last legislature there were only 18 whigs in the lower house."

The editor then gives returns as follows:

Senate.

Whigs	11
Administration	5
Conservatives	2

House.

Whigs	42
Administration	30
Conservatives	5

The congressional election in the third district is extremely close, so much so that it can scarcely be determined with certainty until the official returns are made up. The Peoria Register of the 16th has returns from all the counties in the district except Calhoun, which give Stuart, the whig candidate, 170 votes more than Douglass, his V. B. opponent. Another account contains all the returns except those from the county of Iroquois, and gives Stuart a majority of 12. The St. Louis Bulletin and Republican both regard Mr. S. as elected.

Rhode Island. The election for representatives to the state legislature, took place in Rhode Island on Tuesday. From the Providence Journal of Wednesday, we learn that in Providence, Cranston,

---

Johnston, Scituate, Barrington, Warwick and Smithfield, the representatives chosen last spring are re-elected, without exception. In North Providence, one is re-elected, and the other would have been, had he not declined. As it was, another person of the same politics (W.) is elected in his stead. The last house contained 45 whigs and 27 Van Buren men. The towns above mentioned, have elected 16 whigs and 4 Van Buren—same as before.

The town of Providence, by a vote of 407 to 338, has decided that no licenses shall be granted in that town for the sale of intoxicating liquors for one year from the 1st Monday in October next. North Providence, ditto, 68 majority. Warwick has voted to grant licences.

Missouri. Harrison and Miller, the administration candidates for congress, were nearly 4,000 ahead of their competitors at the last accounts, and ten or twelve counties to be heard from. In the legislature the administration party will have a majority of about 25 on joint ballot.

Alabama. The "Globe" says, that the Wetumpka Argus of August 22 gives returns from 37 counties, which have returned to the legislature 63 members in favor of the sub-treasury, and 28 against it. Eleven counties remain to be heard from, which will increase the majority.

Mr. Crabb (W.) has been elected to congress, to supply the vacancy occasioned by the death of Mr. Lawler.

The democratic state convention of New Jersey assembled at Trenton on Wednesday last and nominated the following congressional ticket; Philemon Dickerson, Manning Force, Peter D. Vroom, Daniel B. Ryall, William R. Cooper and Jos. Kille. The election takes place on the second Tuesday in October.

BANKS, CURRENCY, &c. Philadelphia money market. Bicknell's Reporter of Tuesday says that the money market in that city, for the last week, has been rather tight. The rate out of doors was from 8 to 10 per cent. The banks, although a little cautious, are as liberal as could be expected.

The New York Post states that the secretary of the treasury has purchased 500,000 dollars of the bonds of the Real Estate Bank of the state of Arkansas, from the commissioners now in that city.

New York money market. The Express of Tuesday says—

There has been a sudden change in domestic exchanges to-day. Mississippi has been sold at only 10 per cent. discount, an improvement of four per cent. in as many days. It is now said that the Agricultural Bank of that state has made a loan of six hundred thousand dollars. Exchange on Alabama and Tennessee is down to eight per cent., and Georgia to 3 per cent. These are evidences of a most cheering character, for only 90 days ago exchange on these three first named states was from 20 to 30 per cent.

A new bank is about to go into operation in Cincinnati, under the title of the Mechanics' and Traders' Bank of Cincinnati. Dr. W. Price has been appointed president, and Wm. Surtees, cashier.

The packet ship Francois 1st from Havre, brings 668,000 francs in gold, on account of the Neapolitan indemnity.

Within the last eighteen months the banks in Cincinnati have reduced their line of discounts a million and a half of dollars.

Nashville, Tenn., Aug. 24. The money market has undergone but little change since our last notice. The banks are all preparing for resumption, and we should not be surprised to see that event brought about about six weeks or two months in anticipation of the 1st of January. There is, as we have before remarked, a feeling of opposition to resumption among some of our friends, and it is said out of doors, that the managers of the new banks are among the number. Their notion is to postpone the day to 1st July, 1839, and failing in this, in consequence of the determination of the old banks, their policy will probably be to pay specie in the fall.

The rates on southern money are a little lower than last week; and premium funds not quite so

Chapter 2

H. Niles, the Man and the Editor

AFTER a dinner, a cup of good coffee, and a glass of Madeira, Hezekiah Niles liked to seat himself in his "freedom's chair," once the property of a participant in the Boston Tea Party, light a Havana "segar," and through the medium of his pen hold a "fireside conversation," with his readers.[1]

In this often-enacted scene at his Baltimore home were exemplified the chief interests of this Quaker editor: an appreciation of good food, wine, and tobacco; something concrete to link him with his country's history; love of home and family; and, what was probably always first in his thoughts, his editorial responsibilities to and relations with the readers of his *Register*. For the *Register* was his; in fact, for twenty-five years he was the *Register* and the *Register* was Hezekiah Niles—in type. It is impossible to separate the two. And so, to understand the publication, it is necessary to know the publisher.

Hezekiah Niles was born on October 10, 1777, near Chadd's Ford, Chester County, Pennsylvania, in the farmhouse of James Jefferis. His parents lived in Wilmington, Delaware, but had fled from that city in anticipation of the approach of British troops, some two months before his birth. Taking refuge in the home of a fellow Quaker near the forks of the Brandywine, to which locality many Wilmington residents had temporarily

[1] *Register*, XXI, 196, November 24, 1821. An editorial begins, "It is now more than six months since I held a fireside conversation with my numerous readers and friends, on things of deep interest to them and myself, as joint members of the government of the U. States." To one who listened to the fireside chats of President Franklin D. Roosevelt, the similarity between Niles' editorial introduction and the President's radio introduction is striking. A letter of June 5, 1939, from Stephen Early of the White House secretariat to the author, says that newspapermen, not the White House, "created the phrase 'fireside chat.'" Early did not comment on the similarity of the President's introductory remarks in his radio talks to that used by Niles.

moved, the Niles family found themselves practically in the line of march of Lord Cornwallis, who crossed the Brandywine at Jefferis Ford.

Hezekiah's birth took place within a month after the Battle of Brandywine, a fact which he mentioned in 1825 when plans were being made to have Lafayette attend an anniversary celebration of the battle. When it was safe to do so, his parents returned to Wilmington where his father, also named Hezekiah, was a carpenter and planemaker. Niles took honest pride in the fact that his ancestors had been "able, industrious and sober *mechanics* (as I trust that some half a dozen of my own sons, by the blessing of PROVIDENCE, will be). . . ." [2]

In approximately 1682 or 1683 the great-grandfather of the editor, whose first name was Hezekiah and whose last name was variously spelled Nyle, Nyles, Niels, Nile, Nils, as well as Niles,[3] left England and came to Pennsylvania, settling at or near Philadelphia. His only son, Tobias, a boatbuilder, lived in Philadelphia until his death in 1761.[4] The editor's father moved to Wilmington after his marriage to Mary Way, a daughter of a merchant in that city, and a descendant of one of the companions of William Penn. Thus, the editor of the *Register* traced both his maternal and paternal ancestry to "those who fled for *liberty* and *safety* to *Pennsylvania,* with the illustrious founder of that rich and populous, and patriotic and enlightened state." [5]

[2] *Register*, XIII, 33–34, September 13, 1817; XXV, 146, November 8, 1823; XXVIII, 321–22, July 23, 1825; XXXIX, 250–52, December 11, 1830; XLVI, 131, April 26, 1834. Stone, *op. cit.* 33 [593], 35–36 [595–96]. Sketches of Niles' life, none of them entirely accurate, may be found in J. S. Futhey and Gilbert Cope, *History of Chester County, Pennsylvania* (Philadelphia, 1881), 669–70; J. Thomas Scharf, *History of Delaware* (Philadelphia, 1888), I, 465–66; Edward T. Schultz, *History of Freemasonry in Maryland* . . . (Baltimore, 1885), II, 714–16. Brief sketches are in Allen Johnson and Dumas Malone (eds.), *Dictionary of American Biography* (New York, 1928–1937), XIII, 521–22; *National Cyclopaedia of American Biography* (New York, 1898—), X, 255; James Grant Wilson and John Fiske (eds.), *Appleton's Cyclopaedia of American Biography* (New York, 1888–1889), IV, 521.

[3] Letter to author from Hannah Niles Freeland Miller, March 2, 1939, quoting from receipt book of Tobias Nile, dated 1718, in her possession.

[4] Christ Church Records, Philadelphia. Correspondence from Hannah Niles Freeland Miller. Deeds of County of Philadelphia, Pennsylvania, July 23d, 1828, G. W. R., No. 23, pp. 618–21, cited in Stone, *op. cit.,* 34 [594].

[5] *Register*, XXXIX, 250, December 11, 1830; Monthly Meeting, Friends Society, Wilmington, Delaware, in Friends Library, Swarthmore College, Book I, 274, cited

Just before Hezekiah's fourteenth birthday his father was killed when a falling signpost struck him on the head as he stepped out of the door of his carpenter shop.[6] He was survived by his widow and two sons, Samuel and Hezekiah. The father apparently was a solid citizen. He served as an assistant burgess, and acquired a substantial estate, most of which was left to Samuel, the elder son, although $3,000 went to Hezekiah.[7] Hezekiah's education, which included a knowledge of classical languages, probably was obtained at the Friends School in Wilmington, as his parents were members of the Wilmington Friends meeting. A historian of the state tells of Wilmington's schools of the period and of the employment at the Friends School of a competent teacher of Latin, Greek, and English grammar.[8] In 1794 Hezekiah, then seventeen years old, was apprenticed to Benjamin Johnson, a printer, bookbinder, and bookseller in Philadelphia.[9] Here, through the liberality of his employer, he was allowed free access to the books in the store. In 1823 he wrote "it was my practice to rise early in the summer and seat myself at the front door, where I enjoyed the fresh air, and generally read about an hour, before the rest of the family were stirring. . . ."

The store was located in Market Street, and in addition to having this opportunity to continue his education, Hezekiah saw the nation's great at close range as the seat of government was still in Philadelphia. He related that Washington "often passed me in his morning walk, and . . . frequently seemed to give me an encouraging look, if our eyes happened to meet; to which he would sometimes add a kind nod of recognition." [10] It is not surprising that in this environment the apprentice lad, yet in his teens, became interested in politics and turned to the press as a means of expressing his opinions. Years later he re-

---

in Stone, *op. cit.,* 34 [594]; *Register,* X, 372, August 3, 1816; XVI, 106, April 3, 1819; XLVI, 131, April 26, 1834.

  [6] Wilmington *Delaware Gazette,* October 8, 1791.

  [7] *Register,* XIX, 39, September 16, 1820.

  [8] Scharf, *History of Delaware,* II, 686, 691.

  [9] *Register,* XXIV, 234, June 14, 1823; XXXVIII, 154, April 24, 1830; Wilmington Monthly Meeting, Book III, 65; and Collections of the Genealogical Society of Pennsylvania, Vol. 171, p. 149, cited in Stone, *op. cit.,* 36 [596].

  [10] *Register,* XXIV, 234, June 14, 1823.

called: "In 1794, while an apprentice, I wrote several small articles which were published, (if my memory serves correctly), in col. *Oswald's* paper, printed at Philadelphia, in support of domestic industry, and its essential connexion with the independence of the United States." He also wrote articles supporting Thomas Jefferson for the presidency in 1796, published in the Philadelphia *Aurora* and other Republican papers.

He returned to Wilmington in less than three years, because of the declining business of his employer, and had a brief partnership with James Adams, Jr., son of the first printer in Delaware.[11] About this same time his brother Samuel died, leaving his estate, much of which had come from their father, to him, except for a small annuity to their mother.[12] Shortly thereafter, he formed a partnership with Vincent Bonsal, a Wilmington printer and bookseller, who had a branch store in Baltimore. They specialized in job printing and also printed the *Delaware Gazette* for John Vaughn and Daniel Coleman until it was sold late in 1799.[13] The republication of *The Political Writings of John Dickinson*, of whom Niles was an ardent admirer, proved financially disastrous to the firm, although it is possible that Bonsal had not been honest in his financial dealings with his junior partner. The failure left Niles $25,000 in debt which he *"unfashionably* paid—so that, except what I count on my business, I am yet poor," he wrote to a friend in 1815.[14]

Niles was married before his twenty-first birthday to Anne Ogden, daughter of William Ogden, a Philadelphia tavern keeper.[15] They too were Quakers, although Niles' father-in-law had been temporarily expelled from the society for fighting in the Revolutionary War. An ancestor, David Ogden, had

11 *Register*, XXXIX, 252, December 11, 1830; XXXVIII, 154, April 24, 1830; Douglas C. McMurtrie, *A History of Printing in the United States, The Story of the Introduction of the Press and of its History and Influence during the Pioneer Period in each State of the Union* (New York, 1936), II, *Middle & South Atlantic States*, 248–49.

12 Record of Wills, New Castle County, Delaware, O–I, 174, cited in Stone, *op. cit.,* 37 [597].

13 McMurtrie, *op. cit.,* 251; Anna T. Lincoln, *Wilmington Delaware Three Centuries Under Four Flags 1609–1937* (Rutland, Vt. [c1937]), 355.

14 Scharf, *History of Delaware*, I, 466. Niles to William Darlington, January 12, 1815, Darlington MSS, Library of Congress, in which he wrote, "Bonsal peace to his soul!—was a bad man. I knew it too late."

15 *Claypoole's American Daily Advertiser*, May 19, 1798.

come to America on the same ship with William Penn.[16] Thus, his marriage strengthened the already strong Quaker ties of his forebears.

Niles had the reputation of being a faster type setter, with cleaner proof, than any other compositor in America. Ambitious, he turned also to other fields, entering Wilmington politics, and was elected town clerk in the fall of 1801, receiving more votes than any candidate for any office.[17] He was again chosen clerk in 1804. In the interim he had served one year as an assistant burgess and was elected to this office again in 1805.[18] At the same time he was active in Delaware politics, especially in the organization of the "old democratic" party in that state. Years later he wrote that from 1797 until he moved to Baltimore in 1805 he was personally acquainted with nearly every prominent "democrat" in Delaware. He added: "I was the junior member of the first *regular* democratic meeting or 'caucus,' that, as I believe, was ever held in Delaware, with a general view to the organization of the party; and, until I left the state, had the *honor* of being assailed as one of the five persons whom the 'federalists' called the 'CAUCUS JUNTO'—myself being, for some years past, the only survivor." [19]

Just before leaving Wilmington, Niles made his bow as a publisher. The publication, a literary one, had the double title of *The Apollo or Delaware Weekly Magazine*. The first issue was dated February 12, 1805, contained eight pages, and had a subscription rate of $3.00 per year. It was a short-lived venture, the final issue being printed on August 24, 1805. Much of its contents, which included verse, essays, and short novels, was contributed, but Niles is generally credited with the authorship of a series of humorous essays entitled "Quil Driving by Captain Jeffery Thickneck." [20]

A few months later he moved to Baltimore. There with a

16 Charles B. Ogden, *The Quaker Ogdens in America; David Ogden of ye goode ship "Welcome" and his descendants 1682–1897; their history, biography and genealogy* (Philadelphia, 1898), 61.

17 Scharf, *History of Delaware*, I, 465–66; Wilmington *Mirror of the Times and General Advertiser*, September 12, 1801.

18 *Minutes of Wilmington Burgesses Meetings, 1739–1811*, cited in Stone, *op. cit.*, 39 [599].

19 *Register*, XLVI, 265–66, June 14, 1834.

20 *The Apollo or Delaware Weekly Magazine* (Wilmington, 1805).

partner he purchased the Baltimore *Evening Post,* founded the preceding March. He edited this daily newspaper five and one-half years. In a year he had as a new partner, Captain Leonard Frailey, of the Maryland militia, who remained interested in the establishment until May, 1808. In 1809 Niles offered the *Post* for sale, but shortly thereafter withdrew the offer.[21]

The *Post* was a four-page newspaper, with three, or nearly three, of its pages filled with advertising. Local, national, and foreign news in brief filled page four. Few editorials were carried. The paper was Republican in politics, and a series of editorials which Niles wrote for it, defending the administration's foreign policy, was reprinted in book form in 1809.[22] There was nothing distinctive about the newspaper; nothing to indicate that its editor would within a few years be solely responsible for a publication with nation-wide recognition. The sale of the paper to pay his "honest debts" was announced in its columns on June 10, 1811, and two weeks later the prospectus for the *Weekly Register* appeared.

Niles was in his thirty-fourth year when he started the publication which widened the scope of his influence from a city to a nation. Already a familiar figure on Baltimore streets because of his editorship of the *Post* and his book-selling business, he was soon to become known through the columns of the *Register* to residents of every state. Descriptions of him are scarce. But his keen gray eyes and habit of stooping were noted by two contemporary observers, one of whom mentioned his weather-beaten face "with a sharp eye and compressed lips," while the other described him as "a short stout built man, stooping as he walked, speaking in a high key, addicted to snuff, but with a keen gray eye, that lighted up a plain face with shrewd expression. . . ."[23] The stoop undoubtedly came from bending

21 J. Thomas Scharf, *The Chronicles of Baltimore; Being a Complete History of "Baltimore Town" and Baltimore City from the Earliest Period to the Present Time* (Baltimore, 1874), 88; associated with him was George Bourne; Baltimore *Evening Post,* November 27, 1805; September 12, 1806; November 8, 1809; June 10, 1811.

22 [H. Niles, alias Jerry Didler], *Things As They Are; or Federalism turned inside out!! Being a Collection of Extracts from Federal Papers, &c. and Remarks upon Them, Originally written for, and published in the Evening Post* (Baltimore [1809]).

23 John M. Neal, *Wandering Recollections of a Somewhat Busy Life. An Auto-*

over a desk, reading newspapers, writing copy, and reading
proof. His taste for good wine and imported tobacco led his fellow editors and friends to have some good-natured fun with him
while he was engaged in his editorial campaigns to educate the
public to use American products.[24]

His love for and interest in his family were reflected in his
writings in the *Register* and in his private correspondence, as
well as in the financial arrangements he made for them. His
first wife died on June 2, 1824. Her death, which followed a
long illness, was a blow to Niles. He paid a sincere, honest
tribute to her in an obituary, for which he asked his readers' indulgence for breaking his rule of not noticing the deaths of private persons. Twelve children had been born to them, "four
of whom died soon after their birth, one in infancy, and the sixth
when nearly 22 years old." Mrs. Niles was buried in the Friends'
burying ground at Baltimore.[25]

His wife's death, he wrote, had been hastened by the death
of their second son, Samuel, in Florida, eighteen months
earlier.[26] Samuel had worked for his father as a clerk, but became interested in Florida and had studied Spanish to prepare
himself for a position there. Niles had used his political contacts to obtain the appointment for him and keenly felt the
loss.[27]

He trained his eldest son, William Ogden Niles, as a printer
in the office of the *Register* and employed him as an assistant for

biography (Boston, 1869), 212; John E. Semmes, *John H. B. Latrobe and His Times,
1803–1891* (Baltimore [c1917]), 184, quoting Latrobe, who was associated with Niles
in the management of the Maryland Institute.

[24] *Register*, XXIV, 19, March 15, 1823, quoting the *National Intelligencer*; 18,
quoting a letter from a friend which called attention to the *Intelligencer* article,
concluding, ". . . then to your desk and segar, with what appetite you may."
Register, XXIV, 54–55, March 29, 1823.

[25] *Register*, XXVI, 222–23, June 5, 1824.

[26] *Register*, XXIII, 129, November 2, 1822.

[27] Niles to Darlington, June 3, 1822, asking Darlington's aid in obtaining the
appointment for his son Samuel as secretary to a commission for settling land
claims in Florida; *id.* to *id.*, June 27, 1822, about Samuel's departure for Pensacola,
also mentioning Niles' correspondence with John C. Calhoun about his son, Darlington MSS, Library of Congress. A letter to Dr. James C. Bronaugh from Andrew
Jackson, May 29, 1822, mentions the receipt of a letter from Niles about his son.
This letter is in John Spencer Bassett (ed.), *Correspondence of Andrew Jackson*
(Washington, 1926–1935), III, 163.

a number of years before taking him into partnership. He gave editorial mention to his son's first venture alone into the newspaper field at Albany in 1825 and called upon his New York friends to aid him.[28] This paper, the Albany *Journal and Mercantile Advertiser,* was not a success, and the son apparently returned to his father's office where in 1827 he was taken into partnership. Niles hoped that his son would succeed to the management, but in 1830 the partnership was dissolved, the father writing, "It has so happened, that the editorial business of this work could not be well divided. . . ." He told of his son's purchase of the Frederick (Maryland) *Herald* and again asked the support of his friends, saying, "A little encouragement, at the starting point, may be permanently important to him, and stimulate him to persevere in maintaining those great principles which he has been taught from his childhood." [29]

Two years after the death of his first wife, Niles married Sally Ann Warner, daughter of John Warner, a Wilmington friend.[30] She was much younger than Niles. Eight children were born to them, all of whom survived their father. One, Henry Clay, born in 1828, was the subject of many a postscript in the proud father's correspondence on political matters with the Kentuckian.[31]

He aided his grown sons by lending them money. When he made his will, after a paralytic stroke in 1836, he directed that their notes be canceled, but did not leave them the two thousand dollars that was to go to each of the other ten children then living. The girls' portions were to be held until they reached the age of eighteen, and the sons were to receive their shares when they reached their majority. To his wife he left

[28] *Register,* XXVIII, 129, April 30, 1825.

[29] *Register,* XXXI, 305, January 13, 1827; XXXVI, 378, August 8, 1829; XXXIX, 137, October 23, 1830.

[30] Baltimore *American and Commercial Daily Advertizer,* June 22, 1826.

[31] Niles to Clay, October 28, 1830, "Your little namesake is the finest fellow in Baltimore! And almost every day, taught by his mother, 'hurrahs for Clay.' " *Id.* to *id.,* July 4, 1832, he wrote that his wife was a " 'Clay man'—that is, as much of a man as a gentle woman can be," adding a note about the namesake. Clay in a letter to Niles, November 25, 1828, acknowledged the "high compliment" of having the boy named after him and added, "It is a better evidence of the fidelity of your friendship, than of your discretion, at this time." Clay MSS, Library of Congress.

"two thousand dollars in cash, and all my household and kitchen furniture and plate not hereinafter disposed of, as and for her portion of my estate, and in lieu of dower and third." [32] It so happened that much of the estate, a large portion of which was on the books of the *Register* for overdue subscriptions, was never collected, so that the provisions of the will could not be carried out in full.[33]

Niles' interest in his family was exceeded only by his absorption in his chosen work, to which, he wrote in the early thirties, he had given an average of ten hours, "for *every* 'working day,' in the twenty years past." This steady work, most of which was at his editorial desk, claimed its toll of his health, and after trying the experiment of taking brief vacations away from his duties, he finally was forced to take an extended trip, during which time, however, he contributed articles to the publication.[34]

His pride in the *Register* shines through the pages in innumerable places. Its form he always defended and he ridiculed those who based their estimate of the worth of a publication on its size and weight, "as they do a cheese." [35] Of its contents, he was ever proud and jealous. In the April 22, 1826 issue he asserted:

It is no more required by the law that a *newspaper* shall be printed in folio than in octavo. Neither congress or the postmaster general, has undertaken to say on what size type, or paper, or shape, editors of newspapers shall print their journals; and the REGISTER has more of the pure characteristics of a newspaper than *any* other weekly print issued in the U. States, because that it contains more of the public documents, proceedings of congress and articles of intelligence, foreign and domestic, than any other weekly publication; and the *shape* in which these things are presented has no reference to the character of them.

When errors crept into the columns, he was mortified, and often asked his readers to make corrections in their copies with

[32] Certified copy, Last Will and Testament of Hezekiah Niles, Register of Wills, Baltimore City, Wills Liber D. M. P., No. 17, Folio No. 281, etc. Certified by John H. Bouse, Register of Wills for Baltimore City, May 12, 1939.
[33] Stone, *op. cit.*, 55 [615].
[34] *Register*, XL, 129, April 23, 1831; XLIV, 337, July 20, 1833.
[35] *Register*, IX, 138, October 28, 1815.

a pen.[36] He sometimes explained how a mistake got into type, but he never attempted to justify it, saying, ". . . it was my business to have *read* it." The growing reputation of the *Register* as an accurate, impartial publication caused Niles to be increasingly careful in his editing and proofreading, and he was meticulous in printing corrections of minor misstatements, when called to his attention. Obtaining practically all of his material from newspapers, Niles made many corrections prior to publication, but some errors escaped his eye. He prized the confidence of his readers and asserted that his "sincere devotion to HOLY TRUTH at all seasons, and in laborious exercises to discover it," had built this confidence. His earnest desire was "that whatever shall be advanced as matters of fact in the REGISTER shall not be questioned," and often reiterated that he "endeavored never to misrepresent *facts*. . . ." Realizing that many editors clipped the *Register,* seldom checking its statements for accuracy, he felt his responsibility keenly and appealed to them to correct errors which he aided in disseminating.[37]

Recognizing that his presence was clearly reflected in the typographical make-up and editorial content of the *Register,* Niles almost invariably announced in advance or mentioned afterward any absence from his editorial desk on a publication day. More than a score of these notices appeared at the top of the first column on the first page from time to time. The following, chosen at random, are typical:

> Expecting to be absent next week, and having no one to take his place at the desk, the editor very respectfully asks the indulgence of his readers, if the usual order of things should not be observed in the succeeding number of this paper.

> The editor's absence from home, and a longer detention than was *calculated* upon, has very materially affected the contents of this sheet, and prevented a notice of many things which would otherwise have been attended to.

---

[36] *Register,* X, 33, March 16, 1816; XI, 65, 78–79, September 28, 1816; XIX, 369, February 3, 1821.

[37] *Register,* XIII, 195–96, November 22, 1817; XXI, 273, December 29, 1821; XXVI, 191, May 22, 1824; XXXI, 163, November 11, 1826; XXXV, 113, October 18, 1828; 129, October 25, 1828; XXXVI, 377, August 8, 1829.

The usual prompt attention to many matters requiring his personal services, has not been given for the last two or three weeks, because of the absence of the senior editor from home.

I am sensible that many things must be neglected in the present week—but hope that it will be excused, seeing I am seldom absent from my post.

When he was away for any length of time, he usually sent back letters, enclosing articles and giving instructions on the make-up of the week's issue.[38]

He prided himself on his good health which permitted him to work long hours. In his thirty-sixth year, he apologized to his readers for an attack of rheumatism which nearly denied him the use of his right arm.[39] He boasted to a friend some time later that he had never been sick a day in his life, "except for a little touch of rheumatism," [40] but two years afterwards apologized to his numerous personal correspondents for not having answered their letters, saying that he had been compelled to spend some time in the open air. In the early twenties illness prevented him from working on several different occasions.[41]

In May, 1828, while running across the yard in the rain, he slipped and fell into the lighting area for the lower kitchen of his home, breaking his right arm, an accident which incapacitated him for some time. In August he apologized for inattention in his correspondence and told of the seriousness of the injury. He had been unable to feed himself, and could write only by moving the paper while he held the pen in his hand. Fortunately his son was then junior editor of the paper, and Niles was able to take a vacation trip of several weeks to Delaware and New York. In January, 1829, he fell on the ice, apparently driving a misplaced bone back into place for

---

[38] *Register*, XIII, 209, November 29, 1817; XIX, 353, January 27, 1821; XXVI, 369, August 7, 1824; 394, August 14, 1824; XXXIII, 353, January 26, 1828; XXXIX, 137, October 23, 1830; XLIX, 121, October 24, 1835.

[39] *Register*, V, 220, November 27, 1813.

[40] Niles to Darlington, January 12, 1815, Darlington MSS, Library of Congress.

[41] *Register*, XII, 262, June 21, 1817; XXI, 17, September 8, 1821; 321, January 19, 1822; XXIV, 353, August 9, 1823.

he regained the use of his arm to a considerable extent.[42]

Through the thirties there was an increasing number of references to his health and to the necessity of getting some relaxation from the confining editorial duties. He set the close of the fiftieth volume as a goal he hoped to reach before retirement.[43] While in New York attending the annual exhibit of the American Institute in October, 1835, he suffered a broken left arm; as he was getting out of an omnibus, the horses started, throwing him to the ground. This last injury proved more serious than was at first thought, and nearly six months later, when advertising for an assistant, he reported that he had been unable to dress or undress himself or cut his meat since the accident. His old enemy, rheumatism, also returned, making his use of the pen extremely difficult.[44] Around the first of July, 1836, he suffered a stroke which paralyzed his right side, a fact which he did not make public until his son officially became editor and publisher of the *Register* on September 3. Referring to his condition, the doughty veteran dictated in his valedictory: "This state, there is no doubt, has been caused by my devotion to business, and the necessity that existed of personal exertion for so long a period—having been predisposed to the disorder under which I am now suffering, for several years, without the ability to relax my concerns and take the needful exercise." [45]

Niles evolved a homely philosophy which as often found expression in brief quips at the end of news stories as in his long editorials. Many of these serve to give a picture of the man.

Notwithstanding I may render myself liable to the suspicion of complimenting myself, I cannot refrain from the declaration,—that there is no human being that I respect so much as a plain unsophisticated honest man.

But our opinion does not constitute the right of any matter; nor do we ever wish that it should be so regarded.

[42] *Register,* XXXIV, 153, May 3, 1828; 377, August 9, 1828; Niles to Darlington, January 26, 1829, Darlington MSS, Library of Congress.

[43] *Register,* XXXIX, 274, December 18, 1830; 384, January 22, 1831; XL, 361, July 23, 1831; XLI, 74, October 1, 1831; XLIII, 2, September 1, 1832; XLIV, 417, August 24, 1833; XLV, 1, August 31, 1833; 113, October 19, 1833; XLVI, 298–99, June 28, 1834; XLVIII, 58, March 28, 1835.

[44] *Register,* XLIX, 137, October 31, 1835; L, 89, April 9, 1836.

[45] *Register,* LI, 1, September 3, 1836.

. . . the contents of a journal may be compared to the viands placed on the table of an inn, and it may be that every one cannot be pleased—so all that can be required is, to make a gentlemanly payment of the reckoning and depart in peace; . . .

The great misery is, that too many persons suffer others to *manufacture* opinions for them. . . .[46]

Like many of his contemporaries, he used only his initial in signing his correspondence. "H. Niles" was carried at the top of the first page of each issue of the *Register* during his editorship. Apparently sensitive over the name "Hezekiah," he once wrote that the "whole hog" press "would lose half the spice of their articles against me . . . were it not that my name is *Hezekiah*. I sometimes see it mentioned in every other line." [47]

Members of the bar had no high place in his estimation. Commenting on General Andrew Jackson's difficulties in New Orleans after jailing judges and newspaper editors for alleged infractions of martial law, he wrote, ". . . heaven preserve the reputation of that man who incurs the hatred of *lawyers* and *printers!*" Fifteen years later, in discussing jurisdiction of a pending case, he concluded, "But what case will not be argued —if paid for?" [48] His own profession did not escape his humorous jabs; in an item printed in the December 1, 1821, issue, which told of the burglary of three Boston newspaper offices, he added, "A printing office is about the last place in which a thief should expect to find money."

Called for jury duty, he served like the good citizen he was, but on his return to his editorial desk criticized the system in which the jurors' pay was more than equal to the amounts asked in the suits. Damage suits amused him; the following comment is typical: "SEDUCTION. A person was brought in for damages in the amount of $1,283, for *seducing* the wife of another, who had been married *eighteen years,* and was the mother of *nine children.* 'That's a good one.' " [49]

[46] *Register,* XVII, 198, November 27, 1819; XXI, 179, November 17, 1821; XXVII, 1, September 4, 1824; XXXVIII, 203, May 8, 1830.
[47] *Register,* XXXIX, 250, December 11, 1830.
[48] *Register,* VIII, 145, April 29, 1815; XXXVIII, 1, February 27, 1830.
[49] *Register,* XLIII, 331, January 19, 1833.

Noting the amount of space the press gave the marriage of Miss Fanny Kemble, the actress, to Pierce Butler, Niles dryly remarked that the world would not come to an end because "Miss K. has become Mrs. B.—nor will the stock of beauty or of talent be exhausted by her retirement into married life, and from the stage. . . ." [50]

While humor leavened the pages of the *Register*, Niles more often than not used it to drive home a point he wished to make. He had a strong contempt for dueling and did all in his power to end the practice. For several years, he refused to print accounts of duels, and when he did print an item, left out the names of the participants.[51] He was too good a newspaperman, however, to suppress accounts of engagements between national figures, although, as in the case of Stephen Decatur and James Barron,[52] and Henry Clay and John Randolph,[53] he held the articles to minimum space. Mentioning the Japanese custom, in which each participant disemboweled himself, Niles suggested that the introduction of that system into the United States would reduce the affairs of honor.[54] Printing an item about a duel between Canadian Indians, he quipped, "So we see the savages are rapidly advancing in *civilization*." [55]

He had a solid citizen's pride in his adopted city, although he often referred to his affection for and friends in Wilmington. He encouraged all branches of education, printing many items about the Lancastrian system, giving space to both sides of the question on the value of the classics, and noting with pride the growth of universities in Maryland and elsewhere.

His ingrained respect for law and order caused him strongly to condemn attempts of individuals to take the law into their own hands, even when he sympathized with their cause. His condemnation of effigy burnings was unqualified.

Outstanding among Niles' characteristics was his tolerance. The only notable exceptions to this trait were found in his at-

50 *Register*, XLVI, 260, June 14, 1834.
51 *Register*, XVI, 400, August 7, 1819; XVIII, 326, July 1, 1820; 464, August 26, 1820; XIX, 2, September 2, 1820.
52 *Register*, XVIII, 98–107, April 8, 1820.
53 *Register*, XXX, 115–16, April 15, 1826.
54 *Register*, XXI, 215, December 1, 1821.
55 *Register*, XXV, 54, September 27, 1823.

titude toward England and monarchies. He stoutly defended
foreign-born American citizens from attack, respected the opinions of others, decried the persecution of Jews in Europe and
the hostility to them in America, and advocated burying a man's
faults with him. He was a kindly employer, rearranging publication dates so that his employees could spend the holidays
with their families. That the evils of child labor, however, were
not apparent to him may be seen from his comment, after visit-
ing a factory which employed one hundred girls from six to
twelve years of age, that ". . . this factory is a blessing and
a comfort to many families in its neighborhood." [56]

Niles had a deep and abiding faith in democracy. He thought
the United States government the "grandest experiment" ever
tried, and declared, "The end of government is the happiness
of society." He wrote, ". . . a free republic *is* the strongest
system yet devised for a social compact amongst men." When
others criticized faults of the republic, he replied, "We have
many times said, that we preferred even the licentiousness of
freedom to the calm of despotism—." [57] He had confidence in
the farmers and mechanics and felt that the hope of the nation
lay in them. He sensed and early predicted the rise of Jacksonian democracy, "by the indignant suffrages of a neglected and
injured people." [58]

Niles was almost fanatical in his devotion to the theory of
majority rule, describing it as ". . . the first principle of our
solemn compact with each other . . . the life of the republic. . . ." He felt that the safety of the state was involved in an
"adherence to this sublime principle," and repeatedly called
upon the voters to exercise their right of suffrage and to abide
by the decision of the majority.[59] That this was not merely lip
service to democracy is shown in his determination to submit

[56] *Register*, XII, 227, June 7, 1817.
[57] *Register*, II, 364, August 1, 1812; XIII, 1, August 30, 1817; XV, 1, August 29, 1818; XIX, 387, February 10, 1821.
[58] *Register*, XI, 178, November 16, 1816; 209, November 30, 1816; XII, 69, March 29, 1817; XX, 2, March 3, 1821; 130, April 28, 1821; XXXII, 245, June 9, 1827; XXXVII, 353–55, January 23, 1830; XLII, 1, March 3, 1832.
[59] *Register*, II, 283, June 27, 1812; X, 334–36 (incorrectly numbered, should be 234–36), June 8, 1816; XV, 4, August 29, 1818; XVII, 442, February 26, 1820; XXIV, 209–11, June 7, 1823; 324–25, July 26, 1823.

to the expressed will of the people and withdraw from editorial support of the Bank of the United States and internal improvements after Jackson's victory in 1832.[60]

Convinced that the United States offered the best example of representative government in the world, Niles became one of the nation's leading exponents of nationalism. Through the War of 1812, he pleaded for an American feeling instead of party strife, writing, "I wish that *my* countrymen had the same sense of *national glory* that actuates the *British* nation," and, "At present, we are semi-*Englishmen,* and have not a national *character.*" [61] After the war, he repeatedly expressed the opinion that the people were assuming a "national character," and felt that the farmers and manufacturers, especially the westerners, had much to do with this. He took some credit to himself, noting briefly on a front page in 1817: "It is delightful to see the words 'national character,' 'national feeling,' and the like, coming into *common* use;—and it is, indeed, a luxury to the editor of this paper to believe, that he, as much as any man, has contributed to bring it about.—A pride of country is a bulwark of safety. Let us cherish it—it is the cheapest, as well as the best, defence of the republic." [62] In his opening address to the thirteenth volume, he told his readers: "It has been the great business of the editor of the WEEKLY REGISTER to endeavor to raise up a *national character;* and it shall be persevered in with unwearied assiduity. The people are every day more and more convinced that they have a country and a constitution worth defending. . . ." [63]

His correspondence and nearly every issue of the *Register* edited by him show his intense nationalism. Fourth of July editorials, the "glorious system" which permitted former presidents to live in simplicity and friendship, and the deaths of national figures, all gave him an opportunity to voice his nationalistic sentiments.[64]

60 *Register*, XLIII, 177, November 17, 1832; 209, December 1, 1832.

61 *Register*, V, 127, October 23, 1813; VI, 277, June 25, 1814.

62 *Register*, XII, 321, July 19, 1817.

63 *Register*, XIII, 1-2, August 30, 1817.

64 Niles to D. Chambers, May 16, 1812, Niles MSS, Library of Congress; *Register*, XV, 113, October 17, 1818; XVI, 321, July 10, 1819; XVIII, 329, July 8, 1820; XXIII, 247-48, December 21, 1822; XXVIII, 1, March 5, 1825.

Niles keenly felt the lack of national literature and was particularly bitter against the country's dependence upon England for books and magazines. He encouraged the publication of histories, geographies, encyclopedias, collections of documents and letters, and biographies by American authors.[65] In a two-page open letter to Jefferson and Madison in 1817, he asked the former presidents to lend their active aid to the compilation of "A *spelling-book* and a *reading-book*" for American school children, asserting that such books would "instantly supersede most others used in our schools." [66] He also encouraged literary magazines and societies, and noticed favorably the novels of Washington Irving and James Fenimore Cooper, although he was less favorably impressed by the latter's excursion into political fields.[67]

One would expect to find such an ardent patriot as Niles in favor of a program of national defense. And so he was. The need for an adequate navy, especially, was stressed after the War of 1812 in editorials and in articles by naval officials.[68]

That Niles opposed sectionalism, states' rights, separatist movements, nullification, and secession is not surprising to one who has read this far. From the discontent in New England during the war with Great Britain, through the sectionalism that flared up over the Missouri Compromise, and the states' rights talk that centered around the Creek controversy in Georgia, to the South Carolina opposition to a protective tariff, terminating in the nullification convention and the passage of the Force Bill, Niles used every means at his disposal to convince

[65] *Register*, XI, 84–85, October 5, 1816; XVI, 213–14, May 22, 1819; XX, 113, April 21, 1821; XXI, 134, October 27, 1821; XXII, 289, July 6, 1822; XXXII, 218–24, May 26, 1827; XXXIII, 83, October 6, 1827; XXXIX, 143–44, October 23, 1830; XLI, 475, February 25, 1832; XLIV, 101, April 13, 1833.

[66] *Register*, XIII, 145–47, November 1, 1817. His failure to mention Noah Webster's *American Spelling Book* is hard to explain. Possibly it had not superseded the English schoolbooks in the Baltimore and Maryland schools.

[67] *Register*, XII, 197–98, May 24, 1817; XIV, 199–200, May 16, 1818; XXII, 193, May 25, 1822; XXIII, 354, February 8, 1823; XXX, 234, June 3, 1826; XLV, 169, November 9, 1833; 182–83, November 16, 1833; XLVI, 292, June 21, 1834; 428, August 23, 1834.

[68] Typical of many carried from 1815 to 1821 are: *Register*, IX, 139–43, October 28, 1815; 406, February 10, 1816; XII, 209, May 31, 1817; XVI, 2–3, February 27, 1819; XXI, 113–18, October 20, 1821.

his readers of the absolute necessity of obeying the will of the majority and of maintaining unimpaired the national union of the states.

He frequently quoted Washington on the necessity of maintaining the Union intact, in one signed article going on to say: "Little did that great man believe that in ten or fifteen years after his death, men in *Boston,* the 'cradle of the revolution,' should coldly sit down and calculate *a separation of the states.*" [69]

From November, 1814, through April, 1815, he ran in the *Register* a series of lengthy articles under the title "New England Convention," in which he attempted to prove that the commerce of New England was of less importance than that section believed, that the northeast had profited much during the first eighteen months of the war, that the convention would encourage the enemy and prevent a peace, and that the nation, as a whole, was disgusted with the action taken by the New Englanders.[70]

His strong opposition to the convention did not blind him to the desirability of covering its activities as fully as possible. Under "Events of the War," a not-too-subtle classification, he carried what proceedings were available, chiefly from Hartford papers. More than one half of the issue of January 14, 1815, was given to a copy of the convention's proceedings "to gratify the *curiosity* of his readers." The next week he printed nearly five pages of statistics prepared by the delegates to support their stand.[71]

Sectionalism in Congress over the tariff, the election of a speaker, and in party politics disturbed Niles.[72] Saying he was "neither neutral or indifferent" about the attitude of Georgia on the Creek lands during the presidency of John Quincy

[69] *Register,* VI, 1–4, March 5, 1814.

[70] *Register,*.VII, 185–89, November 26, 1814; 193–97, December 3, 1814; 337–38, January 28, 1815; VIII, 138–41, April 29, 1815.

[71] *Register,* VII, 269–70, December 24, 1814; 280–81, December 31, 1814; 302, January 7, 1815; 305–15, January 14, 1815; 328–32, January 21, 1815; other articles on the convention are in VIII, 65–70, April 1, 1815; XI, 337–38, January 18, 1817, the latter of which ridicules the claims of Massachusetts and Connecticut for reimbursement for militia service during the war.

[72] *Register,* XVIII, 114–15, April 15, 1820; XIX, 177, November 18, 1820; XXV, 2–3, September 6, 1823; Niles to Darlington, October 22, 1820, Darlington MSS, Library of Congress.

Adams, he promised, "This paper will always 'go the whole,' as the saying is, 'for the country.' " [73] The opposition of Virginia and South Carolina to internal improvements on constitutional grounds irked Niles and he wrote: "The states have rights, but the general government has powers,—and it is no less the interest of the people, at large, that the last should be maintained in wholesome operation, than the first be preserved, to check an unwholesome preponderance, and an overshadowing of the powers reserved to states or the people respectively." [74]

As the rumblings of discontent over the tariff grew louder in South Carolina and there was talk of a state nullification convention and of a separation of the Union at the Potomac, Niles left no doubt as to his stand: "But to us—the idea of a dissolution of this union, the hope of all men who know and appreciate human liberty, seems something like that which we attach to personal annihilations. . . ." [75]

While the South Carolina and Georgia legislatures debated what action to take against the "Tariff of Abominations," Niles asserted that ". . . the people will not be *frightened* into submission in 1829 any more than they were in 1814, and the majority shall rule." Of the Georgia protest he said: "It is *ridiculous* in its beginnings, *untrue* in its proposition, and *ignorant* in its conclusion." [76]

Niles' often-expressed belief that the United States government was the best in the world did not prohibit him from criticizing any or all of its three branches. Frequently critical of Congress, especially at the end of protracted sessions, and never hesitating to criticize the executive, he freely commented on the powers of the judiciary. His attitude toward the Supreme Court underwent a change in the decade between 1821 and 1831. At the beginning of this period he admitted feeling veneration at a visit to the chambers of the tribunal, but reminded himself that the judges were only men and proposed a plan of reviewing their decisions.[77] Commenting on the wide-

[73] *Register,* XXVIII, 401, August 27, 1825.
[74] *Register,* XXIX, 161, November 12, 1825.
[75] *Register,* XXXV, 184, November 15, 1828.
[76] *Register,* XXXV, 297, January 3, 1829.
[77] *Register,* XX, 82–83, April 7, 1821.

spread press discussion given the decision in Cohens *vs.* Virginia, he added that it seemed that all who would not subscribe to the court's infallibility were in danger of political excommunications.[78]

Niles' religious philosophy was based on tolerance. In a day when religious discussions formed an important part of everyday conversation, he declined to insert such controversial matter in the *Register,* reserving the right, however, to criticize state religions and the intolerance of various sects and denominations.[79] He delighted in pointing out instances of co-operation between different denominations and was quick to criticize those, including his own Society of Friends, which refused other sects the privilege of using their buildings. Critical of the activities of missionaries at home and abroad, he showed his only religious intolerance toward the Mormons.[80]

Thus, it is in the *Register* where one finds clearly reflected his high standard of ethics that the reader gets a true picture of the religious, social, and political philosophy of the man. The very name of the periodical he chose with care. To him the name expressed what he felt to be its primary function, that is, the registering of significant documents and facts for future use, and he frequently used the word "register" both as a noun and as a verb in explaining his policy.[81] In volume after volume, from his prospectus in the first issue until the time of his retirement, he reiterated that the *"first object,"* "chief purpose," and "primary object," of the *Register* was to record material for the future.[82] In spite of readers' objections, he never wavered

---

[78] *Register,* XX, 289, July 7, 1821.

[79] *Register,* I, 2, September 7, 1811; VII, October 22, 1814; VIII, 127, April 22, 1815; IX, 55, September 23, 1815; XVI, 106, April 3, 1819; XVIII, 82–84, April 1, 1820; XXV, 81, October 11, 1823; 357, February 7, 1824; XXIX, 115, October 22, 1825; XXXVIII, 434, August 14, 1830; XLIV, 369–70, August 3, 1833.

[80] *Register,* XIX, 225, December 9, 1820; XX, 101–102, April 14, 1821; 225, June 9, 1821; 336, July 21, 1821; XXIII, 163, November 16, 1822; XXV, 115–16, October 25, 1823; XXXVIII, 254, May 29, 1830; XL, 353, July 16, 1831.

[81] *Register,* XXVIII, 241, January 18, 1825; XXIX, 289, January 7, 1826; XLII, 19, March 10, 1832; XLVI, 1, March 1, 1834, offer typical examples of scores of such instances.

[82] *Register,* XIV, 89, April 4, 1818; XXX, 89, April 8, 1826; XXXIII, 289, January 5, 1828; XXXVII, 97–98, October 10, 1829; XLIII, 113, October 20, 1832; XLVIII, 337, July 18, 1835. One of the best explanations of his entire editorial philosophy is in a long address to his readers in Volume V, 1–4, September 4, 1813.

from this goal. If his sixteen pages could not accommodate both documents and current news, the news was cast aside or greatly condensed. And many a time he discarded an editorial of his own composition, prepared with much care, in order to carry an official report or communication.[83]

However zealous he was to compile a complete record for posterity, Niles did not by any means neglect the presentation of current news. His prospectus promised, among other things, that the periodical would contain: "A neat summary of the NEWS of the preceding week, and occasionally details of important events abroad and at home, legislative, judicial, and executive—commercial, military and miscellaneous, shall be inserted in every number—so as to present a general view of what is doing in the world." A glance at almost any number will convince the reader that he lived up to this promise. Niles' philosophy included no justification for printing stories about crimes, murders, and hangings. Those that were printed were confined to a few lines in which he condemned the long articles in the daily newspapers and the then common practice of public hangings which were attended in some cases by fifty thousand persons, including many women.[84]

Besides the responsibility of preserving documents for the future and of summarizing significant news for the present, Niles' editorial philosophy embraced a third duty to his readers, that of commenting intelligently upon contemporaneous events. Many points of his personal philosophy, which cannot be divorced from his editorial policy, have already been touched upon in this chapter and others will be discussed at length in succeeding chapters. The following excerpt, however, illustrates his feeling of editorial responsibility: "Our purpose is, to write for and speak to people—not the learned and the wealthy . . . but the *free laboring* people, like ourselves, struggling to get a

---

[83] *Register*, XV, 65, September 26, 1818; XVI, 65, March 20, 1819; XXV, 241, December 20, 1823; XXIX, 417, February 25, 1826; XXXII, 17, March 10, 1827; XXXVII, 97–98, October 10, 1829; XLI, 73, October 1, 1831; XLIII, 1, September 1, 1832; 401, February 16, 1833; XLV, 241, December 14, 1833, are typical of many such expressions.

[84] For his attitude on crime news, see *Register*, XXVI, 52, March 27, 1824; 96, April 10, 1824; XXVII, 341, January 29, 1825; XLV, 169, November 9, 1833; 177, November 16, 1833; 291, December 28, 1833.

little forward in the world, and educate their children, &c." [85]

He also included in his editorial responsibilities that of presenting an impartial picture of the opinions of American newspapers on matters of public concern. It mattered not that he detested nullification; he printed columns of editorial excerpts from representative southern newspapers upholding the tenets of that doctrine.[86] All through his tariff fight he gave full space to the free-trade advocates, and during his ardent battles for internal improvements, he printed the opinions of his opponents.

Niles keenly felt the weight of his editorial responsibility, but he gloried in his independence. "My press is my own" was his boast in 1819, and in 1828 he proudly wrote, "We allow no dictation as to the management of our paper." [87] The following paragraph from a three and one-half page open letter to a member of the New York legislature who had written to Niles suggesting that he change his stand on a political question so well expresses his independence that it is quoted in length:

The REGISTER is as much my property as your farm is yours. Nay, it is more so, for I *made* it—but you did not make the land. No person or party ever had any control over it, myself excepted, and no person or party ever shall. Attempts at *dictation* have been made, and, perhaps, I might have yielded to some *recommendations* with the hope of pecuniary profit; but I set out to keep in *"a gang by myself,"* and there is no *man* can say that I ever stood editorially committed to him. The *people* appear to have been satisfied with this course—they have supported me, and I have done my best to support them; and I believe that they will continue to do so, as long as "measures and not men," are regarded. I am willing to sell my establishment, because of the severity of the labor that its business imposes —but will not sell myself; that is *another affair.* I follow in the wake of no man—never wait to find out whether the POLITICAL PREFECT pitches the tune on *fa, so* or *la*—C sharp or B flat; yet am thankful for advice and willing to receive instruction. But when it assumes the shape of a *threat,* a prompt resolution is ever present to reject it,

[85] *Register,* XXXIX, 217, November 27, 1830.

[86] *Register,* XXXIV, 352–56, July 26, 1828; XXXIX, 2–4, August 28, 1830; 129–32, October 16, 1830; XLIII, 77–78, September 29, 1832; 317–19, January 12, 1833; 345–46, January 19, 1833.

[87] *Register,* XVII, 66, October 2, 1819; XXXV, 19, September 6, 1828,

whether the thing suggested be good or bad in itself. Such, sir, is the perversity of my nature, and "I can't help it." [88]

The integrity of this editor, who never bargained with his principles and who took pride in the fact that his press was his own, arouses admiration. He resented rumors and statements that he had a financial interest in manufacturers or had received favors from the Bank of the United States, and he had only contempt for editors who accepted orders from political or financial leaders. He was even suspicious of the indirect influence of advertisers upon the opinions of editors, one reason that he never admitted advertising to the *Register*'s columns.[89]

Niles believed that a free press was one of the foundation stones of democracy, and he urged the people of the United States to support the press so that it also could be independent. He frequently called attention to the lack of press freedom on the European continent, and criticized members of the Holy Alliance for their censorship of the press in various countries. Not one to shut his eyes to the faults of his own profession, he still believed that ". . . it is better to have a licentious press than one subjected to any other *regulation* than that which is imposed by *public opinion*." [90] In 1817 he even went so far as to argue for the abolition of postage on newspapers in order to increase their circulation.[91] He disliked the political partisanship of the press of the period, but, pointing out that it naturally grew out of the liberty of the press which permitted anyone who wished to do so to start a newspaper, he asked the critics if they would establish a censorship.[92] During President Jackson's second term in office Niles became more critical of the *"organized party-press,"* charging that hundreds of editors over the country followed the editorial lead of Duff Green and later

88 *Register*, XXVI, 204, May 29, 1824.

89 *Register*, IX, 175, November 11, 1815; XI, 3, August 31, 1816; XII, 263, June 21, 1817; XVII, 97, October 16, 1819; XXXII, 178, May 12, 1827; XLIII, 39, September 15, 1832.

90 *Register*, XIII, 381, February 7, 1818; XIV, 172–73, May 2, 1818; XXX, 285, June 17, 1826.

91 *Register*, XIII, 129–30, October 25, 1817; 164, November 8, 1817.

92 *Register*, XXVII, 385–86, February 19, 1825. Also XIII, 99, October 11, 1817; XXXI, 76–77, September 30, 1826; XXXIX, 202, November 20, 1830; 217, November 27, 1830.

of Francis P. Blair, and that obedient editors were rewarded at
the public crib with jobs, the salaries of which aggregated more
than $100,000 per year.[93] Naturally, so ardent an advocate of
press freedom defended freedom of speech, too, and was quick
to resent any infringement against this constitutional guarantee.[94]

The standard of editorial conduct that Niles set for himself
and followed throughout his editorial career and which made
the *Register* so valuable a source to students of the period was
based upon fairness, impartiality, and accuracy. The last point
has already been noticed. He was scrupulously careful to reprint
full quotations or excerpts which presented a true picture of
an opponent's position when engaging in editorial contests, and
he demanded, often vainly, the same courtesy from his antag-
onists.[95] He was ever ready to acknowledge an error in editorial
judgment, and he printed statements from organizations and
men whom he opposed in order that his readers could form their
own opinions. In the first volume he wrote: "Whatever may
be our private opinions, we never will make ourselves liable
to the charge of suppressing or neglecting to insert, any official
paper belonging to a series of them laid off for the Register.
'*All or none,*' is our motto." [96] To this policy he adhered. In
1812 he printed resolutions opposing an excise on whisky, although he personally and editorially favored a heavy tax on it.[97]
Through the War of 1812, he gave space to the minority opposition in the House and the actions taken by various state
legislatures in opposition to it, in spite of his warm support
of the war.[98] A few years later he condemned those who took

[93] *Register*, XLV, 306–309, January 4, 1834. For accounts of the Jackson press,
see Erik McKinley Eriksson, "President Jackson's Propaganda Agencies," in *Pacific
Historical Review* (Berkeley, Calif.), VI, No. 1 (March, 1937), 45–57; William E.
Smith, *The Francis Preston Blair Family in Politics* (New York, 1933), I, 56 ff., 66,
80–81; Amos Kendall, *Autobiography of Amos Kendall,* edited by William Stickney
(New York, 1872), 371–74.

[94] *Register*, XLII, 123, 128–34, April 21, 1832; 153, 157–63, April 28, 1832.

[95] *Register*, XIV, 361, July 25, 1818; XIX, 114, October 21, 1820; XLI, 17, September 10, 1831.

[96] *Register*, I, 296, December 21, 1811.   [97] *Register*, II, 54, March 21, 1812.

[98] *Register*, II, 309–15, July 11, 1812; 417–19, August 29, 1812; III, 22–25, September 12, 1812; 116–18, October 24, 1812; 179, November 21, 1812; 291, January
9, 1813; 305–309, January 16, 1813; VI, 7, March 5, 1814.

the liberty to edit letters and public documents, and during his fight against the Bank of the United States permitted the bank's supporters to state their case in the *Register*.[99] Throughout the entire battle for the protection of domestic manufacturers, he gave the advocates of free trade space, and although he left no doubt as to his stand, he printed pages of material giving the South's side in the tariff controversy.[100] When the dispute reached the stage of threatened nullification and secession, he continued true to his editorial policy of presenting both sides.[101] So, in addition to presenting a complete picture of the press's attitude, as discussed earlier in this chapter, he also gave his readers an impartial presentation of the arguments and beliefs of both parties to the controversy. This impartial presentation of speeches, official pronouncements, and addresses of the nullificationists in no way interfered with the expression of his editorial opposition to such a course of action, as may be easily seen by examining almost any copy of the *Register* of the period in which the controversy raged.

He asserted that Senator George McDuffie's logic was no better than his temper or patriotism, repeatedly criticized the ambitious southern politicians who worked themselves into a frenzy over the tariff, condemned the "indecent and abominable" principles of nullification, and in November, 1832, after South Carolina's denunciation of the 1832 tariff, said that the season for argument was past and that the use of force seemed near at hand.[102] Of Jackson's nullification proclamation, he wrote,

99 *Register*, XI, 401, February 15, 1817; XIV, 281–82, June 20, 1818; XV, 60–61, September 19, 1818; 385, January 9, 1819.

100 *Register*, XVII, 353, January 22, 1820; XVIII, 257, June 10, 1820; XX, 195–96, May 26, 1821; XXV, 234–36, December 13, 1823; XXXIII, 26–32, September 8, 1827; XXXV, 161, November 8, 1828; XXXIX, 243–48, December 4, 1830; 401, February 5, 1831.

101 *Register*, XXV, 225, December 13, 1823; XXXIV, 265, June 21, 1828; XXXV, 199–208, November 22, 1828; 303–10, January 3, 1829; XXXVII, 213, November 28, 1829; 425, February 20, 1830; XXXVIII, 375–80, July 17, 1830; XL, 98–106, April 9, 1831; 437–45, August 20, 1831 (Calhoun's Fort Hill letter); XLII, 412–14, August 4, 1832 (South Carolina Manifesto); XLIII, 87–89, October 6, 1832; 173–75, November 10, 1832 (Governor James Hamilton's message to the South Carolina legislature); 231–39, December 1 and 8, 1832 (South Carolina Exposition), are typical of scores of other articles which might be cited in proof of this impartiality.

102 *Register*, XXXIV, 329, July 19, 1828; XXXV, 315, January 10, 1829; XLII, 419, August 11, 1832; XLIII, 65, September 29, 1832; 167–68, November 10, 1832.

". . . as a whole it must be regarded as worthy of highest commendation, as well as for the matter and manner of the *argument,* as the vigorous patriotism which it instils into the public
mind." [103]

Another rule for his editorial conduct which will bear passing
mention was his attitude toward anonymous communications.
He never knowingly suppressed a fact, but he never hesitated to
consign anonymous letters and articles to the wastebasket, as his
code of editorial ethics designated them as unfair.[104]

Niles worked hard on the *Register,* a fact already mentioned.
Two years after founding the periodical, he wrote: ". . . this
work has cost me more editorial labor and drudgery than is
bestowed on any two daily newspapers in the United States;
leaving out the *National Intelligencer. . . . Every* thing is to
be read, examined, digested, and compared—that, if possible,
the truth may be discovered and preserved." [105] Eighteen months
later, writing to a friend, he said his work on a daily paper had
been mere play compared with his toil on the *Register.* The
selection of his news from his exchanges and of his documentary
material from the flood of official reports which increased annually was a laborious task which occupied "three days a week
to keep myself reasonably well *posted* up on passing events,"
he wrote a friend in 1828. The writing itself was no easy job,
but the selection of the items and the crowding of them into
the sixteen pages of the *Register* each week presented problems
which at times seemed insoluble. Practically every volume
published by him voiced a wish for more room, although he
frequently issued larger numbers, free supplements, or turned
to the use of smaller type. Often he wrote that as many as forty-
eight or sixty pages could not carry the material he had on
hand.[106]

The editorial labor expended upon preparation of articles
in the *Register* was often discussed by the editor in its columns.

[103] *Register,* XLIII, 249, December 15, 1832; the proclamation is on 260–64.
[104] *Register,* IV, 166, May 8, 1813; X, 217, June 1, 1816; XIV, 36, March 14, 1818;
XVI, 121, April 10, 1819; XVIII, 273, June 17, 1820; XXII, 263, June 22, 1822;
XXXIX, 73, September 25, 1830.
[105] *Register,* IV, 409, August 28, 1813.
[106] Niles to Darlington, January 12, 1815; September 5, 1817; March 31, 1828,
Darlington MSS, Library of Congress.

After the end of the War of 1812, he said, regarding the compilation of lists of prize ships captured during that conflict which ran almost weekly for two years, that he had "read the journal of every vessel that was published, and examined, perhaps, *twelve thousand columns* of 'ship news,' " in order to assure himself of accuracy.[107] One of his long, rambling editorials entitled "Desultory Remarks," written from his favorite "Freedom's Chair," quoted, at its start, Cato's *Letters,* Edmund Burke, John Adams, De Ligne, and John Dickinson, an indication of the time and thought expended on editorials.[108]

The selection and condensation of foreign news into the space which he felt he could allot to it was a constant challenge to Niles and he frequently took his readers into his confidence about his perplexity over this influx of news, the gist of which he felt should be a matter of record.[109] On the selection of news, he wrote: "It is easy for a man that holds a free pen to dash off eight or ten pages of a common sized volume, on the familiar subjects of the day . . . but to attempt to cull 'the wheat from the chaff' of the multitudinous reports, surmises and conjectures; to glean the substance of ten thousand columns of what is called *news;* to retain *all* the useful and necessary facts, and reject the vast body of matter which appears to have been made for no other purpose than to *fill up* the newspapers—requires much patience, perseverance and care." [110] He was quite proud of his summarizing ability, however, and in 1820 quoted the editor of the Baltimore *Morning Chronicle* as remarking that his pen had "the condensing power of a 100-horse steam engine." [111]

A lighter side of his daily task is revealed in his accounts of vainly trying to made out the handwriting of correspondents, of the futility of trying to please everyone, and of the cotton manufacturer who praised his tariff stand highly, saying that he read the *Register* every week, borrowing it from a neighbor. Concerning this last practice Niles good-humoredly remarked,

---

107 *Register,* VIII, 405, August 12, 1815.

108 *Register,* XXI, 195, November 24, 1821.

109 *Register,* IV, 72, March 27, 1813; VIII, 258, June 10, 1815; XVII, 161, November 13, 1819; XVIII, 41, March 18, 1820; XX, 167, May 12, 1821.

110 *Register,* XI, 1, August 31, 1816.

111 Niles to Darlington, January 21, 1820, Darlington MSS, Library of Congress.

"We do not exactly print for pay,—but without pay it is certain that we could not print,—." [112]

In addition to reading and selecting documents, speeches, messages, and correspondence to be printed and reading and condensing domestic and foreign news from newspapers and magazines, Niles wrote the editorials or leading articles and read an average of four thousand letters a year which he received. He turned over about three fourths of these to the clerk or friend who handled his business affairs for him, but answered from 1,000 to 1,500 a year himself. He also compiled the indices mailed with the title page of each volume, no small task, although he wrote that he usually accomplished it in about fifteen hours.[113] He always had his readers in mind and if important news was received while the week's edition was on the press, he often stopped the press and inserted it under the heading "Postscript." Sometimes an article prepared with great care was lost; now and then he had his figures tied up in the index to the preceding volume and had to postpone the printing of a statistical article; sometimes extra printers were not available when wanted; but to the veteran editor these were minor problems.[114]

Niles' relations with his fellow editors form an interesting side of his editorial career. In a period when personal attacks by editors on each other were the rule rather than the exception, his restraint was marked, although some of his expressions may seem uncouth to twentieth-century ears.

William Cobbett, Thomas Ritchie, Joseph Gales, Jr., William W. Seaton, and James Wilson were the editors with whom he was on the closest terms, although the names of many others appeared from time to time in his editorials.

Toward Cobbett, Niles varied in his editorial attitude, although he never condemned him as strongly as did the *Edinburgh Review* which in 1827 referred to him as: "The fiercest

[112] *Register*, XX, 339, July 28, 1821; XXIII, 337, February 1, 1823; XXIX, 257–58, December 24, 1825; XXXIII, 2, September 1, 1827.

[113] *Register*, XIII, 33, September 13, 1817; XXVI, 33, March 20, 1824; XXXVI, 378, August 8, 1829; XXXIX, 274, December 18, 1830.

[114] *Register*, IX, 317, January 6, 1816; XX, 145, May 5, 1821; XXI, 368, February 2, 1822; XXIV, 17, March 15, 1823; XLVII, 385, February 7, 1835; 454, February 28, 1835; XLIX, 329, January 16, 1836; 345, January 23, 1836.

and basest libeller of the age, the apostate politician, the fraudulent debtor, the ungrateful friend, whom England has twice spewed out to America, whom America, *though far from squeamish,* has twice vomitted back to England." [115] Immediately after the war, Niles reprinted many of Cobbett's articles, undoubtedly because Cobbett was in opposition to the English government. He devoted 88 pages of a 192-page supplement to Volume VIII to Cobbett's letters from *Cobbett's Weekly Political Register,* and 11 pages of a supplement to Volume IX. In addition, he and his English contemporary, with whom he was inevitably compared, carried on a correspondence by means of open letters in their respective periodicals.[116]

However, when Cobbett made his second trip to the United States and there commenced publication of an American edition of his *Register,* in which he belabored the American government as hard as he had the British, Niles in a two-page open letter accused him of violating the hospitality of the country which gave him an asylum, saying, ". . . as we did not send for you, the least we can expect of you is, that you will behave decorously." [117] Cobbett's reply, calling Niles a grog drinker, which he was not, so infuriated the American editor that he wrote that Cobbett's conduct "forbids all further notice of him," a promise which was broken a month later when he printed from the *Delaware Watchman* a defense of himself and his habits.[118] Hardly mentioned in ten years, the English editor was referred to by Niles in 1826 as the "able and eccentric, ever-variable and generally unprincipled writer" and two years later as "rude and rough—frequently vulgar, sometimes mistaken, and . . . perhaps, the most popular public writer that lives." In 1830 he declared that he had never doubted that Cobbett was "hired to lead the people of the United States astray." Four years later he wrote that Cobbett was "celebrated in 'two worlds'

115 *Register,* XXXIII, 53, September 22, 1827; Cf. *Edinburgh Review* (Edinburgh, Scotland) XLVI, No. XCI, 255, June, 1827; for Cobbett's life see Marjorie Bowen, *Peter Porcupine: Study of William Cobbett* (London, 1936).
116 *Register,* VIII, Supplement, 1–88; IX, Supplement, 55–65; IX, 105–107, October 14, 1815; 173–74, November 11, 1815; X, 171–73, May 11, 1816.
117 *Register,* XIII, 33–34, September 13, 1817.
118 *Register,* XIII, 112, October 11, 1817; 163, November 8, 1817.

for his ruffian like writings and destitution of moral principle,"
and in 1835, when he died, Niles gave him a three-line obituary.[119]

With Thomas Ritchie, editor and publisher of the Richmond
Enquirer, Niles maintained an unbroken and more or less
stormy relationship for twenty-five years. Agreeing on the War
of 1812, a big navy, internal improvements, and the South
American revolutions, they were friendly from 1811 to 1820.[120]
From then on the editors waged almost incessant editorial combat until Niles laid down his pen. The changed political and
economic views of the Virginian caused Niles to chide him and
the fight was on. The two editors respected each other, Niles
writing in 1823 that ". . . while our heads argued our hearts
were at peace," [121] but each delighted in pointing to the editorial
inconsistencies of his antagonist. In this sport, Niles had the
advantage, for while the only question that he reversed himself
on during his editorship was his stand on the Bank of the United
States, Ritchie, politician that he was, changed on internal improvements, the tariff, and in his editorial attitude toward Andrew Jackson as a presidential possibility, shifts which Niles
did not let pass unnoticed.[122]

Niles often charged Ritchie with employing unfair editorial
tactics by lifting out sentences or paragraphs from their context,
thereby giving the *Enquirer*'s readers an erroneous impression
of the *Register*'s arguments, but complimented him when he
quoted the *Register* fully and accurately.[123] If the Virginian
seemed disinclined to engage in an editorial contest of wits,
Niles would prod and jab him with pointed paragraphs until
his opponent unlimbered his pen and accepted the challenge

[119] *Register,* XXX, 20, March 11, 1826; XXXV, 68, September 27, 1828; XXXVIII,
333, July 3, 1830; XLVI, 260, June 14, 1834; XLVIII, 377, August 1, 1835.

[120] *Register,* XVI, 97, April 3, 1819; for a life of Ritchie which stresses his political rather than his editorial activities see Charles H. Ambler, *Thomas Ritchie: A
Study in Virginia Politics* (Richmond, 1913).

[121] *Register,* XXV, 162, November 15, 1823; for other expressions of respect see
Register, XVII, 417, February 12, 1820; XXI, 225, December 8, 1821; XLII, 193,
May 12, 1832; XLVI, 260, June 14, 1834; Richmond *Enquirer,* September 5, 1828;
December 23, 1830; January 13, 1831.

[122] *Register,* XXX, 317, July 1, 1826; XXXV, 330, January 17, 1829; XL, 73,
April 2, 1831; 397–98, July 30, 1831; XLIV, 151, May 4, 1833; Ambler, *Thomas
Ritchie,* 63, 132; 44, 76–77; 68–69, 113–52.

[123] *Register,* XXV, 113, October 25, 1823; XXIX, 289, January 7, 1826; XXXVI,
253, June 6, 1829.

in the approved editorial language of the 1830's, "We neither like the labor of writing long articles, nor can we read without a 'groan' the long namby-pamby, drivelling, 'bald and disjointed cheat,' of our worthy contemporary.—" [124] When Ritchie called Niles' attention to some articles on free trade—the subject of many of their editorial discussions—in another newspaper, Niles refused to be put off saying: "Mr. Ritchie . . . must not think of *turning me over* to any other person. He is a 'philosopher' that I wish to have some talk with. And if it shall not be the good fortune of either to *convert* the other, our respective readers may be amused, if not instructed, by the controversy, between us—being, as we are 'veterans of the *goose*-quill;' and sufficiently, perhaps, impressed with a good opinion of ourselves! *We shall see.*" [125] Ritchie, however, had the last laugh, but Niles, though sick at heart, showed his innate sportsmanship by printing a column of the Virginian's gloating editorial over the passage of the Compromise Tariff in 1833.[126]

Niles for years obtained his reports of the Congressional debates from the *National Intelligencer,* a fact which he usually mentioned at the opening of a session.[127] With its editor, Joseph Gales, Jr., he had a close editorial and personal friendship, although the journals differed on some political questions, notably the Congressional caucus and a high protective tariff. In 1832 Niles paid a well-merited tribute to Gales and William W. Seaton for their "long-established fidelity and unquestioned ability" in reporting the debates, saying: ". . . though 'many a time and oft' 'differences of opinion' and *ink-shedding* controversies have existed between its editors and ourselves—we have *always* had occasion to admire the extraordinary accuracy, the rigid impartiality and indefatigable industry of the 'National Intelligencer,' in its issues of the proceedings and debates of the congress of the United States." [128]

[124] *Register,* XXX, 201, May 20, 1826; XXXV, 33, September 13, 1828; XXXVIII, 301, June 19, 1830; XXXIX, 313–15, January 1, 1831; XL, 234, June 4, 1831; XLI, 97–98, October 8, 1831; XLII, 73, March 31, 1832; 226–28, May 26, 1832; XLIII, 81, October 6, 1832; Richmond *Enquirer,* January 13, 1831.

[125] *Register,* XXXIX, 425, February 12, 1831.

[126] *Register,* XLIV, 20, March 9, 1833.

[127] *Register,* XIII, 314, January 10, 1818; XXXIII, 211, December 1, 1827; XLIII, 249, December 15, 1832; XLV, 225, December 7, 1833.

[128] *Register,* XLIII, 249, December 15, 1832.

48   Niles' Weekly Register

The two editors indulged in banter over minor errors, editorial idiosyncracies, and evasions of arguments, but the chaff
was good natured, as the following from the *Intelligencer* clearly
shows. Writing of one of Niles' trips to the Capitol, Gales
warned that Niles was about ready to get into "Freedom's Chair"
again, saying:

> In good truth, when we saw the honest face of our good friend in
> the lobby of the house of representatives, we could not help thinking
> to ourselves,
>   "A chiel's among you taking notes,
>   "And faith he'll prent 'em." [129]

Niles typically wrote that Gales and Seaton had a "right to
maintain and express their own opinions," but in 1823 he became excessively irked when the Washingtonians refused to
engage in an editorial discussion of the tariff. For weeks on end
he printed a quotation from the *Intelligencer* of March 21 that
the manufacturers of the country were the only prosperous interest and were flourishing at the expense of every other, insist-
ing that the editors prove the statement or apologize for printing it.[130] Their refusal to notice his action by so much as a word
aroused his ire, and he charged them with acting like fish frozen
in a pond and with not being courteous.[131] Furthermore, they
were on opposite sides over the selection of an 1824 presidential
candidate, which led Niles to charge: "Messrs. Gales and Seaton
have lately acted as if they had 'authority' to direct the public
presses of the United States. No sooner does a printer utter a
sentiment contrary to what they regard as *orthodox*, than they
pounce upon him and belabor him most unmercifully. Yes—
they are, they must be, the 'censors of the press'—but I should
like to see from whence they have derived their commission!" [132]
    A year later he wrote that the conduct of the *Intelligencer*'s
editors was such that many believed "they have lost no small

129 *Register*, XXII, 227, June 8, 1822; other examples of editorial raillery may
be found in *Register*, XVII, 1, September 4, 1819; XX, 369–70, August 11, 1821;
XXI, 178, November 17, 1821; XXV, 33–34, September 20, 1823; 337, January 31,
1824.
    130 *Register*, XXIV, 19–20, March 15, 1823; 71, April 5, 1823; 113, April 26, 1823;
129, May 3, 1823; 233, June 14, 1823; 321, July 26, 1823.
    131 *Register*, XXIV, 129, May 3, 1823; 233, June 14, 1823.
    132 *Register*, XXV, 18, September 13, 1823.

share of their discretion," [133] but after these skirmishes in which
nothing but ink was shed, they fought side by side through the
Jacksonian period. In 1830, replying to a letter from Gales,
Niles quoted the price of the *Register* and suggested that they
make a trade as he wished to obtain a copy of the debates.[134] Just
before the 1832 election, optimistically feeling that a large
majority was opposed to Jackson and saying "We must rally
them," he urged Gales to write an "article in your own inimi-
table stile [*sic*] . . . not to exceed a column, or say 1500 wds, &
publish it in a small pica type in your paper. It will thus attract
attention, & be copied every where." A few days later Niles wrote
thanking him for the excellent article which he felt would be
extensively copied.[135] He congratulated the editors on their
election as printer to Congress in 1833, and defended at length
charges and insinuations made against their editorial integrity
by Francis P. Blair in the *Globe,* following revelations of their
indebtedness to the Bank of the United States.[136]

James Wilson, grandfather of Woodrow Wilson, and Niles
"firmly esteemed one another for *thirty years* and upwards . . ."
Niles wrote the year before his retirement. Wilson for years
edited the *Western Herald,* a stanch Whig paper at Steubenville, Ohio. He purchased the Philadelphia *Aurora* from William Duane, another close friend of Niles, in 1822 and ten years
later started to publish the Pittsburgh *Pennsylvania Advocate,*
an undertaking in which Niles wished him success. They supplied each other with ammunition and encouragement in their
battle for protection and each paid tribute to the other in his
respective columns.[137]

Three editors for whom Niles had but little respect because
of their editorial methods were Mordecai M. Noah, editor at
various times of the New York *National Advocate, Morning*

[133] *Register,* XXVII, 21, September 11, 1824.

[134] Niles to Joseph Gales, Jr., December 8, 1830, Joseph Gales, Jr., and William
Winston Seaton Papers, Library of Congress.

[135] *Id.* to *id.,* October 18 and October 23, 1832, Gales and Seaton MSS, Library
of Congress.

[136] *Register,* XLIII, 427, February 23, 1833; XLV, 241–42, December 14, 1833;
306–309, January 4, 1834; XLIX, 242, December 12, 1835.

[137] *Register,* XXIII, 81, October 12, 1822; XXXIX, 233, December 4, 1830; XLIII,
4, September 1, 1832; XLVI, 243, June 7, 1833; XLVIII, 130, April 25, 1835.

Courier and New York Enquirer, and New York *Evening Star;* Duff Green, of the *United States Telegraph,* and Francis P. Blair, of the Washington *Globe.* Of Noah he once wrote, "It would be like breaking a moth, that flutters around the candle, on a wheel, to reason with one who thus trifles with convictions of mean and wanton representation—" [138] With Green, known for his vituperative pen, Niles simply refused to fight. He condemned the "vulgarity and profligacy" of the *Telegraph* and said that he never engaged in "personal brawls—and neither Duff Green, or 'Rough Green' shall cause me to change. . . ." He did not consider the *Telegraph* a respectable paper, and turned down a challenge from Green to an editorial debate on the tariff in 1831, saying he was pledged to Ritchie, "and the gallant general will not expect me to fight two such veterans of the quill . . . on the same subject, and at the same time!" [139] Blair's entrance into the newspaper field in Washington rated one inch of the *Register*'s space. Two years later Niles attacked him for his "scoundrelly insinuation" that Niles changed his attitude on the Bank of the United States because of financial favors. His last brush with the mouthpiece of the Jackson administration came over Blair's articles on the indebtedness of Gales and Seaton to the Bank of the United States. Niles defended his old friends with the not-too-strong argument that their security was sufficient for their loans and that divulging the amount constituted an invasion of their personal privacy.[140]

Because of his custom of ignoring personal attacks and cutting off his exchange list newspapers which persisted in the practice, Niles' relations with most of his contemporaries were pleasant. He encouraged new newspapers and magazines, and paid tribute to editorial friends on their retirement or death. Attacks on him and his policies were referred to with a courteous pen, wielded

138 *Register,* XL, 251, June 11, 1831; other editorial references to Noah may be found in *Register,* XXV, 33, September 20, 1823; XXVI, 19, March 13, 1824; XXVII, 24–28, September 11, 1824; XXXVI, 299, July 4, 1829; XL, 182, May 14, 1831; XLV, 37, September 14, 1833.

139 *Register,* XXXII, 97, April 7, 1827; XXXV, 113, October 18, 1828; XL, 392, July 30, 1831; other editorial notices of Green are in *Register,* XLIII, 10–12, September 1, 1832; XLIX, 98, October 17, 1835.

140 *Register,* XXXIX, 276, December 18, 1830; XLIII, 129, October 27, 1832; XLV, 306–309, January 4, 1834.

with good nature and humor, occasionally with a touch of con-
decension, but seldom with anger.[141]

Niles was shrewd in arriving at his conclusions and was seldom
led astray by wishful thinking. One contemporary American
writer said he was "a shrewd calculator, far-seeing, crafty, and
sagacious; a truly honest man, a patriot, and a Christian. . . .
Without being illiberal, he was never a generous man, and
never unjust." [142]

During the War of 1812 he warned manufacturers that their
present prosperity would not last. Before the news of Jackson's
victory at New Orleans had filtered through the slow channels
of news transmission, Niles predicted that "the British would
sustain one of the greatest losses they ever met with, in their
attack on *New-Orleans*." [143] He forecast the revolution in Spain,
and a year later pooh-poohed the report of the discovery of the
Northwest Passage. Discussing conflicting rumors from South
America, he wrote, "A time of public commotion is not that
which is best fitted to ascertain truth." [144] Exercising the editorial prerogative, he suggested public duckings or legal whip-
pings for those who tell ghost stories to children. He was interested in the United States Military Academy, but felt that it
was kept up at public expense "to educate the fit for *private*
life, the sons of the most wealthy or most influential persons
in the United States." [145]

Niles' onerous duties as editor of the *Register* did not prevent
him from taking part in numerous other activities. He compiled
a number of books, several being collections of essays which first
appeared in the *Register;* served officially for at least two national tariff conventions, editing and publishing their proceedings; was active in Baltimore civic affairs; took part in city, state,

141 *Register*, IX, 389, February 3, 1816; XVI, 108, April 3, 1819; XXII, 69, March
30, 1822; XXIV, 305, July 19, 1823; XXX, 138, April 22, 1826; XXXI, 17, Septem-
ber 9, 1826; XXXIX, 217, November 27, 1830; 252, December 11, 1830; XL, 451–53,
August 27, 1831; XLI, 151, October 22, 1831; XLVI, 189, May 17, 1834; XLVII, 273,
December 27, 1834; 428, February 21, 1835; XLVIII, 115, April 18, 1835; L, 49,
March 26, 1836, are typical of hundreds.

142 Neal, *op. cit.*, 211.

143 *Register*, VI, 217, June 4, 1814; VII, 356, February 4, 1815.

144 *Register*, XVII, 35, September 18, 1819; XVIII, 81, April 1, 1820; 287, June
17, 1820.

145 *Register*, XXII, 33, March 16, 1822; 71, March 30, 1822.

and national politics; and was an active worker and officer in Masonic bodies and typographical associations in Baltimore.

His first publication in pamphlet form was a compilation of editorials written while he was editor of the *Evening Post* and defending Jefferson's foreign policy. The title page bore the following, "By the Editor, Things as they are; or, Federalism turned inside out!! Being a Collection of Extracts from Federal Papers, &c. and Remarks upon Them, Originally written for, and published in the Evening Post. 'O that mine enemy had written a book.' Baltimore: Printed at the Office of the Evening Post, by H. Niles." [146]

Other publications included *Agriculture of the United States, or An Essay concerning Internal Improvements & Domestic Manufacturers, Shewing Their Inseparable Connection with The Business and Interests of Agriculture, In the Establishment of a home-market for bread-stuffs and meats, wool, cotton, flax, hemp, &c. as well as the Supplies that they furnish in aid of the foreign commerce of the United States;* [147] *Politics for Working Men. An Essay on Labor and Subsistence: Addressed to the Free Productive People of the U. States;* [148] and *Journal of the Proceedings of the Friends of Domestic Industry, in General Convention met at the City of New York, October 26, 1831.*[149]

The one volume of any size that Niles published during his years on the *Register* was the 495-page collection of speeches, documents, letters, and other materials of the Revolutionary period entitled, in part, *Principles and Acts of the Revolution in America.*[150]

[146] On the title page of the copy in the Library of Congress is written, "Sept. 15, 1809. Niles, Hezekiah alias Jerry Didler." It contains seventy-five pages.

[147] The title page of this sixteen-page pamphlet carries in small italic type, *"First published in Niles' Register, of March 24, 1827. With additions."*

[148] This was written on July 4, 1831, a fact recorded on the title page. It was reprinted in a sixteen-page pamphlet from the *Register* of July 9, 1831.

[149] This was the proceedings, including the journal and addresses and memorials of the convention of which Niles was the principal secretary.

[150] The full title of this work is *Principles and Acts of the Revolution in America: Or, An Attempt to Collect and Preserve Some of the Speeches, Orations, & Proceedings, with Sketches and Remarks on Men and Things, and Other Fugitive or Neglected Pieces Belonging to the Revolutionary Period in the United States: Which, Happily, Terminated in the Establishment of Their Liberties: with a View to Represent the Feelings That Prevailed in the "Times That Tried Men's Souls," to Excite a Love of Freedom, and Lead the People to Vigilance, as the Condition*

A subscriber wrote to Niles in 1816 suggesting the publication of such a volume. Niles was enthusiastic over the project and immediately wrote to Jefferson,[151] John Adams, and others, asking their co-operation. He requested his readers generally to let him know if they possessed papers of interest to posterity and asked them to tell him whether they would contribute originals or copies. He printed letters and editorials praising the plan,[152] and refused to become discouraged when former President Adams wrote: "In plain English and in a few words, Mr. Niles, I consider the true history of the American revolution, and of the establishment of our present constitution, as lost forever. And nothing but misrepresentation, or partial accounts of it, ever will be recovered." [153] Later Adams relented and sent him several pieces from his own pen to be included in the volume.[154] However, the materials came in slowly and by April, 1818, he was about ready to give up the project, except to publish a special supplement to the *Register* containing what had been sent in.[155] But he changed his mind and went ahead, printing the material when his presses were not otherwise occupied, and the *Register* through 1819, 1820, and 1821 contained references to the progress being made with the volume.[156] Finally, five and one-half years after he began seeking material, the last page of the book was printed, and Niles jubilantly wrote Dr. William Darlington, his friend and correspondent in Congress, that he would soon bring several copies to the Capitol.[157] The announcement of publication brought but few orders, and Niles was left with a large stock on hand, in spite of some clever sales

---

on Which It Is Granted. Dedicated to the Young Men of the United States (Baltimore, 1822).

151 Niles to Jefferson, December 23, 1816, Jefferson MSS, Library of Congress.

152 *Register*, XI, 297, 313, January 4, 1817; 396–97, February 8, 1817; XII, 1–2, March 1, 1817.

153 *Register*, XI, 337, January 18, 1817, quoting letter, dated at Quincy, January 3, 1817.

154 *Register*, XII, 241–43, June 14, 1817; one of these was a pamphlet, "History of the Dispute with America; from its origin in 1754. Written in the year 1774. By John Adams, esq."

155 *Register*, XIV, 106, April 11, 1818.

156 *Register*, XV, 348, January 2, 1819; XVII, 61, September 25, 1819; XVIII, 274, June 17, 1820; XIX, 281, December 30, 1820; XX, 385–86, August 18, 1821.

157 Niles to Darlington, April 16, 1822, Darlington MSS, Library of Congress.

promotion articles in which he reported that only a few copies remained for sale after the subscribers had been supplied.[158] He finally disposed of the volumes by offering one thousand copies as consolation prizes in the lottery he conducted to reduce his stock of *Register* sets and to get some working capital.[159]

As a matter of fact, the volume's material was poorly organized, there was no attempt at chronological order or other classification, and speeches, letters, newspaper articles, and pamphlets appeared in a hodge-podge, discouraging to any but the most ardent seeker after information. The book was reprinted in a somewhat rearranged edition in 1876 with a foreword by Samuel V. Niles, a grandson, and six pages of excerpts from letters recommending republication.[160]

Thus, his two attempts at publishing books of any length were financial failures, the first putting him $25,000 in debt, which he was years in repaying, and the second costing him dearly of time and effort.[161] In his less ambitious ventures, he was more successful. Ten thousand copies of *Things As They Are* were distributed in 1809; the "democratic committee" in Baltimore had borne the expense of publication, and probably distributed the pamphlet free.[162] He estimated that more than one hundred thousand copies of *Agriculture of the United States* reached the public through newspapers and various editions in pamphlet form.[163] Another essay, *Politics for Farmers*, first printed in the *Register* in September, 1830, passed through not less than ninety thousand impressions, he estimated in December of that

---

[158] *Register*, XXII, 113, April 20, 1822; 289, July 6, 1822.

[159] Tickets were sold at $10 each. Prizes included 300 complete sets of the *Register*, valued at $70 each; 500 sets of Volumes XIII–XXIV, valued at $33 each; and 1,000 copies of *Principles and Acts of the Revolution*, valued at $3 each. The lottery was not a financial success.

[160] Hezekiah Niles, *Centennial Offering Republication of the Principles and Acts of the Revolution in America. Dedicated to the Young Men of the United States, fifty-four years ago by the late Hezekiah Niles, Editor of the "Weekly Register"* (New York, 1876).

[161] *Register*, XXV, 146–47, November 8, 1823.

[162] *Register*, XXXVIII, 334, July 3, 1830.

[163] *Register*, XXXII, 353, July 28, 1827; the article may be found in *Register*, XXXII, 49–58, March 24, 1827.

year.[164] Some sixty thousand copies of *Politics for Working Men* were distributed.[165]

In 1827 and again in 1831 Niles took time from his editorial duties to attend and take an active part in conventions held to promote protection of American industry. The first convention was held at Harrisburg, Pennsylvania, from July 30 through August 3, 1827. It had been called by the Pennsylvania Society for the Promotion of Manufacturers and the Mechanical Arts on May 14, and not only manufacturers, but also farmers and other proponents of protection were invited to send delegates. Virginia and Maryland were the only southern states among the thirteen represented.[166] Niles, one of eight delegates from Maryland, was extremely active during the sessions, offering several resolutions and being named chairman of the committee to prepare an address to the people of the United States. A resolution praising his "early, constant and eventually useful exertions in promoting the great cause of American industry and internal improvements," was adopted by the convention.[167]

Niles denied that the convention was in any way interested in candidates in the approaching election except as to their attitude toward the American System.[168] Returning to Baltimore, he turned most of his editorial duties over to his son and spent most of his time for the next two months in the preparation of the convention's address to the people of the country.[169] The address itself occupied nearly twelve pages in the *Register* and was signed by H. Niles, Chairman, dated October 10, 1827.[170] The appendices to the address which were made up of statistics supporting the arguments, and of essays on production and consumption, internal trade, British trade, and other allied subjects, filled many pages in the *Register* during the next two

---

[164] *Register*, XXXIX, 50–55, September 11, 1830; 233, December 4, 1830; see also XXXIX, 89, October 2, 1830; 251, December 11, 1830, and letter from Niles to Darlington, September 10, 1830, Darlington MSS, Library of Congress.

[165] *Register*, XL, 392–93, July 30, 1831; XLI, 99, October 8, 1831.

[166] *Register*, XXXII, 237–40, June 2, 1827; 369, August 4, 1827.

[167] *Register*, XXXII, 388–96, August 11, 1827.

[168] *Register*, XXXII, 353, July 28, 1827; 385, August 11, 1827.

[169] *Register*, XXXIII, 17, September 8, 1827; 97–98, October 13, 1827.

[170] *Register*, XXXIII, 100–111, October 13, 1827.

months.[171] Reviewing the great amount of time and energy that went into the compilation and writing of the address and appendices, time taken without pay from his regular duties, Niles recalled to his readers "that for many years, this work stood *alone* as the steady and zealous advocate of what has been since called the 'American system,' and that now more than one hundred and fifty newspapers in the north, east or west, give a general support to it . . . there is encouragement to hope for better dispositions and better times." He regretted that he was not better fitted to meet the responsibility of preparing the pamphlet and shrewdly predicted that he would be "a mark for any one to shoot at, that pleases—not only with profitable and manly argument, but with satire, reproof and scurrility, and foul and filthy impeachments of motives." [172]

The second tariff convention in which Niles played an important part was held in New York City from October 26 through November 1, 1831. Called as an outgrowth of an earlier convention of New Yorkers, chiefly interested in the growth and manufacture of wool, this second national convention chose Niles temporary secretary and chief of the four permanent secretaries. He also was named chairman of the permanent committee of the convention and charged with the responsibility of preparing a memorial to Congress. This convention, as had the preliminary one, adopted a resolution voicing the thanks of the friends of protection to Niles.[173] Again, he took much time from his editorial duties in gathering the material for and writing the memorial and proceedings of the convention which were not finally ready for distribution until September 1, 1832.[174] In the

171 *Register*, XXXIII, 123–28, October 20, 1827; 138–44, October 27, 1827; 149–60, November 3, 1827; 171–76, November 10, 1827; 188–92, November 17, 1827; 193, 203–208, November 24, 1827.

172 *Register*, XXXIII, 97–98, October 13, 1827; writing to Darlington, September 17, 1827, he said he felt that the address would do some good and that he was more interested in protection than ". . . as to *who* shall be president." November 3, he sent Darlington copies of the completed pamphlet, and asked him to circulate them so that the public mind might have some effect on Congress before it acted on the tariff; Darlington MSS, Library of Congress.

173 *Register*, XL, 242–44, June 4, 1831; XLI, 161, October 29, 1831; 177, 180–92, November 5, 1831.

174 *Register*, XLI, 201, 202–16, November 12, 1831; 242–45, November 26, 1831; 401–13, February 4, 1832; XLII, 90–91, April 7, 1832; XLIII, 1–2, September 1, 1832.

meantime, the memorial to Congress, which made up a part of the pamphlet, had been presented to that body, but too late to affect the pending legislation. Niles wrote a second memorial, addressed to the Senate, supporting Clay's opposition to the House measure, and urging its defeat.[175] This second memorial was also included in the convention report.[176]

Niles' interest in the city in which he spent thirty-one years was expressed in a practical manner by his service on various civic boards and organizations. He was a member of Baltimore City Council for two terms, served on the board of managers of the Maryland Institute, was a director of the state penitentiary, often served as secretary of town meetings, and was a member of the committee on arrangements for the National Republican Convention held in the city in 1831. Early in his career, he was active in Masonic work, serving as Worthy Master of Warren Lodge, Number 51, and in 1818 and 1819 as Grand High Priest of the Grand Chapter.[177] It may be worthy of mention here that he never permitted his Masonic affiliations to affect his handling of statements of those opposed to the order and of news regarding Antimasonic activities, the mystery of the disappearance of William Morgan, and the political activities of the Antimasonic party.[178] Although Niles was an employer rather than an active printer throughout most of his career, he was a member of the Baltimore Typographical Society. In the elaborate parade, held in connection with the groundbreaking ceremonies of the Baltimore & Ohio Railroad, he represented the employers of printers on their float, and in 1830 the Typographical Association presented its flag to him, as senior employer in the city, for custody.[179] Tribute was paid to him at annual meetings of the typographical societies in Washington and Baltimore in 1834 and 1835.[180] As was true of many

175 Niles to Clay, July 4, 1832, Clay MSS, Library of Congress.
176 Hezekiah Niles (ed.), *Journal of the Proceedings of the Friends of Domestic Industry, In General Convention met at the City of New York, October 26, 1831* (Baltimore, 1831).
177 Schultz, *op. cit.*, II, 311–12; 715–16.
178 *Register*, XXXV, 5, August 30, 1828; the ramifications of the Morgan case occupied many columns in the *Register* through 1827, 1828, 1829, 1830, and 1831, too numerous for citation; see especially Volumes XXXII, XXXIII, XXXVIII.
179 *Register*, XXXIV, 322–23, July 12, 1828; XXXIX, 159–62, October 30, 1830.
180 *Register*, XLVI, 114, April 19, 1834; XLIX, 225, December 5, 1835.

notables of his day, he belonged to a volunteer fire company, of which he was several times president.[181]

Niles placed his chosen life work of editing the *Register* above personal considerations and because he thought his acceptance of office might "lessen the general influence" of the paper, he refused to become a candidate for the governor's council in spite of an "almost unanimous desire . . . on the part of our friends in all sections of the state," he wrote Clay in 1830. He expressed to his friend his belief: "The power of my press, because of its consistency, I do think, is second to that of no other in the union, and I cannot consent to put it at hazard; but if my counsels are valued, they shall not be wanted when sought for." [182]

The following year, he apparently changed his mind, for he was defeated as a candidate for the state legislature, a fact over which the St. Louis *Beacon,* reputedly edited by Senator Thomas Hart Benton, expressed pleasure.[183] Some years earlier he had been decidedly receptive to suggestions that he run for Congress. Dependent upon the decision of the incumbent not to run again, Niles had "mentally agreed to stand," he wrote Darlington, but the congressman ran for another term and Niles' appearances at the Capitol were limited to visits made in behalf of protection and of his periodical.[184]

Niles was ever careful to keep his personal political activities and beliefs entirely separate from those expressed in the *Register,* which he held was absolutely nonpartisan as far as men were concerned. His early support of Jefferson has already been mentioned, and he was active in Republican circles in Baltimore for years. He declared he became a "no party" man after the War of 1812, but his vote was always cast for the "Democratic" ticket.[185] As his interest in protection increased, he naturally supported Clay, with whom he was closely associated for years

[181] George W. McCreary, *Ancient and Honorable Mechanical Company of Baltimore. Organized, September 22d, 1763. Provincial Charter, June 26th, 1764. Incorporated by Act of Assembly, No. 127, 1827* . . . (Baltimore, 1901), 7.

[182] Niles to Clay, October 28, 1830, Clay MSS, Library of Congress.

[183] *Register,* XLI, 151, October 22, 1831.

[184] Niles to Darlington, September 7, 1819, and February 28, 1820, Darlington MSS, Library of Congress.

[185] *Register,* XVIII, 449, August 26, 1820; XXV, 132–33, November 1, 1823.

in seeking the adoption of the American System. Niles' correspondence with Darlington, who served several terms in Congress from Pennsylvania, indicated little interest in the election and re-election of James Monroe.[186] He wrote in 1822 that Clay had a design toward the presidential election, "But as yet I feel only a remote, a very remote interest in the thing." In the same letter, he said that the newspapers were being unfair to Calhoun and John Quincy Adams.[187] That fall he expressed respect for several of the candidates, but he felt that none of them combined the various qualities necessary for the office.[188] Early in 1823, he wrote that Maryland was against William H. Crawford, "But we are all waiting to find out whom we shall support." [189] In a letter to Jackson that summer, he wrote: "We are getting quite alive in this city on the presidential election, and though almost to a man opposed to Mr. Crawford are much divided as to whom shall be supported. In this city I apprehend that the *rate* of feeling trends thus—Mr. Adams, yourself, Mr. Clay, Mr. Calhoun, Mr. Crawford. The two first strong, the rest very weak." He went on to say that he was writing him confidentially as a friend, but that his opinion might not be unpleasant, adding that he believed a large majority would be for him, if it were not for their fear of Crawford.[190]

That fall he wrote Darlington of a "very free conversation" he had held with Calhoun which led him to believe that they could unite against Crawford.[191] In January he reported that Jackson was far ahead in Baltimore, but that Adams probably would lead the state. He said that his private wish was for Adams, but that he would be content with any candidate other than Crawford.[192]

During Adams' term, he expressed regret at the political opposition in Congress.[193] Writing to Clay early in 1828, Niles expressed pride in the influence of the *Register*, which he felt

186 Niles to Darlington, February 16 and March 21, 1816, and January 3, 1820, Darlington MSS, Library of Congress.

187 *Id.* to *id.*, June 27, 1822, Darlington MSS, Library of Congress.

188 *Id.* to *id.*, September 24, 1822, Darlington MSS, Library of Congress.

189 *Id.* to *id.*, February 18, 1823, Darlington MSS, Library of Congress.

190 *Id.* to Andrew Jackson, July 23, 1823, Jackson MSS, Library of Congress.

191 *Id.* to Darlington, November 3, 1823, Darlington MSS, Library of Congress.

192 *Id.* to *id.*, January 10, 1824, Darlington MSS, Library of Congress.

193 *Id.* to *id.*, October 23, 1826, Darlington MSS, Library of Congress.

was "quite equal to that of any other paper in the U. S. and rapidly extending," and said that he had no fear of the result of the campaign, "if all exert ourselves as we should." He told the ambitious Kentuckian that he would be the preferred candidate in 1832 for "either the action or re-action *must* favor you & us." [194]

The result of the 1828 election was a disappointment to both men. Clay advised his friend against "gratuitous propositions of support to the new administration or on the other hand a rash and precipitate opposition." [195]

Niles predicted trouble among the Jacksonians,[196] and worked hard for the party and for Clay during Jackson's first term, writing the candidate in October, 1830, that the anti-Jacksonians in Maryland were unanimous in backing him, "but the *reasons* for that opinion are various & partially adverse." His other correspondence with Clay expressed confidence, but pointed to the necessity of hard work.[197]

President Jackson's re-election ended, as far as is known, Niles' political activities. Bowing to the will of the majority, he diverted his energy to an effort to sustain the protective tariff, an undertaking in which he was no more successful than he had been in his battle for internal improvements and the rechartering of the Bank of the United States.

The only time that Niles tried to benefit directly from his political contacts was in the 1824–1825 session of Congress when he sought election as printer to Congress. Rather optimistically, he counted upon the personal friendship of Adams, Jackson, Clay, Calhoun, and John McLean, and he wrote Darlington that he could be of great service to him "by dropping letters to some of your old colleagues." He particularly requested Darlington, who was not in Congress at the time, to write to Calhoun.[198] To Thomas Ritchie and other editorial colleagues who saw that he had little hope of obtaining the place and advised

194 *Id.* to Clay, April 2, 1828, Clay MSS, Library of Congress.
195 Clay to Niles, November 25, 1828, Clay MSS, Library of Congress.
196 Niles to Darlington, January 26, 1829, Darlington MSS, Library of Congress.
197 *Id.* to Clay, September 17, September 18, October 28, 1830, and July 4, 1832, Clay MSS, Library of Congress.
198 *Id.* to Darlington, December 3, 1824, Darlington MSS, Library of Congress.

him against making the attempt, Niles retorted that he had as much right as any to offer himself and that he had been solicited to seek the position two years earlier, but had not done so because he thought Gales and Seaton were entitled to two terms.[199] When he received only 40 votes as against 141 for the editors of the *Intelligencer,* he wrote, "It was the *first* time that I ever sought public employment, and it probably will be the last. . . ." [200] That he had been too sanguine of success, there is no question, but he wrote two years later, denying that he was again an applicant for the post, that he had been "seduced into an application for the place . . . in 1825, and abandoned by those who led him into the proceeding. . . . Thereby 'hangs a tale' never yet told—and which, probably, never will be." [201]

A man's contemporaries may not be the best judges of his worth, but their opinions at least show the place he occupies in their estimation. Niles had many admirers, and he also had enemies. One who took as definite a stand as he did on the public questions of the day was certain to create a following and set up an opposition. His relations with his fellow editors, especially those on the larger and more influential newspapers, have been examined, but it might be well in passing to call attention to the attitude of the press in general toward him. In 1817 the editor of the Richmond *Compiler* suggested that Niles draw up some canons for the regulation of the press, an instance of the faint stirrings of editorial ethics which finally found fruition in the code drawn up by the American Society of Newspaper Editors in 1923. Niles declined to act on the suggestion, but agreed to compile facts about the number of papers in the country.[202] Editors of the Norfolk *Herald, People's Press* of Batavia, New York, Norwich *Courier,* and Lexington *Intelligencer* were among the many who expressed their praise of the editor during his career.[203] The Milledgeville *Georgia Journal* qualified its compliment by saying that when

199 *Register,* XXVII, 321, January 22, 1825.
200 *Register,* XXVII, 401, 414, February 26, 1825.
201 *Register,* XXXII, 97, April 7, 1827.
202 *Register,* XIII, 210, November 29, 1817.
203 *Register,* XXI, 193, November 24, 1821; XXXII, 323, July 14, 1827; XXXV, 116, October 18, 1828; XLVIII, 58, March 28, 1835.

he stayed away from the American System he was "generally a
man of good, sound, practical every day sense." [204] A western
editor favored him for president, a fact which Niles passed off
with a laugh.[205] Others, of opposite political and economic beliefs, assailed him, but recognized his position, the New York
Evening Post charging that one could not find in Clay's orations, ". . . a single argument which cannot be traced to the
dull pages of Niles' Register, and the interminable essays of
Mathew Carey." [206]

Seldom did a meeting of friends of domestic industry adjourn
in the late twenties and early thirties without adopting a resolution thanking Hezekiah Niles, and very often his friend,
Mathew Carey, for the aid they had given American manufacturers. These resolutions came from such widely separated localities as Goose Creek Meetinghouse, Loudon County, Virginia; Utica, New York; Pittsfield, Massachusetts; Hudson, New
York; New York City; and Cambridge, Maryland.[207] Admirers
sent him gifts, including cloth for suits, casks of wine, damask
tablecloths, and numerous other examples of the progress of
American manufacturers.[208] With the prevailing system of toasts
drunk at every dinner meeting, it was inevitable that Niles
should be the recipient of many such expressions of esteem. He
was hailed as "The great champion of the American System,"
"the consistent, faithful and successful advocate of American
industry," and his "talents, patriotism and perseverance" were
praised.[209] Now and then at an antitariff meeting, his enemies
also toasted—or roasted—him. A Major James Jones at Sumpter-
ville, South Carolina, proposed this sentiment: "Hezekiah
Niles and Mathew Carey—the big ourang-outang and baboon

[204] *Register*, XXXVI, 97–98, April 11, 1829.
[205] *Register*, XLI, 265, December 10, 1831.
[206] *Register*, XXXVIII, 82, March 27, 1830.
[207] *Register*, XXXIII, 358–59, January 26, 1828; XXXIX, 155, October 30, 1830; XL, 233, June 4, 1831; XLI, 151, October 22, 1831.
[208] *Register*, XVIII, 45, March 18, 1820; XXVIII, 305–306, July 16, 1825; XXXVIII, 65, March 20, 1830, are a few of the many places where thanks are expressed for gifts.
[209] *Register*, XXXIV, 416, August 23, 1828; XXXVIII, 387, July 24, 1830; XL, 167, May 7, 1831; others are mentioned in XXXII, 324, July 14, 1827; XXXIV, 393, August 16, 1828; XXXVIII, 365, July 17, 1830.

of the 'monkey system;' we blush for our humanity when they dictate to twelve millions of freemen." [210]

His enemies frequently attacked him in "coarsely written" anonymous letters which Niles threw away, although he requested the writers to pay the postage on such abusive communications.[211] The fact that he received many crank letters and had been tarred and feathered, hanged and burned in effigy a number of times led him to express unconcern over the furore raised by the Washington *Globe* about the receipt of threatening letters by President Jackson.[212]

Niles' name lives in two cities in the Middle West, Niles, Ohio, and Niles, Michigan. When he received a letter postmarked "Niles" in 1829, he acknowledged the compliment paid him and expressed the hope that he was deserving of such honor.[213] The rapid growth of the Michigan village pleased him; he occasionally printed items about it from western papers, and when its first newspaper, the Niles *Gazette and Advertiser,* appeared he gave it and the town a notice.[214]

His retirement because of ill health has already been commented upon. He made his will on July 6, 1836, signing it with his left hand because of his paralyzed right side.[215] Two months later he said farewell to his life's work in the following words: ". . . I know my own resources, and the vainness of a hope of relying on any other. The work is my own, whether it be good or bad; and has been persevered in with invincible industry, and oftentimes under distressing circumstances, until, at length, I am, temporarily at least placed in a condition that compels a retirement from its active duties. . . . I retire from the editorial seat with feelings of gratitude and without hostility to any human being." [216]

[210] *Register,* XXVIII, 398, July 31, 1830, to which Niles urbanely replied that dictating to 12,000,000 ". . . is something like a compliment. . . ."

[211] *Register,* XLIII, 2, September 1, 1832.

[212] *Register,* XLVII, 409, February 14, 1835.

[213] *Register,* XXXVII, 161, November 7, 1829; *National Encyclopaedia of American Biography* (1898—), X, 255.

[214] *Register,* XLVIII, 130, April 25, 1835; XLIX, 122, October 24, 1835.

[215] Certified Copy Last Will and Testament of Hezekiah Niles, Register of Wills, Baltimore City, Wills Liber, D. M. P., No. 17, Folio No. 281.

[216] *Register,* LI, 1, September 3, 1836.

In the fall he returned to Wilmington where he had many friends with whom he had kept in touch throughout his absence of thirty-one years. But his physical condition prevented him from getting much enjoyment from his well-earned leisure. He suffered greatly and death, which came on April 2, 1839, undoubtedly was a relief from the enforced painful inactivity which followed a life of diligent and uninterrupted industry.

The press in general gave generous space to Niles' passing. The *Daily National Intelligencer,* Washington *Globe, Delaware State Journal* and *Delaware Gazette,* both of Wilmington, the Baltimore *Sun,* Baltimore *Republican,* Baltimore *Patriot and Commercial Gazette, Poulson's American Daily Advertiser* of Philadelphia, the Boston *Daily Courier,* Boston *Daily Evening Transcript,* Springfield (Massachusetts) *Republican* are among newspapers in which obituaries have been located, and it is probable that a search would reveal many similar notices. As was the custom of the day, many of these articles were copied from exchanges, and it is apparent that most of them were based upon the tributes originally appearing in the two Wilmington papers and in the *Sun* at Baltimore which had been started after his retirement. The *Sun* mentioned especially his services to the typographical profession and to the public, concluding: "Such a man is a true patriot, and as long as the United States shall preserve its independence, so long shall the name of Hezekiah Niles, the founder of Niles' Register, be revered, and his career be quoted as an example for imitation, by all who desire to obtain that highest and noblest title: a good and honest man, in private life; in public, a pure disinterested patriot." [217]

The *Daily National Intelligencer* on April 4 quoted the Baltimore *Chronicle* in stressing his ". . . frank, honorable, independent, and truly republican spirit, simple in his manners, and habits, affectionate to his family, liberal to those who he employed in the prosecution of his business, disinterested and public spirited." [218]

Two days later the *Intelligencer* printed a longer notice from

[217] Baltimore *Sun,* April 3, 1839.
[218] Washington (D. C.) *Daily National Intelligencer,* April 4, 1839.

the *Delaware State Journal,* which mentioned his "forcible, perspicuous, and original" style of writing, his unusual memory, and his ardent patriotism.[219]

The *Register* printed the announcement of its founder's death in a seven and one-half inch article in the first column of the first page with column rules and cut off rules turned. William Ogden Niles had gone to Wilmington to be at his father's bedside. A brief notice above the obituary said that the event which compelled the editor's absence made an apology for the contents of the present number unnecessary. Strangely enough, viewed in the light of present-day newspaper practice, the son apparently had prepared no obituary of his father in spite of his long illness. The *Register* merely reprinted the first obituary article from the *Delaware State Journal,* errors and all.[220] A week later the son paid a brief tribute to his parent and predecessor in the editorial chair. He promised to present a history "of his life and writings to the public, through the pages of this work; in which we will endeavor to do justice to his memory, by exhibiting his devotion to his beloved country and his desire to promote the happiness of his fellow men," a plan, like so many others of the son, never carried out.[221]

[219] *Daily National Intelligencer,* April 6, 1839; for entire obituary see Wilmington *Delaware State Journal,* April 2 and April 5, in the latter of which several errors in the first article were corrected.

[220] *Register,* LVI, 81, April 6, 1839; other obituaries were printed in Baltimore *Republican,* April 4, 1839; Boston *Courier,* April 6, 1839; Boston *Daily Evening Transcript,* April 6, 1839; *Delaware Gazette* (Wilmington), April 5, 1839; *Poulson's American Daily Advertiser* (Philadelphia), April 4, 1839; Springfield (Mass.) *Republican,* April 13, 1839; Washington *Globe,* April 5, 1839.

[221] *Register,* LVI, 97, April 13, 1839.

Chapter 3

Other Editors of the *Register*

WILLIAM OGDEN NILES, eldest son of Hezekiah, edited the *Register* from September 3, 1836, to October 12, 1839. It was he who moved the publication office to Washington, and changed the name to *Niles' National Register*.[1] When he became editor he promised to endeavor to carry out his father's policies unchanged,[2] but in spite of his previous association with his father on the *Register* and his varied newspaper work, the job was too much for him.[3] From the first number published under his editorship to the final one, carrying his embittered farewell to his readers, the *Register* reflected his inability to fill his father's shoes.[4]

He improved its format and typographical appearance and bought modern equipment, but he edited with scissors and paste. As an editor he became increasingly absorbed in the activities of Congress and filled more and more columns of the *Register* with abridged reports of the debates. To allot practically all the space to the debates was not good editorial judgment because the weekly publication could not hope to compete with such dailies as the *National Intelligencer* and the Washington *Globe*, which specialized in this type of reporting.

The son's intentions were good, but like most editors of the period and unlike his father, he gave evidence of being more interested in politics than in journalism. After he moved to Washington he covered Congress himself for the *Register*, al-

1 *Register*, LII, 353, August 5, 1837; LIII, 1, September 2, 1837.

2 Proposed policies were printed in *Register*, LI, 1, September 3, 1836.

3 In 1825 he started the Albany *Journal and Mercantile Advertiser*, a triweekly, and from 1830 to 1836 he published the Frederick (Md.) *Herald*, a weekly, which he purchased when he and his father dissolved their qualified partnership; see *Register*, XXVIII, 129, April 30, 1825 and XXXIX, 137, October 23, 1830.

4 *Register*, LI, 1, September 3, 1836, through LVII, 113, October 19, 1839.

though he continued the practice of his father of condensing the reports of the *National Intelligencer* and the Washington *Globe*.[5] He lacked not only his father's skill with the pen, but also his ability to select and condense news.[6] His preoccupation with Congressional and political matters failed to present the wide picture of the contemporaneous scene which his father had so well done. Ambitious, as shown by his plans for improving the publication, for getting printing from Congress, and by the hiring of his own reporters at the Capitol, he lacked the business ability of his father.[7] The new editor was apparently unable to meet the notes he had given his father in payment for the establishment and probably unable to meet his payroll, for the periodical was suspended through May, June, and most of July, 1839.[8] The period of suspension followed almost immediately after the death of Hezekiah Niles, and shortly after publication was resumed the *Register* was offered for sale.[9]

William Ogden Niles' feelings toward his father's second wife, who, as administratrix of his estate, decided to sell the *Register*, were bitter. In his valedictory to his readers, he mentioned that he had "fondly hoped that death alone would sever" his connection with the *Register* which he had hoped "would long, very long, remain in the family of its founder, as an enduring evidence of sacred regard for one of the dearest aspirations of his heart." He went on to add with a note of defiant pride "that amidst the conflicting emotions of the present moment I have the proud consolation that I have surrendered the 'REGISTER,' unimpaired in its character as an historical record and with a subscription list as large, if not larger, than it was when I received it from the hands of my father." [10]

In the number which announced that the *Register* was for

5 *Register*, LIII, 1, September 2, 1837; 17, September 9, 1837.
6 An example of the son's florid style may be found in *Register*, LIV, 257, June 23, 1838.
7 *Register*, LIV, 257, June 23, 1838; LV, 209, December 1, 1838.
8 *Register*, LVI, 321, July 20, 1839. The missing issues were later printed by William Ogden Niles and his successor so that subscribers had a complete volume. For detailed description of his financial difficulties see *Register*, LIX (address accompanying title page).
9 *Register*, LVII, 1, August 31, 1839; 17, September 7, 1839; 33, September 14, 1839.
10 *Register*, LVII, 113, October 19, 1839.

sale, he inserted a notice saying that he would soon be "at liberty," and asking for an editorial job in any of the large cities or in one of the prosperous towns in the West. He pointed to his experience of "more than fifteen years" as "assistant editor" of the *Register*, and his conduct for six years of a Whig political paper.[11]

He returned to the political-paper field in August, 1840, when he started publication of the *Daily Evening Gazette* in Baltimore.[12] That same year he compiled, chiefly from the columns of the *Register*, a ninety-five page campaign biography of William Henry Harrison, entitled *The Tippecanoe Text-Book, Compiled from Niles' Register and Other Authentic Records.* The book contained eight highly laudatory chapters of the Whig candidate.

The death of a son, Hezekiah, a midshipman in the navy, was given space in the *Register* in 1841, although no mention was made in the obituary, which was reprinted from the Baltimore *American*, of the father's occupation at the time.[13] William Ogden Niles died in Philadelphia on July 8, 1858, from paralysis and apoplexy. At the time of his death he was employed by the United States Pension Bureau.[14]

Jeremiah Hughes, editor and publisher of *Niles' National Register* for eight and one-half years, was second among the four editors of the periodical in point of tenure and influence. An old and valued friend of the first editor, he had been active for thirty years in Maryland journalism.[15] For many years he was editor of the *Maryland Republican*, published at the state capital, and he was credited with doing much to improve that city's harbor and to encourage the erection of public buildings. During the War of 1812, he was adjutant general of the militia of Maryland.[16]

While serving as state printer in 1834, he was criticized on

---

11 *Register*, LVII, 1, August 31, 1839; his interpretation of "assistant" was broad as he enjoyed a qualified partnership with his father from 1827 to 1830; he probably had served his apprenticeship and had been employed in the office earlier.

12 *Register*, LVIII, 401, August 29, 1840; Scharf, *Chronicles of Baltimore*, 94.

13 *Register*, LXI, 256, December 18, 1841.

14 Scharf, *History of Delaware*, I, 466.

15 *Register*, LVII, 113, October 19, 1839.

16 *Register*, LXXIV, 400, December 20, 1848, which contains an obituary reprinted from the *Annapolis* [sic] [*Maryland*] *Republican*.

the floor of the House of Delegates for opposing editorially the stage appearance in Annapolis of Colonel R. M. Johnson and the part the House was allegedly playing in sponsoring the performance, which Hughes felt was merely a build-up of Johnson's vice-presidential candidacy. However, his legislative friends rallied to his support and the proposed resolutions of censure were withdrawn.[17]

His editorial motto, "By his works ye shall know him," was expressed in his bow to his patrons in which he paid tribute to his friend, Hezekiah Niles, and promised "To collect materials . . . for the future history of the passing age, and to afford a standard and impartial record of public documents, incidents and decisions, which may be referred to as authority." [18]

Hughes took over the *Register* under inauspicious circumstances. Publication had been resumed for only three months after a period of two and one-half months during which the periodical did not appear. Subscribers undoubtedly were wary of sending in their hard-earned money to a shaky enterprise in spite of its history of nearly twenty-eight years of unbroken publication. He set about to make up the missing numbers and within three months had printed all of them and was engaged in compiling indices for three preceding volumes, a task neglected by his immediate predecessor in spite of promises.[19] He wrote truly enough that no one but newspaper publishers could estimate the extra labor imposed upon him and apologized for the irregularity of the *Register*'s appearance during this "tour of double duty." [20] By May, he had compiled and mailed to subscribers the missing indices, including the one to the volume completed on February 29, 1840, no small accomplishment for an editor who was at the same time preparing and editing copy for a sixteen-page weekly.[21]

In a prospectus accompanying the title page and index to the fifty-seventh volume, he described his plans for the *Register,* which embraced a thorough coverage of all significant national and foreign news.[22] The lack of original material and editorial

---

17 *Register*, XLV, 384–86, February 8, 1834.
18 *Register*, LVII, 113, October 13, 1839.   19 *Register*, LVI, 321, July 20, 1839.
20 *Register*, LVII, 337, January 25, 1840.   21 *Register*, LVIII, 129, May 2, 1840.
22 *Register*, LVII, iii, preceding index.

comment in the early volumes of the *Register* under his editorship is noticeable, but later Hughes wrote many vigorous editorials on controversial questions.

The financial difficulties which had been a worry to Hezekiah
Niles through his quarter century as publisher, and to his son,
were complicated further for the third editor-owner because of
the fact that subscribers who owed long-overdue accounts apparently had been antagonized by attempts at collection. In an
address to his readers early in 1841, Hughes mentioned these
"most embarrassing and sometimes provoking difficulties" arising from the fact that the establishment had had three proprietors within the past five years. He informed his subscribers
that subscriptions through August, 1836, should be paid to
Philip Reigart, acting agent for the administrators of the estate
of Hezekiah Niles. Those from September, 1836, through February, 1839, were payable to Thomas Hill, agent and assignee
of William Ogden Niles, for his creditors, and from March,
1839, to himself.[23]

Hughes maintained the policy of presenting both sides of
questions without relation to the editorial stand of the *Register*
and resumed Hezekiah Niles' practice of writing annual New
Year's editorials.[24] A friend of temperance, he gave frequent space
to the meetings of temperance societies.[25] In handling his campaign against war with Great Britain over Oregon, in which he
criticized the administration for its belligerent attitude when
the nation was unprepared for war, he adopted a technique still
used by newspaper editors. It was that of carrying the same or a
similar headline over editorial articles week after week, with
the idea that the reiteration would awaken in the reader's consciousness an awareness of the situation. In November and December, 1845, the headline, "IS WAR BREWING? Are We Ready?"
was used. The first four months of 1846 saw the following headlines used twelve times: [26]

23 *Register*, LIX, address accompanying title page.

24 *Register*, LXIII, 273, December 31, 1842; LXIV, 193, May 27, 1843; LXIX, 273,
January 3, 1846.

25 *Register*, LXII, 289, July 9, 1842; LXVI, 256, June 15, 1844; LXVII, 16, September 7, 1844; LXXII, 254–55, June 19, 1847.

26 *Register*, LXIX, 148, 187, 228, 241, 284, 289, 305, 321, 340, 353, 369, 385, November 8, 1845 through February 21, 1846; LXX 17, 33, 49, 65, March 14 through
April 4, 1846.

ARE WE TO HAVE WAR OR PEACE?

SHALL WE HAVE WAR OR PEACE?

SHALL WE HAVE PEACE OR WAR?

His relations with contemporaries in the newspaper field were similar to those of Hezekiah Niles. Early in 1845 he reported the rumored transfer of the *Globe* to Thomas Ritchie and John P. Heiss, and the sale of the *Madisonian*.[27] When the *Globe* became the Washington *Union,* he acknowledged that Ritchie "probably contributed more than any other man in the union towards elevating Mr. POLK to the presidency—." He printed without comment the opinion of a correspondent of the Baltimore *Patriot* that the Virginia editor and politician would find in Washington a far different atmosphere than he was accustomed to in Richmond. Carrying from the *Globe* of April 14 the statement of Francis Preston Blair and John C. Rives, its outgoing proprietors, and from the *Union* of May 1 the new editor's address, he also added to his readers' information about the press in the nation's capital by printing from the *National Intelligencer* of May 3 a two-column background story on the government press.[28] When the *Intelligencer* and the *Union* came to grips, as they often did, he printed excerpts from their intellectual combats.[29]

The final number of the seventy-third volume appeared on February 26, 1848, but there was no notice in the issue of the impending four months' suspension. In the lower right-hand corner of the last page of the index, which usually went out to subscribers some few weeks after the last number of the volume was published, this notice was printed:

It has become necessary to suspend for a few weeks the publication of NILES' NATIONAL REGISTER. The publication will be resumed as speedily as possible, in new type and an improved appearance, which nothing but the want of adequate support and funds, has so long delayed.

[27] *Register,* LXVIII, 96, April 12, 1845.

[28] *Register,* LXVIII, 153–54, May 10, 1845.

[29] *Register,* LXX, 4–5, March 7, 1846, where nearly five columns from both papers are reprinted, is typical.

Such of our friends as are in arrear [*sic*] for subscription are very earnestly requested to aid us by remitting per mail.[30]

Hughes was sixty-five years old and did not feel equal to the task of continuing the publication of the *Register* under adverse financial conditions. He found a buyer and wrote his valedictory to his patrons in the first issue published under the new ownership. In it he referred to his fervent determination to meet the responsibility of editing the *Register*, which he said he had done "amidst such a series of embarrassments, difficulties and disheartening circumstances as few publishers have been subjected to."

That he felt he had done well was indicated in these two sentences: "The material for nine years of eventful history to our country has been 'Registered,' as we believe, and certainly as we intended, impartially selected and condensed to our number of pages with unremitting toil, knowing that by our works we were to be judged. To the future HISTORIAN we commit the record, and await the final judgment with full confidence."[31]

Six months later Jeremiah Hughes was dead. The *Maryland Republican*'s obituary of its former editor paid homage to his good works and mentioned especially his exhaustless energy, his perseverance, and his active and enlarged mind.[32] That the evening of his editorial days was spent on the *Register* was of unquestioned benefit to that periodical.

George Beatty purchased the *Register* from Jeremiah Hughes, moved its office to Philadelphia,[33] where he got out the fifty-two issues of two volumes with fair regularity, and made a futile attempt to keep the publication alive by selling advertising.[34] This last-minute injection of additional revenue failed to sup-

[30] *Register*, LXXIII, iii (incorrectly numbered, should be viii).

[31] *Register*, LXXIV, 1, July 5, 1848.

[32] *Register*, LXXIV, 400, December 20, 1848, which carried the obituary without credit. On the first page of the next issue (LXXIV, 401, December 27, 1848), was a notation that the article had been taken from the *Annapolis* [*sic*] [*Maryland*] *Republican*. An earlier brief death notice was printed in *Register*, LXXIV, 352, November 29, 1848.

[33] *Register*, LXXIV, 1, July 5, 1848.

[34] *Register*, LXXVI, September 14, 21, 28, 1849. These three numbers are rare. The Library of Congress has them, each of the three copies being autographed, "P. Force."

ply the needed spark, and the publication, famous in its day throughout the United States and in foreign countries, died.

The new owner-editor was a young man whom his predecessor styled "active, and enterprising," but his enterprise could not take the place of editorial experience he admittedly lacked.[35] The fifty-five numbers published under his direction are evidence of his ineptitude as an editor. He entered into his new work with enthusiasm and optimism and a realization of the responsibility he was assuming, but the problem of keeping unbroken the recording of a chain of events begun by the founder nearly thirty-seven years earlier proved too difficult for him to solve.[36]

The *Register* had not been published during March, April, May, and June, 1848, during which time the political parties had held their conventions and made their nominations for the fall campaign. That a report of their proceedings be printed in the *Register* was entirely fitting in order to have no gaps in the periodical's record for the future. But instead of intelligently and succinctly summarizing the proceedings, platforms, and nominations of the Whigs, Democrats, and Barnburners, he carried column after column on the conventions, including such details as lists of delegates and papers accompanying the credentials committee's report, months after the conventions and weeks after the election had been held.[37] In an address, closing the first volume under his editorship, he asked indulgence for the errors of inexperience and promised to issue the first number of the next volume on the regular day of publication.[38] This failure to meet deadlines showed his lack of newspaper background and undoubtedly irked subscribers who had received their papers with clocklike regularity for years except when the mails failed. After six months, he resorted to the expedient of reducing the subscription price, which had stood at $5.00 a year during the entire life of the periodical, to $4.00,

---

[35] *Register*, LXXIV, 1, July 5, 1848; 401, December 27, 1848.

[36] For detailed statement of his hopes and objectives see the column-long address to readers and five separate notices, occupying the next column in *Register*, LXXIV, 1–2, July 5, 1848.

[37] *Register*, LXXIV, 349, November 29, 1848; 376–80, December 13, 1848.

[38] *Register*, LXXIV, 401, December 27, 1848.

when paid in advance. Group subscriptions of three for $10.00 and seven for $20.00 also were offered.[39]

Beatty repeatedly expressed a high conception of the function of the *Register* and promised the exercise of unwearied pains in collecting accurate and impartial statements concerning national and state governments, but his ability to carry out his promises was circumscribed by his lack of editorial experience.[40]

In the final number of the seventy-fifth volume, which like the preceding issue consisted of only eight instead of the usual sixteen pages, appeared this announcement: "TO SUBSCRIBERS. —The next number of the *Register* will be delayed until after the middle of July, in order to complete the arrangements for issuing it in an improved form." It was concluded with two paragraphs appealing to subscribers to remit.[41] Publication, however, was not resumed until September 14 when the first of three issues, numbered, respectively, 11, 12, and 13, appeared. He planned to make up the ten missing issues, but never did. His office had been moved to his residence during the interim, an evidence of his financial situation. The subscription price, in advance, was further reduced to $3.00.[42]

From a journalistic point of view, Beatty's editorship was the least satisfactory of the four editorial regimes of the *Register*. The value of the volumes printed after Hughes' retirement does not compare with that of any of the seventy-three volumes published before. Volumes LXXIV and LXXV and the three issues of LXXVI represent the product of a novice unable to cope with the multitudinous problems faced by the editor of a periodical of national scope.

[39] *Register*, LXXV, 1, January 3, 1849.
[40] *Register*, LXXV, 17, January 10, 1849.
[41] *Register*, LXXV, 393, June 27, 1849.
[42] *Register*, LXXVI, advertising cover (unnumbered), September 14, 1849; repeated in the two succeeding issues.

Chapter 4

News and Editorials

THE *Register* was both a newspaper and a magazine. Possessing certain of the characteristics of these two types of publication, the periodical actually was a weekly news magazine specializing in printing official documents, governmental reports, Congressional speeches on matters of great public moment, and diplomatic correspondence, with a summary of the significant news of national interest. In addition, in the first half of its thirty-eight-year career, it campaigned unceasingly through editorial and statistical articles for the American System, including a protective tariff for American manufacturers, federal government expenditures for internal improvements, higher wages for labor, a national banking system, and an increase in population.

Before discussing in detail the various classifications of material carried in its columns, the contents of two numbers of the *Register,* as typical, will be briefly listed. The number for June 12, 1813, contained the governor's speech to the Massachusetts legislature, the report of the United States Treasury, "Events of the War," the weekly list of "American Prizes" (ships captured), proceedings of Congress, ten or eleven brief news items in the department called "A Chronicle," and a "Postscript" containing three brief war items.

The March 12, 1825, number, which Niles said fulfilled the design of the work, contained a note on the contents, a brief mention of John Quincy Adams' inaugural address, cabinet appointments, a mention of the secrecy being removed from the Senate vote on Clay's confirmation as secretary of state, naval promotions, an article on the rejection of a slave-trade convention with Colombia, an article on a treaty with the Creeks, ceding land to Georgia, the King's speech to Parliament, a description of the inauguration ceremonies, Andrew Jackson's letter to Samuel Swartwout, G. Kremer's address of February 25, statements of William Brent, Peter Little, and William Dudley Digges, all on the Jackson-Clay controversy, Francis Johnson's address to the public, proceedings of the House and the Senate, and five miscellaneous items in "A Chronicle."

There were times when the press of Congressional proceedings and a plethora of official reports filled the periodical's columns to the practical exclusion of every other type of news or article. This usually occurred at the beginning and near the end of Congressional sessions.

Its book size and $5.00 subscription price occasionally brought a complaint from a reader, but Niles stoutly maintained that it contained as much reading matter as ten or twelve weekly papers and as much as the average of the daily papers, eliminating advertising.

Now and then a note on the first page of an issue called attention to the contents, of which the following is typical:

The present sheet has a greater variety of articles than usual—some of them are as follows: the official report concerning the conflagration of the treasury building—a circular from the postmaster general on abuses of the *franking privilege*—a long account of a grand military celebration at *Charleston, S. C.* with the speeches of gov. *Hayne* and gen. *Hamilton*—the speech of Mr. Tyler, at a public dinner given to him in Gloucester county, Virginia—the *emperor of China*'s prayer for rain—a letter from Mr. *Calhoun,* on being invited to a public dinner at Edgefield—law case concerning naturalization happening in South Carolina—message of the governor of Massachusetts concerning a certain act of incorporation—present state of Mexico, (official)—Foreign news, with the proclamation of King Otho, of Greece, French "free trade," &c. &c.[1]

Naturally, the periodical's contents reflected events of the times, and certain of the volumes when studied a century after publication leave definite impressions in the mind of the reader. News of the War of 1812, as might be expected, predominated in the columns during the war years. Politics and Lafayette's visit to the United States dominated the pages of the twenty-seventh volume; the forty-ninth volume was filled with aboli-

[1] *Register*, XLIV, 113, April 20, 1833.

tionist disputes and difficulties; the fiftieth was devoted to Texas more than to any other item of intelligence; the sixtieth contained a great deal of Congressional material, especially on the pre-emption bill and the various bank bills; the sixty-second gave many pages to the Northeastern boundary dispute; and the sixty-fourth presented a complete picture of the early stages of the 1844 presidential campaign.

Forty-three of the fifty volumes edited by Hezekiah Niles contain considerable original material in the form of essays written to disseminate his views on political economy, editorials advocating the American System, statistical and argumentative articles supporting his economic theories, and verbose editorials with the title "Desultory Remarks," which well describes them. Beginning with the forty-fourth volume, March 2, 1833, the editorial and original matter declined noticeably and there was a concurrent increase in the amount of factual material derived from official sources and other newspapers. The three volumes published at Washington, D. C., by William Ogden Niles, as well as the two earlier ones under his editorship, were given over to a great extent to the debates in Congress. A greater variety of content is evident in the fifty-sixth volume, and Jeremiah Hughes, the new owner, outlined in the prospectus accompanying the fifty-seventh volume's index and title page, his nine-point program for the *Register*'s content. He proposed to present news and documents under the following departments:

Foreign Articles
National Concerns
Affairs of the States of the Union
Passing Incidents
Law and Cases in Court
Political
Inventions, Improvements, the Arts and Literature
Congressional Proceedings
A Chronicle [2]

This plan of presentation was followed as closely as one can expect any periodical dealing with news events to conform to a pattern.

The issue of June 10, 1843, carried a variety of material typi-

[2] *Register*, LVII, iii, preceding index.

cal of the *Register*'s contents during the forties when Congress was not in session. Eight columns of news, chiefly governmental, from Great Britain, and shorter items from France, Spain, Cuba, Portugal, Germany, Turkey, India, Sandwich Islands, China, Yucatan, and Mexico filled the first four pages. Texas news occupied just over two pages, an editorial of more than a column advocated a commercial treaty with England, two columns were given over to army and navy news, and about a page and a half to the "States of the Union" department containing items from Pennsylvania, South Carolina, Indiana, Florida, Iowa, and Oregon. Miscellaneous news, including a speech of Daniel Webster, articles on the Canadian census and Canadian tariff, public-school music, state repudiation, southwestern borders, and Peter the Great's will, filled two pages. Slightly more than a page was devoted to politics, with John Tyler, John C. Calhoun, and Webster being given most of the attention. Two pages on the Sandwich Islands, including some correspondence between a British ship commander and the King of the Islands, were followed by nearly a page on trade with Bremen. As usual, the last page was occupied by the department, "A Chronicle," which this week contained thirty-one items on as many different subjects.

From the viewpoint of the political historian, the issue of May 4, 1844, is filled with interest. In the sixteen pages may be found, in the following order: a brief editorial on the Texas letters of Henry Clay and Martin Van Buren, the proceedings of the Whig National Convention which nominated Clay and Frelinghuysen, a brief report on the Young Men's Whig Ratifying Convention, the Texas annexation treaty, President Tyler's message and documents accompanying the treaty, Clay's Raleigh letter, Van Buren's Lindenwald letter, a defense of Clay against the old "bargain and corruption" charge, a brief account of proceedings in the Senate and House, and a page of miscellaneous items.

An analysis of these two issues, which represent a fair sampling of the *Register*'s contents, clearly indicates why the periodical has been so much used by students of the period.

In 1848 and 1849 there was much less variety, and the publication presented a dreary parade of not-too-judiciously selected documents and official papers, often printed months after their news interest to contemporaries had died down.

The well-defined plan of the founder to edit the *Register* primarily for future readers, but with the contemporary subscribers kept in mind, rather naturally divides the description of its contents into two main parts: First, articles of interest to contemporary readers, and second, material chosen with an eye toward future reference. As it has worked out, much of the material selected obviously because of its contemporary interest has added greatly to the value of the *Register* as a contemporary source for scholars. Niles was not unaware that such material would prove valuable. The contemporary news will be examined here under the following heads: (1) Difference in nineteenth- and twentieth-century handling of news; (2) big news stories; (3) governmental news; (4) news from states; (5) foreign news; (6) mirroring contemporary editorial opinion; (7) miscellany.

The *Register*'s editors constantly kept in mind the national character of its circulation, hence, any comparison or contrast should be made with a magazine of similar broad appeal, such as *Time,* rather than with a daily newspaper, the appeal of which is primarily to citizens of the city in which it is published.

Names were often omitted in items referring to officials, the editors apparently assuming that their readers knew the occupants of government posts. For example:

The President of the United States has been quite ill with a billious [*sic*] fever, but not considered dangerous. He is now said to be convalescent.[3]

The vice president of the United States has dislocated his shoulder by a fall.[4]

The airy dismissal of the following event in six words appalls a twentieth-century journalist or radio commentator: "Many articles in type omitted— But nothing important. *Bonaparte* has landed at St. Helena."[5]

When more than one hundred persons perished in a fire on the Mississippi River steamboat, *Brandywine,* in 1832, one and

[3] *Register,* IV, 296, July 3, 1813.   [4] *Register,* XVI, 40, March 6, 1819.
[5] *Register,* IX, 244, December 2, 1815.

one-half inches were given the catastrophe.[6] However, an attempt upon the life of President Andrew Jackson, by a dismissed naval officer, filled five pages.[7]

A picture of Baltimore in the thirties may be obtained from this item: "Our city has been filled with strangers. It was hardly possible to obtain accommodations at our numerous and large hotels. The autumn business has commenced and the rail road is pouring-in great supplies from the west. We have had Mr. Durant's second ascention [sic]—the great fall races—the French opera—the performance of Mezeppa [sic]—and splendid displays of fire works, all tending to excite and keep up the attention of many. Among the visitors were Mr. *Van Buren,* vice president of the U. States, and John Sergeant, esq. of Philadelphia." [8]

Such spot news as stories of fires, explosions, shipwrecks, and other accidents was carried only if of national significance. Hezekiah Niles usually wrote his news articles from information received from other newspapers, but his son copied items directly from the newspapers, editing only as to length. Hughes used both methods, often combining them. Following the custom of the day, editorial comment was a part of many of the news stories. The impersonal method of writing news had not been adopted and the separation of the news and editorial pages was yet to come. The leading paragraph of an article on the 1837 "flour riots" in New York City demonstrates how opinion appeared in the news columns: "The following particulars of the late riot in New York are from the New York Commercial Advertiser of the 14th inst. and are placed on record to enable the future historian to trace the downward course of this republic; for we are fully convinced that unless such disgraceful acts are promptly punished by the arm of public justice, the spirit which dictated them will openly reveal itself against other interests, also deemed sacred, and substitute the law of force, for the statute and moral law, and ultimately overthrow every thing deemed valuable in our political and civil institutions." [9]

6 *Register,* XLII, 153, April 28, 1832.
7 *Register,* XLIV, 170–75, May 11, 1833.
8 *Register,* XLV, 113, October 19, 1833.
9 *Register,* LI, 403, February 25, 1837.

The explosion on the *Princeton* on February 28, 1844, in which Secretary of State Abel P. Upshur and Secretary of the Navy Thomas W. Gilmer lost their lives, and President Tyler escaped only because he had gone below deck, was given three and one-half columns, chiefly taken from the *National Intelligencer* and the Washington *Globe* of February 29 and March 1. A week later more than two pages were devoted to the explosion, including an excellent eye-witness account by a correspondent of the Philadelphia *Public Ledger*.[10]

The marriage of President Tyler to Miss Julia Gardner, whose father had been killed in the *Princeton* disaster, occupied only a few inches with the following humorous introduction: "PRESIDENT TYLER, accompanied by his private secretary, JOHN TYLER, Jr. and Capt. STOCKTON, of the U. S. navy, left the seat of government on the 25th inst. in the railroad line, and reached the city of New York on the same day. It is understood that the object of the president's visit is ANNEXATION in a direction where the senate cannot 'head' him with their *veto*." This was followed by a brief account of the marriage and of the couple's return to Washington.[11]

The end of a war, the death of the first United States President to die in office, the visit of a Revolutionary hero, the mysterious disappearance and rumored murder of a secret-society member, and the rebellion of a group within a state against the commonwealth's constituted authority all are events which fall into the category of big news stories. The news handling of each will be described briefly.

The sluggishness of news transmission in the early 1800's is illustrated by the fact that the news of the Battle of New Orleans, fought on January 8, 1815, was printed in the *Register* on February 11, and that the Treaty of Ghent, ending the war, signed on December 24, 1814, was not printed until February 18. The end of the war brought a typographical and verbal splurge which bears description.

A cut of the American eagle was carried at the head of the first column under which was the headline "Glorious News!" in 12-point type, followed by a line of 8-point italic, "*Orleans*

10 *Register*, LXVI, 1–2, March 2, 1844; 19–22, March 9, 1844.
11 *Register*, LXVI, 275, June 29, 1844.

saved and peace concluded." Unusual as this was in a publication which started many stories without any kind of a headline or caption, there was more. The third deck of this rudimentary headline printed in 5-point type was

> "The star spangled banner in triumph
> shall wave
> "O'er the land of the free and the
> home of the brave."

The lead on the story follows: "The matters detailed and recorded in the present number of the REGISTER, are of incalculable importance. The enemy has retired in disgrace from New-Orleans, and peace was signed at Ghent on the 24th December, on honorable terms: At least, so we believe from the *dolefuls* of the British ministerialists. For particulars, see the several heads."

After a paragraph about a mass of interesting material which the editor hoped to get into the next number, the article went on: *"Who would not be an American? Long live the republic! All hail! last asylum of oppressed humanity! Peace is signed in the arms of victory."*

Then followed five pages of official reports from General Jackson, Adjutant General Robert Butler, Daniel T. Patterson, commanding the naval force at New Orleans, and other miscellaneous correspondence, topped off with one and one-half pages of excerpts, from English newspapers and pro-British papers in the United States, predicting a British victory at New Orleans. Hezekiah Niles dissected and ridiculed the predictions with obvious pleasure.[12]

The appetite of the *Register*'s readers had been whetted for this morsel of news by the previous week's number in which seven and one-half pages of letters, Niles wrote, were

. . . supported by such a host of testimony that the most skeptical cannot refuse entire belief to them, however extraordinary some of the parts may appear. Glory be to GOD, that the barbarians have been defeated, and that at *Orleans,* the intended plunderers have found their grave! Glory to *Jackson, Carroll, and Coffee.* . . .

Hail glorious people—worthy, thrice worthy, to enjoy the bless-

12 *Register,* VII, 385–89, February 18, 1815.

ings which heaven in bounteous profusion has heaped on your country! Never may its luxuriant soil be trodden unrevenged by insolent foreigners in arms!

This display of rhetorical pyrotechnics was followed by a number of official communications which reported the victory and by letters from General Jackson and others written both before and after the battle.[13]

The news of the death of President William Henry Harrison was almost a week old when the *Register* appeared, but in spite of this interval, which gave plenty of time for the preparation of articles, only five of the sixteen pages were taken up with stories concerning Harrison's death and the accession of John Tyler to office. The column rules on all sixteen pages of the issue were turned to denote mourning. The story was started on the third page, under "National Affairs," and was made up of a brief factual announcement, the statement signed by the cabinet, a column from the *Madisonian* of April 6, a column from the *National Intelligencer* of April 5, brief excerpts from the *Globe* of April 4 and the Baltimore *American* of April 5, the report of the physicians, the cabinet's notification to Tyler, arrangements for the funeral, including the general orders of the army and navy, three and one-half columns from the *Intelligencer* of April 9 concerning the funeral, the oath taken by Tyler, and the constitutional provisions for the succession to the presidency.[14]

Four pages in the next week's issue, led off by a eulogistic editorial, related in detail the resolutions passed by state legislatures and city councils, and gave plans for observances in many cities. Excerpts from the comments of representative American newspapers filled two pages. Succeeding issues carried more of the same type of material and during the summer an item described the final interment of the President's remains on the hill overlooking the Ohio River.[15]

[13] *Register*, VII, 369, 372–81, February 11, 1815.

[14] *Register*, LX, 83–88, April 10, 1841; an equal amount of space in the same issue was given over to a continuation of the three-month-old debate on the pre-emption bill.

[15] *Register*, LX, 97–103, April 17, 1841; 113–15, April 24, 1841; 149–52, May 8, 1841; 323, July 24, 1841.

The third big story examined is in reality a series of stories for it concerned the visit of the Marquis de Lafayette to the United States in 1824–1825. Ardent admirer of his country's Revolutionary War history that Hezekiah Niles was, it was to be expected that he would welcome the coming of the Frenchman who had aided the colonies in their hour of need. This he did, and from August 15, 1824, when the nation's guest landed at New York City, until September 17, 1825, at which time his leave-taking of President Adams at the White House and his departure for France were described in detail, most of the issues of the *Register* contained accounts of his travels. Two weeks after his arrival, Niles set up a standing head, "The Nation's Guest," which was carried for a year over accounts of Lafayette's triumphal tour through all sections of the United States. Elated as he was over the General's visit, Niles disliked seeing his countrymen debase themselves in their enthusiasm and he penned the following rebuke, part of a longer editorial: "At *one* place they failed so far in self-respect as to contend with *horses* for the privilege of drawing the revolutionary chief in his carriage! It is to be hoped that the general will not be thus *insulted* again—for insulted he must be, when he sees the sovereigns of this great and glorious country, aiming at the most magnificent destinies, converted into asses or other beasts of burden. It is his desire to be treated like a *man,* not as a titled knave or brainless dandy . . . . let us remember that we are men like unto himself, and *republicans.*"

Some thirteen pages were filled with accounts of his reception in various New York towns before he arrived in Baltimore early in October, when eleven and one-half pages of one number described the celebrations in Philadelphia, Delaware, and Baltimore. Niles took pride in the orderliness of the Baltimore crowd of fifty thousand or more, walking the streets to view the illumination in honor of the distinguished visitor with such decorum that ". . . the most delicate female might have walked alone without meeting with an incident to give a fear to her innocence." When Congress held a reception for the aged patriot in December, it was Niles' privilege to be present, and he reported that Clay was heard by all and the General by most of those present in spite of the great press of people, "male and female." The Masonic dinner in Baltimore, which Niles undoubtedly attended, was described, and the Act of Congress voting $200,000 in cash and a township to Lafayette was printed in full, as were speeches for and against the bill. Through the spring and summer of 1825, the *Register* followed Lafayette's progress, an amazing itinerary for a man of his age, covering more than five thousand miles in ninety-nine days. Niles' farewell editorial is interesting because of its lapse into the plain language of the Society of Friends, seldom met with in his writings: "Highly favored man—who has thyself seen and felt all that a grateful *posterity* can confer for imperishable deeds of virtue, farewell!—and, if so it yet shall be, that the evening of thy days and thy night of death are passed in this land of the free, every house will be opened to receive thee, or every heart be engaged to invoke eternal blessings upon thee." [16]

The handling of the case of William Morgan, whose mysterious disappearance and reputed murder had far-reaching political effects and implications, has already been referred to in Chapter II. From 1826 through 1830, items on the abduction and the subsequent legislative investigations, resolutions, rumors, and trials were printed in the *Register*. In spite of his Masonic affiliations, Niles wrote that there was no excuse for such an act and that ". . . if the act was that of masons, they should, if possible, be more severely dealt with, on the assurance that they ought to have been as sensible of the weakness as of the baseness of the deed." He refused to carry controversial articles on the case, but steadfastly reported the official aspects, such as grand jury investigations, legislative actions, results of trials, and reports of special counsels to the governor of New York. He especially commended the action of De Witt Clinton, as governor of New York, in removing Eli Bruce, sheriff of Niagara County, for being implicated in Morgan's abduction.

A good contemporary account, including proclamations, messages, and correspondence, of Dorr's Rebellion may be found in the pages of the sixty-second volume of the *Register*. Practically every number from March through August, 1842, contained documentary and official material concerning the revolt,

---

[16] *Register*, XXIX, 2, September 2, 1825; Volumes XXVI through XXIX contain few issues which do not carry articles about his travels.

with newspaper articles chiefly from the Providence *Evening Journal* and New York *American,* giving additional details. The refusal of Governor Henry Hubbard of New Hampshire to honor a requisition from the Rhode Island executive asking the surrender of Thomas W. Dorr to Rhode Island officials was carried later, as were the accounts of the attempts of Dorr's friends to gain freedom for him after his imprisonment.[17]

The quadrennial inaugurations of Presidents of the United States have long been the occasion for lengthy descriptive stories in the nation's press. But the *Register* in its coverage of the ten inaugural ceremonies which occurred during its life condensed the descriptions to an almost irreducible minimum, devoting most of its space each time to the inaugural address of the newly inducted executive. President Madison's second inauguration was covered simply by giving his inaugural address with five lines of description.[18] When James Monroe was sworn in as the country's chief magistrate four paragraphs described the "simple, but grand, animating and impressive" ceremony, with three pages given over to a complete report of his address. Four years later a brief paragraph which mentioned that the "great hall of the house of representatives, . . . was completely filled with people" told of the administering of the oath by Chief Justice John Marshall. The address again filled three and one-half pages.[19] John Quincy Adams' inaugural ceremonies, as described by the *National Intelligencer* and *National Journal,* occupied parts of two pages more than a week after they took place.[20]

Andrew Jackson's two inaugurations were briefly described, with his speeches carried in full, the 1833 address occupying less than one and one-quarter columns of small type.[21] William Ogden Niles held up the publication of the *Register* three days in order to carry an account of Martin Van Buren's inaugura-

[17] *Register,* LXIII, 72–73, October 1, 1842; LXVII, 22–23, September 14, 1844; 189–91, November 23, 1844; 361–63, February 8, 1845, this last being a succinct outline of the entire affair.

[18] *Register,* IV, 15, March 6, 1813.

[19] *Register,* XII, 17–20, March 8, 1817; XX, 17–21, March 10, 1821.

[20] *Register,* XXVIII, 19–20, March 12, 1825; the address was printed in the preceding issue on pp. 8–11, with half a column of descriptive matter.

[21] *Register,* XXXVI, 28–29, March 7, 1829; XLIV, 21–22, March 9, 1833.

tion, and then had to content himself with less than a column
of reprinted description from the *National Intelligencer,* which
told of the "immense multitude, gathered from all quarters
of the country," which witnessed the ceremony on the eastern
front of the Capitol. The *Intelligencer,* in opposition to the
administration, mentioned the distribution of Jackson's farewell address in pamphlet form and praised the temper of the
presidential address but editorially wondered, "Whether beneath this smooth and glossy surface there be any lurking
evils. . . ." A week later the *Register* printed Van Buren's address, preceded by three fourths of a column of grandiloquent
description from the Washington *Globe,* in which the "whit-
ened head of the toil-worn general" was mentioned.[22]

William Henry Harrison's address filled three and one-half
pages of the *Register* two days after the inauguration, and a
week later four columns of descriptive matter were reprinted
from the *Intelligencer.*[23] The rainy-day ceremonies at James K.
Polk's induction into office brought mention of the "display of
umbrellas" which John Quincy Adams so humorously mentioned in his diary, and the two columns of description were
followed by two pages containing his address which spoke a
good word for the annexation of Texas and affirmed the right
of the United States "to that portion of our territory which
lies beyond the Rocky Mountains."[24] General Zachary Taylor's
induction into the presidency "in presence of the Senate of the
United States, the judges of the Supreme Court, the late Cabinet, the Diplomatic Corps of the city, and an immense assemblage of citizens from various parts of our Union" was the last
such ceremony fated to be described in the *Register.* The names
of the new cabinet followed a brief descriptive paragraph and
in the same number the old soldier's short address was printed.
A week later just over three columns on the ceremonies were
printed from the *Intelligencer* of March 6.[25]

Obituaries of national figures were given space in the *Register*

22 *Register,* LII, 16, March 4, 1837; 18–20, March 11, 1837.
23 *Register,* LX, 1–4, March 6, 1841; 18–19, March 13, 1841.
24 *Register,* LXVIII, 1–3, March 8, 1845; John Quincy Adams, *Memoirs of John
Quincy Adams, comprising Portions of his Diary from 1795 to 1848,* edited by
Charles Francis Adams (Philadelphia, 1874–1877), XII, 178–79.
25 *Register,* LXXV, 145, 150, March 7, 1849; 161–63, March 14, 1849.

throughout its career. Brief mention was made of the deaths of Revolutionary War soldiers, but to requests of subscribers and friends that notices be carried of the passing of private individuals, Niles called attention to the rule which he had set up to prevent such articles from occupying too much of his valuable and limited space.[26] One may find in its columns obituaries of Benjamin Rush, Robert Fulton, Pope Leo XII, Charles Carroll, the last surviving signer of the Declaration of Independence, John Randolph, William Wirt, William H. Crawford, whose presidential aspirations Hezekiah Niles fought so hard against, Aaron Burr, Mathew Carey, who died a few months after Niles' death, Robert Y. Hayne, the wife of President Tyler, Noah Webster, and Joseph Story, associate justice of the United States Supreme Court for thirty years.[27]

The deaths of former Presidents of the United States were reported at length, usually accompanied by a roundup of contemporary editorial comment from representative newspapers. When Thomas Jefferson and John Adams died on the same day, July 4, 1826, the *Register* in five succeeding issues printed eulogies of the two men and descriptions of the ceremonies honoring their memories held in many parts of the nation.[28]

Monroe's death received brief mention in one issue, with three pages of a succeeding number carrying a biographical sketch, accounts of the funeral, and newspaper comments.[29] The death of James Madison received only half a column of the *Register*'s space, but four months later a five-page eulogy delivered by James Barbour was reprinted from the *National Intelligencer*.[30]

[26] *Register*, XX, 306, July 14, 1821.

[27] *Register*, IV, 136, April 24, 1813; VIII, 430 (incorrectly paged, should be 14), March 4, 1815; XXXVI, 121–22, April 18, 1829; XLIII, 178, November 17, 1832; XLIV, 217, June 1, 1833; 238–39, June 8, 1833; XLV, 425, February 22, 1834; XLVII, 51, September 27, 1834; LI, 33, September 17, 1836; LVII, 49, September 21, 1839 (from the Philadelphia *United States Gazette*); 81–82, October 5, 1839; LXIII, 36, September 17, 1842; LXIV, 224, June 3, 1843; LXIX, 55–56, September 27, 1845.

[28] *Register*, XXX, 329, July 8, 1826; the news of Adams' death had not yet reached Baltimore, but Jefferson's passing was given news and editorial mention; XXX, 345–52, July 15, 1826; 368–75, July 22, 1826; 383–85, July 29, 1826; 397–408, August 5, 1826.

[29] *Register*, XL, 321, July 9, 1831; 369–72, July 23, 1831.

[30] *Register*, L, 297, July 2, 1836; LI, 170–75, November 12, 1836.

The turning of the column rules as a symbol of mourning for President Harrison's death has been noted, and this practice was followed by Hughes, when Andrew Jackson died on June 8, 1845, although only two pages, instead of all sixteen, carried the heavy black lines. Seven and one-half columns were filled with a brief editorial comment, Sam Houston's letter of June 8 to President Polk, the President's order setting June 17 as an official day of mourning, the general order of George Bancroft, secretary of the navy, and acting secretary of war, and two and one-half columns of a diary on the last days of the former President, kept by William Tyack and sent to Paul T. E. Hubles, of New York City.[31] The death of John Quincy Adams, following his dramatic collapse on the floor of the House, also received typographical notice with the four horizontal rules below the nameplate of the *Register* being turned, instead of the vertical column rules.[32] Lafayette's death brought a summary of editorial comment in which New York and London papers were quoted at length.[33] John Marshall's death occasioned several pages of tributes, including the dissent of the New York *Evening Post,* which remarked that his doctrines were of the ultrafederal or aristocratic kind, his decisions on the side of the implied powers, and "his situation, . . . at the head of an important tribunal . . . has always been to us a source of lively regret."[34]

News of the affairs of the national government occupied more space in the *Register's* columns than that devoted to any other classification of its contents. Indeed at times it filled all sixteen pages to the exclusion of other types of news. Governmental news falls naturally into the divisions of the three branches of the government. Congressional activities were reported through abridged reports of debates, complete speeches on important questions, some resolutions and laws, and by a list of laws and

---

[31] *Register,* LXVIII, 241–43, June 21, 1845; other notices on 382–86 (incorrectly paged, should be 282–86), July 5, 1845.

[32] *Register,* LXXIII, 401, February 26, 1848; as this was the final number printed prior to the four months' suspension, a selection of contemporary editorial opinion on his death is not to be found in the *Register.*

[33] *Register,* XLVI, 291, June 21, 1834, mentioned the receipt by mail of New York papers in mourning for Lafayette's death on May 20; XLVI, 332–34, July 12, 1834, quotes London *True Sun* and New York *Journal of Commerce,* among others.

[34] *Register,* XLVIII, 321–22, July 11, 1835; 339–41, July 18, 1835.

resolutions passed at each session, usually carried immediately after adjournment.[35] The executive branch was covered by printing all presidential messages, reports of cabinet officials, diplomatic correspondence, often *in extenso*, and treaties. Less fully covered was the judicial arm of the government, but not a few of its decisions were printed in full.[36]

The reader in the first half of the nineteenth century who wished to follow the varied activities of his government found in the *Register* no predigested mental fare for easy assimilation. The facts were there, but they were buried in the excess verbiage of legal language, annual reports, and papers written with an eye toward the political future of the writer, whether he be President, cabinet official, member of Congress, or diplomatic representative. No one winnowed the wordy documents, sifting out significant statements and writing therefrom interpretative articles, thus furnishing the reader with ready-made opinions. Unlike practically all the other editors in the country, Niles wanted his readers to form their own opinions on political questions. He fought hard for measures in which he believed. But at the same time, he usually printed official documents such as presidential messages, diplomatic correspondence, and treaties, without comment in the same number. His opinions, more often than not, were withheld until the reader had had sufficient time to peruse the documents leisurely and arrive at his own judgment.[37] Occasionally, it is true, he expressed an opinion in the same number, as, for example, when he wrote on December 7, 1822, that Monroe's message of December 3 did not "contain anything new or important," and when on December

[35] Typical lists may be found in *Register*, IV, 18–19, March 13, 1813; XXIV, 14–16, March 8, 1823; XXXII, 30–32, March 10, 1827; LII, 25–26, March 11, 1837; LXIV, 28–29, March 11, 1843; LXXV, 166–67, March 14, 1849.

[36] The admiralty court's decision in the case of the brig *Tulip* is printed in *Register*, III, 71–76, October 3, 1812; McCulloch *vs.* Maryland in XVI, 68–76, March 20, 1819; Cohens *vs.* the State of Virginia in XX, 155–67, May 5 and May 12, 1821; Gibbon *vs.* Ogden in XXVI, 54–62, March 27, 1824; the *Amistad* case in LX, 40–42, March 20, 1841.

[37] For example, Monroe's message of December 2, 1817, was printed in the *Register*, XIII, 236–40, December 6, 1817, and was not commented upon until XIII, 259, December 20, 1817; Monroe's last message to Congress, delivered on December 7, 1824, was printed in the *Register*, XXVII, 323–33, December 11, 1824, and discussed editorially in XXVII, 257, December 25, 1824.

10, 1825, he called John Quincy Adams' first message to Congress, "a clear and intelligent, as well as eloquent exposition of the state of our affairs." On occasion he summed up the contents of a message, and his masterly and succinct summarization of President Jackson's message of December 7, 1830, shows that his famed condensing power was applicable to official documents as well as to newspaper articles.[38] But generally the matter was printed in its raw state with its digestion dependent upon the mental processes of the individual reader. Thus, while Niles followed the accepted newspaper practice of the day in combining news reporting and editorial comment in the same article, in reporting foreign news in most cases and certainly in summarizing the noncontroversial and nonpolitical news of the United States, he was several editorial generations ahead of his contemporaries in his reporting of political and governmental news. The very fact that he printed material on both sides of every political controversy occurring during his editorship sets him apart from his contemporaries of the period in which nearly every newspaper published was fiercely and unfairly partisan.

After the election of each Congress the *Register* usually carried a complete roster, listing the members according to party affiliation and often designating new members. As has been stated, the *Register* obtained its reports of the debates in Congress from the *National Intelligencer* as, indeed, did many of the nation's newspapers. Although abridging the *Intelligencer*'s reports, the *Register* frequently found its columns overflowing with the stream of the proceedings, which neither the issuance of eight-page supplements nor the use of small type could completely absorb. However, the task of condensing the reports was usually ably done, and it must be remembered that the *Intelligencer* was a daily paper of "blanket" size, while the *Register* was published only once a week in a book format throughout two thirds of its career. When the amount of Congressional, and other material got completely out of hand Niles issued a supplement, usually of 192 pages, which sold for $1.00, an amount which barely covered the expense of printing, paper, and ink. Such supplements were issued to nine volumes,[39] but

---

[38] *Register*, XXXIX, 249, December 11, 1830.

[39] Volumes V, VII, VIII, IX, XV, XVI, XXIII, XXXVIII, XLIII; the supplement

today are not always found in the bound volumes in libraries for the subscriber did not receive one unless he ordered it. These book-size supplements, one of which contained 264 pages,[40] are not to be confused with the free eight-page and sixteen-page supplements issued to subscribers with many numbers and discussed in Chapter 1.[41]

Material other than governmental news was printed in the supplements; for example, biographies of army and naval officers who died in the War of 1812 occupied nearly a third of those to the fifth and seventh volumes. Many articles were reprinted from contemporary magazines, the *Port Folio, Analectic,* and *Museum* being well represented. Reprinting of material from magazines, especially by newspapers, was very generally done and the periodicals regarded it as good advertising, providing credit was given. As has been pointed out Niles was extremely careful to see that proper credit was given in the *Register* and was frequently irritated at the free use of material from the *Register* without credit by other papers. Copyright legislation was vague and only the ethical question of giving due credit was involved in the practice.

The *Register*'s news from the executive branch included every message sent by the executive to Congress and treaties negotiated with Indians and foreign countries. The large number of agreements reached with various Indian tribes caused Niles to summarize these treaties, but conventions negotiated with foreign countries were printed in full, when made public. Diplomatic correspondence, as sent to the Senate by the executive, was frequently printed at great length, an eight-page supplement and an entire sixteen-page number being turned over, for instance, to the Adams-Onìs correspondence in 1818.[42] Presi-

to Volume XXIII was originally planned for the preceding volume and at the top of each page is printed "Supplement to Volume XXII." The title page, however, is marked "Supplement to Volume the Twenty-third of Niles' Weekly Register," and an editorial note explains the discrepancy.

[40] *Register*, XLIII, Supplement.

[41] Typical examples of these gratuitous supplements may be found in *Register*, XXXII, 65–80, March 24, 1827; XXXV, 273–80, December 20, 1828; XXXVIII, 169–76, April 24, 1830; XXXIX, 33–40, September 4, 1830.

[42] *Register*, XIV, 65–72, March 21, 1818, and 73–88, March 28, 1818; other correspondence of Monroe and Adams with Onis may be found in XII, 21–25, March 8, 1817; 60–67, March 22 and March 29, 1817; XIV, 5–8, February 28, 1818; 58–60,

dential appointments were carried in many issues, usually after ratification by the Senate.

Reports by cabinet officials were printed verbatim. Niles, commenting briefly in 1827 on the report of Richard Rush, secretary of the treasury, said that he made a practice of inserting such official reports because "They shew the business and affairs of the nation in a very masterly manner, and with all the frankness and simplicity of truth—which would make known everything, conceal nothing useful to be known." [43]

One also finds in the volumes of the *Register*'s first twenty years many messages of governors to state legislatures, either in full or in abstracted form, and frequent accounts of legislative action upon affairs of national interest. In the late twenties the *Register* made a determined attempt to collect brief but significant items of general news from its exchanges from all states in the Union. Abandoned to some extent in the last few years of Hezekiah Niles' editorship, this practice was resumed by Jeremiah Hughes, late in 1839, and from then on in the department, "States of the Union," news items from states and territories told of interesting and significant events.[44] The reporting of news was often supplemented by a presentation of nation-wide editorial opinion.

Foreign intelligence took precedence after national and state news; it consisted of summarized accounts of longer news articles in the London and New York press, and of documents, including proclamations, treaties, decrees, speeches, and diplomatic correspondence. Momentous events were given space relative to their importance, with over half the *Register* sometimes being given over to European occurrences. This state of affairs, however, did not occur often. For the first few years foreign news was printed unclassified under the heading "Foreign News" or "Foreign Articles," but by 1817 an attempt to classify the items according to the countries of their origin was being made.

Obtaining his foreign news chiefly from New York news-

March 21, 1818. Diplomatic correspondence on other affairs, XXII, 235–38, June 8, 1822; XXVII, 171–85, November 13 and November 20, 1824; 203–15, November 27 and December 4, 1824.

[43] *Register*, XXXIII, 241, December 15, 1827.

[44] *Register*, LVII, 166–69, November 9, 1839; LXI, 289–96, January 8, 1842; LXVIII, 131, May 3, 1845.

papers, which had translated and rewritten the European journals, Niles did not have the background or the means to check
its accuracy as was the case with news from his own country.
He warned readers against accepting everything reported, and
at times printed articles, the truth of which he questioned either
because of conflicting reports or of known censorship.[45] In spite
of these handicaps, and the irregularity of the arrival of news
from Europe—as late as 1822, eighty days once elapsed without
news from England or France—the *Register* gave to its far-flung
reading public a fairly satisfactory picture of the European
scene, something that few daily newspapers of the day even
attempted.[46]

If the news from Europe seemed trivial, he so told his readers,
but when it was of interest he waded through page after page of
newspapers, laboriously selecting documents and condensing
the prolix articles as best he could. In keeping with the practice of the time, editorializing was found in many articles, especially those concerned with the Holy Alliance, revolutions in
various countries, and England.[47] Parliamentary debates, if of
interest to United States readers, were carried in abridged form
from London papers. The death of Napoleon occupied considerable space in the *Register,* which had sympathized with
him in his exile.[48]

To one interested in the journalism and the social fabric of
any given period, the study of its newspapers or magazines is a
fascinating one; one with temptations on almost every page to
lure the student away from the course decided upon. In the vast
amount of miscellany found in the *Register,* this temptation
lurks in many forms; yet a passing glance or two at the mine of
contemporaneous material found therein merely serves to give
a more nearly complete picture of the periodical's contents. In
the December 25, 1815, issue, an item from the Brattleboro
Vermont Reporter told of a recently deceased farmer who had

45 *Register*, VI, 72, March 26, 1814; 120, April 16, 1814; 136, April 23, 1814; IX,
117, October 14, 1815.

46 *Register*, XXI, 353, February 2, 1822.

47 *Register*, XX, 151, May 5, 1821, which carries the *"Great and glorious news!!!"*
of "All Italy . . . in flame!," and XXXIX, 33, 37–47, September 4 and September 11, 1830, in which the overthrow of the Bourbons is discussed, are examples.

48 *Register*, XXI, 5–8, September 1, 1821; 18–20, September 8, 1821.

married two sisters, established two homes, and whose two wives and twenty-six children "maintained the utmost harmony and affection. . . ." A plan furnished by a farmer for the rotation of crops, the recipe for the ink with which the *Register* was printed, an aeronaut's account of a balloon ascension, and geographical facts about the Great Lakes were all printed, adding to the amusement and information of the readers.[49]

One sympathizes with the victim of the following tragic accident, but is hard put to suppress a smile at the description:

MELANCHOLY. On saturday morning last, Mr. Jesse Converse met with a most unfortunate end, while at his work in his sawmill, on Muddy creek. Some unknown cause brought him in contact with the saw, and he was sawed entirely through diagonally, from the shoulder to the hip.

Crawford Messenger [50]

A remedy for frost-bitten feet, a description of a stationary steam engine, a method to exterminate wild garlic, statistics on churches and church members, an item on height of mountains, a warning against sleeping in a closed room with burning charcoal, many statistical articles on the newspaper press, more than a column on the daguerreotype, description of the public-school system in Cincinnati, and an item on the founding of an American Medical Association indicate the variety of informational material prepared in condensed form for readers.[51]

The humorous newspaper controversy centering around James Gordon Bennett's fortunately unsuccessful campaign to substitute "Allegania" for "United States" as a name for the nation, was given space,[52] as was an explanation of the origin of the phrase "talking turkey," [53] and a dig at the Polk administration that "O. K." must mean " 'Oll this Kontinent'—Ore-

[49] *Register*, XI, 148, November 2, 1816; XVII, 64, September 25, 1819; XIX, 133, October 28, 1820; XXIX, 149–50, November 5, 1825.

[50] *Register*, XLIX, 156, November 7, 1835.

[51] *Register*, IV, 40, March 13, 1813; IX, 77–78, September 30, 1815; X, 33, March 16, 1816; XII, 400, August 16, 1817; 416, August 23, 1817; XX, 80, March 31, 1821; 387, August 18, 1821; XXIII, 370, February 15, 1823; XXIV, 98, April 19, 1823; XXVI, 32, March 13, 1824; LVI, 322, July 20, 1839; LVII, 73, September 28, 1839; LXI, 214–15, December 4, 1841; LXXII, 161–62, May 15, 1847.

[52] *Register*, LXVIII, 98, April 19, 1845.

[53] *Register*, LII, 224, June 3, 1837.

gon, Kalifornia, Kanada, and Kuba." [54] Commenting on a "world's convention" called by Robert Owen to meet in New York, Hughes wrote in 1845: "Whether Mr. Owen has got hold of the secret yet of putting society in tune and keeping it so, is the question. He seems really to think he has, and that of itself is the occasion of some scepticism." [55]

One could go on for pages citing examples of miscellaneous news items carried by the *Register* throughout its career, but space does not permit. For fifteen years most of these items, except those used for filler, were carried in the department headed "A Chronicle." In 1826, the heading was changed to "Items," later to "Domestic Items," and then to "Interesting Items." After his son left for Frederick, Maryland, Hezekiah Niles returned to the use of "A Chronicle," and in this he was followed by Jeremiah Hughes, who, however, devoted the leading item of this department to a business review.[56] Later this type of news almost monopolized that department, until a new one, "Trade and Commerce," was set up. Hughes also carried a "Conventions" department which briefly noted national conventions.[57]

Significant stories sometimes escape the notice of contemporary journalists. The daily press, for example, gave but a few matter-of-fact lines to the first successful experiment of sending a message from Washington to Baltimore by telegraph.[58] The *Register*, however, recognized in this demonstration an epoch-making event and, in spite of the necessity of reporting the results of the national conventions of two political parties held in its home city, gave more than three fourths of a column to "Morse's Electro-Magnetic Telegraph." The description of the event of May 24, 1844, was interspersed with editorial comment

[54] *Register*, LXIX, 48, September 20, 1845.

[55] *Register*, LXIX, 80, October 4, 1845.

[56] *Register*, LVIII, 416, August 29, 1840; LXV, 32, September 9, 1843; LXIX, 112, October 18, 1845.

[57] *Register*, LXVIII, 199–203, May 31, 1845; 222–23, June 7, 1845; LXXII, 263, June 26, 1847.

[58] For an account of its handling by the Baltimore newspapers, especially the *Sun*, see Gerald W. Johnson, Frank R. Kent, H. L. Mencken, Hamilton Owens, *1837–1937, The Sunpapers of Baltimore* (New York, 1937), 66–71. The message, "What hath God wrought?" was sent on May 24, 1844, from Washington to Baltimore.

on the significance of the invention and bears quoting in part: "Communication was established between the two cities on the 24th of May, 1844, which we may assume as a new era in the diffusion of information. The vast importance of this contrivance, when carried out into all the ramifications of which it is susceptible, can hardly be guessed at,—much less now estimated. Space is, as it were, annihilated, so far as respects the intercourse of thought. Think of the fact, that men standing as they actually now can *and* do, 40 miles apart, conversing with each other . . . just as speedily as if they were in the same apartment!"

The article went on to predict that very soon men in New York and Boston would be conversing with those in New Orleans and St. Louis "with the same facility that a Washington reporter now communicates with his editor in Baltimore." Its use by business and professional men was accurately predicted and its value in emergencies stressed.[59]

That the *Register*'s editor was more perspicacious than his brethren in the daily field may have been due to the fact that he had been watching the progress of the invention and some months earlier had devoted more than a column to a technical description of it.[60] In the *Register*'s account of the Democratic National Convention which had nominated James K. Polk for the presidency early in the week appeared the following paragraphs:

> In twenty minutes after this result was announced, the response at the Capitol at Washington, was received by the convention by means of Morse's Electric Magnetic Telegraph.
> The democratic members of congress, to their democratic brethren in convention assembled, send greeting, three cheers for James K. Polk.

The article then told of the nomination of Silas Wright for Vice President, of his refusal by telegraph, and of his second refusal after being asked to reconsider. Some members of the convention, apparently not trusting the newfangled invention, insisted upon sending a delegation to Washington to get Wright's answer personally, and he was informed by wire that five dele-

59 *Register*, LXVI, 211, June 1, 1844.
60 *Register*, LXV, 139, October 28, 1843.

gates had been appointed to proceed to Washington to confer with him.[61]

Three weeks later, a five-column article on the telegraph was printed. Headed by a long historical account of the various methods of communication, the story included a good description of the apparatus and of its operation, and some nationalistic editorializing on its invention in "Republican America." It regretted that the bill providing for funds to extend the line to Philadelphia or New York was not acted upon by the recently adjourned Congress, predicting: "The utility of the invention is established beyond all controversy, and a few years will see its ramifications extended to every considerable town in the Union." [62]

The next few years saw many items about the extension of the telegraph, the method by which it was financed, and its use by businessmen. The *Register* opposed a government monopoly of the new invention, although it had favored appropriations to aid in its development. Its use in speeding transmission of presidential messages as far west as Buffalo in 1846, and St. Louis in 1847, was noted and commented upon editorially.[63]

Thus, in the miscellaneous content of the *Register*, one may view through contemporary eyes the development of such important inventions as the telegraph and photography, the humor and the tragedy of everyday events, and the varied informational service supplied by that publication to its subscribers.

As has been said before, much of this contemporary material is invaluable to the reader of today. But in addition much material was printed by Niles primarily for its usefulness in the future, either by his own readers or their descendants. Constitutions of the thirteen original states, of each new state as it entered the Union, and revised constitutions as adopted, may be found in the *Register* or in supplements.[64] The frequent

[61] *Register*, LXVI, 218, June 1, 1844.

[62] *Register*, LXVI, 261–63, June 22, 1844.

[63] *Register*, LXXI, 243–44, December 10, 1846; LXXIII, 272, December 25, 1847.

[64] Complete citations are out of the question; the following are illustrative: New Hampshire, *Register*, III, 97–99, October 17, 1812; 113–15, October 24, 1812; Connecticut, XV, 65–70, September 26, 1818; Alabama, XVII, 45–53, September 18 and September 25, 1819; Maine, XIX, 26–36, September 9 and September 16, 1820; New York, XXIII, 172–76, November 16, 1822; Virginia, XXXVII, 380–85, January

printing of an "Army Register" preserved in handy form information about army officers, and tabulated articles about naval ships and officers complemented it. The journal of the Stamp Act Congress of 1765, the Articles of Confederation, the Constitution of the United States, the Declaration of Independence, facts on the ratification of the Constitution, Washington's Farewell Address, and rather interestingly, John Jay's letter of March 29, 1811, to Richard Peters expressing surprise that a copy of this address in Hamilton's writing had been found among his papers, may all be found in the *Register*.[65]

That it served as a sort of *World Almanac* to the public may be deduced from the fact that such miscellaneous facts as lists of governors, college presidents, tabulated election statistics, statistical analyses of Congress, and lists of foreign diplomats at Washington were printed from time to time.[66]

Population figures were carried in the *Register* when released after each decennial census, and it is interesting to compare them with the predictions made by Hezekiah Niles and printed in the *Register* in 1816, 1822, and 1834. Listing the probable population in 1753, 1783, 1784 and the census reports for 1790, 1800, and 1810, Niles prepared a table in 1816 estimating the probable population in 1820, with the percentage of increase in each state.[67] In his first estimate, he was less accurate than in his two succeeding attempts, but he was very close to the actual returns for the eastern states. He estimated in 1816 that the 1820 population would be 9,964,178. Since it actually was 9,638,191, he had overestimated the increase by some 325,000. He blamed this discrepancy on the "prostration of domestic industry,"

30, 1830; Mississippi, XLV, 12–16, August 31, 1833; Pennsylvania, LIV, 84–87, April 7, 1838; Texas, LXX, 56–60, March 28, 1846.

[65] Typical army lists, *Register*, VIII, 226–31, May 27, 1815; XX, 196–202, May 26, 1821; XXII, 381–82, August 10, 1822; naval lists, VIII, 235–36, June 3, 1815; IX, 85–91, September 30 and October 7, 1815; XXIX, 370, February 4, 1826; other official documents, II, 337–42, July 25, 1812; 353–55, August 1, 1812; III, 65–66, October 3, 1812; 81–83, October 10, 1812; 103, October 17, 1812; 385–87, February 20, 1813; 401–403, February 27, 1813; IV, 281–84, July 3, 1813; XXXI, 122–24, October 21, 1826.

[66] *Register*, XXI, 305, January 12, 1822; XXII, 246, June 15, 1822; 267, June 22, 1822; XXIII, 322, January 25, 1823; XXIV, 389, August 23, 1823; XXXII, 233–35, June 2, 1827; LXI, 211, December 4, 1841; LXXII, 49, March 27, 1847; 241, June 19, 1847.

[67] *Register*, XI, 35, September 14, 1816.

which "not only checked emigration, but also severely retarded the natural increase."[68] In July, 1822, he made his forecast for 1830, taking two pages to explain his conclusions and to elucidate his methods of reasoning by which he compiled his figures. He gave his rates of increase for the four official census reports and predicted a 32.25 per cent increase for the decade from 1820 to 1830.[69] His prediction of 12,789,505 was a surprisingly accurate one, the official total being 12,866,020. Thus, he came within 76,515, an error in underestimation of less than five eighths of one per cent. More than half of his error was due to underestimating the increase of the slave population, his forecast being 47,050 below the fact.[70]

In 1834, printing a table showing predicted and official figures for 1820 and 1830, he made his state-by-state estimate for 1840. Estimating a 31.25 per cent increase for the period, he arrived at 16,899,693 as the probable total in 1840. The actual figure was 17,069,453, his error in this prediction approximating one per cent.[71]

Articles of this type made the *Register* of real value to its readers who regarded it as a weekly newspaper and to those who used it as a reference work in their libraries. It must be admitted that much of the material was and is hard to find. The indices to the volumes, sent out free with each title page, were inadequate. Although many contained more than two thousand items, the number was insufficient for the 416 or more closely printed pages. Niles recognized this need for a more nearly complete index, and at the close of the first series of twelve volumes made several attempts to compile one himself. Then he paid $300 for the preparation of an index which he found unsatisfactory and threw away.[72] Through friends, he

[68] *Register*, XX, 33, March 17, 1821; 241, June 16, 1821; 402, August 25, 1821; XXI, 289, January 5, 1822; see *Compendium of the Enumeration of the Inhabitants and Statistics of the United States as Obtained at the Department of State, from the Returns of the Sixth Census, by Counties and Principal Towns . . . to which is Added an Abstract of Each Preceding Census* (Washington, 1841), 373.

[69] *Register*, XXII, 341–47, July 27, 1822.

[70] *Register*, XLIII, 27–38, September 8 and September 15, 1832; see *Compendium . . . of the . . . Sixth Census*, 375.

[71] *Register*, XLVI, 425, August 23, 1834; LX, 273, July 3, 1841; LXI, 113–15, October 23, 1841; see *Compendium . . . of the . . . Sixth Census*, 102.

[72] *Register*, XIV, 193–94, May 16, 1818.

finally found John Neal, by his own admission "a poet, in the flower of early manhood—say twenty-six or thereabouts," who worked sixteen hours a day, including "sabbaths; and never taking an hour for exercise or amusement, for four full months;" in completing an index for what he reported as twelve volumes, but which Niles wrote was only ten. However, after some haggling, Niles paid him the agreed sum of $200 and in addition presented him with a set of bound *Registers*.[73] This index was printed in a 254-page volume of the same format as the *Register* and sold for $3.00.[74] It was the only index, other than the short ones accompanying each volume, ever printed, although in 1831 Niles told his readers of plans to prepare one covering the periodical to date.[75]

As has been frequently noted, most of the *Register*'s news came from other newspapers, chiefly rewritten during Hezekiah Niles' editorship, and often thereafter merely clipped. Credit was usually given to the publication from which it was taken, although at times a compilation from several might be credited to London or New York papers without naming them individually. This method was followed by daily papers as well and a publication of nation-wide circulation such as the *National Intelligencer* or the *Register* not only was an original source of much news, but also was a distributor of a great deal of news gathered from its exchanges, which often were not available to newspapers in other sections of the country. For instance, the *Register* reprinted an article on the navigation of the Roanoke from the *National Intelligencer,* which had clipped it from the *Norfolk Herald*.[76] It is altogether probable that a number of editors obtained their first knowledge of the article in the *Register* and copied it therefrom. Frequently, rewritten and clipped stories were used without credit by some editors, giving rise to the erroneous crediting of articles to newspapers which merely reprinted them. Niles mentioned such a case in 1820, when an article which he had written some months earlier about the West was published in Kaskaskia, Illinois, as an orig-

---

[73] Neal, *op. cit.,* 210–14; *Register*, XIV, 193, May 16, 1818.
[74] *Index to Niles' Weekly Register.*
[75] *Register*, XXXIX, 327, January 1, 1831.
[76] *Register*, X, 326, July 13, 1816.

inal five weeks after the first publication, and in another month had returned to the eastern seaboard where newspapers were crediting it to the Kaskaskia paper.[77]

Niles' use of the *National Intelligencer* has been commented upon in connection with Congressional debates and other official papers. He also used the *National Journal* at certain periods, and to a lesser extent, the *United States Telegraph* and the Washington *Globe,* especially during Jackson's two terms.[78] The Baltimore daily papers often supplied Niles with news they had received. The Philadelphia *Aurora,* under the editorship of William Duane, was the source of much news, especially about South America.[79] Some typical numbers reveal the following newspapers credited with articles: June 21, 1823, Richmond *Enquirer,* New York *Commercial Advertiser,* Louisville *Argus,* Zanesville *Messenger,* Steubenville *Western Herald* of Ohio, and *Arkansas Gazette;* August 23, 1823, *Bell's Weekly Messenger* of London, *National Intelligencer, Onondaga Gazette* of Syracuse, New York *Statesman,* Providence *Journal,* New York *American,* the London *Times,* Vienna *Austrian Observer.* In the August 29, 1829, issue, there were twenty stories, for which thirteen different newspapers and magazines were cited as sources. The November 8, 1834, issue quoted twenty-seven newspapers in addition to unnamed New York and London papers, as sources for the articles carried on fifteen pages.

Newspapers from Washington; Richmond; New York; Augusta, Maine; Harrisburg, Pennsylvania; Louisiana; Troy and Albany, New York; Winchester, Virginia; Baltimore; Erie; Mobile; and Liverpool, England, were given credit in the February 14, 1835, issue, a list not by any means unusual. On one page of the March 26, 1836, issue were reprinted excerpts of articles from the New York *Evening Star,* Natchez *Courier,* Philadelphia *National Gazette,* Newark *Daily Advertiser,* Chicago *Daily American,* Hudson *Gazette,* Columbia (Pennsylvania) *Register,* Philadelphia *Saturday Morning Herald,* Baltimore

---

[77] *Register,* XVIII, 273, June 17, 1820.

[78] *Register,* XXVII, 337, January 29, 1825; typical references to the latter two papers are found in XXXVI, 1, February 28, 1829, and XLVII, 113, October 25, 1834; from 1829 through 1837 there were many such references.

[79] *Register,* XIII, 221–22, November 29, 1817.

American, and Winchester *Republican.* The three years of William Ogden Niles' editorship provide a fertile field for the seeker of extracts from other publications. Hughes did much less writing than the elder Niles, and consequently more of his material also was derived from contemporary publications.

Foreign news reached the *Register's* readers through various paths of communication, some of them exceedingly devious. For example, the news of the 1819–1820 revolution in Spain was received by the *Register* almost simultaneously from three sources: First, the *United States Gazette* of Philadelphia printed the journal of a Captain Ramberger of the ship *Mendoza,* which had sailed from Cadiz on January 5, evading an embargo. The captain was represented as being "one of the most respectable of his profession, and of unquestionable veracity." Second, a letter to a gentleman in Philadelphia from Cadiz, dated January 5 and 6, was printed in the *Gazette.* Third, the New York *Mercantile Advertiser* printed an extract from a letter from Havana, dated February 16, telling of the arrival there of a Spanish packet from Cadiz. To these reports Niles added a half column of his own editorial comment.[80]

Much news was obtained from British newspapers to which Niles apparently had free access. Not only English, but European and South American news was obtained from the London press. On November 2, 1816, he credited the New York *Evening Post* for a translation of the declaration of independence of the United Provinces of Rio de la Plata from the Buenos Aires *Gazette* of August 17. Four years later, he "took the opportunity to remark that on the present occasion, as is very often the case, we are chiefly indebted to the New-York *Commercial Advertiser*" for foreign news.[81] Frequently the credit was only to New York or London papers, but on April 25, 1829, he mentioned specifically the New York *Herald* as the source of some foreign news, which in turn obtained it from Liverpool and London papers. Many reports from South America reached the American press by way of English newspapers at Jamaica.[82] Most of the news

---

[80] *Register,* XVIII, 1–2, March 4, 1820.
[81] *Register,* XVIII, 385, July 29, 1820.
[82] *Register,* IX, 202, November 18, 1815; XVII, 141, October 30, 1819; XVIII, 162, April 29, 1820; XXVII, 388–89, February 19, 1825, this last item being from

from continental Europe was filtered through the English news-paper and periodical press, although in some cases the trans-lations from the Spanish or the French were made by American newspapers, which the *Register* copied.[83]

Not an inconsiderable part of the foreign news was obtained by the *Register*'s first editor from the books of the Baltimore Coffee House and the Merchants Coffee House, names which may be found frequently in the "Foreign Articles" department, especially during the second decade of the century. Ship captains would write in these books news which they themselves had witnessed, information given them by other captains encoun-tered in foreign ports, and excerpts from foreign newspapers. Sometimes conversation with ships' officers met in the coffee houses or at the Exchange and Commercial Reading Rooms uncovered additional information which was made available to *Register* readers, although what is now known as the interview had not yet been developed by American newspapermen.[84]

Another source of news made use of by Hezekiah Niles was letters from friends and subscribers and, as was the custom with all newspapers, letters received by persons willing to make the contents public. In 1815 the editor thanked a "warm friend of the *Weekly Register,* at *Buenos Ayres* (personally un-known) . . ." for his letter and a file of South American news-papers.[85] A subscriber living in Scotland wrote from time to time

the *Public Advertiser* of Kingston, Jamaica, which copied it from the *Impreso de Lima,* brought to Kingston by a sloop of war.

[83] *Register,* XII, 411–12, August 23, 1817; XXIII, 60–63, citing among others, *Edinburg* [sic] *Scotsman, Edinburg* [sic] *Review;* XXV, 39, September 20, 1823, unnamed London papers and *Edinburgh Scotsman;* 91–95, October 11, 1823; 153–54, November 8, 1823.

[84] *Register,* V, 303–304, January 1, 1814; VIII, 137, April 29, 1815; X, 8, March 2, 1816; 199–200, May 18, 1816; 319, July 6, 1816; XI, 188–89, November 16, 1816; XIV, 241, June 6, 1818; XLVIII, 233–34, June 6, 1835, contain European and South American news items obtained by Niles from books in the two coffee houses; the reading room is described in Charles Varle, *A Complete View of Baltimore, with a Statistical Sketch, Of all the commercial, mercantile, manufacturing, liter-ary, scientific, and religious institutions and establishments, in the same, and in its vicinity for fifteen miles round, derived from personal observation and research into the most authentic sources of information. To which is added, A Detailed Statement of an Excursion on the Baltimore and Ohio Rail Road, to the Point of Rocks, giving an interesting description of said road, &c. And an Advertising Directory* (Baltimore, 1833), 36–37.

[85] *Register,* IX, 300, December 23, 1815.

News and Editorials   105

and sent Scotch newspapers.[86] Much of his Mexican news came
from letters.[87] Sometimes letters contained conflicting reports
in which case Niles printed both and let his reader make his
own decision.[88] Niles did not hesitate to ask his subscribers'
aid in gathering information, as for instance in 1818, when he
asked gentlemen living in New Hampshire, New Jersey, Delaware, Virginia, North and South Carolina, Georgia, Kentucky,
Tennessee, Louisiana, Illinois, and Missouri to send him information regarding banks in their respective states.[89]

News transmission before the day of railroads and the telegraph, both of which came into common use during the *Register*'s span of life, was slow and uncertain. Snow in winter and
mud in spring delayed the mail coaches. After the receipt of the
newspapers, Niles liked to take time to read different accounts
before preparing his articles, but when important news was
carried in the columns of exchanges, he worked expeditiously,
either handing a clipped article to the compositor to be set up
in type at once or writing a brief bulletin which he inserted in
the *Register,* even if part of the week's edition were already
printed. Sometimes he told the date on which the original
article was printed, but more often than not he merely credited
the newspaper. The delay in the receipt of the news from the Battle of New Orleans has been mentioned; two issues in January,
1815, discussed the "entire failure of the mail" and the fact that
five weeks had elapsed since word had been received from that
city.[90] News from Baltimore papers was often printed the day
following publication and this was sometimes true of the Washington journals. That from New York papers had a time lag of
at least seven days, and articles from the western papers often
were printed a month, six weeks, or two months after original
publication. The time element in much of the periodical's contents was of no great importance.

Telegraph was first employed in transmitting a presidential
message on December 3, 1844, when an abstract of President
Tyler's final message to Congress was received in Baltimore

[86] *Register,* XXV, 35, September 20, 1823.
[87] *Register,* XII, 58, March 22, 1817.
[88] *Register,* XIV, 271–72, June 13, 1818.
[89] *Register,* XV, 190, November 14, 1818.
[90] *Register,* VII, 334, January 21, 1815; 345, January 28, 1815.

"twenty minutes from the time the message was handed to the presiding officers of each house." The entire message, however, was brought by train in one hour and twenty minutes. It reached New York at eight minutes after ten o'clock that evening and all New York papers of Wednesday printed it.[91]

For years the elapsed time from original publication of foreign news to its appearance in the *Register*'s columns was around six weeks or even two months during the winter. As has been pointed out, Niles obtained much of his foreign news from New York and Boston newspapers, and often several days were lost after it had been printed in this country. With the development of faster sailing vessels and the employment of packet ships, this time lag was reduced to a month. The application of steam power to vessels greatly reduced the time of a transatlantic crossing, and in the late thirties and early forties the *Register* frequently printed European news in three weeks or even less after it had been printed in Liverpool, London, or Paris. In 1844 the *Great Western* crossed from Liverpool to New York in fourteen days and the *Hibernia* made the crossing to Boston in twelve days.[92] In spite of this speed, which enabled American newspapers to print foreign news within three weeks of its occurrence, there were often long gaps when no news was received, one of twenty-six days being noted in 1840 and one of twenty-one days in 1845. News from China was more than three months in arriving as late as 1844.[93]

The development of news transmission from horse-express riders, through the use of the railroads, to the operation of the telegraph, with a combination of all three means of communication being used in the late forties, had little to do directly with the *Register*, but by reading its columns one may follow the contemporary evolution of news communication.

91 *Register*, LXVII, 209, December 7, 1844.
92 *Register*, LXVII, 1, September 7, 1844.
93 *Register*, LVIII, 321, July 25, 1840; LXVII, 97, October 17 (misdated, should be October 19), 1844; LXVIII, 97, April 19, 1845.

Chapter 5

The Tariff and the Bank

THE *Register* was the vehicle of the economic beliefs of Hezekiah Niles for a quarter of a century. In its columns he expounded his nationalistic economic doctrines, the adoption of which he was convinced would bring economic independence from other nations, especially Great Britain. A confirmed opponent of the free-trade doctrines of Adam Smith, Niles, shortly after he founded the *Register,* became leader in the fight for protection of domestic industry. Marshaling his arguments and those of his contemporaries, he fought the fight more or less continually from the publication of the first number until the principle went down to temporary defeat in the Compromise Tariff of 1833. In this period of twenty-one and one-half years, economic subjects received more space in the *Register* than any other type of article, news of the national government excepted. The periodical has been styled "probably the most important primary source to the student of American economic history of the period." [1]

Niles and Mathew Carey, with whom he was closely associated, were recognized as leaders of American economic thought by friends and foes. Niles was often quoted as an authority on the floor of Congress, in state legislatures, and by the press on both sides of the controversy over protection. His economic essays, reprinted from the *Register* by himself and other friends of domestic industry, were circulated by the thousands of copies in friendly newspapers and in pamphlet form. He was indefatigable in his efforts to convert the citizens of the United States to his doctrine which he felt provided the only sure road to national economic independence and national prosperity. The keynote of his economic philosophy was national prosperity

[1] Stone, *op. cit.,* 8 [568].

which he believed could be achieved only when the nation became economically self-sufficient. He recognized that agriculture and commerce monopolized the capital and the interest of practically the entire population. Therefore in the first number of the *Register* Niles set out to arouse an interest in domestic manufacturers, the products of which would enable the country to supply itself with necessities and even luxuries, and the development of which would bring economic freedom "from the workshops of the world."

If Niles is to be believed, and there is no reason to doubt him, his opinions regarding the importance of domestic industry were formed early. In 1830, reviewing his long fight in behalf of a protective tariff, he wrote that the *"starting place"* of his opinions was a procession of "gentlemen clothed entirely in home-productions, in about 1786, at Wilmington," to which his father had taken him, a boy of nine or ten. While still in his teens, he wrote articles for a Philadelphia paper "in support of domestic industry, and its essential connexion with the independence of the United States." Upon his return to Wilmington he joined a debating society, one of the members of which, "an unlettered blacksmith," David Chandler by name, greatly influenced Niles, yet a minor, in forming his opinions on labor.[2] The importance of home manufacturers was discussed in the *Apollo*,[3] his magazine venture in 1805, but the subject received little attention in the Baltimore *Evening Post* because the period of his editorship coincided with the Embargo Act of 1807 and the Non-Intercourse Law of 1809. The stimulus given infant industries by these two acts and the inability to obtain foreign products encouraged Niles, who, late in 1812, expressed editorial astonishment at the progress of manufactures and urged that the *"double duties* on dry goods" be continued.[4]

The *Register* had carried statistical and informational articles throughout the year on the establishment and output of American "manufactories," and its editor saw the War of 1812 as a distinct advantage to them. He warned, however, that English products must be discriminated against, and accurately pre-

2 *Register*, XXXIX, 252, December 11, 1830.
3 *The Apollo* (Wilmington), March 16, 1805.
4 *Register*, III, 189, November 21, 1812.

dicted that the mother country at the close of the conflict would employ the dumping tactics used so successfully by her at the close of the Revolutionary War.[5] During the war years the *Register* lost no opportunity to encourage American manufacturers by printing enthusiastic articles on the growth of all branches of industry with special attention paid to the growth of wool and the manufacture of woolen goods, the cotton-spinning industry, and the increase of factories, particularly in the West. He warned the manufacturers, however, against profiteering, and suggested that they maintain the quality of their products that the protection given them be merited. He also urged the importance of putting some of their money aside to meet the certain shock of peace.

Having mentioned after the close of the war the likelihood of a reduction of existing duties, under which manufacturers had flourished, he argued that protective duties were needed if American manufacturers were to continue.[6] He praised the progress of the recently established factories, but said that they must be protected for yet awhile "to meet, on equal grounds, the more wealthy and older institutions of Europe." Declaring that the government owed the same duty to these infant industries that a mother owes to her children, he pleaded, "But we must creep before we can walk. Protect the manufacturers for the present, and in a little time, they will protect themselves and us." [7] The *Register* followed the course of the tariff measure through Congress, and its editor kept in close touch with the various developments by means of letters to a Congressional friend.[8] The law, as approved on April 27, 1816, to go into effect on June 30, was printed.[9]

The passage of this tariff, probably the last to be considered "in a broad and rational spirit," marked a turning point in economic legislation because protection was adopted "as a

[5] *Register*, II, 227–28, June 6, 1812; 300, July 4, 1812; 331–32, 336, July 18, 1812; III, 8–9, September 5, 1812.

[6] *Register*, IX, 2, September 2, 1815.

[7] *Register*, IX, 437–47, February 24, 1816; X, 81, 82–84, April 6, 1816.

[8] Niles to Darlington, March 21, 1816; April 5, 1816, Darlington MSS, Library of Congress; in the later letter he said that he was not entirely pleased with the measure but that he hoped it might work out "*tolerably* well."

[9] *Register*, X, 160–62, May 4, 1816.

fundamental basis of the fiscal system and revenue was sub-
ordinated to industrial needs." [10] Through the summer of 1817
Niles carried a series of four articles on political economy in
which he listed nine reasons why industry should be protected,
supporting his arguments with statistics. The editor endeavored
to write on political economy, as he called it, so that the working man would understand.

The public needed to know more about economics and fiscal
operations, he felt. Taxpayers should understand the taxing
system. In 1821, while discussing scarcity and supply, he argued
that a surplus of only one one-hundredth part of a supply of a
commodity reduced the price of the entire supply and that a
similar deficiency raised the price, adding that it "would benefit
the growers of that stock to destroy the surplus, and so keep it
out of the market." [11]

The period of serious financial stringency in 1819, brought
about, at least in part, by the expansion of industry during the
embargo and war periods, saw the manufacturers awakening to
the need of a system of protective duties. Associations were
formed in areas affected; addresses were made to the public;
and memorials to Congress appeared in increasing numbers.
The *Register* printed many of these appeals in full. Thirteen
articles based upon a series of essays and addresses of the Philadelphia Society for the Promotion of Domestic Industry were
printed during 1819, Niles adding his remarks in brackets or
in footnotes.[12] April, May, and June of 1820 saw column after
column in the *Register* given over to outlining the provisions
of the proposed tariff measure, which, however, finally was defeated in the Senate. Niles' correspondence reflected his disappointment at the rejection of the bill.[13] Editorially, however,
he wrote that the postponement of protection might be a good
thing for its friends in that the panic was cutting down im-
portations and thus encouraging domestic industry; also that

10 Davis Rich Dewey, *Financial History of the United States* (8th rev. ed.; New
York, 1922), 162–63.

11 *Register*, XXI, 273, December 29, 1821.

12 *Register*, XVI, 134–37, April 17, 1819, almost weekly through XVI, 434–37,
August 28, 1819.

13 Niles to Darlington, April 26 and May 3, 1820, Darlington MSS, Library of
Congress.

the reduction of income from import duties could not be charged against a higher tariff by its enemies.[14]

Through the next few years the *Register* gave much space to the condition of industry and the need for protection. When tariff legislation was defeated early in 1823, Niles wrote a friend in Congress: "Some bill of the sort *must* & *will* be passed. Is it not possible that a certain man may ride to the presidency upon it? He *surely* will mount it, & trust the issue upon it . . . & for myself, without regard for any man, I shall *go* for it—though not in any *personal* tract just now." [15]

Clay undoubtedly was the "certain man" referred to in the letter. Niles' pride in his own sponsorship of domestic industry was expressed in an editorial in March, 1823, in which he wrote: "I believe that I am now about the *oldest* public writer—(as we editors are honorably called.) in favor of domestic manufacturers in the United States. I commenced the *campaign* about eighteen years ago, with nearly the same views, and to help to bring about the same purposes that I now aim at." [16]

The progress of the 1824 tariff bill, wherein protection was extended to other industries, was closely followed by the *Register*.[17] With the passage of the bill, Niles hoped to retire from the tariff controversy "as the *leading* editorial subject of this work." He restated his disinterestedness in the question except insofar as it "would benefit the *whole* people of the United States," but warned that he stood ready to fight for the principle again if it became necessary.[18] That necessity arose almost at once and continued without a break throughout the next nine years. Articles in 1825 and 1826 chiefly dwelt upon the number of factories and their products.

The demand of the woolen manufacturers for higher duties, followed by similar demands from other branches of industry, was reported and editorially supported in the *Register*. Answer-

14 *Register*, XVIII, 297, June 24, 1820.
15 Niles to Darlington, February 18, 1823, Darlington MSS, Library of Congress.
16 *Register*, XXIV, 19, March 15, 1823.
17 From January through May nearly every number contained articles and editorials on the legislation; the bill as originally introduced is in *Register*, XXV, 315-17, January 17, 1824; as passed by the House, XXVI, 121-24, April 24, 1824; comments and articles in support, XXV, 289-90, January 10, 1824; XXVI, 65-68, April 3, 1824; 113-14, April 24, 1824.
18 *Register*, XXVI, 129-30, May 1, 1824.

ing critics, Niles wrote that he had not one cent invested in
any business but the *Register,* and that his support of protection
had cost him money in canceled subscriptions. By 1828 the
Register was battling vigorously for the so-called American
System. This phrase, apparently borrowed from the oratorical
efforts of Henry Clay, was first used in the *Register* on May 15,
1824, and in the next nine years was to appear frequently in its
columns.[19] Niles, Carey, and Clay were everywhere recognized
as the leading exponents of the system, destined to go down to
defeat before President Jackson.

That Niles was not oblivious of the changes wrought by the
industrial revolution is indicated by an editorial written in 1825
in which he found himself wondering what the state of society
would be like if ever there were a general surplus production.
He predicted that persons then living would see great changes
in the moral, social, and political conditions of society and questioned whether surplus production might not bring idleness
and a retrogression of society.[20]

The intricate and devious course of the Tariff of Abominations through Congress was followed in detail by the *Register*
during the first six months of 1828. The act, as signed by President John Quincy Adams on May 19, was printed five days
later.[21] Niles in correspondence expressed displeasure at the
political motives which gave birth to the bill.[22] Shortly after its
passage, he asserted that the "opponents of the protecting principle" who "*loaded* the bill to sink it," and then were defeated
in their "*left-handed* legislation," should bear the burden of
reproach; but he clearly saw that the condemnation would fall
upon the "old and steady friends of domestic industry" who
permitted their enemies to outmaneuver them.[23]

The 1828 tariff marked the high point of protection in the
United States before the Civil War. Niles spent the next four
years in defending his protective principles and in attacking

[19] *Register,* XXVI, 161, May 15, 1824; Clay's speech containing the phrase is in
XXVI, 384, August 7, 1824.
[20] *Register,* XXVIII, 113–14, April 23, 1825.
[21] *Register,* XXXIV, 203–205, May 24, 1828.
[22] Niles to Darlington, March 31, 1828, Darlington MSS, Library of Congress.
[23] *Register,* XXXIV, 249, June 14, 1828.

the sectional opposition, the leadership of which centered in South Carolina. It was in this quadrennium that the bulk of Niles' writing in defense of the American System was concentrated. The student of a protective tariff will probably find in the thirty-fourth to the forty-second volumes of the *Register* all the arguments available at that time. Niles' various essays on protection first appeared in the *Register*, as did the reports of the tariff conventions held at Harrisburg in 1827 and in New York in 1831.

In the minds of many the phrase, the American System, is always associated with Henry Clay, who defended it with eloquence on the floor of the House and the Senate for years, and from whom Niles unquestionably picked it up. However, it is interesting to discover from a perusal of the *Register* that Jefferson had used the expression in a slightly different form in a letter on June 26, 1817, in which he wrote: "The history of the last twenty years has been a sufficient lesson for us all to depend for necessaries on *ourselves alone;* and I hope that twenty years more will place the *American hemisphere under a system of its own,* essentially peaceable and industrious, and not needing to extract its *comforts* out of the eternal fires raging in the old world." [24]

The phrase with another connotation was used years earlier by Alexander Hamilton in the *Federalist* when he wrote: "Let the thirteen states, bound together in a strict and indissoluble union, concur in erecting one great *American System,* superior to the control of all transatlantic force or influence, and able to dictate the terms of the connexion between the old and the new world." [25]

Niles fought for his beloved principle of majority rule and ridiculed the idea that the principle of protection which had

[24] Letter written to the secretary of the American Society for Promoting Manufactures, reprinted from the Charleston *Courier* in *Register*, XXXVIII, 294, June 12, 1830.

[25] *Register*, XXXIX, 139, October 23, 1830; cf. Henry Cabot Lodge (ed.), *The Federalist A Commentary on The Constitution of the United States Being A Collection of Essays written in support of the Constitution agreed upon September 17, 1787, By the Federal Convention Reprinted from the original Text of Alexander Hamilton, John Jay, and James Madison* (New York, 1889), 67.

been recognized by *"every* congress and *every* executive, from Washington to John Quincy Adams," was now pronounced *"unconstitutional, tyrannical* and *unjust."* He argued that four fifths of the citizens wanted a tariff and that the other fifth would also benefit by it. He devoted practically the entire September 20, 1828, number to the tariff, printing several hundred extra copies, five hundred of which he sent to friends in Congress for distribution among their constituents and elsewhere. Throughout 1829 articles defending the American System appeared frequently as propaganda against the attempts made by the new administration to lower the tariff, although Niles did not "esteem it expedient" to defend the 1828 measure.

The next two years were discouraging ones for the *Register*'s editor. The exuberant editorials in the southern press over the Maysville veto and their predictions that the protecting system would be the next to go brought an answering rallying cry to the friends of domestic industry in the *Register*.[26] An essay, "Politics for Farmers," appeared on September 11, 1830, to be followed by an enthusiastic description of the American Institute's annual fair in New York, which Niles attended.[27] In 1831 the tone of the propaganda campaign was one of enthusiasm for the American System. Landholders and factory owners were urged to induce the laboring classes to "read and reflect" upon the need for a protective tariff. The effects of the American System, which he pledged himself to support as long as he could "talk or write about it with the hope of being useful," were outlined in a number of editorials, supported by letters. Another of his essays, "Politics for Working Men," written on July 4, 1831, and designed to explain in simple language the theories of protection, closed with this appeal to the working people:

I ask you not to vote for this man or that man, or any particular man—but this I exhort, and entreat you to do—by all that is good for the nation, by all that is beneficial for yourselves, to give your suffrages to no human being who does not stand broadly pledged, manfully and honestly "committed," and unquestionably devoted, to the preservation of the AMERICAN SYSTEM—the fountain of public wealth, the guarantee of private comfort—proclaiming plenty and

26 *Register*, XXXVIII, 319–21, June 26, 1830; 349–53, July 10, 1830.
27 *Register*, XXXIX, 153–54, 162–65, October 30, 1830.

securing peace—offering relief to the opposed of all nations, and *establishing the independence of these United States.*

I am your friend,
H. Niles, printer.

Baltimore, July 4, 1831.[28]

Fighting as he was for the principle of protection Niles was true to his editorial principle of fairness and impartiality and gave notices and an entirely adequate coverage to the free-trade convention, held in New York City, starting September 30, 1831. He questioned, however, whether such a thing as true free trade existed.[29]

The first six months of 1832 saw the *Register* to all intents and purposes given over to the tariff fight. Clay's series of speeches in defense of the American System; the speech of Senator Robert Y. Hayne, of South Carolina, opposing Clay's first speech; the majority and minority reports of the House commitee on ways and means of which George McDuffie, of South Carolina, was chairman; the report submitted by Louis McLane, secretary of the treasury, generally regarded as having administration backing; and the bill as drawn by John Quincy Adams, chairman of the House committee on manufactures, formed the documentary background for a series of editorials that fought a good fight for the American System. Niles feared that the temper of the House was "totally unfitted for that sober and solid examination" which the tariff question deserved, and in the same article, which ran nearly seven pages in length, hotly denied that he had misrepresented facts in his defense of the tariff principle. "IF IT CANNOT STAND ON TRUTH—LET IT FALL!" he wrote in reply to the charges of the Washington *Globe.*[30] On July 14 he reported its passage in final form, and the next week, in an editorial on the record of the recently adjourned Congress, wrote that he felt that the *"constitutionality and expediency of the protecting system"* had been upheld although the internal improvements plank in his American-System platform had been ripped out.[31] After the victory Niles was apprehensive

28 *Register*, XL, 321–27, July 9, 1831, this quotation being on p. 327.
29 *Register*, XL, 305–306, July 2, 1831; XLI, 129, 135–41, October 15, 1831; 156–58, October 22, 1831; 166, October 29, 1831.
30 *Register*, XLII, 272, June 9, 1832.   31 *Register*, XLII, 353, July 14, 1832.

lest the American System be weakened by attacks from both sides —from opponents as well as from some of its former friends who were irked because certain industries had, in their eyes, received insufficient protection. He said he would try to ward off both attacks and pointed to his long and earnest devotion to the cause of domestic industry, at times, "highly detrimental to his pecuniary concerns," as proof that he was entitled to the confidence "of every true friend of the system." [32]

Niles was not one to shut his eyes to realities, and in the same number which conceded the re-election of President Jackson and acknowledged the *Register*'s submission to the will of the majority as expressed at the polls, he sounded the warning that the principle of protection was "in imminent danger." [33] He at first refused to believe that Congress would repeal a law not yet in operation; however, at the introduction of the Verplanck bill, he opened his two months' campaign with a four-page editorial. Therein he defended protective tariff and attacked the "DICTATION" of measures by 250,000 people in South Carolina when 1,500,000 in Pennsylvania and many more elsewhere stood opposed. Extra copies containing this appeal were sent to members of Congress and other nonsubscribers.[34] Pointing to the compromise in the Act of 1832, he expressed the hope that both parties might accept the proposal to permit the measure to operate for at least a brief period; [35] but a week later, the desertion of Clay, who apparently had not taken his friend and supporter into his confidence, was a severe blow, all the more so because of its unexpectedness. He wrote: "Mr. Clay's NEW TARIFF PROJECT will be received like a crash of thunder in the winter season, and some will hardly trust the evidence of their senses on a first examination of it—so radical and sudden is the change proposed. . . ."

Niles said that Clay's speech had not convinced him of the "*necessity* of abandoning the principle of protection," and he could not agree with the Kentuckian that the compromise measure did not constitute an abandonment. He reiterated his

[32] *Register*, XLII, 385, July 28, 1832.

[33] *Register*, XLIII, 177, November 17, 1832.

[34] *Register*, XLIII, 265, December 22, 1832; 281–85, December 29, 1832; a "hasty transcript" of the Verplanck Bill is on 290–91.

[35] *Register*, XLIII, 298, January 5, 1833; 313, January 12, 1833.

plea to let the tariff alone until the next session of Congress.[36] Its passage by the two houses was recorded, with an editorial expressing Niles' disappointment. Mathew Carey's withdrawal from the advocacy of protection because of the lack of support by manufacturers caused Niles to give some serious thought to his own future course. He felt that anything worth doing at all was "worth doing well, with all one's heart," and said that the flag of the American System would never be flown at half-mast in the *Register*. He decided to take the matter under advisement, but in the meantime said that the law must be obeyed.[37]

On January 3, 1835, in an article praising the House for refusing to admit iron for railroads free, Niles acknowledged editorially that he had begun "to entertain a better opinion" of the compromise measure. It was late in 1840 before the tariff again occupied much space in the *Register*. Jeremiah Hughes, then owner-editor, was an advocate of reciprocity rather than of protection.[38] Later he supported a return to "a good tariff," and welcomed the settlement of the controversy by the measure which finally won President John Tyler's approval on August 30, 1842.[39] By 1844 the *Register* had returned to warm support of the protective policy and its editorials sounded much like the ones of 1828–1832.[40] This similarity was heightened in 1845 when the passage of a free-trade bill loomed. The *Register* said that the proposed measure had been drawn up to meet the wishes of "the British government, the British merchants, the British capitalists, and the British manufacturers, all of whom are known to be actively engaged through their agents, to effect a change so vital to them and so fatal to our manufacturing. . . ." The day after its enactment the *Register* roundly condemned the Walker Tariff of July 30, 1846, and reiterated the belief that British influence had had much to do with its

36 *Register*, XLIII, 401–402, February 16, 1833.

37 *Register*, XLIV, 1, March 2, 1833; 17–18, March 9, 1833; 34–35, March 16, 1833; 103–104, April 13, 1833.

38 *Register*, LX, 307–308, July 17, 1841; 385–86, August 21, 1841; LXI, 49, September 25, 1841.

39 *Register*, LXII, 84, April 9, 1842; LXIII, 17–18, September 10, 1842; the act was printed in LXIII, 5–10, September 3, 1842.

40 *Register*, XLV, 401, February 24, 1844; LXVI, 177–78, May 18, 1844; LXVIII, 348–51, August 2, 1845; LXIX, 57–60, September 27, 1845; 128, October 25, 1845; 141–43, November 1, 1845.

passage. It printed the brief new law and, "as an appropriate companion," the new tariff law recently passed in Great Britain was reprinted from the *Times*.[41] The announcement of the nineteenth annual fair of the American Institute was made the occasion of an attack on the Walker Tariff and an appeal for economic independence strongly reminiscent of those of Hezekiah Niles. It closed, "Oh for an AMERICAN feeling—an AMERICAN spirit—another effective assertion of AMERICAN INDEPENDENCE." A week later were printed excerpts from Canadian and English newspapers praising the tariff and from American newspapers citing lower wages and unemployment as immediate effects.[42] On this pessimistic note ended the *Register*'s long advocacy of the principle of a tariff to protect American industry.

The attitude of the *Register* and of Hezekiah Niles toward the Second Bank of the United States makes an involved and intricate story, to do justice to which would take far more space than can be allotted in this work. It was the only matter of policy on which the founder-editor reversed his position. In 1831–1832 Niles campaigned arduously to obtain a new charter for the same institution that he had fought tooth and nail in the late teens and early twenties. Proud of the consistency of his opinions, Niles was forced to acknowledge that his ideas toward the financial institution had changed over a period of years.[43]

The first bill to establish the bank was vetoed by President Madison on January 30, 1815, for which action he was editorially thanked by the *Register*. The next measure, drawn to meet the executive's objections, received his approval on April 10, 1816.[44] Niles' correspondence with Dr. William Darlington, Pennsylvania Congressman, indicated his opposition. On March 1 he wrote, "I doubt both its constitutionality and its expediency." [45]

41 *Register*, LXX, 324, July 25, 1846; 345–51, August 1, 1846.

42 *Register*, LXXI, 32, September 12, 1846; 45–47, September 19, 1846.

43 *Register*, XLII, 417, August 11, 1832; 433–36, August 18, 1832.

44 *Register*, VII, 364, February 4, 1815; the veto message is on 366–67; earlier editorial opposition to the bank may be found in VII, 335, January 21, 1815; passage of the revised measure is mentioned in *Register*, X, 111, April 13, 1816; the act itself is printed in X, 129–35, April 20, 1816.

45 Niles to Darlington, March 1, 1816, Darlington MSS, Library of Congress.

During 1816 the *Register*'s notices of the bank were confined to factual reporting of the stock subscription, the naming of the directors and officers, and the fixing of salaries.[46] Two distinct editorial campaigns were opened in 1818 in the *Register*, one against the Bank of the United States and the other against the evils of the paper-money system. Denouncing the influence of banking on the freedom of the press, he gloried in the fact that his only patron was the "people at large; and, blessed be Providence for it, those institutions have not any hold upon *me*." In the same article he suggested that the states tax the mother bank out of existence if it refused to furnish drafts at par for bills payable by the same bank, no matter from where they were issued. He denied any special enmity against the United States Bank or any bank, saying that in printing the series he felt that he was doing his duty.[47] In a "Septennial Retrospect," looking over the period since the founding of the *Register*, he devoted several paragraphs to arguments upholding the right of states to tax the bank and called attention to plans in Ohio, Pennsylvania, and Maryland to pass such legislation.[48]

Chief Justice John Marshall's decision in McCulloch *vs.* Maryland was a severe blow to the editor. He had followed the legal course of the case and recognized its importance, writing that much would depend upon the decision as to the constitutional principles involved.[49] But he could not go along with the chief justice in his sanction of the doctrine of implied powers. As soon at it was available to him, he printed the decision in full, in the same number declaring that it was the most important decision ever pronounced by the "exalted tribunal." He admitted that the court should be respected, but questioned the reverence with which members were held by some, saying, ". . . we have yet to learn that its members are superior to the common feelings and frailties of men, and that they cannot be mistaken." He felt that the decision established the principle "that congress may grant *monopolies*, almost at discretion, to any set of men, and for almost any purpose, if the price is paid

[46] *Register*, X, 197–98, May 18, 1816; 366, July 27, 1816; 381, August 3, 1816; XI, 16, August 31, 1816; 176, November 9, 1816; 191, November 16, 1816.
[47] *Register*, XIV, 1–5, February 28, 1818; 17, March 7, 1818.
[48] *Register*, XV, 3–4, August 29, 1818.
[49] *Register*, XV, 362, January 9, 1819; XVI, 1, February 27, 1819.

for them, or without any pecuniary consideration at all." Even the style in which the opinion was written came in for criticism: "We frankly confess *our* opinion, that the writer of the *opinion* in question, has not added any thing to this stock of reputation by writing it—*it is excessively labored.*" [50]

On October 27, 1821, he wrote that his "late silence about the bank must not be construed into a belief that it was constitutionally established, or that it has always been honestly conducted." Three years later he made the occasion of the laying of a cornerstone of the Boston branch of the bank on July 4 the point of departure for a three-page attack on the "cold, calculating, selfish, *soul-less*" corporation.[51]

His concurrent campaign against the issuance of insufficiently backed paper money by state banks was based less on political prejudice and more on sound economic reasoning. The brunt of the attack was borne by a series of seven articles entitled "The Paper System," ostensibly written by "the pen of a master, in the hand of a gentleman," but certainly suggested, if not actually composed by Niles. The series covered the history of banking in the United States, the evils of paper currency, the lack of suitable restrictions upon the setting up of banks, the effect of paper money on farmers, and a history of banking in England.[52]

The first indication of Niles' changed feeling toward the Bank of the United States appeared in an editorial late in 1827 opposing the sale of the stock owned by the government.[53] Two years later the editor criticized President Jackson for questioning the bank's expediency and constitutionality. Niles took the stand that seven years before the expiration of the charter was too early to open discussion on its renewal. He said his opinions had not been changed but admitted that they had been "much softened by time and circumstances." He felt that the bank had "rendered essential services toward 'establishing a uniform and sound currency,' . . ." [54]

[50] *Register*, XVI, 65, March 20, 1819.
[51] *Register*, XXVI, 337-39, July 24, 1824.
[52] *Register*, XIV, 141-42, April 25, 1818; 153-56, May 2, 1818; 180-84, May 9, 1818; 194-98, May 16, 1818; 242-46, June 6, 1818; 273-77, June 13, 1818; 284-87, June 20, 1818; 426-28, August 22, 1818.
[53] *Register*, XXXIII, 241, December 15, 1827.
[54] *Register*, XXXVII, 257-58, December 19, 1829.

In 1831 Niles lined up definitely on the side of the bank when he wrote that between supporting the "present bank of the United States, with some few modifications of its privileges and powers," and adopting Jackson's plan, he was for the present institution with all its evils.[55] When Clay and the National Republicans decided to make a campaign issue of the bank, Niles covered the Congressional fight, which was opened by the introduction of the memorial on January 9, 1832, asking recharter.[56] The investigation of the bank brought three separate reports, so voluminous that the *Register* was unable to print them. However, they were commented upon.[57] Niles was too realistic to hope for anything but a veto from the President on the bank bill. The veto message occupied four pages of small type in a number turned over almost entirely to the proceedings in Congress.[58] The Philadelphia *Inquirer*, an administration paper, rightly remarked that the veto "puts the question to the people—which do you prefer, Jackson or the bank?" [59] In this race, Niles was backing the wrong horse. But in the next few months he did all that he could through the columns of the *Register* to convince the public that the prosperity of the nation depended upon the continued operation of the financial institution. He laid the blame for the slowing up of business to the veto, rather than to the bank's action in restricting credit.[60]

Niles' national prominence in the journalistic field naturally called attention to his change in front on the bank question. He fought hard on both occasions. In the thirties his editorial opponents lost no opportunity to recall to him his stand of the teens and early twenties. Thomas Ritchie, his opponent in many an inky battle over the tariff, led the charge. [61] Niles endured the jibes of his old friend and opponent, but when editors

[55] *Register*, XL, 114, April 16, 1831.

[56] *Register*, XLI and XLII, from January through July, 1832.

[57] *Register*, XLII, 185, May 5, 1832; 209, May 19, 1832. An excellent account of the bank fight may be found in Carl Brent Swisher, *Roger B. Taney* (New York, 1935), IX, 160–84.

[58] *Register*, XLII, 365–68, July 14, 1832.

[59] *Register*, XLII, 353, July 14, 1832.

[60] *Register*, XLIII, 17–18, September 8, 1832; 49–51, September 22, 1832; 73, September 29, 1832.

[61] *Register*, XL, 397–98, July 30, 1831.

of other Jackson papers implied, if they did not actually charge, that his change of attitude had been brought about by loans or favors from the bank, he flatly declared that

. . . he never personally received a solitary accommodation, or favor, from that bank, (nor any other person for him), in any manner whatsoever, directly or indirectly, since its establishment to the present day—
. . . But, in common with others, he has received great benefits from the bank—in remittances from his subscribers. He used to pay six or eight hundred dollars a year *in shavings of bank notes,* and now does not pay one hundred. . . .[62]

The verdict of the voters in re-electing President Jackson was taken by Niles to indicate approval of the President's stand on the bank issue and he thereupon withdrew the *Register* from the bank controversy in deference to the legally expressed wishes of the majority.[63]

The final chapter in the *Register*'s relations with the bank dealt with the removal of government deposits carried out in the early part of Jackson's second administration under the leadership of Amos Kendall and Roger B. Taney. For the most part this story was handled impersonally and was told through Congressional debates, messages from the President and cabinet officials, correspondence and reports of committees.[64]

Newspaper editorials and articles containing rumors of the removal were quoted at length. The decision and the resultant cabinet shake-up occupied nearly five pages of the September 28, 1833, number. Niles wrote that the vote sustaining the removal was a party one and charged that many who opposed the action

[62] *Register*, XLIII, 39, September 15, 1832.
[63] *Register*, XLIII, 177, November 17, 1832.
[64] In Volumes XLIV, XLV, and XLVI of the *Register* will be found a great amount of material on this question which caused Jackson to revamp his official family; typical are: XLIV, 108–12, April 13, 1833, Congressional debate; XLV, 73–77, September 28, 1833, Jackson's communication of September 18, 1833, read to his cabinet; XLV, 205–206, November 23, 1833; 236–39, December 7, 1833, correspondence between William J. Duane, removed secretary of the treasury, and the President; XLV, 258–64, December 14, 1833, report on the removal of the deposits made by Taney to both houses of Congress on December 4, 1833; XLV, 313–19; 319–26, January 4, 1834; 335–44, January 11, 1834; 349–60, January 18, 1834, speeches of Polk, McDuffie, and Clay; XLV, 418–24, February 15, 1834; XLVI, 38–48, March 15, 1834; 54–64, March 22, 1834, Congressional committee reports.

cast their ballots in favor of it because "the president must be supported!" The Senate's rejection of Taney as secretary of the treasury was not surprising to Niles, who asserted that that body "had already pronounced its judgment on Mr. Taney, in declaring that his reasons assigned for the removal of the deposites [*sic*] were insufficient, &c." [65]

In an open letter in reply to charges that the opposition to Jackson on the bank was purely political and led by "such men as Clay, Webster and H. Niles," the editor asserted that his attitude had nothing to do with politics. He outlined six conditions under which the bank's charter might well be renewed in an effort to meet the objections raised by opponents.[66]

Thus the two great economic questions of the day, the tariff and the Bank of the United States, were covered in the *Register*. Economic questions then as now were inextricably involved in the politics of the day and the *Register*'s coverage of the American political scene from 1811 to 1849 will next be examined.

[65] *Register*, XLVI, 97, April 12, 1834; 187, May 17, 1834; 297, June 28, 1834.
[66] *Register*, XLVI, 18–21, March 8, 1834.

Chapter 6

The *Register* and Politics

THE results of ten presidential elections are recorded in the *Register*. From the re-election of James Madison in 1812 through the election of General Zachary Taylor in 1848, one may read in its columns the political history of the nation. And it is an impartial, nonpartisan history that one finds here. In each of the ten elections which occurred during the *Register*'s career, the activities of both or all sides were reported fully and fairly; in not a single instance was a candidate supported. Measures, not men, were the criteria used in determining the *Register*'s stand on political issues, and measures, not men, were supported or opposed. The reader cannot find an editorial advocating or opposing the election of an individual in the *Register*. He can find any number of them taking a vigorous stand on campaign issues, especially in the political battles of 1824, 1828, and 1832.

That a newspaper or periodical should adopt such a policy regarding politics was almost unheard of at that time. The period during which the *Register* was published was characterized by the most partisan political journalism in the history of American newspapers. Every historian of American journalism has classified it as the period of the political-party press and most of them are outspoken in their denunciation of the utter domination of the press by politicians.[1]

[1] For detailed discussions and analyses of this period in American journalism the following may be consulted with profit: Willard Grosvenor Bleyer, *Main Currents in the History of American Journalism* (Boston, c1927), 130–53; Frederic Hudson, *Journalism in the United States from 1690 to 1872* (New York, 1873), 141–407; Alfred McClung Lee, *The Daily Newspaper in America: The Evolution of a Social Instrument* (New York, 1937), 178; James Melvin Lee, *History of American Journalism* (New York, c1923); 140–63; Frank Luther Mott, *American Journalism: A History of Newspapers in the United States through 250 Years, 1690 to 1940* (New York, 1941), 167–326; Frank Luther Mott, *Jefferson and the Press* (Baton Rouge, 1943); George Henry Payne, *History of Journalism in the United States* (New York, 1920), 153–239.

Hezekiah Niles was personally a Republican and for nearly six years he edited a daily newspaper of that political complexion. But when he published the prospectus of the periodical upon which his fame rests, he announced the nonpartisan character of the *Register,* a character maintained throughout its life. He wrote:

> It shall be open to all parties, temper, moderation and dignity being preserved. . . . The news-papers of the day, devoted to *party* and *partizans,* seldom dare to *"tell the truth, the whole truth, and nothing but the truth"* . . . the dignity of the press is prostrated to the will of aspiring individuals. . . . The editor does not intend to interfere in the petty disputes between the *ins* and *outs.* . . . Its politics shall be *American*—not passive and lukewarm, but active and vigilant—not to support individuals, but to subserve the interests of the people, so far as he shall be able to discern in what their interest lies.[2]

He accepted the responsibility of presenting both sides of great national questions in order "to preserve a history of the feelings of the times on men and things." [3] From this course he never deviated. Electioneering in the press was condemned practically biennially. He felt he was neither a man-worshiper nor an office hunter, and he operated editorially in a " 'gang by himself'—owe-ing [sic] much to the public, but nothing to party in his business." [4]

Niles prided himself on the fact that personal attacks upon political candidates, the chief content of many of the day's newspapers, were not printed in the *Register.* At the close of the sixth year of publication, in a two-and-one-half-page editorial, looking back over the period, Niles wrote that the *Register* had "Established a new era, if the phrase is not too pompous for the occasion, . . . in passing through the warmest period of politics, and most warmly engaged in them, without a solitary personal attack—a descent to remarks upon *men,* so much easier to an editor than the support of principles." [5]

Still warmer periods were to come while he occupied the editorial chair, but in spite of his personal disappointment over

[2] *Register,* I, 2–3, September 7, 1811.   [3] *Register,* I, 1, September 7, 1811.
[4] *Register,* XIX, 388, February 10, 1821.
[5] *Register,* XII, 401–404, August 23, 1817.

defeat of measures and of men, nothing reflecting upon the character or private life of a candidate for office was printed.[6] His "measures, not men" policy was well expressed in an editorial printed August 25, 1821, as follows, "The proprietor of a press stands as a sort of centinel, and he must not cry 'all's well,' when an enemy is within reach of his point, without being thought a traitor. We have no choice about men—we do not care who it is that makes or executes the law, provided it is good in itself. We have nothing to gain or lose by a change of *persons* —the congressman and the common laborer are equal in our eyes, if each performs his part honestly."

Starting his sixteenth year as editor of the *Register*, Niles mentioned his "rigid impartiality" in the selection of political news and his practice of seeking articles on the opposite side when one side of a controversy had been given space in the periodical.[7] Before examining briefly the *Register*'s stands in the national campaigns from 1812 to 1848, a few of its editorial expressions on politics and elections will be noted. It favored a uniform method of choosing presidential electors, opposing their choice by the state legislatures.[8] Election of the executive by the House of Representatives was said to have been "productive of more ill-blood and enmity among the people than any other two events that have happened in our political history—"[9] A six-year or eight-year single term for the President was suggested.[10] The practice of calling parties after candidates such as "Jackson-men" and "Adams-men" irked the *Register*'s editor, although in 1834, after arriving upon Whig as the name for the opposition party, he finally settled on the term "Jacksonian" for the Jackson–Van Buren group.[11] Niles disliked the

[6] In *Register*, XXII, 193–94, May 25, 1822, commenting upon the attacks being made upon cabinet members under discussion as candidates for the presidency, he wrote, "It cannot be supposed that Messrs. Adams, Crawford, or Calhoun, Mr. Clay and others spoken of as fitted to succeed to the chief magistracy of the United States, are cold enemies of their country, destitute of talents, or without moral principles."

[7] *Register*, XXXI, 1, September 2, 1826.

[8] *Register*, XXV, 65–67, October 4, 1823.

[9] *Register*, XXXI, 66–67, September 30, 1826.

[10] *Register*, XXXII, 339, July 21, 1827.

[11] *Register*, XXXVII, 165, November 7, 1829; XLVI, 115, April 19, 1834; 130, April 26, 1834; 409, August 16, 1834; XLVII, 17–18, September 13, 1834.

use of the words "the government" as applied to the executive, feeling that the sovereignty rested with the people.[12] In the controversy over the "instruction" of members of Congress by their constituents, Niles took little part other than to report it, although he recognized its "general right" to which there must be "many serious exceptions. . . ."[13]

The caucus which chose Madison as the Republican candidate was duly reported. In the same issue an editorial differed with the President's critics, saying that his public acts were marked by "an uniformly *non-submitting* spirit."[14] Nominations for vice president and actions of state legislatures were reported. Niles felt that the re-election of Madison would show Great Britain that the country was united against her in the war.[15] Just before the end of the war became known to the *Register*, Niles had opposed suggestions that the President be removed from office, saying that while he was not an "ardent admirer" of the executive, he felt that it was infamous for "insolent foreigners" to interfere in domestic political affairs.[16] This reference indicated his belief that English influence was back of the suggestions emanating from New England.

The choice of James Monroe over William H. Crawford at the Republican Congressional caucus of March 16, 1816, was reported in detail, without editorial comment. A four-page biography of Monroe had been reprinted from the *National Advocate* in an earlier number. But outside of printing some correspondence from the candidates and a comment on the decline of federalism in New England, little space was devoted to the election.[17] Niles sincerely believed that the so-called era of good feelings was not an unmixed blessing to the country. A strong believer in the two-party system, in which the opposition maintained a close surveillance over the party in power, he wrote that the "state of *apathy*" which prevailed under the new

[12] *Register*, XLV, 209, November 30, 1833.
[13] *Register*, XLVII, 129–31, November 1, 1834.
[14] *Register*, II, 192–93, 197, May 23, 1812.
[15] *Register*, II, 235, June 6, 1812; 276, June 27, 1812; 321–22, July 18, 1812; 396, August 15, 1812; III, 17–19, September 12, 1812; 131–33, October 31, 1812.
[16] *Register*, VII, 337, January 28, 1815.
[17] *Register*, X, 4–8, March 2, 1816; 59–60, March 23, 1816; 162–63, 168, May 4, 1816.

era represented a retrogression in the nation's history.[18] In 1819 he wrote that he was not interested in the President's re-election, "though generally pleased with his administration, because we have fallen into the opinion that the republic would be better served, if the presidency were held for four years only." [19] By the fall of 1820 he saw Monroe's re-election as inevitable, but, commenting upon reports of attempts to get up an antislavery ticket in Pennsylvania, he suggested to his "southern friends" that they support "a gentleman from a different section, as his successor." [20] A brief factual item told of the nearly unanimous electoral vote received by the President.[21] The *Register* later became somewhat more critical of Monroe's administrations, its editor asserting that during his two terms the "prosperity and the general happiness" of the country had retrograded. Niles reiterated that the criticism had nothing to do with the man, but was based on an honest conviction that policies were at fault.[22] Motivated by his sense of fair play, however, the editor came to the defense of the executive near the end of his second term when he was being generally attacked, writing, "I am not one of those who 'fell down and worshipped' Mr. Monroe, when the sun of his greatness was at its meridian, nor will I be among his enemies *because* his political power is about to pass into other hands. He was praised without decency, and now is abused without shame." [23]

It was during Monroe's second term that Niles won what was undoubtedly his most spectacular victory in the field of politics. Fighting for a principle and against a custom, he set out to kill the Congressional caucus method of choosing presidential candidates. And kill it he did, in spite of having such worthy journalistic opponents as the *National Intelligencer*, Richmond *Enquirer*, Albany *Argus*, and Philadelphia *American Sentinel*. This method of choosing the party candidates had

[18] *Register*, XX, 132, April 28, 1821; other comments on this era may be found in *Register*, XIII, 163, November 8, 1817; XX, 97, April 14, 1821; 338, July 28, 1821; see Frank R. Kent, *The Democratic Party, A History* (New York, c1928), 63.

[19] *Register*, XVI, 25–26, March 6, 1819.

[20] *Register*, XIX, 129, October 28, 1820.

[21] *Register*, XIX, 256, December 16, 1820.

[22] *Register*, XIX, 391, February 10, 1821; XX, 341, July 28, 1821; 373–74, August 11, 1821; XXI, 203, November 24, 1821.

[23] *Register*, XXVI, 151, May 8, 1824.

been in use since 1800.[24] Niles had defended the caucus in 1812 and four years later had been silent, or at least noncommittal on the meeting.[25] It was the 1816 caucus, he wrote seven years later, *"that destroyed my confidence in that plan for collecting and uniting public opinion, and brought me to the conclusion that it ought not to be tolerated any longer."* [26] Mild criticism of the practice was voiced in 1820.[27] In 1822 he gave notice that he was going to express his opinion decisively on the "dirty thing that is called a *caucus.*" He went ahead in the same editorial to charge that the practice was "not only injurious, but absolutely dangerous to the liberties of the country," and added, ". . . I would rather learn that the halls of congress were converted into common brothels, than that caucuses of the description stated should be held in them; I would rather that the sovereignty of these states should be re-transferred to England, than that the people should be bound to submit to the dictates of such an assemblage." [28]

This was strong language indeed for an editor who usually employed a restrained vocabulary and who bitterly hated England. But it was only the opening salvo of an editorial barrage of propaganda against the caucus that was laid down in the columns of the *Register* through 1823 and into the early months of 1824, when, at last, the battle was won. Niles wrote on March 1, 1823: "And, if there must needs be a caucus, the members of congress are the worst of all men to hold it, and Washington the worst fitted, of all places, for its convention." Two months later, pointing out that Jackson, Clay, and Calhoun were all Republicans and that Adams was also, although he once had been a Federalist, Niles urged that the choice be left to the people. He feared the result of an election by the House, but said that a caucus nomination would not lessen the probability of such an outcome. He argued that a Congressional caucus was

[24] For a succinct history of the Congressional caucus, based largely on material from the *Register*, see M. Ostrogorski, "The Rise and Fall of the Nominating Caucus, Legislative and Congressional," *American Historical Review* (New York, 1895—), V, 253–83, December, 1899.

[25] *Register*, X, 59–60, March 23, 1816.

[26] *Register*, XXV, 257, December 27, 1823.

[27] *Register*, XVIII, 97, April 8, 1820; 113, April 15, 1820.

[28] *Register*, XXI, 338–39, January 26, 1822.

unconstitutional. The choice of the executive by the legislative branch was a distinct evil, he felt, saying, "There are temptations enough laid in the way of members of congress already, without investing them with power to *elect*, or *direct the election* of, a president of the United States." [29]

His editorial opponents, especially the *National Intelligencer* and the Richmond *Enquirer*, made much of the fact that the *Register* had supported caucuses in 1812 and 1816, and considerable space in the editorials which ran in nearly every number of the *Register* the last six months of 1823 was given over to arguments attempting to justify his changed position. Niles maintained that his support of the earlier caucuses was based upon their consideration of measures, not men, a position not too easily defended. To an impartial observer, it appears that his stand against the attacks of Joseph Gales, Jr., and Thomas Ritchie would have been strengthened had he admitted that he had changed his mind regarding the caucus.

He was on surer ground when he argued that while the earlier caucuses had been based upon the will of the people, several states through their legislatures and by other means had expressed opposition to a caucus as a method of naming the 1824 candidates.[30] The fact that there was only one political party and that it was virtually impossible to determine from their records or their statements the political lines separating Adams, Calhoun, Clay, Crawford, and Jackson furnished Niles with ammunition for his fight. True to his editorial ethics, even in the hottest part of the battle, he printed resolutions and excerpts from editorials favoring the caucus.[31]

Two months before the last Congressional caucus was held, Niles optimistically predicted that the caucus question "may be regarded as *hors du combat*," adding that if one was held

[29] *Register*, XXIV, 131–33, May 3, 1823; cf. Edward Stanwood, *A History of the Presidency from 1788 to 1897* (rev. ed.; Boston, 1928), I, 126–27; for some of Niles' reasons, chief of which was that a caucus was not authorized by the Constitution and therefore did not exist because it was not among the delegated powers, see *Register*, XXIV, 194–97, May 31, 1823; also XXV, 3–4, September 6, 1823; 97–103, October 18, 1823.

[30] *Register*, XXIV, 322–25, July 26, 1823; XXV, 40–41, September 20, 1823; 137–39, November 1, 1823; 258, 260, December 27, 1823; 281–84, January 3, 1824.

[31] *Register*, XXV, 81, October 11, 1823; 131–33, November 1, 1823; 145–46, November 8, 1823; 273, January 3, 1824.

the recommended candidate would receive no more support than had the meeting not taken place.[32] In the last two numbers of 1823, Niles printed, upon request, a brief factual résumé of Congressional caucuses since 1800, adding that the editor of the New York *Statesman,* then in Washington, reported that eighteen states were opposed to a caucus.[33] With victory within his grasp, he kept up the editorial bombardment into the new year.[34] Two weeks before the slim meeting of 66 of the 216 Republican members of Congress, the editor confidently and accurately predicted that not more than "60 or 70 members will attend—and it is said to be ascertained that 160 are opposed to the proceeding." [35] This confidence, however, did not in any way affect his editorial attacks in the next two numbers which carried last-minute editorials.

Niles packed up and went to Washington for a week and, as a spectator, attended the caucus held on February 14. A dozen pages of the next two numbers of the *Register* were filled with accounts of the meeting and his editorial reactions to it. In the issue of February 21, 1824, most of the space was taken up by the *National Intelligencer*'s "official account" of the caucus and to an address to the Republicans of the nation by those who attended, defending their action. Niles analyzed the membership of Congress and of the caucus and argued that at least fourteen of those present acted against the wishes of their constituents. His own editorial remarks were carried in the number published two weeks after the meeting. They filled six pages, reviewing in some detail the entire history of the caucus method of naming candidates. The account was filled with humor. He wrote that after adjournment he went to Brown's Hotel where he found more than one hundred men collected to hear and discuss the news. "I endeavored to ascertain the opinion of those thus accidentally collected, which had unanimously seemed

---

[32] *Register,* XXV, 162–63, November 15, 1823.

[33] *Register,* XXV, 244–45, December 20, 1823; 258, 259, December 27, 1823.

[34] *Register,* XXV, 291, January 10, 1824; letter to Darlington, January 10, 1824, Darlington MSS, Library of Congress, in which Niles wrote: "I am perfectly sick of *congressional caucusses* [sic]. I believe that there was & perhaps yet is a foul conspiracy of profligate men who expected to impose a president on the people against their wishes."

[35] *Register,* XXV, 337, January 31, 1824.

to be—*that the mountain had labored and produced a mouse,* or that the caucus gentlemen had *'burst their boiler,'* or wrecked their friend on a 'snag.' "

His main argument against following the recommendation of the meeting was that all previous caucuses had represented a majority of the Republican members of Congress, while this group was representative of only a small minority.[36] He continued his attack on the caucus through the summer and fall, charging that the candidates named were "evidently offensive" to the great majority of the voters, although in these articles he refrained from mentioning William H. Crawford or Albert Gallatin by name. If the newspapers could be taken as an index of public opinion, "never was any political measure quite so unpopular in the United States," as the caucus, he wrote a month after the meeting.[37] A few weeks later he supported this statement with figures stating that only 3 of 35 papers in Virginia, 10 of 125 in New York, 3 of 100 in Pennsylvania, and 1 of 48 in Ohio favored the caucus and its choice.[38] Through September and October, Niles summed up in a series of six articles entitled "The Sovereignty of the People" his stand against the caucus system. In these essays, which filled nearly thirty pages, many of his earlier arguments were restated. He particularly attacked the "Richmond Junto" and argued that the choice of Gallatin for the vice-presidency was merely a device to snare the votes of New York and Pennsylvania.[39] There is no way to determine the exact influence the *Register* exerted in eliminating the Congressional caucus as a method of naming presidential and vice-presidential candidates, but the fact that the caucus plan was defeated in spite of such powerful editorial advocates as the *National Intelligencer* and the Richmond *Enquirer* indicates that Niles' sustained campaign against it had an effect upon the outcome. Nearly five years later, shortly after Andrew Jackson's first inauguration, Niles warned against a rumored revival

[36] *Register,* XXV, 401–406, February 28, 1824.
[37] *Register,* XXVI, 19, March 13, 1824.
[38] *Register,* XXVI, 99, April 17, 1824; figures were given on other states also.
[39] The six essays may be found in *Register,* XXVII, 1–5, September 4, 1824; 17–21, September 11, 1824; 33–39, September 18, 1824; 49–53, September 25, 1824; 65–68, October 2, 1824; 97–100, October 16, 1824.

of the caucus plan.[40] Having been in on the kill, he had no wish to see the plan resurrected by politicians.

Concurrently with its fight against the caucus, the *Register* reported the varied political activities preceding the choice of a successor to President Monroe. From the organization of the Seventeenth Congress in December, 1821, to some weeks after the election in the House on February 9, 1825, hundreds of news items described the early start and progress of the campaigns of the candidates. The fact that members of Congress, nearly three years before the next presidential election, were determining their stands on legislation with an eye toward the election instead of considering the proposed laws on their merits, astonished and disturbed the *Register*'s editor who made a trip to Washington in January, 1822. He listed as candidates at the moment, John Quincy Adams, John C. Calhoun, Henry Clay, De Witt Clinton, then governor of New York, William H. Crawford, William Lowndes, of South Carolina, and Smith Thompson and Daniel D. Tompkins, both of New York.[41] The name of Andrew Jackson appeared in the *Register*'s columns as a candidate when the nominating resolution of the Tennessee legislature was printed without comment some six months later.[42] By early 1823, Old Hickory's name was being mentioned with increasing frequency, and on April 5, 1823, announcing a series of articles on the candidates, he listed, alphabetically, Adams, Calhoun, Clay, Crawford, and Jackson as "the only persons who are seriously spoken of just now."

The student interested in the 1824 election campaign will find in the 1823 and 1824 issues of the *Register* a vast amount of factual material about the candidates, descriptions of the politically motivated actions of Congress, resolutions passed by state legislatures and by meetings of citizens, editorial opinions from newspapers on every side of the controversy, results of straw votes and unofficial polls taken in city and hamlet, addresses of various organizations urging the voters to support this or that candidate, and reports on the activities and the

[40] *Register*, XXXVI, 198, May 23, 1829.
[41] *Register*, XXI, 338, January 26, 1822.
[42] *Register*, XXII, 402, August 24, 1822.

health of the contending candidates, showing how little the coverage of a national election in this country has changed in the past century.

Niles' personal preferences in the campaign did not color the editorial stand taken by the *Register*. As early as November 9, 1822, he predicted that the election would be decided in the House, an eventuality which he felt was "truly alarming." Commenting on the number of candidates in Monroe's cabinet, he wrote on August 2, 1823: ". . . If *I* were president, I would hold very few 'cabinet councils,' if things were conditioned as they are now. Admit that the secretaries of state, of the treasury and war, are the most honorable men living, still it is *human nature* that the person shall take a most favorable view of that which will promote his own purposes."

He announced on September 6, 1823, that as editor he would "not abuse, or especially support any one," adding that he would vote as he pleased and let others do the same. The report that Jackson would be elected to the Senate by the Tennessee legislature received his editorial approval because Adams, Calhoun, Clay, and Crawford were in Washington, and the General, by such a move, would be on equal footing with his opponents.[43] Brief expressions of editorial opinion may be found frequently, but the *Register* maintained a hands-off attitude regarding the candidates, except insofar as its campaign against the caucus was directed against Crawford's chances. On March 6, 1824, Niles wrote: ". . . I have not any person or personal objects in view. . . . the election of more than one of the candidates would not grieve me. . . . This paper never has been the partizan of any *man*, nor can it become so." On the eve of the election he defended the absence of an editorial endorsement or support for one of the candidates, urged the readers to study their public acts, and reiterated that the *Register* had never been given up to "personal electioneering." [44]

Declining to make a last-minute prediction as to the outcome of the election, the *Register* through November and December printed the returns as they filtered in from the various states where different methods of electing electors were used. From

43 *Register*, XXV, 97, October 18, 1823; 114, October 25, 1823.
44 *Register*, XXVII, 100, October 16, 1824.

the start it was fairly evident that the *Register*'s prediction of a House election would be borne out, but it was not until December that the identity of the third man to go before that body was disclosed. The first number of the new year carried the final results.[45]

Of the three candidates from whom the members of the House, voting by states, were to choose the executive, the *Register* had given by far the most news space to Andrew Jackson —not as a candidate, but in reporting his military activities through the War of 1812, the recognition he received from the nation following the Battle of New Orleans, and his later activities in Florida. Brief items throughout 1815 described receptions and gifts to the Hero of New Orleans. In 1818 the *Register* stoutly defended the General in the controversy that raged around the invasion of West Florida and the executions of Alexander Arbuthnot and Captain Robert Cherry Ambrister. Niles in March and April, 1819, practically turned the periodical over to the charges and countercharges made in reports and correspondence. He left no doubt of his stand when he wrote: "The fact is—that ninety nine hundredths of the people believe that General Jackson acted on every occasion for the good of his country, and success universally crowned his efforts. He has suffered more hardships and encountered higher responsibilities, than any man living in the United States, to serve us—and has his rewards in the sanction of his government and the approbation of the people." [46]

Jackson's appointment some two years later as governor of Florida won the *Register*'s approval. His clash with the Spanish military authorities occupied a great deal of space in the closing months of 1821, with the *Register* upholding Jackson's conduct.[47]

The notices about John Quincy Adams in the *Register* were of a less sensational nature. His name, however, had appeared in the columns regularly from the time he helped negotiate the Treaty of Ghent. Niles praised his handling of the office of

[45] *Register*, XXVII, 273, January 1, 1825.

[46] *Register*, XVI, 45, March 13, 1819.

[47] *Register*, XX, 36, March 17, 1821; 98, April 14, 1821; see nearly every issue of Volumes XX and XXI.

secretary of state frequently, especially in connection with the correspondence with Spain over the Floridas.[48] The famous Fourth of July speech delivered by the secretary in Washington in 1821 was printed in full and its "warmth of feeling" lauded.[49] Adams' career had been less spectacular than that of his opponent, but it had been fully and appreciatively recorded in the *Register*. William H. Crawford, whom Niles personally opposed, was mentioned much less frequently in the periodical, although his activities as a senator and as secretary of the treasury were given a normal amount of space. On December 22, 1821, the *Register,* commenting on the treasury report, expressed the belief that Crawford was not particularly well fitted for his post. In 1824 the *Register* attempted to arrive at an approximation of truth concerning the conflicting reports on the state of Crawford's health.[50]

As the time approached when the House would ballot on the presidency, Niles made several trips to Washington and sent back articles to the *Register*. In the middle of January he wrote that the result was as much in doubt as it had been six months earlier. He expressed pleasure at the good feelings among the supporters of the contending candidates. This was a fortnight before the storm broke. Four days before the House election the *Register* printed the letter making the "corrupt-bargain" charge from the *Columbian Observer* of January 28, Clay's card from the *National Intelligencer* of January 31, calling the writer of the letter "a base and infamous calumniator, a dastard and a liar," and the card of George Kremer, Pennsylvania Congressman, printed February 3. In the same issue Clay's appeal to the House to investigate the truth of the charges appeared.[51] The first number after the election carried the result, some eight pages of debate on the Clay investigation motion, and an edi-

[48] *Register,* XV, 364–65, January 9, 1819; XVII, 281, December 25, 1819; XXI, 365, February 2, 1822.

[49] The speech was printed in *Register,* XX, 326–32, July 21, 1821; comment on it was carried in the preceding issue, XX, 305, July 14, 1821; for a careful interpretation of the address as an example of Adams' nationalistic feeling and its reception in the United States and abroad, see Edward Howland Tatum, Jr., *The United States and Europe 1815–1823: A Study in the Background of the Monroe Doctrine* (Berkeley, 1936), 241–50.

[50] *Register,* XXVI, 240, June 12, 1824; XXVII, 53, September 25, 1824.

[51] *Register,* XXVII, 305, January 15, 1825; 353, 366–67, February 5, 1825.

torial article descriptive of the scene in the House of Representatives during the balloting. Niles had been present in the gallery. His hope for harmony, expressed in the editorial, was soon to be blasted. He wrote: "It has always been understood, and I believe correctly, that Messrs. Adams and Jackson have entertained the highest personal respect and esteem for one another; and I think it probable that three-fourths of those who desire the election of either, would have taken the other, as a second choice. . . . Under such a state of feeling, let us hope that harmony may be preserved in the nation, and that the late great parties will go hand in hand to promote the public good." [52]

The columns of the *Register* through March, April, and May of 1825 were filled with charges and statements concerning Clay's part in the election of John Quincy Adams. Niles expressed regret at the necessity of giving so much space to the "unpleasant affair," but called attention to the uniform practice of the work which was that "in all matters of controversy, *both sides* shall be treated impartially, whatever our own opinion of the case may be." There followed correspondence of Jackson, letters and addresses of George Kremer, statements of congressmen on the dispute, statements and correspondence of Clay, and letters and newspaper statements of Clay's friends and supporters. Both sides were given an opportunity to state their cases fully.

Niles was still friendly toward Jackson and in the April 2, 1825, number described at length a conversation he had held with the General the morning of the House election. Saying that in previous conversations the question of the presidency had not come up, but that Jackson brought it up at this time, he told of the expression by the General of his gratification at the support of the public and his belief that the citizens would be satisfied with the result of the impending House election, which "he seemed to think it most probable . . . would devolve on Mr. Adams." The editor went on to describe Jackson's

[52] *Register*, XXVII, 372-79, 382-83, 384, February 12, 1825; for a description of Adams' meeting with Jackson the evening following the election see Adams, *Memoirs*, VI, 502; Marquis James, *Andrew Jackson Portrait of a President* (Indianapolis, c1937), 129; John Spencer Bassett, *The Life of Andrew Jackson* (new ed.; New York, 1925), 365-66; other references by Adams to Jackson may be found in *Memoirs*, IV, 247, 248; VI, 274, 332.

observation that many representatives were unpleasantly situ-
ated in that they were compelled to act against Adams or himself. The warrior added that "it was a matter of small moment
to the people who was their president, provided he administered
the government rightfully."

Niles refused to believe that either Jackson or Adams "could
have descended to any act of meanness, or dirty intrigue, to
have obtained that most honorable station." The editorial went
on to say that Jackson's conduct following the election had been
marked by a "magnanimity as distinguished as the moderation
of his successful competitor has been remarkable." Pleading that
the "calling of *hard names* be stopped," he besought the public
to cease wantonly depreciating the character of such men as
Adams, Jackson, Clay, Crawford, and Calhoun.

But the calling of hard names had scarcely begun. There was
no break in the campaign of Jackson for the presidency and his
every move, directed by William B. Lewis, was made with a
view toward the election of 1828. The reader of the *Register*
from 1825 to 1828 found plenty of factual and documentary
material about the approaching election, and the unusual
amount of interest in the campaign caused Niles to set up a
department under the head "Elections and Electioneering" in
which he succeeded very well in his attempt to present an impartial picture of the campaign.[53]

Eighteen months before the election the editor, having re-
luctantly decided that the contest was going to be a heated and
violent one, questioned in an editorial in the March 19, 1827,
issue the necessity of heaping such abuse upon the candidates
and announced the *Register*'s policy. The paper would not enter the political arena and would pay no attention to party
moves. Measures would be supported. As a matter of record,
therefore, none of the scurrility which marked the campaign is
to be found in the *Register*. To read the stories as to Jackson's
marital status, one must go to the Cincinnati *Gazette*, edited by
Charles Hammond, who collected the material, or to the few

[53] *Register*, XXXI, 66–67, September 30, 1826; 82–85, October 7, 1826; 178, November 18, 1826; 193–94, November 25, 1826; 258–59, December 23, 1826; XXXII,
102–103, April 7, 1827; 114–17, April 14, 1827; 197–99, May 19, 1827; 356, July 28,
1827; XXXIII, 129, October 27, 1827; 195–96, November 24, 1827; 212–13, December 1, 1827, are typical examples of articles carried almost every week.

other newspapers that reprinted his charges.[54] Not a hint of
the nature of the stories retailed about the two candidates was
printed by Niles. Near the close of the contest, he wrote that
the struggle had been "severe and ruthless" with "a more
general grossness of assault upon distinguished individuals than
we ever before witnessed." He regretted the lengths to which
both sides had gone.[55]

In the meantime, practically every number of the *Register*
carried reports of speeches and the usual campaign activities
from all sections of the country. By early 1828 the trend toward
Jackson was unmistakable in returns from choice of electors.
The election returns printed in October and November from
the first left no doubt as to the result.[56]

An editorial, reviewing the past and venturing some observations upon the future, so well summarized the political situation in 1828 that it is quoted here at length:

THE ELECTION—The most anxious and ardent, as well as the most
rude and ruthless political contest that ever took place in the United
States, is now decided in the election of a large majority of electors
pledged to the support of gen. ANDREW JACKSON, for the presidency
—the most honorable office in the gift of any people on earth. This
struggle, which really commenced before the present administration
was formed, has been carried on, in attack or defence, with unprecedented zeal and acrimony—too often disgraceful to the freedom of
opinion and of the press, remorseless of public reputation and private
honor, and disregardful even of the sacred obligations belonging to
personal communication and individual confidence. If the hun-
dredth part of what has been said against distinguished men, hith-
erto the pride and ornament of our country, might be accepted as
plain unvarnished truth, they should rather be committed to our
penitentiaries for life, than be held up as examples before the people.
Certainly we are the friends of free discussion; but have always deplored that licentiousness which degrades the character of our nation,

[54] Francis Phelps Weisenburger, "A Life of Charles Hammond," *Ohio State
Archaeological and Historical Society Quarterly* (Columbus, 1887—), XLIII, No. 4
(October, 1934), 383–85. Other references to scurrilous stories about Jackson's
marriage may be found in James, *op. cit.*, 153–58; Bassett, *Life of Jackson*, 394.
[55] *Register*, XXXV, 33, September 13, 1828.
[56] *Register*, XXXIII, 332–34, January 19, 1828; 356–57, January 26, 1828; XXXV,
98–99, October 11, 1828; 129–30, 147–48, October 25, 1828; 161, 166–67, November
8, 1828; 177–78, November 15, 1828.

and would reduce to its own level the most worthy and best of our citizens, and render them fit associates only for the meanest and basest of the human race. . . .

The friends of gen. JACKSON have calculated much on the reformations that he will bring about; those of Mr. ADAMS have believed that our affairs were administered in the most able and best manner practicable, and with an intense and enlightened view to promote the public good.—Results will prove which of the parties have been mistaken. And, however sincere may have been the approbation of any of the measures of the present administration—it is obligatory on them to judge that which is about to commence by its fruits, and not themselves fall into that error which they rightfully condemned in their opponents. . . .

. . . And, while we believe that gen. Jackson, as president of the United States, cannot accomplish the wishes of his too sanguine friends, we are entirely willing to hope that he will also dispel the fears of his most decided opponents. We dare not yield to an opinion, that the duration of this republic depends upon the election of its chief magistrate, however interesting such election may be. Mr. Adams will retire from office with unsullied hands, with a private character that has resisted any hostile test, and a public reputation increased by every assault made upon it—and we anxiously desire that gen. Jackson, having served the period for which he shall be elected, may return again to private life with the same degree of approbation that led to his present exalted standing in the republic.[57]

The *Register* judged the first administration of President Jackson as it had asked the opposition to do, that is, by its fruits. That most of the fruit was bitter to Niles goes without saying, but the editorial opposition which developed, as the administration's policies were formulated, in no way interfered with accurate and impartial reporting of national affairs. The President-elect's arrival in Washington and his failure to call

[57] *Register*, XXXV, 193–94, November 22, 1828; among many accounts of this election the following are of interest: Edward Channing, *History of the United States* (New York, 1905–1925), V, 365–70; Dixon Ryan Fox, *Decline of Aristocracy in the Politics of New York* (New York, 1910), 348–50; William O. Lynch, *Fifty Years of Party Warfare (1789–1837)* (Indianapolis, 1931), 349–62; William McDonald, *Jacksonian Democracy 1829–1837* (Volume XV of *The American Nation*) (New York, 1906), 28–42; William E. Smith, *The Francis Preston Blair Family in Politics* (New York, 1933), I, 30, 37–47; Edward Stanwood, *A History of the Presidency from 1788 to 1897*, 2 vols. (rev. ed.; Boston, 1928), I, 142–149.

upon President Adams were noted.[58] The *Register* did not criticize the make-up of the new cabinet although it feared that the
members would not encourage domestic industry and internal
improvements. Jackson's first message to Congress which had
received praise "so high as to defeat its purpose," and had been
condemned "in a manner not less repulsive," was impartially
discussed.[59]

Jackson's use of the veto brought many verbal attacks from
Niles who felt strongly that the President abused the power.
Eleven months after the Maysville Road Bill had been rejected
by Jackson, Niles unlimbered his pen and dashed off a two and
one-half page editorial on the presidential veto. The Executive
had bowed to "sheer expediency" in setting aside the matured
opinions of 173 members of the Senate and the House, Niles
charged. He closed with the observation that he meant no dis-
respect to the President—and could not "do otherwise than believe that he yielded up his own judgment to the wishes of those
round about him," [60] a remark not so far from the truth if Martin Van Buren is to be believed.[61] Attacks on the exercise of the
veto power continued. Niles argued that for one man to have
so much power as up to two thirds of the legislative body was
incompatible with representative government.[62] When Jackson
vetoed the bill rechartering the Bank of the United States, Niles
wrote a one and one-half column satirical editorial, the content

[58] *Register*, XXXV, 401, February 14, 1829; XXXVI, 49, March 21, 1829; cf.
Adams, *Memoirs*, VIII, 99–102; Adams denied in his diary that he approved the
newspaper attacks on Mrs. Jackson, given by the *United States Telegraph* as the
cause of Jackson's decision not to call on Adams; in this connection it is interesting to note that Jackson had rebuked Duff Green, editor of the *Telegraph*, for
attacking "female charecter" [sic] when Green had printed stories about Mrs.
Adams; see Bassett, *Correspondence*, III, 377; an absorbing account of Jackson's
two presidential terms is Claude G. Bowers, *The Party Battles of the Jackson
Period* (Boston, 1922).

[59] *Register*, XXXVI, 17, March 7, 1829; 34, March 14, 1829; XXXVII, 257–58,
December 19, 1829.

[60] *Register*, XL, 146–49, April 30, 1831.

[61] See John C. Fitzpatrick (ed.), *The Autobiography of Martin Van Buren*,
American Historical Association *Annual Report*, 1918, II (Washington, 1920);
321–22; Bassett, *Life of Jackson*, 486; Smith, *The Francis Preston Blair Family in
Politics*, I, 57.

[62] *Register*, XLII, 22, March 10, 1832.

of which was based on the criticism of the veto rather than on the issue involved. The editor asserted that neither the King of England nor the French monarch would dare to exercise so much power. He jibed at the American public for avoiding the use of the "plain old honest English words *forbid* and *forbids."* He argued that only unconstitutionality of a bill should justify its rejection by the Executive, and charged that a veto based on expediency was "a plain and palpable act of DESPOTISM." [63]

The interminable debates and correspondence on the rejection by the Senate of Van Buren's appointment as minister to Great Britain were printed as a matter of record without comment.[64] Thus one may say that his attitude toward the administration was critical but fair.

The imbroglio which resulted in the turnover of the cabinet was reported *in extenso* in the *Register.* The voluminous correspondence of Vice President Calhoun and the President, and of virtually every member of the cabinet, plus columns of editorial opinions on the dispute, occupied space in nearly every number of the *Register* published from February 12 through December 3, 1831. Calhoun's address to the public, giving his reasons for making public correspondence with President Jackson, was printed early. An editorial reported that the Washington *Globe* was on the side of the President and Van Buren, with the *United States Telegraph* presenting the case of Vice President Calhoun and his friends in the cabinet. First rumors of the cabinet breakup were printed in the April 9 number of the *Register* when brief excerpts from the *Pennsylvania Inquirer* and Norfolk *Herald* reported the resignation or removal of Samuel D. Ingham as secretary of the treasury. Niles also commented on the rumor that John Branch, secretary of the navy, would be asked to resign. Two weeks later the wholesale dissolution of the advisory body was likened to "a clap of thunder in a cloudless sky," in spite of previous rumors. In this number the letters of John H. Eaton and Martin Van Buren, resigning their posts as secretaries of war and state, together

[63] *Register,* XLII, 401–402, August 4, 1832; later condemnation of the veto power may be found in *Register,* XLIII, 403, February 16, 1833.

[64] *Register,* XLI, 416–34, February 4 and February 11, 1832; 453–66, February 18 and February 25, 1832; XLII, 19, March 10, 1832; 37–40, March 17, 1832; 67–68, March 24, 1832.

with the President's replies, were printed.[65] There followed a
five months' parade of letters of resignation, notes of acceptance,
charges by Ingham of threatened attacks by friends of the President and their denials, and the mass of correspondence which
made public all of the serio-comic aspects of the Calhoun-Jackson
break and the Peggy Eaton angle. In no other place has so much
contemporary material on this much-discussed party rift been
deposited as in the closely packed columns of the *Register.*

In addition to the documentary material, the editorial controversies which raged, especially in the *Globe* and the *Telegraph,* were reported in sufficient detail to give the reader a
complete picture of press opinion of the day. Editorials in the
Register itself were largely limited to nonpartisan comment
on the various involved charges made by participants against
each other and to regret that the editor's duty as a "faithful
chronicler" compelled him to print so many "highly-spiced political articles."

By November, Niles was headlining the seemingly never-
ending stream of correspondence "THE SICKENING SUBJECT," and
writing that he felt bound to pursue the matter in order to
compile a full record, but "earnestly wishing to conclude the
whole branch of this wretched concern now, and forever." [66]

The campaign of 1832 marked the start of a new era in the
history of American politics. National conventions of political
parties to choose candidates and to draw up platforms were first
used.[67] The Antimasonic party made its unsuccessful appearance as a party with a national ticket.[68] The Working Men's
party was making its influence felt on the political scene, al-

[65] *Register*, XL, 129, 143–44, April 23, 1831.

[66] *Register*, XLI, 230–31, November 19, 1831.

[67] The 1832 campaign has been reported on in detail in S. R. Gammon, *Presidential Campaign of 1832* (The Johns Hopkins University *Studies in Historical
and Political Science*, XL, No. 1, Baltimore, 1922). It is examined in Kent, *op. cit.*,
87–90; Stuart Lewis, *Party Principles and Practical Politics* (New York, 1928),
62–66; Lynch, *op. cit.*, 390–423; Stanwood, *History of the Presidency*, I, 161–77;
James Albert Woodburn, *American Politics: . . .* (New York, 1924), 43, 291–92.

[68] Charles McCarthy, *The Antimasonic Party: A Study of Political Antimasonry
in the United States, 1827–1840*, American Historical Association *Annual Report*,
1902, I (Washington, 1903), which used contemporary newspapers extensively, is
an excellent monograph. Chap. XXII, 531–36, describes the excursion of the party
into national politics.

though it had no party ticket.[69] Internal improvements, the removal of the Indian tribes from Georgia and Alabama, the public land question, and the question of the Bank of the United States were issues.

The *Register* covered all angles of this bitterly fought campaign. And despite the editor's close friendship for and personal activities in behalf of Henry Clay, the periodical reported the events leading up to the election fairly and remained true to its motto of measures not men. Before the breakup of the cabinet, Niles wrote that there were four parties, or factions, in Congress. He listed them as the original friends of President Jackson; the anti-Jackson party; the old "Crawford" party, chiefly friends of Van Buren; and the friends of Vice President Calhoun.[70] On March 5, 1831, he commented on the unprecedented political excitement in the nation's capital. Two months later in a signed statement he denied that he and others friendly to the American System had met representatives of the Antimasonic party in New York in an attempt to decide upon a candidate satisfactory to both groups.[71]

The activities of Clay, long active in American politics, had been the subject of many a story in the *Register* almost from its inception.[72] In the 1824 presidential campaign, Niles had printed an editorial lauding the "manly frankness" of Clay and quoting his friends as believing that he would be the successor to President Monroe.[73] Clay's appearance as the logical candidate of the anti-Jacksonians in the 1832 campaign naturally kept him in the public eye from the start of Jackson's first term. His speeches were reported and his trips described, but in no more detail than those of Jackson, Calhoun, and other political leaders. In March, 1830, Niles expressed regret that the New York *Evening Post* should have charged that Clay's arguments for

[69] John R. Commons (ed.), *History of Labour in the United States* (New York, 1921), I, 185–326.

[70] *Register,* XXXVIII, 202–203, May 8, 1830.

[71] *Register,* XL, 217–18, May 28, 1831; the charge had been printed in the *Morning Courier and New York Enquirer.*

[72] For a few typical examples of the many to be found in the columns from 1812 to 1828, see *Register,* I, 336, January 4, 1812; XII, 38–39, March 15, 1817; XX, 84, April 7, 1821; XXIII, 227, December 14, 1822; XXVIII, 296–97, July 9, 1825; XXXV, 43–45, September 13, 1828.

[73] *Register,* XXVI, 218–19, June 5, 1824.

the American System could all be traced to the "dull pages of Niles' Register, and the interminable essays of Mathew Carey." [74] Late that summer he printed Clay's speech delivered August 3 in Cincinnati, justifying the amount of space it filled by remarking that it really contained Clay's platform for the campaign.[75] His friendliness toward Clay, however, did not stop him from rebuking an editor who started a paper with the name, *The Henry Clay,* in Woodstock, Vermont, on the grounds that measures, not individuals, were to be supported or opposed.

Toward President Jackson as a candidate to succeed himself, the *Register* conducted itself on a high plane. Editorials were in opposition to his policies or his methods, not to him personally. In 1830, when New York newspapers were engaged in controversy with the *United States Telegraph* over the announcement by the *Morning Courier and New York Enquirer* that the President would run for a second term, Niles wrote that he understood that the President had "very properly, declined saying whether he will, or will not be, a candidate for reelection." [76] In January, 1831, he reprinted from the Washington *Globe,* the new official organ, that the President would "not decline the summons" to serve a second term.[77] The *Register* played no part in disseminating rumors about the President's health, merely remarking on the conflicting accounts and giving a factual statement as to the Chief Executive's age.[78]

The organization of the Working Men's party in New York, damned in the press generally, received Niles' blessing: "The 'working people' have always constituted the body of the solid, true and faithful democratic party—and, though we like not divisions of the citizens into particular sects, . . . we are not sorry that the free laboring classes are rallying themselves, to resist oppression. The power is in them—and they have only to use it, in self-defence." [79]

He foresaw the uncertainty which followed the introduction of third-party candidates into election contests, but did not con-

[74] *Register*, XXXVIII, 82, March 27, 1830.
[75] *Register*, XXXIX, 17, 25–32, September 4, 1830.
[76] *Register*, XXXVIII, 108–109, April 3, 1830.
[77] *Register*, XXXIX, 385, January 29, 1831.
[78] *Register*, XLI, 443, February 18, 1832; XLIII, 19, September 8, 1832.
[79] *Register*, XXXVIII, 231–32, May 22, 1830.

demn the party's backers on that ground.[80] Having given space
to the state Antimasonic conventions, especially in New York,
Niles reported on the national convention which met in Philadelphia on September 11, 1830, and issued a call for a national
nominating convention to be held in Baltimore on September
26, 1831.[81] This meeting, which convened in the district courtroom after having been refused the use of Independence Hall,
was the first national party convention held in the United
States.[82] Ninety-six delegates from New York, Massachusetts,
Connecticut, Vermont, Rhode Island, Pennsylvania, New Jersey, Delaware, Ohio, Maryland, and the Territory of Michigan
were present. In observing this newspaper account of the first
national party convention in the country, it is interesting to note
that so far as is known the first suggestion in a newspaper for
a national party nominating convention was printed in the
Register, in February, 1822. It was in the form of an anonymous
letter to H. Niles and preceded by some six months a similar
suggestion made by Thomas Ritchie in the Richmond *Enquirer.*[83] Because of lack of space Niles refused to print all the
charges and countercharges made concerning the organization
of the Antimasonic party. The nominations of William Wirt
for President and Amos Ellmaker for Vice President by the
Antimasonic party were duly recorded on October 1, "mechanical necessity" prohibiting Niles from printing details of
the convention. Succeeding issues carried the minutes of the
convention, its address to the people of the nation, and a list of
delegates. Niles expressed surprise at Wirt's nomination, his acceptance, and "more especially at its *ratification* by the convention." He told of his high respect for Wirt, but added that
he was quite certain that they disagreed on the American System.[84]

80 *Register,* XXXIX, 19, September 4, 1830.

81 *Register,* XXXIX, 58, September 18, 1830; 91, October 2, 1830.

82 Gammon, *op. cit.,* 38. Lewis, *op. cit.,* 66, calls the Baltimore Antimasonic
convention the first, apparently overlooking the one in Philadelphia, which chose
no candidates; Stanwood, *History of the Presidency,* I, 154, mentions the Philadelphia convention, as does McCarthy, *op. cit.,* briefly on p. 536.

83 Gammon, *op. cit.,* 16; *Register,* XXI, 403–404, February 23, 1822.

84 *Register,* XLI, 74, 83–87, October 1, 1831; 107–10, October 8, 1831; 131, October 15, 1831; 166–74, October 29, 1831.

The National Republican Convention, which met in Baltimore from December 12 to 16, 1831, was covered briefly in the
December 17 number of the *Register*. Two columns were devoted to the high spots of the five-day convention, at which Niles
was a delegate. The letters of acceptance from Clay and John
Sargeant, of Pennsylvania, the vice-presidential nominee, were
carried. Three fourths of the December 24 number was turned
over to a day-by-day chronological account of the convention, a
list of delegates, and the inevitable address to the people of the
United States. The National Republican Convention of Young
Men, which met in Washington, D. C., May 7 to 12, 1832, to
ratify the nominations of the December convention and undoubtedly to arouse enthusiasm among the younger voters,
received space.[85] The result of the Jackson convention to nom-
inate a candidate for the vice-presidency, which met in Baltimore from May 21 to May 23, 1832, was recorded in the May
26 number, with an account from the "official" publication, the
Baltimore *Republican*, supplying details. Throughout the periods preceding and following the conventions, the *Register* had
carried many articles on nominations made by various state conventions, state elections and their results as an indication of the
attitude toward the national situation, as well as editorial comments and reports of meetings.

Niles closed the coverage of the campaign by printing a
roundup of predictions and claims made by the rival parties in
eighteen of the states, in most of which there were three tickets.[86]
After the electors had been chosen in most states but before the
results were known to him, Niles wrote:

In this ardent controversy, which has cast out, we think, a larger
amount of gross and rude, and strange and curious matter than any
previous one, we have endeavored to render justice to men and their
motives, generally—and, while standing free from assaults upon individuals, have seldom used "hard words," even when, without any just
reason, assailed. We have not entered into personal electioneering,
though supporting, (and in strict conformity with the original prospectus of this work), certain *measures* of lofty interest, or regarded
essential to the welfare of the people of the United States—such as a

[85] *Register*, XLII, 206, May 12, 1832; 218–19, May 19, 1832; 236–38, May 26, 1832.
[86] *Register*, XLIII, 133–40, October 27, 1832.

protecting tariff, internal improvements, and a sound national currency, under the *restricted* new charter proposed for the bank of the United States. . . .

But, as before observed, the ballot boxes may have decided every question of this sort, and it will become all parties to reconcile themselves to results—as well as they can and this maxim recommended to others, we shall strive to practice ourselves, in all moderation, and with a decent respect for the opinions of others, while maintaining our own.[87]

This last paragraph indicated that Niles anticipated the outcome. Each number of the *Register* in November, 1832, carried reports from states, but after Pennsylvania's heavy majority for Jackson was reported on November 10, there was little, if any, doubt as to the result. The editor of the *Register,* true to his editorial ethics rather than to his political preferences, sat down and penned a page editorial in which he coolly and sanely analyzed the campaign issues and withdrew himself and the *Register* from further opposition to the will of the majority of the voters. There was no bitterness, in spite of his disappointment at the decision, as the following excerpts show:

The presidential election has so far proceeded as to render the result certain, that "ANDREW JACKSON, of Tennessee," will be reelected president and "MARTIN VAN BUREN, of New York," be elected vice president of the United States, if they shall live until the meeting of the electoral colleges in December next. And the majority for both will be large and decided, and must be respected as "the will of the people."

Two great questions would seem to be settled by this election: the right of congress to appropriate money for *internal improvements* is generally denied—and the unconstitutionality and inexpediency of *a bank of the United States* . . . affirmed. On these points president JACKSON freely exercised the objectionable and repulsive power of the veto, and cast himself upon the support of the people against the acts of both houses of congress. . . .

With respect to these leading measures of policy, we intend to "practice on the maxims which we have recommended to others," under like circumstances,—and submit to the public will, as expressed by the voice of the majority, constitutionally proclaimed—

[87] *Register,* XLIII, 145, November 3, 1832.

and while maintaining our private opinions concerning them, we shall yield to a strict obedience to the *legal* decisions which have been thus made, and retire from the part which we have taken in the discussion of these subjects—until the effects of such decisions shall become manifest, and EXPERIENCE lead us all into a better understanding of the necessity and propriety of either, or both.[88]

The writing of this editorial signified the beginning of the end of a distinct period in the history of the *Register*. Defeated by the will of the majority on the bank issue and on internal improvements, the *Register* suffered another serious reverse within four months when the Compromise Tariff of 1833 was adopted. Niles, at this third major setback, withdrew from editorial discussion of his pet scheme, a tariff to protect American industry. For more than twenty years the periodical had battled editorially for its economic measures, which were inevitably a part of the political scene. For the next sixteen years its columns served chiefly to record political events and to mirror the opinions of the contending parties as expressed in their personal party organs. The events of the months from President Jackson's second election to the approval of the compromise tariff measure fathered by Henry Clay, former champion of the American System, thus marked the ending of one era and the opening of another in the *Register's* policy of handling political and economic questions.

The *Register* continued to criticize the use of the veto by Jackson, disagreed with him over his handling of the French spoliation claims,[89] reported and condemned two attacks made upon the President's life,[90] covered in detail his eastern trip of 1833, and printed factual articles on the number of changes in the cabinet.[91] When Harvard awarded an honorary LL.D. to the President, Niles reported and defended the conferring of

[88] *Register*, XLIII, 177, November 17, 1832.

[89] *Register*, XLIV, 17–18, March 9, 1833; 51, March 23, 1833; on the claims Niles felt that the issue was money, not national honor; see *Register*, XLVI, 201, May 24, 1834; XLVII, 82, October 11, 1834; 258, December 20, 1834; 314–15, January 10, 1835; 441–42, February 28, 1835; XLVIII, 1, March 7, 1835; 217, May 30, 1835; XLIX, 361, January 30, 1836; 425, February 20, 1836.

[90] *Register*, XLIV, 161, May 11, 1833; XLVII, 385–86, 390–92, February 7, 1835.

[91] *Register*, XLIV, 233, June 8, 1833; 256, June 15, 1833; 265, June 22, 1833; 281, June 29, 1833; 321–23, July 13, 1833; 360–61, July 27, 1833; XLV, 172–73, November 9, 1833; XLVI, 313, July 5, 1834; 347, July 19, 1834.

the honor. He jeered at Jackson's friends who felt it was "treason" to call the President "Dr. Jackson" and said that if the use of the title was disrespectful he should not have accepted the degree.[92] As the Old Hero's second term drew to a close, the Senate debates on the resolution introduced by Thomas Hart Benton on March 16, 1836, to expunge the resolution of December 26, 1833, censuring the President, occupied many columns. Saying that it would be charged with personal bias because of the political nature of the question, the *Register* declared that it could not "refrain from saying, that this act of the senate is a palpable violation of the constitution, and has established a precedent of a most fatal tendency." [93] Jackson's farewell message, his departure from Washington, and his reception at the Hermitage terminated the reporting of his presidential activities, although he was to appear often thereafter in the role of an unofficial adviser, especially on the matter of the annexation of Texas.[94]

The *Register* reported the progress of the campaigns of General William Henry Harrison,[95] Daniel Webster,[96] Hugh L. White, of Tennessee, and, of course, that of the administration's favorite, Vice President Van Buren.[97] The convention which nominated Van Buren for President, and Richard M. Johnson, of Kentucky, for Vice President, was accorded an unusual amount of space, including editorials from other newspapers.[98]

[92] *Register*, XLIV, 305, July 6, 1833; 323, July 13, 1833; Niles' attitude was in marked contrast to that of John Quincy Adams who refused to be present to witness his alma mater's "disgrace in conferring her highest literary honors upon a barbarian who could not write a sentence of grammar and hardly could spell his own name." (Adams, *Memoirs*, VIII, 546.)

[93] *Register*, LI, 321, January 21, 1837; speeches and Jackson's messages on the resolution may be found in *Register*, XLVI, 138–44, April 26, 1834; L, 60–61, March 26, 1836; 168–84, May 7, 1836; LI, 406–409, February 25, 1837; LII, 57–60, March 25, 1837; 120, April 22, 1837.

[94] *Register*, LII, 17, 20–24, March 11, 1837; 104, April 15, 1837; 193, May 27, 1837.

[95] *Register*, XLIX, 97, October 17, 1835; 169–70, November 14, 1835; L, 1, March 5, 1836; 33, March 19, 1836; 125–28, April 16, 1836; LI, 23–25, September 10, 1836.

[96] *Register*, XLVIII, 243–44, June 6, 1835; XLIX, 19, September 12, 1835.

[97] *Register*, XLVII, 313, January 10, 1835; XLIX, 52, September 26, 1835; 177–80, November 14, 1835.

[98] *Register*, XLVIII, 201, 206–207, May 23, 1835; 217, 226–29, May 30, 1835; 233, 244–48, June 6, 1835; 249, 257–58, June 13, 1835.

Election returns were carried in the November numbers, the presidential results on December 17, and a week later was printed the note that the vice-presidency would be determined in the Senate.[99]

The early impetus given the 1840 candidacy of William Henry Harrison as a result of his nomination by Ohio Whigs on July 4, 1837, was reprinted from the columns of the *Ohio State Journal*.[100] The *Register*, edited during this period by William Ogden Niles and later by Jeremiah Hughes, probably gave more space to the reporting of political activities than it had done under the editorship of its founder. However, impartiality was still the rule and it was adhered to rigidly.[101] The nomination by the Antimasonic National Convention, November 11 and 12, 1838, of Harrison for President and Daniel Webster for Vice President, was reprinted from *Poulson's American Daily Advertiser* of Philadelphia.[102] A year later the selection of James G. Birney as the Abolition choice for President, was recorded.[103] Shortly thereafter the selection by the Whigs of William Henry Harrison and John Tyler as party standard-bearers was described in detail.[104] The roundabout method of obtaining news at this time is well illustrated by the article on the National Democratic Convention, which met in Baltimore, where the *Register* was published, on May 5 and 6, 1840. The *Register's* account was taken from the columns of the Washington *Globe*, which had in turn reprinted it from the Baltimore *Republican*.[105] The *Register* expressed no opinion on the victory of the Hero of Tippecanoe, merely noting the great excitement

99 *Register*, LI, 241, December 17, 1836; 257, December 24, 1836.

100 *Register*, LII, 328-29, July 22, 1837.

101 Hughes wrote, "We have conscientiously endeavored to give an impartial view of the *doings* and *sayings* of each party, so far as our limits enabled us," in *Register*, LIX, 130, October 31, 1840; accounts of Whig meetings were balanced by those of the Democrats; see almost any number in 1840, especially through August, September, and October; typical are *Register*, LVIII, 4-10, March 7, 1840; 19-22, March 14, 1840; 281-83, July 4, 1840; 292-95, July 11, 1840; 407-11, August 29, 1840; LIX, 6-15, September 5, 1840; 91-95, October 10, 1840.

102 *Register*, LV, 177, November 17, 1838; 221, December 1, 1838.

103 *Register*, LVII, 240, December 7, 1839.

104 *Register*, LVII, 248-52, December 14, 1839; acceptances of the candidates were printed in LVII, 379, February 8, 1840.

105 *Register*, LVIII, 147-52, May 9, 1840; 182-87, May 23, 1840.

over the contest and reprinting the opposing editorial reactions
to the outcome from the *National Intelligencer* and the Washington *Globe*.[106] This policy of mirroring, rather than expressing, opinion was excellently exemplified in the November 28,
1840, number which carried election editorials from Bangor,
Providence, New York, Philadelphia, Baltimore, Washington,
Richmond, Savannah, and Boston newspapers.

The political confusion and the involved party politics arising from the accession of Tyler to the presidency were impersonally reported. The *Register* expressed disgust at the "idle
controversy" over what Tyler should be called, when he became
President, in which several daily newspapers participated, but
beyond that opinion, which had nothing to do with the man,
it remained silent.[107] The resignation of the entire cabinet, with
the exception of Daniel Webster, following close upon the President's veto of the fiscal corporation bill, was adequately covered,
chiefly by reprinting the correspondence in the case and the
address of the Whig senators and representatives to the people.[108] The reprinted editorial comment of some twelve representative Whig newspapers on the new cabinet served to give
the *Register*'s readers a sampling of party opinion on the political dispute.[109]

The presidential race which received by far the most space
of the ten reported in the *Register* was that of 1844. It is ques-
tionable if any campaign for the presidency has been so thor-
oughly and impartially covered in all angles by one publication
as the *Register* reported this one. From November 13, 1841,
when General Winfield Scott's naïve letter of October 25 giving
his views on national issues was printed without comment,
until November 9, 1844, when the returns indicated the almost
certain victory of James K. Polk, the student of American journalism and its relations to American politics may find in the
Register's columns samplings of editorial opinions on every side
of the election—an election which crowned with success the

[106] *Register*, LIX, 162–63, November 14, 1840; election returns were printed in
LIX, 177, November 21, 1840; 210, December 5, 1840; 273, January 2, 1841.
[107] *Register*, LX, 113, April 24, 1841.
[108] *Register*, LXI, 33–36, September 18, 1841; 53–54, September 25, 1841.
[109] *Register*, LXI, 98–100, October 16, 1841.

efforts in behalf of the first "dark horse" candidate in the history of politics in the United States.

That this complete coverage was the result of a well-planned editorial policy, which incidentally kept the *Register* itself entirely neutral throughout the entire campaign, is indicated in an editorial printed just after the 1842 Congressional elections, an excerpt from which follows: "As preliminary to the campaign we have kept up the record of partizan maneuvers in various directions, with a view to counteracting forces for the contest. We shall endeavor to give an impartial history of the coming contest—or rather to furnish authentic items under this head from which an impartial history may be written hereafter." [110]

The *Register* printed not only the 1841 letter of General Winfield Scott, but also a later one in which he said he was not a candidate but would run if nominated.[111] By midsummer, 1842, the candidates in the public eye were listed as John C. Calhoun, General Scott, James Buchanan, Martin Van Buren, Clay, and President Tyler. Late that fall nominations of Lewis Cass at Harrisburg and of Thomas Hart Benton in Missouri were noted, as were newspaper comments on coming conventions.[112]

The first half of 1843 saw almost weekly reports on political addresses and state conventions. By July the *Register* reported: "It is evident that the Whigs rely much upon having but one prominent candidate for the presidency,—Henry Clay, of Kentucky, whilst their opponents are divided between five prominent aspirants, Mr. Van Buren, Mr. Calhoun, Col. Richard M. Johnson, General Cass, and James Buchanan." [113]

In addition to the weekly coverage obtained by printing abstracts from representative newspapers and occasionally summarizing the reports, Hughes attempted a political summary about once a month in which he felt that he was giving his readers "a tolerably correct idea of how matters stand, so far at least

[110] *Register*, LXIII, 183, November 19, 1842.

[111] *Register*, LXI, 169–70, November 13, 1841; LXIII, 77, October 1, 1842.

[112] *Register*, LXII, 357, August 6, 1842; LXIII, 145, November 5, 1842; 201–203, November 26, 1842; 214, December 3, 1842.

[113] *Register*, LXIV, 314–17, July 15, 1843.

as they are represented by the leading journals engaged in the political controversy which is now going on and waxing warm." These political-roundup articles contained excerpts from newspapers of all shades of political opinion the country over, more than a score of newspapers being quoted in the August 19 number.[114]

James K. Polk's appearance in the campaign late in the year, when he was nominated for the vice-presidency by the Democratic state convention of Tennessee at Nashville on November 23, was reported.[115] Election year saw an increase in the space given over to politics. One month before the Democratic National Convention, Van Buren's nomination was as "confidently expected" as was that of Clay by the Whigs.[116] Two weeks later the picture was completely changed as the result of the Virginia elections in which the Van Buren faction lost. Thomas Ritchie's action in introducing resolutions at the Shockho Hill Democratic Association meeting in Richmond, asking the Democratic State Central Committee, of which he was chairman, to poll Virginia Democrats to discover their reaction to relieving the national-convention delegates from their instructions to vote for Van Buren, was rightly interpreted as a death blow to the former President's chances to obtain the nomination. Before the Democrats convened many of Van Buren's supporters had deserted him. Hughes commented on the gloomy aspect of Van Buren's chances, but felt that a last-minute attempt to change front or officers on the part of the Democrats would be "extremely hazardous." [117]

In the meantime, Clay's Raleigh letter of April 17 to the *National Intelligencer*, expressing practically the same sentiments as Van Buren had voiced in opposing the annexation of Texas, had been printed and commented upon. The Whig National Convention and the ratifying convention of the Young Whigs choosing and approving Clay and Theodore Frelinghuysen, of New Jersey, as candidates, were reported fully. Clay's decision, expressed in a letter of May 3 to the *Intelligencer*, to

114 *Register*, LXIV, 389–97, August 19, 1843; LXV, 19–27, September 9, 1843; 172–73, November 11, 1843.
115 *Register*, LXV, 231, December 9, 1843.
116 *Register*, LXVI, 130–32, April 27, 1844.
117 *Register*, LXVI, 161–63, May 11, 1844; 178–79, May 18, 1844.

refrain from making speeches and attending meetings during the campaign, which, unfortunately for him, did not include a ban of letter writing also, was printed.[118]

The Democratic National Convention held in the Egyptian Saloon of the Odd Fellows Hall was given seven and one-half pages in the June 1 number. Interesting angles of the story included the telegraph message from the Democratic Congressional members at the Capitol, received twenty minutes after Polk had been chosen on the ninth ballot, Silas Wright's reiterated refusal by telegraph of the nomination for the vice-presidency, and the decision to retain the two-thirds rule which spelled disaster to the hopes of Van Buren. The *Register's* editorial on the choice of the Democratic nominee, brief as it was, voiced such a sound judgment on political trends that it is reprinted here:

> What an eventful week amongst politicians? How many will wake up from its incidents, and look around with perfect wonderment at the revolution of affairs. *New men* and *new measures,* are suddenly presented. "Old things are done away, behold all things have become new." Van Buren, Calhoun, Cass, Buchanan, Stewart, and even Old Tecumseh, are to be forgotten, and all the political canvassing of the last three years as to their respective claims to the presidency, goes for nothing. What a fitful world is this of ours? *President-making,* in an elective republic, is always a matter of absorbing interest. Ours will become more and more so. Those who think they have witnessed such excitements as will hardly ever occur again, on such occasions, are vastly mistaken. Every new generation will give additional magnitude and rally more imposing incidents to the selection of a CHIEF for the nation.[119]

The scenes of utmost confusion which prevailed at the Tyler convention were reported in the same number. A week later the *Register* reprinted from the *National Intelligencer* of June 4 a comment on the fact that the only mention—or hint—of Polk's candidacy seen in the press prior to the convention was in the Nashville *Union* of May 23, which predicted that after two or three ballotings there would be "cordial, harmonious and strong union" upon the "claims of Mr. POLK and others,"

[118] *Register,* LXVI, 146–49, 152–53, 158–59, May 4, 1844; 161, May 11, 1844.
[119] *Register,* LXVI, 224, June 1, 1844.

to which the Whig organ added, "The inference is irresistible that the arrangement for withdrawing Mr. VAN BUREN, and *bringing forward* Mr. POLK, was made at Nashville, or in the neighborhood of that city."[120]

The Democratic resolutions urging "re-occupation of Oregon and the re-annexation of Texas at the earliest practicable period" were printed in the same issue as the battle lines for the campaign were drawn. The activities of the candidates and the "busy bustle of partizans" furnished such a mass of news and editorial matter that the *Register* was hard put to print even brief summaries. Tyler's withdrawal from the contest was hinted at in July, and on August 24 the rumors were confirmed, with the listing of Clay, Polk, and James G. Birney, the Abolition candidate, as the field from which the choice was to be made.

The unprecedented numbers attending the political rallies of both parties were mentioned in the summer by the editor, who took time and space to denounce the evils of gambling which he felt were encouraged by the newspapers which paraded the election wagers in their columns.[121] The result of the August elections in a number of states convinced this Whig editor of the nonpartisan *Register* that Polk and Dallas had reinvigorated the Democratic party whose tone had become "as confident as that of the Whig presses."[122]

Letters from Clay, Polk, and Andrew Jackson were printed in full. The Kentuckian's tariff stand was restated in his letter of June 29 to Fred J. Cope, in which he unequivocally came out in favor of protection and of the Tariff of 1842. But his attempt to please both sides in the Texas controversy served to cloud rather than clarify his early stand on annexation as expressed in his Raleigh letter. The *Register* printed his first Alabama letter, written July 1, in which he said he had no objection to the annexation if the Union were not seriously jeopardized, and his second Alabama letter, dated July 27, which declared he would be glad to see annexation "without dishonor—without war, and with the common consent of the

---

[120] *Register*, LXVI, 235, June 8, 1844.
[121] *Register*, LXVI, 314–15, July 13, 1844; 325, July 20, 1844.
[122] *Register*, LXVI, 437, August 31, 1844.

Union." [123] Clay's epistolary foundering grew more pitiable as
the campaign progressed and was climaxed in his letter of September 23, to Joseph Gales, Jr., and William W.

Seaton, of the
National Intelligencer, in which he vainly struggled to extricate
himself from the confusion caused by his three previous letters
on the Texas question. In this final pronouncement, which certainly served to antagonize any converts made by his Alabama
letters, he made a feeble attempt to return to the position of
his Raleigh letter, which had irked the annexationists. [124]

Polk fared better in the impression made by his letters. True,
he equivocated a bit on the tariff early in the campaign, but he
later pointed triumphantly to a letter of May 29, 1843, in which
he had expressed opposition to protection, and to his votes on
tariff measures as proof of his free-trade stand. [125] Polk was on
the popular side of the annexation question; there was no question as to where he and his party stood. He had the warm support of Andrew Jackson, vigorously expressed on a number of
occasions by the retired warrior from his retreat at the Hermitage. [126]

As the campaign grew hotter, the *Register* maintained its
impartiality, printing the stories and denials that Polk's ancestors were Tories during the Revolution, and relating how
the "Villainous Forgery" of the story of forty slaves with JKP
branded on their shoulders was started in the Ithaca *Journal,*
an Abolition paper. [127]

As the date for the decision approached, predictions of a
Democratic victory were reprinted from Democratic papers,
although the Richmond *Enquirer*'s estimate was offset by a
National Intelligencer article recalling that Ritchie in 1840
had predicted a victory for Van Buren. Hughes abstracted the
predictions of many newspapers, but he took occasion to call
attention to the extravagant claims of both parties and to
remark that "band-wagon philosophy" was good politics and that

[123] *Register,* LXVI, 325, July 20, 1844; 372, August 3, 1844; 439, August 31, 1844.
[124] *Register,* LXVII, 74, October 5, 1844.
[125] *Register,* LXVI, 234-35, June 8, 1844; 295, July 6, 1844; 343, July 27, 1844.
[126] *Register,* LXVI, 280, June 29, 1844; 372, August 3, 1844; LXVII, 75-77, October 5, 1844.
[127] *Register,* LXVI, 372-73, August 3, 1844; 418-19, August 24, 1844; LXVII, 73,
October 5, 1844.

no "general should ever allow his men to doubt of a victory." [128]

In marked contrast to earlier elections, the probable result of the 1844 contest was printed in the *Register,* published four days after most of the states voted. Without conceding the victory to Polk in so many words, Hughes pointed out that all the doubtful states but Delaware would have to go for Clay in order to elect him. The editor, writing about the unusual amount of space the campaign had filled during the past several months, said he had had a complaint from only one person. However, he doubted if so much room would again be appropriated to recording a party contest. He reiterated his honest attempt to be impartial and briefly outlined his procedure "to register faithfully the progress of the campaign." [129] The next number confirmed the early indications concerning the result. The same week Hughes wrote a strictly historical editorial on the progress and outcome of the campaign, analyzing the reasons for Clay's defeat. He showed that the votes polled by the Abolitionists in New York probably cost Clay that state's electoral vote, which would have reversed the result.[130] Coverage of the campaign was brought to a close by reprinting editorial extracts from American and English newspapers and by printing the popular vote with an analysis of Whig gains and losses.[131]

General Zachary Taylor had early won the admiration of the *Register*'s editor, who wrote on June 20, 1846, that his letters were "admirable specimens of composition." This praise of the writing ability of "Old Rough and Ready" was followed by an account of a meeting held on May 11, in Trenton, New Jersey, at which the General was nominated for the presidency. That fall a letter from General Taylor to a New Yorker expressing pleasure that a New York meeting had not nominated him was printed.[132] By the next spring a "very distinct movement" in favor of the General was noted by the *Register* which reported that many Whig journals had placed his name at the

---

128 *Register,* LXVII, 103–105, October 19, 1844; 117–19, 120–27, October 26, 1844.

129 *Register,* LXVII, 145, 149, 160, November 9, 1844.

130 *Register,* LXVII, 161, 165–67, November 16, 1844; 177, November 23, 1844.

131 *Register,* LXVII, 167–70, November 16, 1844; 185, November 23, 1844; 242–44, December 21, 1844; 280–81, January 4, 1845; 297, January 11, 1845.

132 *Register,* LXXI, 20–21, September 12, 1846.

head of their columns as their favorite candidate, while some administration papers were claiming him as a Democrat. In the same article the Baltimore *Sun,* an administration paper, was quoted as praising Taylor's "true political independence." Whigs in Philadelphia had nominated him for the presidency, and the New York *Journal of Commerce* predicted that both Whigs and Democrats were likely to take up the General.[133]

By this time the newspapers of the country were "teeming" with Taylor meetings, the *Register* reported in an election article which also mentioned Benton and Polk as candidates. The *Register* also teemed with Taylor letters. During the summer and fall of 1847 at least a dozen letters were written by the General from Mexico and upon his return to the United States were given space. His confidential letter of March 4, written from Agua Nueva to General E. G. W. Butler, of Iberville, Louisiana, was reprinted in full from the New Orleans *Picayune* of April 14, after having been quoted in part.[134] In this letter the General wrote that he had been nominated by "a few newspaper editors and others . . . without my knowledge, wishes or consent."

In the next letter carried by the *Register,* reprinted from the New Orleans *Bulletin* of May 20, the General wrote to "a distinguished citizen" of Louisiana:

In regard to the presidency, I will not say that I will not serve, if the good people of the country were to require me to do so, however much it is opposed to my wishes, for I am free to say, that I have no aspirations for the situation. . . .

It has ever been, and still is, my anxious wish that some one of the most experienced, talented, and virtuous statesmen of the country, should be chosen to that high place at the next election. . . .

I must, however, be allowed to say, that I have not the vanity to consider myself qualified for so high and responsible a station. . . .[135]

In July the *Register* printed two more letters from the General, the first from the Cincinnati *Signal,* whose editor, James W. Taylor, had forwarded an Ohio nomination to him and had received a reply dated May 18, from near Monterey. The Gen-

133 *Register,* LXXII, 112, April 17, 1847.
134 *Register,* LXXII, 128, April 24, 1847; 135–36, May 1, 1847.
135 *Register,* LXXII, 193, May 29, 1847.

eral wrote that his own personal views were better withheld until the end of the war, but that his services were at the "will and call of my country, and . . . I am not prepared to say that I shall refuse if the country calls me to the presidential office, but . . . in no case can I permit myself to be the candidate of any party, or yield myself to any party schemes." The second letter was dated May 29, and reiterated his stand that he would "not be the candidate of any party or party clique." The Democratic papers by this time were beginning to ridicule the idea of a President without a party.[136]

A letter to a Florida Democrat written June 9 and published in the *Floridian* of August 7 showed that the General's correspondents were not all Whigs. After North Carolina Whigs had nominated him, Taylor wrote on August 1, "I have *not* the assurance that my abilities are suited to the discharge of such responsible duties as rest upon the office of chief magistracy." Ten days later he wrote his famous letter to Dr. F. S. Bronson of Charleston, South Carolina, in which he made the amazing revelation for a candidate for the presidency that he had never voted. This letter, reprinted from the *National Intelligencer,* also carried the statement that if called to the office by the people he would deem it his duty to accept. His statement about his never having voted concluding with a bid for Whig support follows: *"I have never yet exercised the privilege of voting, but had I been called upon at the last presidential election to do so, I should most certainly have cast my vote for Mr. Clay."* [137]

A letter written on August 3, in reply to a forged letter from Joseph R. Ingersoll, was quoted indirectly in the *Register* in October, the recipient having refused to make the contents public because his name had been forged to the letter sent to the General. In this letter, according to the *Morning Courier and New York Enquirer,* from which the *Register* obtained the indirect quotation, Taylor said he was a decided Whig, but not an "ultra partisan" one. This letter was finally made public at a Taylor meeting in Philadelphia on February 22, 1848, and

[136] *Register,* LXXII, 288, July 3, 1847; 333, 335, July 24, 1847.
[137] *Register,* LXXII, 389, August 21, 1847; LXXIII, 79, October 2, 1847; 83, October 9, 1847; 126–27, October 23, 1847.

was printed in full in the *Register* four days later, the last number before the periodical's four months' suspension.[138]

By the first of the year the General's determination to maintain his position in the presidential contest was shown by an article reprinted from the Baltimore *American,* whose Washington correspondent wrote that he had seen a letter from Taylor

> Which dispels altogether the idea that the General will defer to Mr. Clay or submit his claims to a *whig* national convention. The writer says:—"It is important in this particular, that General Taylor regards himself as already nominated by a portion of the people in their primary assemblies, and that *he regards himself as already committed by such nominations.* The people are at liberty, he says, to vote for him or not, as they think best, but *he shall not decline*—not even in favor of Mr. Clay, as has been suggested, though believing most sincerely that many whom he could name, Mr. Clay among the number, are far better fitted than himself, to perform the duties of the high office of president of the United States.[139]

This same number, incidentally, published a letter written at Brazos Island, Texas, on November 25 by Taylor to Pennsylvania Democrats who had nominated him on October 9. Most of these issues which carried the letters also carried notices of meetings in all sections of the country at which the General was enthusiastically endorsed. A review of a campaign biography was reprinted from the *Southern Quarterly Review,* in which the writer had said that Taylor was "a man whom neither Mexicans nor biographers" could put down. The Fourth of July celebration, held July 5 at Monterey, at which General Taylor was toasted by fellow officers as the next President, was described at some length in a *National Intelligencer* article which the *Register* reprinted.[140] The returning hero's reception at New Orleans was described for *Register* readers in the New Orleans *Mercury* article of October 4, reprinted in the Christmas issue.[141]

From this recital of the correspondence of General Taylor,

[138] *Register,* LXXIII, 126, October 23, 1847; 406–407, February 26, 1848.
[139] *Register,* LXXIII, 277, January 1, 1848.
[140] *Register,* LXXII, 220–22, June 5, 1847; 361–62, August 7, 1847.
[141] *Register,* LXXIII, 257, December 25, 1847.

one should not get the impression that only his candidacy was given space in the *Register*. As a matter of fact, almost every number containing a letter from him included a summarized account from other newspapers of the activities of all candidates and their adherents. Speeches by Daniel Webster, Thomas Hart Benton's nomination by Missourians and his withdrawal, the activities of Clay and his friends, efforts in behalf of Lewis Cass and James Buchanan by Democratic supporters, and nominations of the Liberty party and the Free-Soilers, all received space throughout 1847. Not many editorials were written by the *Register* editor, who apparently was satisfied to record the material from which history could be written. However, on May 15, 1847, the increasing power of the executive branch of the government was discussed as was the frequently offered suggestion to limit the presidency to one term. The successful fight against the Congressional caucus was adverted to with the admonition that the national party convention method also could be abused. The confusion of both parties over potential candidates and the issues of the campaign, chiefly in relation to the conduct of the war, formed the subject of an editorial early in 1848.[142] Noting that General Taylor's friends had held by far the most meetings, an election article two weeks later listed the candidates and their whereabouts as follows: "General CASS, Vice President DALLAS, Mr. Secretary BUCHANAN, Judge WOODBURY, Senator CALHOUN and HENRY CLAY, are all at the city of Washington. General TAYLOR was at New Orleans at the latest dates from thence. General SCOTT is in Mexico, and is suspended from command of the army and ordered to Puebla to submit to a court of inquiry. The whereabouts of the anti-slavery and other partizan candidates we are not apprised of." [143]

The suspension of the *Register* through March, April, May, and June brought to a virtual close its coverage of the presidential campaign. By the time it resumed publication in July, the Whig, Democratic, and Barnburners conventions had been held and candidates chosen. The results were summarized as a matter of record in the first number published and newspaper comment on the effect of the nomination of Van Buren reprinted

[142] *Register*, LXXIII, 320, January 15, 1848.
[143] *Register*, LXXIII, 339, January 29, 1848.

The *Register* and Politics 163

from representative newspapers. Through the summer, scattered items were reprinted from newspapers, and acceptances of Taylor and Fillmore, Lewis Cass and W. O. Butler, and Van Buren printed. Convention proceedings were printed months later.[144] The coverage of the 1848 campaign was in sharp contrast to that of the preceding one, but little space being given as late as the closing month of the campaign.[145] Results of the Taylor victory were briefly summarized, with editorial extracts from the *National Intelligencer* and the Washington *Union*.[146]

Thus ended thirty-seven years of political reporting. Serving chiefly to reflect the editorial opinions of others, the *Register* fought hard during its first twenty years for issues, but never in a partisan way. Advocates of all parties always were granted space. Its columns mirror the most nearly complete and most nearly accurate picture of the American political scene from 1811 to 1849 to be found in any one contemporary publication.

[144] *Register*, LXXIV, 7–9, 9–10, July 5, 1848; 19, July 12, 1848; 38, July 19, 1848; 69, August 2, 1848; 109–10, August 16, 1848; 324–29, November 22, 1848; 348–49, November 29, 1848.

[145] *Register*, LXXIV, 209, October 4, 1848; 247–48, October 18, 1848.

[146] *Register*, LXXIV, 320, November 15, 1848; see also LXXIV, 329, November 22, 1848; LXXV, 24–25, January 10, 1849.

Chapter 7

Anglo-American Relations

FO R twenty-five years the *Register* was unmistakably an outspoken Anglophobe organ. Founded on the eve of the second war with Great Britain, it enthusiastically supported the "war hawks" and seldom deviated from an attitude of animosity toward the mother country during the quarter century that Hezekiah Niles determined its editorial policies.

Niles came honestly by his lifelong hatred of England, for just before his birth in 1777, his mother was threatened by the bayonet of one of the "king's brave grenadiers . . . to kill, as he gallantly said, two rebels at once." [1] His writings before he founded the *Register* reflected his anti-British and antimonarchical feelings, which practically amounted to a phobia, and when he founded the *Register,* he sounded his monarchomachic editorial philosophy in the first issue. [2]

The government's connection with the Church of England was condemned from the beginning. Its "pensioned priesthood" made it the "grand agent of knavery, the choice engine of tyrants" and "there is no government in *Europe,* that of *Turkey* and *Spain* excepted, so intollerant [sic] as the government of *Great Britain,* in religious affairs," are typical excerpts. [3]

The divine-right theory and the legitimacy of kings also were anathema to the *Register* which lost no opportunity to

1 *Register*, XIII, 33, September 13, 1817. Niles liked to repeat this story in type and it appears a number of times in articles. See XXV, 146, November 8, 1823; XXVIII, 321-22, July 23, 1825; XXXIX, 250, December 11, 1830; XLVI, 131, April 26, 1834.

2 [H. Niles., Alias Jerry Didler], *Things As They Are; or, Federalism turned inside out!! Being a Collection of Extracts from Federal Papers, &c and Remarks upon Them, Originally written for, and published in the Evening Post* (Baltimore, 1809?); *Register*, I, 9, September 7, 1811.

3 *Register*, I, 130, October 26, 1811; III, 347-48, January 20, 1813; XXXIX, 18, September 4, 1830.

deride them. Ridiculing propaganda that England was fighting for the liberties of Europe, the *Register* said, ". . . when England [shall] cease to be a robber and man-stealer on the ocean, some credit may be due her exalted pretension.[4] In 1813, in discussing the "deliverance" of Europe by Russia, Prussia, and England, Niles wrote that such a claim reminded him of ". . . a veteran bawd lecturing on chastity, and should have the same weight." [5]

When France was defeated in 1814, the *Register* on June 25 said it would have been a "subject for universal rejoicing" had England fallen as well. The latter nation was charged with ransacking "the dominions of Satan himself" for allies in the war against France and an ironic pen described the union of the "cross of St. George and the crescent of Mahomet—the British bayonet and the savage scalping knife . . . to preserve the religion and liberties of the world."

Americans along the eastern seaboard were friendly to England in the early years of the century because of trade relations. Niles never quit trying to prove that foreign commerce was of little importance in comparison with commerce between the states, but he realized that many New Englanders continued to be favorable to England because it was "the source of their profits. . . ." [6]

To him, impressment was the chief point at issue between the two nations. He wrote dozens of editorials immediately preceding and during the War of 1812 attacking this practice and demanding that England desist from it. Charging that every British war vessel was partly manned with impressed Americans, he pointed out that American acquiescence in the practice was inconsistent with sovereignty and independence. The depth of Niles' feeling regarding impressment may be gauged from this statement written two months before the declaration of war: "Accursed be the American government, and every individual of it, who by the omission or commission of any thing, shall agree to make peace with Great Britain, until ample provision shall be made for our impressed seamen, and security

4 *Register*, I, 405, February 1, 1812.
5 *Register*, V, 84, October 2, 1813.
6 *Register*, II, 331, July 18, 1812.

shall be given for the prevention of such abominable outrages in future." [7]

Niles touchingly referred to the ". . . neighbors and friends, groaning out a weary life on board the vessels . . . whipped, spurned and kicked . . . basely and deliberately murdered . . ." in an editorial on the declaration of war and insisted that rather than admit the principle, a war of extermination must be engaged in.[8] In his fight against impressment, Niles often used ammunition supplied by fellow editors; late in 1813 he quoted extensively from the Boston *Patriot* and the *Pennsylvania Republican* in arguing that as Great Britain "naturalizes and protects foreigners how can she deny the United States the same right?" [9]

All the devices employed by the modern propagandist were used by Niles to arouse hatred against enemy England. Almost every printable epithet was used and some verging on unprintable. In one editorial, England was called

. . . the common robber, the man-stealer, the scalper of women and children and prisoners, the incendiary and the ravisher . . . the enemy of our fathers, and our present unprincipled foe . . . the cause of every war that has afflicted the civilized world for fifty years past, the common pest of society and plague of the earth . . . the cold-calculating assassin of thirty millions of people in *India,* the ferocious murderer in Ireland, the minister of famine and pestilence [*sic*] in America . . . the most profligate and corrupt government in the universe . . . a government so polluted, so gangrened with every abomination, that it must perish of its own action, sooner or later. . . . [A] nation red to her arm-pits in the blood of innocence. . . .[10]

Then, as now, the most effective printed propaganda was in atrocity stories about the enemy soldiers. The *Register* printed many of these, obtaining them from army and navy officers, from letters, and by reprinting stories from other newspapers and periodicals. No story was too brutal to be placed before the readers and all, apparently, were accepted as gospel truth.

Before the declaration of war, England was accused of encouraging the Indians to commit "horrible murders." English

[7] *Register*, II, 119, April 18, 1812.   [8] *Register*, II, 283, June 27. 1812,
[9] *Register*, V, 237–40, December 4, 1813.
[10] *Register*, V, 144–45, October 30, 1813.

officers were charged with condoning and permitting the torture and killing of wounded American soldiers after the battle of Frenchtown. The British navy was reported to have fired upon "men, women, and children—the sick and the healthy," who were sea bathing at Rockaway Beach, near New York. Soldiers were said to have entered the home of a poor widow and to have broken her piano, chairs, sideboard, and table each in two pieces, telling her that she now had two of each. Niles wrote that he would like to make a schoolbook of these disgraceful incidents "so that . . . every child should be taught to hate the deeds of Englishmen." [11]

The burning of the White House and the Capitol at Washington aroused intense resentment and was generally criticized in the European and even in the English press. Niles saw such actions as a demonstration of the "hate with which *we* have always said Great Britain regarded us. . . ." Decrying the use of the invader's torch, he paid tribute to the valor of the British soldiery in capturing Washington, but called the burning of public buildings a disgrace.[12]

But it was the stories of the violation of American womanhood by the British and their Indian allies that made the strongest appeal to the emotions of the reader, and Niles, in spite of a high ethical code of editorial conduct and a tendency to criticize the London press for retailing scandal, printed many of these tales. A particularly blood-curdling one is credited to a letter from a "gentleman at Kaskaskia" which described the murder and kidnaping of some frontier American families by Indians. "The situation of Mrs. Kennedy was shocking beyond description. She having been pregnant, her body was found entirely naked, cut open and the child taken out and hung up on a peg in the chimney. Her entrails were scattered all about the door and the hogs were eating them." [13]

Of the British invasion of Virginia in 1813, a story related that the officer in charge offered his men "three days plunder, *and the free use of a number of fine women*, besides a hand-

[11] *Register*, VI, 410, August 13, 1814.

[12] *Register*, VII, 1, September 10, 1814; 275–76, December 31, 1814; 336, January 21, 1815.

[13] *Register*, IV, 135, April 24, 1813.

some bounty." The same article related that "The admirals then permitted their men to strip these unhappy women naked, and with drawn bayonets, drive them through the streets before them." Niles, after styling this an "eternal stigma on the British character," added, "My heart bleeds for these unfortunate females." [14] Another story described the raping of an American woman by seven British soldiers in the presence of her husband.[15] The Boston *Patriot* furnished the following item: ". . . THE BRITISH OFFICERS STRIPPED YOUNG LADIES ENTIRELY NAKED, and obliged them to stand before them in that condition for an hour and a half; when they, the British officers, at length permitted these distressed females again to clothe themselves." [16] Merely as an aside, it may be remarked that the English papers were printing similar stories about American troops in Canada, and that Henry Clay was described in a London newspaper as the man who killed Tecumseh and "cut several razor strops out of his back after he was dead." [17]

Niles' enthusiasm at times led him away from absolute accuracy in reporting American naval victories in the War of 1812.[18] He made no pretense of impartiality in the international field during the war. In an address to his readers, he referred to his freedom from political partisanship, adding: "But—in regard to the war against *Great Britain*—though we would not knowingly insinuate a falsehood, or distort a fact, we cannot, dare not, will not, stand with our arms folded, *neutral* and *insensible*. By diligent investigation, truth shall be ascertained, and faithfully recorded in the "Events of the war"—yet we will use our best efforts to rouse and encourage our fellow-citizens to such deeds of patriotism as may lead to a glorious termination

[14] *Register*, IV, 332–37, July 24, 1813.
[15] *Register*, VI, 210, May 28, 1814.
[16] *Register*, VII, 136, November 5, 1814.
[17] *Register*, VII, 280, December 31, 1814.
[18] Theodore Roosevelt in *The Naval War of 1812 or the History of the United States during the Last War with Great Britain* (New York, 1882), after acknowledging that for sources he was most indebted to the *Register* and to the *Naval Chronicle* (London, 1799–1818), compared the misstatements of Niles regarding the British with those of William James, author of the *Naval History of Great Britain* (London, 1847), about the Americans, but praised each for the accuracy concerning his respective country's navy; IV, 16, 410.

of the controversy, so far forth as the same shall be in our power." [19]

Niles kept his ear close to the ground and in December, 1814, reported that the "general opinion" was that peace would be signed at Ghent. When the peace treaty was completed, the *Register* carried it in full.[20] The militant editor was so happy over the postwar victory at New Orleans that he said nothing about the fact that impressment was not mentioned in the document.

The Treaty of Ghent ushered in no era of good feelings between the United States and Great Britain. On the contrary, the antagonisms aroused and the hatreds rekindled by the war seemed to be intensified by the peace which was unsatisfactory to both combatants. In 1815, when American prisoners of war began to return home, Niles' indignation at their stories was expressed in a wrathy editorial which called attention to the "deep guilt and terrible depravity of our late enemy" and admonished his readers:

We may, possibly, aspire to the Divine principle of *forgiveness,* but must, indeed, be lost to common prudence if we strive to *forget* the outrages of Englishmen. The real character of the British nation has been sedulously concealed by a prostitute press in the United States from a large portion of our people, and the pulpit has lent its aid to extol, almost with the attributes of DIVINITY, a nation that has carried destruction and crime into the remotest parts of the earth— that has desolated immense regions of country, and caused the premature death of uncounted millions of men: That allies itself with negro slaves or savages, Turks or Christians, and supports, by turns the religion of the SON of GOD, or the worship of *Juggernaut,* as subserves its purpose of trade or ambition: and though peace is made with English *men,* we are as much opposed to and at war with English *principles* and *practices* as ever we were.[21]

Through the summer of 1815, many articles were carried on the Dartmoor Prison massacre of April 6, 1815, in which seven Americans were killed and sixty-three wounded. News stories,

[19] *Register,* IV, 1, March 6, 1813.
[20] *Register,* VII, 240, December 10, 1814; 397–400, February 18, 1815.
[21] *Register,* VIII, 127, April 22, 1815.

editorial comments, documents, including correspondence, reports, and depositions of American officers, told the story of the massacre to the *Register*'s readers. Niles felt that the report of the joint commission which investigated the affair was neither fair nor accurate.[22]

Niles constantly deplored the extent of British influence in the United States and spent much of his editorial and personal life in trying to awaken in Americans a nationalism which he felt was lacking. Books by British authors were frequently denounced in the *Register* as purveyors of false ideas regarding monarchies and as being filled with pro-British and antirepublican propaganda. Works written by English travelers in America were subject to a particularly heavy editorial bombardment. In 1812 the *Register* printed four installments of what apparently was planned as a longer series on "Travellers in America." Niles charged that authors were well paid by the British ministers for their works, specifically mentioning Smythe, Moore, Ashe, and Parkinson. He declared, "The base fabrications of these English hirelings are insults which should be resented by every respectable tourist."[23]

Thomas Ashe's *Travels in America* was discussed in detail in the next three articles of the series. Long excerpts were quoted and objectionable phrases italicized. In the last of the three articles, two columns were devoted to pointing out errors in grammar, page by page, through the book. As a matter of fact, Ashe's volume was unfavorable to the United States, but not abusively so. It painted lurid pictures of frontier customs and contained many Munchausen-like exaggerations.[24] The press of war news and documents pertaining to the conduct of the war unfortunately interrupted this highly interesting, if somewhat biased, series.

[22] *Register*, VIII, 267–71, June 17, 1815; 283, June 24, 1815; 321–28, July 8, 1815; 354–60, July 22, 1815; 389–92, August 5, 1815.

[23] *Register*, II, 94, April 11, 1812.

[24] *Register*, II, 114–18, April 18, 1812; 141–43, May 2, 1812; 162–63, May 9, 1812; cf. Thomas Ashe, *Travels in America, Performed in 1806, for the Purpose of Exploring the Rivers Alleghany, Monongahela, Ohio, and Mississippi, and Ascertaining the Produce and Condition of their Banks and Vicinity* (London, 1808), 97–101; 265–78; Ashe's attitude is commented on in Allan Nevins, *American Social History As Recorded by British Travelers* (New York, c1923), 8, 58.

Other literary productions which were a source of constant concern to Niles were English schoolbooks and novels. In 1815, he declared that of the "many causes of the deleterious *British* influence that even yet so extensively prevails in the United States, notwithstanding the barbarism of character exhibited in the late war . . . I have always considered the introduction and use of British compilations in our *schools,* as perhaps the most powerful; assisted as they are by the after readings by our youth of the vile trash that reaches us under the denomination of novels." [25]

These "royal SCHOOL BOOKS, and lord-and-lady novels" gave false impressions and American "teachers should 'tell the truth and fear it not,' and our children ought to be told that kings are mere flesh and blood, liable to all weaknesses, and seldom possessing half the virtues, of the 'beggar of the dunghill,' " he asserted. The fact that there were no histories of merit written by Americans bothered Niles, and he welcomed the announced publication of an Americanized Universal History of the World in 1816.[26]

An English statement that books could be sent from England more cheaply than they could be printed in the United States irked the printer-editor. He offered to pay $25,000 annually for the privilege of printing books on American presses, using American type and American paper if he were allowed to export $100,000 worth of them each year to England. Under such an arrangement, he would make an annual profit of $25,000 to $30,000, he claimed.[27]

American antagonism toward Great Britain was not alleviated by the attitude of the English reviews during the third and fourth decades of the century. In fact, their articles acted as a constant irritant to the sensitive feelings of the citizens of the new world who resented criticism, but who, paradoxically, read everything that the vitriolic quarterlies in England and Scotland saw fit to print about America. The British reviews were reprinted as soon as they reached the United States. The *Regis-*

[25] *Register,* VIII, 305–306, July 1, 1815.
[26] *Register,* XI, 84, October 5, 1816; 198–99, November 23, 1816; XII, 69, March 29, 1817; XIII, 115, October 18, 1817.
[27] *Register,* IX, 137, October 28, 1815.

ter supplied its subscribers with excerpts from many of the vituperative articles, thus doing its bit to keep alive the feeling of bitterness between the countries.

The United States and its citizens were attacked so constantly and so unfairly in articles of all types in the British quarterlies that it is not surprising that a hypersensitivity was developed which reacted to criticism even of faults and evils acknowledged by many Americans themselves. The *Quarterly Review* which, the editor of the Baltimore *Chronicle* observed, commonly saluted America "with a swill-pail of abuse," was quoted on the personal scurrility of members of Congress elected by a keg of brandy. The same magazine criticized the "spiteful and insulting spirit" that Americans evinced toward England, and one of its book reviews strongly condemned a work on the United States because it was friendly to the new country.[28]

The English newspaper press, too, was not above printing vicious attacks on the United States and when these articles were reprinted in American newspapers with appropriate rejoinders little was accomplished in the way of arriving at a better understanding between the two peoples. In London, the *Courier* of September 12, 1822, commenting on those English reformers who held up the United States as a model, attacked the "puerile absurdity" of such a course and said that England "must, in fact, retrograde three or four centuries, in arts, literature, in civilization, in conquests; and then, having lopped off all *our* wide spreading branches of power and dominion—having extinguished *our* taste for refinement and luxury—having lowered the standard of *our* intellectual character . . . *we* may fit ourselves with the garb of republican simplicity." The *True Briton*'s reference to Americans as brethren by birth, *"though they may have emanated from a guilty and degraded stock,"* [29] and the London *Literary Gazette*'s splenetic notice of the Bunker Hill celebration in Boston were carried in the *Register*'s columns with comments and headlines in the same vein.[30]

---

[28] *Register*, XX, 226, June 9, 1821; XXI, 38–39, September 15, 1821; XXIII, 7, September 7, 1822.

[29] *Register*, XXIII, 116, October 26, 1822; 179, November 23, 1822.

[30] *Register*, XXIX, 66, October 1, 1825.

During the twenties and thirties the *Register* reprinted many items from the English newspaper and periodical press. In spite of his expressed opposition to American dependence upon England for ideas and literature, Niles nevertheless obtained considerable material for his periodical from that source. Much of this matter was purely informational or technical and therefore had no ill effect upon Anglo-American relations, but even in the thirties such articles as the following from the London *Monthly Review* were printed: "They, (the United States), have no HISTORY worth reading, not a canto of *poetry*, no *memoirs*, no *collections* of SPEECHES, no *miscellaneous works* of amusement, very few *travels*, and not even a single good *sermon*." [31] The fact that there was more than a modicum of truth in the statement probably only added to American resentment. An article from the *Athenaeum*, given circulation in the *Courier* and then in the *Register*, charged that Americans talked only of the dollar, which was their god, and that when seated they always had their feet up on the wall or out of open windows through which "tobacco juice squirted . . . like a fire of rockets." [32]

In the middle twenties Niles relaxed his unceasing opposition to England and the English long enough to reprint excerpts of friendly editorials on President Monroe's final message to Congress from the *Times* and the *Public Ledger,* which, he wrote, were written in a "kind, liberal and manly manner." [33] Great Britain's recognition of the South American republics also caused an appreciable warming in his feeling regarding England, although he gave the credit to the people rather than to the government.[34] A friendlier attitude was manifest toward the United States in some of the reviews and journals during the thirties, and the *Register's* reprinted abstracts were about equally divided between complimentary and critical ones, often woven into the same articles.[35]

The steady stream of books about the United States continued

[31] *Register*, XL, 396, July 30, 1831, quoting *London Monthly Review* (London, 1749–1844), April, 1831.
[32] *Register*, XLVII, 235, December 13, 1834.
[33] *Register*, XXVIII, 1–2, March 5, 1825.
[34] *Register*, XXVIII, 67, April 2, 1825.
[35] *Register*, XLI, 2, September 3, 1831; XLVIII, 117–18, April 18, 1835.

to flow from English authors and English presses throughout the twenties, thirties, and forties, but fewer and fewer of them were reviewed, or even noticed, in the *Register*. Errors in fact were noted, but the comment was more often than not good natured raillery at some ridiculous statement instead of the unrestrained bitterness with which the earlier productions had been greeted.[36] Mrs. Trollope's *Domestic Manners of the Americans* was the only book which caused Niles to dip his pen into vitriol and even here the attack seemed to lack the fire and vigor of his earlier writing. Mentioning that the newspapers were filled with extracts from and remarks about her book, he asked why not leave her and Captain Basil Hall, another author-traveler, alone? "They cannot do us any harm. We do not see why so much attention should be paid to such animals. And, as they have a talent for scribbling, we are ready to excuse anything which they *can* say concerning us, if they will endeavor to keep their own *Burkers* and other *murderers*, their *forgers*, and *robbers*, and *thieves*, with their *prostitutes*, and ship-loads of *paupers*, at home. They cannot influence those intelligent and worthy and sound-hearted Englishmen to whom we are always willing to tender the right hand of friendship, and accept as fellow citizens." [37]

After this editorial on Mrs. Trollope, the *Register* printed little, if anything, for ten years on English books about America, but the coming of Charles Dickens in 1842 broke this long silence. The primary purpose of his visit was to urge the passage of an international copyright law and his open propagandizing in favor of the measure and his none-too-tactful references to American editors aroused a storm of opposition which destroyed any chance the measure ever had of enactment.

The *Register* printed without comment nearly three columns from the *National Intelligencer,* including a letter from Dickens, an address to the American public from twelve leading English authors among whom were Alfred Tennyson, Leigh Hunt, Henry Hallam, Sydney Smith, and Thomas Hood, a

---

36 *Register*, XX, 292, July 7, 1821; 409–10, August 25, 1821; XXI, 32, September 8, 1821; XXV, 134, November 1, 1823; XXIX, 321–23, January 21, 1826; XXXIII, 50–51, September 22, 1827; XXXIV, 218, May 31, 1828; XXXVII, 295, January 2, 1830; XLV, 50–51, September 21, 1833.

37 *Register*, XLIII, 67, September 29, 1832.

letter from these same writers to Dickens, and a letter from Thomas Carlyle to Dickens, comparing copyright violation to stealing.[38] Several months later an outspoken circular by Dickens in the London *Chronicle,* giving a résumé of his efforts in behalf of the legislation was printed. In this report Dickens wrote that James Fenimore Cooper, Washington Irving, William H. Prescott, and many others, had signed a petition and that Henry Clay had presented it to Congress. He warned English authors against American newspaper editors, many of whom, he charged, had an interest "in the existing system of piracy and plunder." Describing them as "men of very low attainments and of more than indifferent reputation," he suggested that British authors hold correspondence only with respectable American publishing houses.[39] This letter not unnaturally brought a counterattack from the American press. The *Register* asserted that had the European advocates of the copyright measure left the American people to decide for themselves, it might have passed, but that it met its death blow in Dickens' visit. The same editorial commented on the author's *American Notes,* which was reprinted in numerous pirated editions within a few hours after its arrival on the *Great Western.* Thousands of copies were being sold on New York streets at twelve and one-half cents each, nineteen hours after the ship docked. Philadelphians snapped up 1,500 copies as quickly as they could be handed to purchasers, and the same was true of other cities. The *Register's* comment was temperate, compared with many. "The work will sadly lower the estimate in which the author was held —both as a writer and a man, although there are many well written and some wholesome paragraphs in it. The chapter upon slavery in America is decidedly the most outrageous libel upon our country which we have met with in any of the British authors." [40]

Works of many English writers of this period went unnoticed in the *Register,* although the publications of Captain Frederick Marryat and Sir Charles Lyell received mention.[41]

[38] *Register,* LXII, 183-84, May 21, 1842.
[39] *Register,* LXII, 389, August 20, 1842.
[40] *Register,* LXIII, 176, November 12, 1842.
[41] *Register,* LXV, 214-15, December 2, 1843; LXVIII, 405-406, August 30, 1845.

The condition of the masses in England, Scotland, and Ireland offered a target at which the *Register* aimed some of its most sarcastic editorial barbs. Niles neglected few opportunities to contrast the condition of the common people in the United States with that of the same classes in the British Isles. "The crisis seems at hand, which may shake to atoms the British system of finance and government," he wrote in 1816.[42] Late in 1819 he began to advocate revolution as the only solution. In a three and one-half page editorial in October, he wrote: ". . . on the score of the purest humanity . . . we believe that a reform, or revolution, in England, may be considerately advocated. We are friendly to the English people. . . . But considering their government as the common enemy of mankind and as especially hostile to our prosperity, we sincerely wish its destruction; and believe that, cost what it may, the benefits thereby to be conferred on the world at large will be very cheaply purchased." [43]

Because William Cobbett was in opposition to the government during much of this period, Niles reprinted many editorials from *Cobbett's Weekly Political Register*, devoting 100 pages in a supplement to Volume VIII to Cobbett's writings.[44] When Cobbett fled from England to America for the second time, Niles noted his arrival in New York and transferred his admiration to Thomas Jonathan Wooler, editor of the *Black Dwarf*, who had frequent troubles over libel.[45] In 1831 Niles wrote that the English people were "maddened with suffering" and he questioned if reform could be accomplished without revolution, a reiteration of his statement made fourteen years earlier.[46] The reform elections, the passage of the reform bill, and its defeat by the House of Lords brought this suggestion: "Some speculate on a revolution in England—or, at least, calculate dangerous proceedings of the people, to obtain *by force* what the 'hospital of incurables' has denied them: but the king, if resolved to carry the point, may easily *manufacture* a 'batch of peers,' and settle the affair at once."

[42] *Register*, XI, 209–10, November 30, 1816.

[43] *Register*, XVII, 133–36, October 30, 1819.

[44] *Register*, VIII, Supplement; other Cobbett articles, VIII, 49–55, March 25, 1815; 372–75, July 29, 1815; 392–93, August 5, 1815; X, 102, April 13, 1816.

[45] *Register*, XII, 172, May 10, 1817; XIII, 21–26, September 6, 1817.

[46] *Register*, XXXIX, 425, February 12, 1831.

The danger of civil war or revolution seemed real to Niles, who would have been delighted to see the monarchy overthrown but who sincerely sympathized with the plight of the masses. When the Lords gave in and approved the reform measure, the *Register* described its passage and the attitude of the London press toward it.[47]

Niles never softened in his attitude toward the English throne; article after article during his editorship reflected his active animus against royalty. He was firmly convinced that nations governed by kings hated the United States because it "presented to their subjects a *'dangerous example of successful rebellion.'* " Discussing English news stories about the expected confinement of Princess Charlotte, he ended a long footnote with, "But we do not wish her any harm, except that she may not become a breeder of princes." In the following number, which reported her death, he made a halfhearted and not very generous apology for having laughed at what he called the "stupid pomp and silly regulations" concerning her lying in. But even here he inserted a dig at royalty by mentioning that she was the only legitimate child of the prince regent and that neither the Duke of York nor any of his numerous brothers and sisters had a legitimate child.[48]

When the Queen of England died in 1818, Niles, in discussing the lack of foreign news, wrote that he had little of importance to record ". . . except an account of the decease of the queen of England—the old lady died on the 17th of November. . . ."[49] And in 1820, when the mad king finally passed away, Niles wrote, "The old king, George William Frederick Guelph, died at Windsor castle on the 29th of January."[50]

Royal marriages and the private lives of members of the royal family were frequently denounced in the *Register* in plain-spoken terms.[51] Niles seldom resorted to vulgarity found in

[47] *Register*, XL, 417–20, August 13, 1831; XLI, 233, November 26, 1831; 255–56, December 6, 1831; 297, December 24, 1831; XLII, 374, July 21, 1832; 388, July 28, 1832.

[48] *Register*, XIII, 1, August 30, 1817; 298, January 3, 1818; 322, January 10, 1818.

[49] *Register*, XV, 361, January 9, 1819.

[50] *Register*, XVIII, 47, March 18, 1820.

[51] *Register*, VIII, 439, August 26, 1815; X, 338–39, July 20, 1816; 406–408, August 17, 1816.

many of the publications of the time, but in discussing the anticipated and actual births of children to members of England's royal family, he overstepped the bounds of good taste more than once. The natural interest that the English had in the birth of an heir to the throne was not understood by Niles who ridiculed the amount of space given to such news in the English press.[52] He styled a London article "comical" which described the birth of a stillborn child to the Duchess of Cumberland.[53] When the English press carried the news that the wives of the four British royal dukes, who were married soon after Charlotte's death, were all expecting children, Niles repeatedly used poor taste in headlines and comments on the items in the *Register*.[54] The news of the birth of the future Queen of England on May 24, 1819, was carried on July 17, in this three-line item, "The British are lucky of late—the duchess of Kent has lately had a little baby that may be a mistress for them!"[55]

Always a stanch believer in the worth of the working classes of a nation, Niles often contrasted their condition with that of royalty. Accounts of elaborate social affairs particularly annoyed him, and he added to descriptions of them such statements as: "On the *same day,* three millions of people *who contributed to the cost of this dinner,* scantily dined on *cold potatoes!*" and "The same evening that the countess gave this ball, 1 or 200,000 persons in England, after a hard day's work, went supperless to bed. . . ."[56]

In 1821 he ridiculed the extensive preparations for the coronation of George IV, but after the coronation he relented sufficiently to give nearly eight pages to accounts of the ceremony.[57] When George died and was succeeded by William IV, Niles wrote a clumsily sarcastic editorial, followed by a number of criticisms of the new sixty-four-year-old monarch.[58] That his

52 *Register*, XI, 10, August 31, 1816.
53 *Register*, XII, 105, April 12, 1817.
54 *Register*, XVI, 158, April 24, 1819; 220, May 22, 1819; 381, July 31, 1819.
55 *Register*, XVI, 345, July 17, 1819.
56 *Register*, XI, 9, August 31, 1816; XVI, 413, August 14, 1819.
57 *Register*, XX, 349, July 28, 1821; 364, August 4, 1821; 381, August 11, 1821; XXI, 54–61, September 22, 1821.
58 *Register*, XXXVIII, 431, 435–38, August 14, 1830; XXXIX, 20, September 4, 1830.

attitude toward royalty had changed little since 1811 and 1820 may be seen from the following extract written in 1834:

> What is the king of England, for an example? The shattered *re-mains* of one of the most dissolute of his kind—a superannuated ig-noramus—a machine in the hands of others—without any settled and well organized will of his own, but subject to the dictations of those round about him; and totally incapable of understanding or right-fully administering the laws, for the good of his country. It is well for him, that, generally speaking, his *keepers* have been rather clever persons—but of himself, what is he? Divest him of his royalty, and throw him into the crowd—and what would *he* be? [59]

Niles' retirement just before Victoria became Queen brought a different tone to the *Register's* references to royalty. Friend-liness replaced animosity and interest was evinced in the young Queen's accession and coronation, her appearances before Par-liament, and in her marriage and the birth of her children.[60] The editorial attitude of the *Register* in the last dozen years of its existence toward the British royal family could not have been objected to by the most ardent Victorian. That this changed attitude was due in part to the wholesomeness which Victoria brought to court circles was undoubtedly true, but it also was a significant indication of the closer feeling that was growing between the two nations.

Another phase of Anglo-American relations productive of friction between the countries and criticism in the *Register* was the rivalry which developed on the sea, in commerce and in naval affairs. The United States was disturbed by the finan-cial, commercial, and naval power of England on the Continent and throughout the world. Great Britain expressed what seemed to the Americans an undue interest in the size of the American navy. The Lords debated the necessity of building larger ships in order to meet the United States on the sea on equal terms, an event which did nothing to lessen American suspicion of

[59] *Register*, XLVII, 6, September 6, 1834.

[60] *Register*, LI, 48, September 17, 1836; LII, 337, July 29, 1837; 413–15, August 26, 1837; LIII, 3–4, September 2, 1837; LIV, 350–52, July 28, 1838; LVII, 289, Jan-uary 4, 1840; LVIII, 17, March 14, 1840; 33–37, March 21, 1840; LXI, 129, October 30, 1841; 161, November 13, 1841; 225, December 11, 1841; LXII, 257, June 25, 1842; LXVII, 1, September 7, 1844.

England's motives.[61] Not only commerce between the two nations, but rivalry for the carrying trade of the world brought the two countries into conflict. Niles, in 1818, quoting an article from the Dublin *Freeman's Journal*, which mentioned that the United States had failed successively in negotiating commercial treaties with Naples, Spain, France, Sweden, and the Netherlands, made this charge: "It is the secret work of Great Britain, and its object is to check or destroy our naval means by reducing or destroying the commerce of the United States. Let our *statesmen* look to it." [62]

Britain's efforts to maintain a world-wide market for her products were frequently commented upon, and in 1820 the *Register* called attention to the formation of a rich and extensive trade association of English manufacturers which was planning to dump English goods in America at a loss of more than one million dollars, if necessary, in order to stifle American competition.[63]

The publication of an anonymous pamphlet, *The Colonial Policy of Great Britain, considered with Relation to her North American Provinces, and West India Possessions; wherein the Dangerous Tendency of American Competition is Developed, and the Necessity of Recommending a Colonial System on a Vigorous and Extensive Scale, Exhibited and Defended; with Plans for the Promotion of Emigration, and Strictures on the Treaty of Ghent* convinced Americans that England looked upon the commercial, naval, and territorial growth of the United States with envy and fear. The *Register* reviewed the pamphlet in detail, saying that although it was "full of misrepresentation, and written in a spirit of blind, inveterate hostility" it was recommended to Americans so that they may ". . . be fully apprised of the mean, pitiable, self-deluding schemes that are proposed and acted upon, to check our irresistable [*sic*] advancement. . . ." [64]

Less than a year after the Treaty of Ghent had been signed, Niles mapped out a plan of naval warfare to be used by Ameri-

---

[61] *Register*, XVI, 398, August 7, 1819.

[62] *Register*, XIV, 406–407, August 14, 1818.

[63] *Register*, XVIII, 151, April 22, 1820.

[64] *Register*, XI, 5–7, August 31, 1816.

cans ". . . if, unfortunately they should ever be involved in war with *England* again." Briefly, it was to build a large number of speedy ten- to sixteen-gun ships which would *"destroy* the commerce of a nation like England" by sinking all ships captured.[65] A year later, quoting London newspapers that the English were planning a respectable naval force on the Great Lakes, Niles suggested that this country keep an eye on England, and, incidentally, keep its own ships in "a tolerable state for actual service. . . ."[66]

Two phases of English foreign relations which received especial attention in the *Register* were that nation's treatment of the exiled Napoleon and England's interest in the Floridas and Cuba. The United States in general, and the *Register* in particular, were friendly to France but unfriendly to the Bourbons. Because of this friendliness for the French, the Republican newspapers in America had much to say concerning England's action in exiling Napoleon and the treatment he received at St. Helena. The *National Intelligencer* and the Boston *Patriot* both condemned England's "narrow meanness" in this regard. Niles wrote, "The exultation of the British over the fallen *Napoleon Bonaparte,* is disgraceful to the character of their country. The lion preys not on dead carcases." [67] Many articles concerning Napoleon's dissatisfaction with St. Helena were carried.

Through the long period of negotiation that preceded ratification of the treaty with Spain ceding the Floridas to the United States, American distrust of Great Britain was repeatedly voiced in the *Register.* As early as 1816 Niles printed the rumor that Spain had ceded the Floridas to England. At that time he wrote, "We cannot believe, however, that Great Britain is anxious for another war with the United States—." Three years later, after the treaty had been negotiated and was waiting the long-delayed ratification by Spain, Niles quoted an article from the *British Statesman* which criticized the "wily policy" of the United States in ". . . obtaining the possession of these provinces," which gave them ". . . a solid power in the West Indies,

65 *Register,* VIII, 405, August 12, 1815.
66 *Register,* XI, 30, September 7, 1816.
67 *Register,* IX, 70, September 30, 1815.

which may be as detrimental to us as beneficial to her." [68] Niles was unwilling to believe that England would take Spain's part in the controversy, but in the October 16, 1819, issue, he wrote ". . . there is very little doubt but that Ferdinand has refused to ratify the treaty through British interference." There was much newspaper speculation on the causes back of the rejection of the treaty, but Niles assured his readers that he seriously questioned if Great Britain would risk a war with the United States which would curtail, if not kill, her commerce with that country and South America.[69]

It was at this point that England's interest in Cuba began to play an important part in the editorial discussion of the Florida treaty. Rumors that England had forbidden Spain to transfer the Floridas to the United States unless she ceded Cuba to her were circulated in the United States and England.[70] Despite his antagonism toward England, Niles was opposed to steps which might bring about a war with either England or Spain or both. He protested editorially against the recommendation of the House committee on foreign relations that the House authorize the President to take steps to occupy the Floridas, and feared that England would use such a step as a pretext to "accomplish her darling scheme of acquiring Cuba." He wrote: "If this valuable island ever becomes her dependency, the effect will be many times more injurious to us than if she possessed the mouths of the Mississippi, for we could not hope to dispossess her of it; and Cuba, in the hands of a power like Great Britain, would more severely annoy our trade, than it could be annoyed by a position on the Mississippi itself." [71]

Fear that England would obtain Cuba from Spain continued to haunt Niles who wrote many editorials on the subject. One discussed rumors that in the event of war between France and Spain, England would lend money to the latter from whom she would receive "a sort of a mortgage on *Cuba*." Another, commenting on the "probable *occupancy of the island of Cuba by*

[68] *Register*, IX, 405, February 10, 1816; XVI, 161–62, May 1, 1819, quoting *British Statesman* (London, February 10 to December 11, 1819), March 26, 1819.

[69] *Register*, XVII, 113–15, October 23, 1819.

[70] *Register*, XVII, 103, October 16, 1819; 194, November 27, 1819; 210, December 4, 1819.

[71] *Register*, XVIII, 46–47, March 18, 1820.

the British," declared: "Every good feeling of our heart is now allied to the cause of Spain, though it is possible that we may get into a controversy with *her friend,* if the possession of Cuba shall be transferred as reported. This, however, may be averted by the people of that fine island establishing a provisional government for themselves. . . . [72]

A little later he reassured his readers that Great Britain's occupancy of the island was unlikely because of the opposition of the West India sugar interests and of the people of Cuba. England's only reason for wanting Cuba would be to command the Gulf of Mexico, he asserted. Because of this strategic location of Cuba, as well as her trade with the United States, Niles opposed its cession to Great Britain or any strong power. It must be noted that he never advocated annexation to the United States, however. He argued that it was to the interest of both the United States and Great Britain that Cuba remain under the dominion of Spain or become independent. [73]

Four days after Monroe's message was read to Congress on December 2, 1823, Niles, as was his custom with all presidential messages, printed it in full and invited his readers to a "careful perusal" of it. Noting that part of the now-famous message which termed the extension of the European political system to the Western Hemisphere as "dangerous to our peace and safety," Niles wrote: "Every thinking American will accord in this opinion—but the *expression* of it, on an occasion like the present, convinces us that there must be some special *reason* for putting it forth. It has been universally believed that the members of the 'holy alliance' entertained the design of reducing all governments to their own standard of right . . . but we hardly thought that they had proceeded so far as we are now disposed to believe that they have done." [74]

That the doctrine may have been directed at England as well as at the Holy Alliance apparently did not occur to Niles, who, three weeks after his comments on Monroe's message, editorially approved an Anglo-American joint action to guarantee the

---

[72] *Register,* XXIII, 305, January 18, 1823; XXIV, 17, March 15, 1823.

[73] *Register,* XXIV, 72–73, April 5, 1823; XXV, 210, December 6, 1823.

[74] *Register,* XXV, 209, December 6, 1823; in this same editorial Niles mentioned the possibility that England might have been compelled to fall in with that design.

integrity of the South American nations. It was hard for this Anglophobe editor to advocate such co-operation. After giving vent to his anti-British feelings, however, by saying that protection under British cannon was hardly less injurious than the enmity of the allied powers, he admitted "that some not very intimate arrangement might be made" to forestall the attempts of the Holy Alliance.[75]

Even before Monroe's message was received in England and on the Continent, England's probable course of action caused much editorial speculation. Two and one-half months after the delivery of the message, the English and French editorial reactions were printed in the *Register*. England's "general approbation," Niles felt, ". . . shews that the feelings of the people of that kingdom fully accord with Mr. Monroe's view of the condition of the new states of South America. . . ." The *Courier, Globe and Traveller,* and the London *Times,* the Liverpool *Advertiser* and *Bell's Weekly Messenger,* all of which warmly commended the tone of the message and asserted that it settled once and for all time the question of the independence and recognition of the South American republics, were quoted. The *Times* even defended the United States and its President against an attack in the Paris *Etoile,* a ministerial paper, which questioned "by what title then are the *two Americas* to be under his (Monroe's) immediate dependence, from Hudson's bay to Cape Horn?" This Paris newspaper charged that the policy had received no sanction and, "in short, that the opinions of Mr. Monroe are as yet, merely the opinions of a private individual."[76]

In 1825, just below an editorial somewhat grudgingly congratulating Great Britain on her new attitude toward the United States, the *Register* carried the news from a London paper that George Canning, British foreign minister, had notified the foreign ambassadors of the decision of England to send chargés d'affaires to Colombia, Mexico, and Buenos Aires, and to enter into treaties of commerce with them, noting six weeks later that the *"holy allies* are exceedingly *bothered* by the conduct of

[75] *Register,* XXV, 261, December 27, 1823.
[76] *Register,* XXV, 401, 410–13, February 28, 1824.

Great Britain in acknowledging the independence of the new American republics." [77]

It was not only in his stories and editorials on the diplomatic relations of the two countries, but also in the recording of run-of-the-mine everyday events that Niles let his anti-British bias express itself. In reading the *Register* over a period of years the careful reader cannot miss the jabs and jibes at England which appear in item after item. The custom of wife-selling, the sport of prizefighting, the influence of women's styles, the lack of military courtesy in evacuating army posts, and the stamp tax on English newspapers, all served to put the English in a bad light for the *Register*'s readers. Great Britain was charged with causing Indian troubles in the Floridas and in the Northwest, with stealing American inventions, and with dumping its paupers and pickpockets in the United States.[78] As southern opposition to the protective tariff increased in the late twenties and early thirties, British agents were charged with encouraging the nullificationists and secessionists.[79] Not only money, but muskets would be supplied when called for by South Carolina, Niles asserted, and he felt certain that British gold was being used to corrupt the representatives of the people and to support the antitariff press.[80] Similar items by the hundreds may be culled from the columns of the periodical. No reader was left in doubt as to its feeling toward Great Britain.

As early as on November 24, 1827, the *Register* carried an editorial on the necessity of determining the boundary between Maine and New Brunswick, but the controversy did not wax warm until after Hezekiah Niles' death. The possibility of a Canadian insurrection was discussed by Niles less than a year before his retirement when he wrote that such action was a "moral certainty" and predicted union with the United States.[81] However, this chapter of Anglo-American relations, which in-

---

[77] *Register*, XXVIII, 2, March 5, 1825; 119, April 23, 1825.

[78] Such references may be found in nearly every one of the fifty volumes edited by Niles.

[79] *Register*, XXXV, 49, September 20, 1828.

[80] *Register*, XXXV, 281, December 27, 1828; XXXVIII, 333, July 3, 1830; XXXIX, 2–3, August 28, 1830; XL, 177, May 14, 1831.

[81] *Register*, XLIX, 37, September 10, 1835.

cluded the unsuccessful Canadian insurrections and the accompanying *Caroline* affair and McLeod trial, also was written after his death.

Through the period of the various abortive Canadian riots, insurrections, and invasions of 1837–1838, the *Register* was edited by William Ogden Niles, who rarely expressed an opinion in the periodical, and so it is more as a repository of contemporary newspaper accounts than as an organ of opinion that the periodical is worthy of examination. Canadian, New York, and New England newspapers were the source of most of these articles. In November and December, 1837, the Baltimore *American*, Montreal *Courier*, New York *Evening Post*, Albany *Argus*, Burlington *Free Press*, New York *Commercial Advertiser*, *Franklin Journal* of St. Alban's, Vermont, Burlington *Sentinel*, Albany *Advertiser*, Montreal *Gazette*, Buffalo *Daily Advertiser*, and Montreal *Herald* supplied news articles describing riots in Montreal, clashes between loyalists and "Sons of Liberty," and the attack on the village of St. Charles.[82]

The seizure, burning, and destruction of the American steamer *Caroline* on December 29, 1837, by the Canadian militia occasioned a flood of news and documentary material but no comment from the *Register*. President Martin Van Buren's neutrality proclamation, Colonel Allan N. McNab's report on the *Caroline* capture, the surrender of American invading forces near the border in Vermont, and excerpts from diplomatic correspondence on the affair were printed.[83] In spite of a number of provocative incidents, such as the attack on the British steamboat *Sir Robert Peel* and the firing of the American ship *Telegraph*, the American newspaper press, as quoted extensively in the *Register*, generally condemned the hotheaded activities of the participants on both sides and supported the administration's attempt to iron out the border difficulties.[84] The Detroit *Daily Advertiser*, Toledo *Blade*, Detroit *Post*, Kingston *Chron-*

---

[82] *Register*, LIII, 163, November 11, 1837; 179, November 18, 1837; 209–10, December 2, 1837; 227–29, December 9, 1837; 241–42, December 16, 1837.

[83] *Register*, LIII, 289–90, January 6, 1838; 305, January 13, 1838; 321–23, January 20, 1838; LIV, 17, March 10, 1838; 52, March 24, 1838.

[84] *Register*, LIV, 225–26, June 9, 1838; 241–42, June 16, 1838; LV, 189–92, November 17, 1838; 199–204, November 24, 1838; 279–81, December 29, 1838.

icle, and Warrentown *Jeffersonian* were quoted in one number criticizing American attempts to invade Canada.[85]

During 1839 and 1840 the news spotlight of British-American relations swung back to the Maine–New Brunswick sector where the warlike preparations of Maine for the threatened Aroostook War engaged the attention of English and American executive and diplomatic officials. In the closing months of William Odgen Niles' editorship, the *Register* printed a great deal of news and editorial comment on the dispute from English, Canadian, and American newspapers. This included the period of the Forsyth-Fox memorandum and the agreement finally arrived at between Governor John Fairfield of Maine and Sir John Harvey, lieutenant governor of New Brunswick, in the negotiations conducted by General Winfield Scott. Newspapers from London, New York, Boston, Maine, and Nova Scotia were quoted.[86]

The *Register*, in expressing its confidence that the question would be settled amicably, uttered a note of warning to Great Britain that nothing could be "more certain than that in case of a rupture between the two countries, the Canadas would throw off their allegiance and act with the United States against Great Britain as a common enemy.[87] A month later, however, it adopted a much more conciliatory tone in an editorial congratulating its readers upon the pacific aspect of the boundary question and praising General Scott for bringing about the agreement between Maine and New Brunswick. A hiatus of nearly a year concerning the boundary dispute in the *Register*'s columns was ended by the publication in the early months of 1840 of much of the correspondence between British and Canadian officials on the one side and Americans on the other.[88]

The year 1841 saw the equilibrium of Anglo-American relations jarred by the idle boast of a drunken Canadian in a New York tavern. Alexander McLeod's claim that he had killed

[85] *Register*, LV, 257, December 22, 1838.

[86] *Register*, LV, 289, January 5, 1839; 401, 402–403, February 23, 1839; LVI, 1–2, 16, March 2, 1839; 17–18, March 9, 1839; 33–35, March 16, 1839; 49–50, March 23, 1839; 70–72, March 30, 1839; 83–84, April 6, 1839.

[87] *Register*, LVI, 1, March 2, 1839.

[88] *Register*, LVI, 81, April 6, 1839; LVII, 389–91, February 15, 1840; 401–402, February 22, 1840; LVIII, 67–69, April 4, 1840; 273–74, July 4, 1840.

Amos Durfee on the *Caroline* threatened international amity and the relations between the national and state governments within the United States. The *Register* covered the case amply and efficiently from the arrest to the comments of the English newspapers on the acquittal. This coverage, which extended over eleven months, included the printing of much of the diplomatic correspondence on the case, rather full accounts of the involved legal moves made preceding the trial, Congressional and Parliamentary debates, and a brief summary on the trial itself. Quite correctly, the *Register* made no comment on the pending case, but at its conclusion expressed its gratification that the "long agony" was over, settling at least one point of altercation between the United States and Great Britain and avoiding a "vexed question" between the United States government and a state authority.

English newspapers were quoted throughout the period, and at the trial's conclusion, the *Sun, Morning Chronicle,* and *Herald,* were quoted expressing satisfaction at the conduct and result of the trial. The *Times,* however, a correspondent reported, indulged in "brutal sarcasms against the court, the jury, the American people and their government" in a "most malignant article." [89]

With the McLeod case disposed of without a serious diplomatic rift, the Northeastern Boundary question again engaged the *Register*'s attention. Scattered items had been carried during 1841, but the news of the appointment of Lord Ashburton as a special minister to the United States to negotiate on the boundary opened the floodgates of news, editorials, and documents.[90] Jeremiah Hughes, now editor, from the first took a conciliatory attitude in editorials.

Through 1845 and the first half of 1846, another boundary, that of Oregon, was discussed on both sides of the Atlantic. The *Register* faithfully reported English and American attitudes.

[89] *Register,* LIX, 290–91, January 9, 1841; 306–307, January 16, 1841; LX, 36–37, March 20, 1841; 53, March 27, 1841; 132–35, May 1, 1841; 146–47, May 8, 1841; 179, May 22, 1841; 229–32, June 12, 1841; 274–81, July 3, 1841; 307, July 17, 1841; 324–30, July 24, 1841; LXI, 51–52, 60–62, September 25, 1841; 90, October 9, 1841; 104–108, October 16, 1841; 119–25, October 23, 1841; 187–91, November 20, 1841; 193, November 27, 1841.
[90] See Volumes LIX, LX, LXI, LXII, through LXIII.

President Polk's outspoken inaugural declaration of the right of the United States to the Oregon country was sharply condemned by the *Times,* which belligerently declared that ". . . the territory of the Oregon will never be wrested from the British crown, to which it belongs, but by war." [91]

Back in 1825 Niles, who had but little interest in the area west of the Rockies, had expressed the hope that the project to build a chain of military posts to the Pacific and to found a colony near the mouth of the Columbia would be postponed because it was not to the interest of the old or the new states "that a current of population should now be forced beyond the present settled boundaries of the republic." [92] But the stream of emigration continued, and in the early forties the *Register,* under Jeremiah Hughes' direction, carried many articles on Orgeon, including letters from colonists, most of whom were loud in their praises of the Northwest.[93] English reviews carrying articles supporting the British claim to the area were quoted at length. The American side was represented chiefly at this time by Congressional reports with practically no comment until after the election of 1844.[94]

The *Register* consistently opposed war with Great Britain over Oregon, and, after the election of 1844, expressed the hope that the negotiations between the two countries would be resumed in an amicable spirit. It refused to take sides until more time was available for examining documents. The press generally, one may deduce from quotations in the *Register,* regarded a resort to war over the matter as unlikely,[95] but the *Times* on April 5, 1845, deplored the "ill regulated, overbearing, and

[91] *Register,* LXVIII, 1–3, March 8, 1845; 97, April 19, 1845; cf. the *Times,* March 27, 1845, first leader, p. 4.

[92] *Register,* XXIX, 151, November 5, 1825.

[93] *Register,* LVIII, 403, August 29, 1840; LXII, 184–87, May 21, 1842; LXV, 137, October 28, 1843; LXVIII, 130, November 2, 1844.

[94] *Register,* LIII, 342, January 27, 1838; LV, 139–45, October 27, 1838; LVI, 234–39, June 8, 1839; LIX, 338, January 30, 1841; LXIV, 40–42, March 18, 1843, in which is reprinted an article from *Fisher's Colonial Magazine* (London, 1840–1845) for January, 1843; 121–22, April 22, 1843; 345, July 29, 1843; LXV, 104–105, October 14, 1843, quotes the *Edinburgh Review;* 173–75, November 11, 1843, carries a seven-column letter from an American (Peter A. Brown) upholding the United States title to the territory.

[95] *Register,* LXVII, 179, November 23, 1844; LXVIII, 104–105, April 19, 1845, quoting the Albany *Argus.*

aggressive spirit of the American democracy" for not being willing to leave the Oregon question as it was (that is, joint occupation) for fifty years to come. "The Thunderer" pontificated that the pretension of the United States amounted to the "clearest *causa belli* which had ever yet arisen between Great Britain and the American union." In the same tone, the government organ went on to warn the United States that it faced two wars for which it was "very ill-prepared." That this was not merely the editorial effusions of an anti-American leader-writer was indicated in an excerpt from *Willmer & Smith's European Times* of the same date which stated that the *Times* probably reflected the attitude of the government and exercised much control over public opinion in England.[96]

Had Hezekiah Niles been at the editorial desk of the *Register*, its readers certainly would have been treated to one of his acrimonious philippics against England for which he was so well known, but he had been in his grave for six years. Jeremiah Hughes, as has been said, had a friendlier feeling toward the mother country. Printing summaries of the House of Lords and Commons debates, he remarked that the rival claims instead of being negotiated and adjusted by diplomats had been thrown to the legislatures and the people of the two countries, ". . . amongst whom, such questions are very apt, instead of being adjusted, to foment and grow into broils." [97] In one number, editorials from the following newspapers showed varying shades of opinion: New York *Evening Post,* Washington *Union,* New York *News,* Charleston *Mercury, Madisonian,* Baltimore *American,* New York *Journal of Commerce, Pennsylvanian,* and from England and Ireland, the *Times,* the London *Morning Post,* and the *Nation* of Dublin.[98]

Newspapers quoted favoring arbitration or some other type of amicable adjustment of the territorial dispute included the New York *Commercial Advertiser,* Charleston *Courier,* the *National Intelligencer,* and the *Examiner,* the *Standard,* and

96 *Register,* LXVIII, 114–15, April 26, 1845, quoting the *Times,* April 5, 1845; cf. the *Times,* April 5, 1845, which carried much of the Oregon debate on p. 2 and a leader on p. 6.
97 *Register,* LXVIII, 113, April 26, 1845.
98 *Register,* LXVIII, 184–85, May 24, 1845.

the *Times,* all of London.[99] A three-page article from the *National Intelligencer,* reviewing the history of the Oregon negotiation of 1823–1824, aided in rounding out the background of the reader. From the same paper was reprinted a seventeen-page article in four installments which had been condensed from a six-hundred-page book describing the two expeditions of John C. Frémont to the Rockies in 1842 and to northern California and Oregon in 1844.[100]

During the last two months of 1845 the editorial headline "IS WAR BREWING? Are We Ready?" appeared in several numbers on articles directed at the administration for exposing the country to danger of war without being prepared for it, rather than at England. In fact, the *Register* bitterly opposed a war, and used factual material on England's military and naval strength, ridicule of the value of the territory in question, and ironical allusions to the expansionist dreams of the territory grabbers in many editorials. The Washington *Union* demanded all of Oregon or none.[101] Representative daily newspaper editorials and Daniel Webster's Faneuil Hall speech of November 7 advocating coolness were quoted in the same number. President Polk's first annual message to Congress on December 2, 1845, occupied nearly six pages in the *Register,* and the editor used space on the first and last pages of the same number to comment on it.[102]

Nearly thirteen of the sixteen pages of the December 27, 1845, number were given over to the Pakenham-Calhoun and Pakenham-Buchanan correspondence on the Oregon dispute. In the same number it was stated that it was apparent that neither the government nor the people in the United States were considering a war with England, which the *Register* felt would be "absolutely preposterous." During the first four months of 1846 while both houses of Congress debated the question at length before finally passing on April 23

[99] *Register,* LXVIII, 205–207, May 31, 1845; 236–39, June 14, 1845.

[100] *Register,* LXVIII, 364–67, August 9, 1845; LXIX, 26–31, September 13, 1845; 43–47, September 20, 1845; 61–63, September 27, 1845; 75–79, October 4, 1845.

[101] *Register,* LXIX, 148–50, 160, November 8, 1845; 187–88, November 22, 1845; 228, December 13, 1845.

[102] *Register,* LXIX, 164–68, November 15, 1845; 217–23, December 6, 1845.

the joint resolution authorizing the President to terminate the joint-occupancy treaty, every number of the *Register* contained editorial material pertaining to the question. Using a standing headline, "ARE WE TO HAVE WAR OR PEACE?" which was later alternated between "SHALL WE HAVE WAR, OR PEACE?" and "SHALL WE HAVE PEACE OR WAR?" Hughes utilized column after column to discuss the problem from all angles.[103]

Newspaper articles from Washington letter writers, as the correspondents then were called, and editorial comments on their rumors indicated strongly the feeling that the forty-ninth parallel was the sensible solution to the dispute. The line-up in Congress with Senators Lewis Cass of Michigan, William Allen of Ohio, Edward A. Hannegan of Indiana, and Sidney Breese of Illinois leading the "Fifty-four Forty" war faction, and John C. Calhoun the group in favor of the forty-ninth degree, if offered by Great Britain, was reviewed in detail. Only a diplomatic point of honor as to which country should make the first advance seemed to stand in the way of ultimate solution, and this, the *Register* asserted, was "too small an affair for comment, amongst men of common sense." [104] The *Register* consistently campaigned for peace, but at the same time criticized the Polk administration for taking no steps to prepare for war.[105]

The outbreak of the Mexican War naturally pre-empted space in the *Register* for several weeks, but the main speeches in the debate on Oregon were printed, even after the treaty had been submitted to the Senate and ratified. The final steps in this long dispute, the Senate approval of Pakenham's proposal on June 12, and the ratification of the treaty on June 16, were carried in detail in the *Register* through the summer and fall of 1846.[106]

Thus, over a period of eighteen months, the *Register* presented a complete picture of the Oregon question, including all shades of English and American editorial opinion, at the

103 *Register*, LXIX, 284, January 3, 1846, to LXX, 115, April 25, 1846.

104 *Register*, LXX, 17, March 14, 1846; 33, March 21, 1846.

105 *Register*, LXX, 49–50, March 28, 1846; 209, June 6, 1846.

106 *Register*, LXX, 208, May 30, 1846; 218–23, June 6, 1846; 225, 235–39, June 13, 1846; 241, June 20, 1846; 257, June 27, 1846; 314–19, July 18, 1846; 322, July 25, 1846; 374–78, August 15, 1846; 389–94, August 22, 1846; LXXI, 106–11, October 17, 1846.

same time consistently maintaining an editorial policy which favored an amicable adjustment of the dispute. The picture of Anglo-American relations that the reader of the *Register* from 1811 to 1849 carries away with him is a clear, but not necessarily consistent, one. The periodical's attitude was determined by its editor-owners. Hezekiah Niles did not like England, and he permitted this dislike to color nearly everything he printed about that country, in spite of a well-deserved reputation for impartiality in regard to the American political scene. William Ogden Niles expressed but few opinions, but he reprinted the editorial opinions of others. Jeremiah Hughes brought to the periodical a feeling of friendliness toward England which caused him to urge strongly the adjustment of disputes with that country without a resort to war. Anglo-American relations were friendlier at mid-century than they were in the earlier decades, and the *Register,* consciously or not, may have reflected the public opinion in the United States toward the mother country.

Chapter 8

Latin America

ANOTHER field of international relations to which the *Register* devoted a great deal of space and on which it took a well-defined editorial position was that relating to the colonies of Spain in the Western Hemisphere, and, in fact, to the entire area, whether called Latin America or Hispanic America, including Brazil and the islands in the Caribbean.

Thousands of news items, many of them containing expressions of editorial opinion; hundreds of documents, including manifestoes, proclamations, decrees, treaties, and diplomatic correspondence; and numbers of informative articles were printed about the nations in South America and the southern portion of the North American continent.

From the first page of the second issue of the periodical, which carried the "Declaration of Rights by the People of Venezuela," to the last number, in which several Mexican news items were printed, few copies appeared without some reference to the countries below the Rio Grande. Throughout the first decade of the *Register*'s career, the amount of material about Mexico, Central America, and South America is especially noticeable, as is the frequent expression of editorial opinion.

Editorialized news items, of which the following is a good example, may be found time and again: "We have cheering intelligence from *South America*. The particulars are not stated, but the following are given as facts—*Montevideo* was closely besieged by the patriot army May 20—the cause of liberty is well sustained in the provinces of *Buenos Ayres*—the patriotism of *Chili* is alert and active—*Peru* is decidedly opposed to royalty. In the provinces of *Caracas*, the flame of liberty burns with renewed vigor; the greater part of the country appears to be in the hands of the whigs—the capital city and port of Laguira, we learn, have fallen before them." [1]

In 1815 Hezekiah Niles wrote that the people of Cartagena were "full of enthusiasm, and panting to punish the slaves sent to deprive them of their freedom." In the same article, he commented on American indifference to the revolutionary struggles in the south, saying:

It is astonishing how indifferent the great body of the people of the United States appear as to the events in these extensive regions. This may partly arise from our ignorance of their real situation and of what is going on. It is strange that the feelings of the nation should have been so excited for the "deliverance" of old *Spain* from Boneparte, when so little interest is excited for the *real* deliverance of the new world from the dominion of a knave, fool and bigot. The freedom of *Mexico* alone, is indeed, fifty times more important to the United States than the rescue of Spain from the hands of Napoleon was, in a commercial point of view, independent of those desires which, as republicans, we ought to have for its emancipation; and I seriously wish that circumstances were such that we could give them a helping hand. *Perish the "legitimates," live the people, say I—Up republics; down royalty.* [2]

When Luis de Onís, minister from Spain, demanded prosecution of "insurgents and incendiaries" who were raising troops in the United States to aid the South American rebels and protested against the admission to United States ports of ships from Cartagena, Buenos Aires, and other revolutionary ports, Niles styled Spain's pretensions as "preposterous," calling Onís' letters "a farrago of nonsense." [3]

The revolutionary groups were referred to as "patriots" in most news stories and editorials, while the royalist forces were variously called "finished villains," "tory priests," and "murderers." He compared the South American struggle with that of the North American colonies against England, but predicted that it would be a long one. He did not encourage Americans to join the revolutionary forces, unless they were willing to renounce their United States citizenship, pointing out that it was

[1] *Register*, V, 32, September 11, 1813.
[2] *Register*, IX, 170, November 4, 1815.
[3] *Register*, IX, 392–97, February 3, 1816.

"the natural as well as the national law" that one so doing relinquished all claims on his country for protection.[4]

When Henry Clay on March 24, 1818, after a winter of debate on neutrality regarding the South American nations, offered an amendment to the appropriation bill providing funds for the outfit and salary of a minister to Buenos Aires, the *Register* devoted eight and one-half pages to his speech, saying that it would "command attention, even from those who may not approve of the proposition." Two weeks later an equal amount of space was given to the speech of John Forsyth, of Georgia, opposing the plan.[5] That fall, after months of unofficial approval through brief sentences in news items and headlines, Niles wrote an editorial unequivocally favoring recognition of the United Provinces of Rio de la Plata, declaring that he doubted if by so doing the United States would incur the enmity of any great power in Europe.[6]

When recognition was finally recommended by Monroe on March 8, 1822, Niles carried the message and an editorial, expressing hope that the recognition would be granted that "we may regain the ground that we have lost, by a rather *too* neutral conduct." He mentioned rumors of the dissatisfaction of Russia, Great Britain, Spain, and Portugal at the recommendation, but was doubtful as to their accuracy.[7] Volumes covering 1818 to 1822 carried a great deal of news, documentary, and editorial material on South America and the revolution in Spain, including forty pages of a supplement in 1819 on Joel R. Poinsett's report on South America and official correspondence.[8] The surrender of Chiloé, bringing "extinction of the Spanish power on the continent of America," was commented on in 1826, and an address of John Williams, chargé d'affaires in Central America, to Don Manuel José Arce, president of that nation, was printed, as was

---

[4] *Register*, IX, 364, January 20, 1816; XII, 34, March 15, 1817; 168–69, May 3, 1817; 174, May 10, 1817; XIII, 117, October 18, 1817; 143, October 25, 1817; XIV, 132, April 18, 1818; XV, 78–79, September 26, 1818; XVI, 206, May 15, 1819; XX, 126, April 21, 1821.

[5] *Register*, XIV, 121–30, April 18, 1818; 156–65, May 2, 1818.

[6] *Register*, XV, 129, October 24, 1818.

[7] *Register*, XXII, 33, March 16, 1822.

[8] *Register*, XVI, Supplement, 46–85.

a treaty between that federation and the United States signed on December 5, 1825, by H. Clay and Antonio José Cañas.[9] Venezuela and New Granada, which united to form Colombia, probably received more space than any other section of the continent, chiefly because of the involved and long-drawn-out bloody conflicts waged there between royalist and revolutionary forces. A manifesto of the general congress of Venezuela was printed in 1811.[10] From then through 1822, when the constitution officially adopted at Cúcuta, August 30, 1821, was printed,[11] manifestoes, protests, decrees, and speeches gave an official picture of the new nation's activities.[12] Statistical articles, friendly editorial comments on the prohibition of the slave trade, and a story on the arrival of a group of Colombian youths in the United States to be educated indicated the feeling toward the neighbor nation. The description of the arrival in Colombia of Richard Clough Anderson, first United States minister to the republic, was translated from a Bogotá newspaper, and the treaty negotiated by him, "the first of its kind concluded with the new states of the south," was printed with editorial approval.[13]

News from the United Provinces of Rio de la Plata probably came next in volume. An informational article on the United Provinces covering two and one-half pages was printed in 1813.[14] Two years later Niles expressed satisfaction that "Royalty and toryism" were quite under foot. He printed a letter from Buenos Aires which thanked him for being "the only American editor who has deemed the important changes operating in this country worthy a marked attention," but Niles wrote that justice compelled him to decline the compliment because several other editors were interested, adding, ". . . thousands of our citizens

---

[9] *Register*, XXX, 156–57, April 29, 1826; 439–40, August 19, 1826; XXXI, 172–76, November 11, 1826.

[10] *Register*, I, 105–10, October 19, 1811; 121–25, October 26, 1811.

[11] *Register*, XXII, 229–31, June 8, 1822.

[12] *Register*, XX, 8–10, March 3, 1821; XXIII, 263–64, December 28, 1822; XXIV, 46–48, March 22, 1823; 245–47, June 21, 1823.

[13] *Register*, XXI, 274, December 29, 1821; XXIV, 209, June 7, 1823; 253, June 21, 1823; XXVI, 23–24, March 13, 1824; XXVIII, 209, June 4, 1825; 241, 252–56, June 18, 1825.

[14] *Register*, V, 81–83, October 2, 1813.

. . . regret that the world is so circumstanced at present, as to make it imprudent and improper for us to give that open and honest aid, which political feeling and commercial interest so powerfully plead for." [15]

News stories through the next few years were concerned chiefly with the rapid changes in government in the provinces, especially Buenos Aires.[16] The preliminary convention of peace between representatives of Buenos Aires and of Spain signed on July 4, 1823, was printed on September 13. Articles had been printed from time to time giving geographical and commercial information about the confederation, thus giving interested Americans an opportunity to learn about a little-known region.[17]

As might be expected, Niles' attitude toward Brazil at no time reflected the enthusiasm that he expressed regarding the fortunes of the Spanish-American republics. He reprinted without comment, from the *National Intelligencer*, the proclamation of December 16, 1815, proclaiming Brazil a kingdom,[18] and over the period of the next five years printed frequent items that the country was ripe for revolt, extremely unsettled, and in a confused state. When the Portuguese Cortes passed a resolution suggesting that the prince regent travel in Europe to visit the principal courts in order to complete his political education, Niles said the United States would have been a much better place to send him; "for, here, he would learn the true principles of liberty, and witness the true science of government in full operation." [19] The manifesto of the prince regent dated August 1, 1822, which preceded the declaration of independence from Portugal the following month, was printed, as were other developments.[20]

The treaty of peace and alliance signed August 29, 1825, between Portugal and Brazil, in which the former recognized the

15 *Register*, IX, 260, December 9, 1815; 285, December 23, 1815.

16 *Register*, XVII, 429, February 19, 1820; XVIII, 241, June 3, 1820; XIX, 46–47, September 16, 1820; 140, October 28, 1820.

17 *Register*, XV, 183–84, November 7, 1818; XXIX, 37, September 17, 1825.

18 *Register*, X, 72–73, March 30, 1816.

19 *Register*, XXII, 269–70, June 22, 1822.

20 *Register*, XXIII, 124–27, October 26, 1822; 142–44, November 2, 1822; cf. William Spence Robertson, *Hispanic-American Relations with the United States* (New York, 1923), 24.

complete independence of its former colony and sister monarchy, was carried by the *Register* that fall.[21]

Coverage of other South American countries can only be touched upon. News from Chile included an account of the arrival of Joel Roberts Poinsett at Santiago in 1811, and his reception there, biographical sketches of José San Martín and Bernardo O'Higgins, and many of their decrees and proclamations, the replacing of the latter's autocratic government by a junta, and the reception of the first United States minister to the country. Many miscellaneous items on Peru preceded the exultant editorial following the Battle of Ayacucho, the news of which Niles wrote "will warm the heart of every friend of liberty and the rights of man." This news was chiefly in the form of official army orders and correspondence from General Antonio José de Sucre to Simón Bolívar and a proclamation by the latter.[22]

Naturally many of the news items in the decades from 1811 to 1831 carried mention of Bolívar, the Liberator, the number referring to his activities being noticeably greater after 1816 when he returned to Venezuela to renew his fight against the royalists.[23] He was compared with Washington in 1821, and a quotation from his speech after being made president of Colombia caused Niles to write that every day he rose in the estimation of those who heard about him. Bolívar was quoted as saying, "A man like me, is a dangerous citizen in a popular government—is a direct menace to the national sovereignty. I wish to become a citizen, in order to be free, and that all may be so too. I prefer the title of *citizen* to that of *liberator*—because this emanates from war, and that from the laws. Exchange, sir, all my honors for that of a *good* citizen."[24]

[21] *Register*, XXIX, 174–75, November 12, 1825.

[22] *Register*, II, 327, 335, July 18, 1812; IV, 376, August 7, 1813; VII, 285, December 31, 1814; XIV, 113–16, April 11, 1818; 384–87, August 1, 1818; 437, August 22, 1818; XVI, 335, July 10, 1819; XXIV, 205–206, May 31, 1823; XXVI, 398, August 14, 1824; XXVIII, 1, 6–8, March 5, 1825; 156–58, May 7, 1825, are typical.

[23] Typical of many articles to be found in the *Register* are X, 367–68, July 27, 1816; 432, August 24, 1816; XI, 32, September 7, 1816; 380, February 1, 1817; XII, 78, March 29, 1817; XIV, 325–27, July 4, 1818; XVI, 128, April 10, 1819; XVII, 94–95, October 9, 1819; 174, November 13, 1819; XVIII, 398, July 29, 1820.

[24] *Register*, XXI, 143–44, October 27, 1821; 223, December 1, 1821; 257, December 22, 1821; 290, January 5, 1822.

The difficulties among and within the newly formed nations of South America which seemed to make necessary the continued use of military force by the leaders brought the first deviation from the paeans of praise the *Register* had printed about the Liberator. In 1828 Niles wrote:

> Though unwilling to believe all that we hear, we feel compelled to apprehend that this distinguished leader has lost all claims to the title once so liberally bestowed upon him—"*the Washington of the south.*" Indeed, we begin to think as if nature had thrown the mould away "in which the father of his country was formed." Bolivar, lately re-invested with extraordinary powers, appears to exercise them with extraordinary force. Distinguished men have been imprisoned without charge of offences, and it seems as thought criminal to inquire why they were arrested. A late letter says, "Every thing is conducted at the point of the bayonet." Many persons are put to death at the discretion of military commanders, and without much ceremony. This is a fearful state of things.[25]

From a journalist's point of view, the source of the *Register's* news from South America before the days of cable and radio communication is of interest. Much of it came from newspapers in the United States which, in the case of South America, translated articles from the Spanish-language newspapers. The *Aurora*, Baltimore *American,* Boston *Daily Advertiser,* and Boston *Courier* supplied articles which Niles used, in addition to those from the *National Intelligencer* and the New York dailies. Among the southern newspapers which the *Register* apparently received direct were the *Gazeta, El Censor,* and *La Prensa Argentina,* of Buenos Aires; Puerto Rico *Gazette,* and Bogotá *Constitucional.*[26]

In addition to the London newspapers, the use of which has been referred to, English-language newspapers at Kingston, Jamaica, and St. Thomas now and then supplied news from South America.[27] Letters received by Hezekiah Niles from subscribers, friends, and acquaintances and those printed first in

---

[25] *Register*, XXXIV, 100, April 5, 1828.

[26] *Register*, XI, 46–47, September 14, 1816; XIII, 12–13, August 30, 1817; 61–62, September 20, 1817; XXII, 325, July 20, 1822; XXIV, 303–304, July 12, 1823; XXIX, 124–25, October 22, 1825; XXX, 354–55, July 15, 1826; XXXII, 384, August 4, 1827.

[27] *Register*, X, 215, May 25, 1816; XXIV, 78–79, April 5, 1823; XXXVIII, 51, March 13, 1830.

other newspapers constituted an important source of information about the South American republics. Mention of intelligence received in letters was frequently made.[28] Late in 1818 several long articles were made up of letters from Henry M. Brackenridge, who accompanied the Rodney-Graham-Bland mission as secretary.[29] In 1823 Niles printed letters from his friend, Colonel Charles Todd, special agent sent from Washington to Bogotá, preceding recognition of Colombia.[30] Coffeehouse books and the files of newspapers available there in the Exchange Reading Room at Baltimore also furnished news items. Usually the captain bringing the news, and his ship was mentioned as well as the coffeehouse, as for example in 1816 when the *Coquette* brought news to the Merchants Coffee House on February 8, from Santa Marta, of the capture of Santa Fe by the royalists. As late as 1841, the brig *Susan,* Captain Laudeman, from Montevideo, brought a number of South American papers and the *British Packet* from Buenos Aires. News from ship captains was made public at many ports, Baltimore, New York, and Salem being frequently mentioned.[31]

The first damper on Niles' enthusiasm for the South American patriots came from their privateering activities, which he felt often were "mere acts of *piracy*." [32] In 1819 he wrote:

We yield to no one in our devotion to the cause of liberty in South America. The patriot cause has been as our own, since its beginning. But it is now disgraced by numerous vessels, bearing independent flags, whose *sole* purpose is plunder. The seas teem with sheer pirates, robbing all persons that they think they can do with safety to themselves. . . . Let us not, however, impute these things to the patriots of South America, whose local governments are ignorant even of the names of many of the cruisers sailing under their flags! . . . They are most commonly under the flag of Artigas; and indeed, it does not

28 *Register*, XIV, 261–64, June 13, 1818; 288–89, June 20, 1818.
29 *Register*, XV, 185, 188–90, November 14, 1818; 202–205, November 21, 1818.
30 *Register*, XXIV, 49, March 29, 1823, the letter being dated "Bagota" January 18; other articles based on letters, XIV, 361–64, July 25, 1818; 430–32, August 22, 1818; XV, 166–67, November 7, 1818; XVII, 158–59, November 6, 1819; XXII, 309, July 13, 1822; XXX, 251–52, June 10, 1826.
31 *Register*, IX, 402, February 10, 1816; X, 112, April 13, 1816; XIII, 95, October 4, 1817; XIV, 209–11, May 23, 1818; XVI, 256, June 5, 1819; LX, 33, March 20, 1841.
32 *Register*, XV, 89, October 3, 1818.

appear now that the flag can be regarded as any thing more than that of mere *pirates*.[33]

Niles was sufficiently versed in the problems of statecraft not to expect perfection in the operation of the new republics, his tolerance being well expressed in the following excerpt from a long editorial concerning troubles in Chile in 1825:

We must not expect that a people, so long capriciously governed and enslaved as were those of Mexico and South America should, (with the mere emancipation of themselves and their country from the dominion of royal and priestly authorities so abominable as those of Spain), suddenly enter upon and pursue that steadiness of course and liberality in all things, which distinguished those of the more enlightened, and more fortunate, colonies, which now compose the United States, wherein the principles of liberty and the rights of man, were, perhaps, quite as well understood before the revolution as since. . . . A generation, perhaps, must pass away before those who have been accustomed to see and feel power without regard to right, can be made fully sensible of what is a government of the laws.[34]

Doubt began to appear in his writing, however, at the adoption of the constitution of Bolivia which created "Bolivar dictator—absolute sovereign!" Although two months later he said he had not seen any disposition on the part of the Liberator "to act otherwise than becomes a patriot." He felt that republican principles were but little understood when the state of a people depended so much on the conduct of one man, and he editorially regretted "the lust for power and love of office, and the predominance of the military spirit and authority, together with a want of knowledge as to what are civil rights . . ." evident in all the new states.[35]

The reader of the *Register* over the late twenties may trace the growing doubt in Niles' mind as to the ability of the South Americans to govern themselves. On November 15, 1828, he wrote: "The suppression of one insurrectionary movement has been only the precursor to another, more destructive of the

[33] *Register*, XVI, 112, April 3, 1819.

[34] *Register*, XXIX, 104–105, October 15, 1825.

[35] *Register*, XXXI, 242, December 16, 1826; 369, February 10, 1827; XXXII, 99, April 7, 1827; 161, May 5, 1827.

principles of good order, leaving us in doubt whether the country is regulated by laws, or one general scene of anarchy and confusion, filled with factions, each distrusting the other and anxious to advance an individual interest."

He put his finger on at least one of the main causes for the frequent conspiracies and revolutions when, discussing the latest flare-up between Peru and Colombia, he wrote: "We have lost much of the fond hope we entertained of the establishment of the new southern republics—and are satisfied that, for the preservation of free governments, a much greater degree of intelligence in the people is necessary, than the inhabitants thereof possess." [36]

This feeling of disappointment was succeeded by one of utter discouragement, and through the next few years he voiced bitter criticism of the military and religious leaders time and again. The following typical excerpts show:

The curse of *general-ism* and of *priestcraft* still bears heavily on Mexico and Peru, and, indeed, on all the new *republics* of the south.

* * *

There is no just hope of permanent peace and safety, in any of these republics, until the generals and priests are rendered severely subject to the civil law.[37]

"Republics!" Aye, republics in name, but despotism in fact—the prey of unprincipled soldiers and sordid and ambitious priests and politicians. . . .[38]

The state [sic] of *Mexico, Peru,* &c. are about as unpropitious as their worst enemies can desire that they should be. We are forced to confess our belief—that the inhabitants of them are incapable of self-government, and must have a *master.*[39]

In the quarter of a century of his editorship, Niles changed his attitude toward the South American states from eager enthusiasm, willing to overlook errors in judgment and procedure, to dispirited disillusionment, based soundly enough on a keen

[36] *Register,* XXXV, 213, November 29, 1828.
[37] *Register,* XLVI, 365–66, July 26, 1834.
[38] *Register,* XLVII, 379, January 31, 1835.
[39] *Register,* XLVIII, 116, April 18, 1835.

observation of the reasons back of the repeated revolutions in the republics.

His editorial reactions toward Mexico and its military chieftains followed an almost identical course during the same period. In spite of his enthusiasm for the cause of independence, he upheld President Madison's neutrality proclamation of September 1, 1815.[40]

Of a practical turn of mind, he saw material as well as spiritual benefits as a resultant of Mexican independence, writing:

> Where is the republican that does not sigh for the emancipation of Mexico? Who that is free, will deny the blessing to his brother, or be indifferent of his struggles to win it of tyranny? Who is there in the United States, merchant or manufacturer, planter or artizan, that would not be benefited by the liberation of this great empire from Spain, and in its exaltation to the rank of a sovereign and independent state? The advancement of republican principles, as well as of the commercial interests of our country, are alike engaged on the side of the *patriots* of Spanish America, whose success would open a source of trade to us more important than any we have with the old world. In the present state of nations, policy, perhaps, may require the government of the United States to be neutral on this great question, but it is impossible to divest the people of their wishes for the prosperity of the patriots.[41]

The tenth volume of the *Register,* published in 1816, bore the following dedication on its title page: "To the Patriots of Mexico and South America, contending for liberty and independence, and to all others struggling to obtain civil and religious freedom: The editor dedicates this volume of the Weekly Register. Imploring for them—Washingtons in the field, Franklins in the cabinet, and Reeds in their deliberative assemblies— The Happiest Unions of valor with discretion; sagacity with honesty; and fidelity with disinterestedness." [42]

The first considerable cloud to darken the enthusiasm of the *Register*'s editor for Mexico was formed by the setting up of the short-lived empire of Augustín de Iturbide in 1822. Niles left no doubt as to his feeling toward the form of government,

---

40 *Register,* IX, 33, September 16, 1815.
41 *Register,* IX, 69–70, September 30, 1815.
42 *Register,* X, reverse of title page.

writing that "It prostrates every hope that we entertained of his republican principles." [43] On May 10, 1823, he told of the abdication on March 19 of Emperor Augustín, saying that his "former tyranny and present pusillanimity has [sic] disgusted the Mexicans." He guessed incorrectly that Iturbide would not be allowed to leave the country.

The consideration by Mexico of a constitution for a federal republic of sovereign and independent states failed to arouse Niles' enthusiasm because of the provision establishing the Roman Catholic religion.[44]

Niles was distrustful of a military government and on October 1, 1831, he wrote, "Let the generals become farmers, and manufacturers, and all will be well." A year later he asserted, "There will not be peace and safety in the south until the *generals* are in a state of submission to the laws, and the arbitrary spirit of the sword given up to the decisions of the legislative and judicial authorities, ordained by the people." [45] On September 6, 1834, he expressed the fear that Santa Anna was "steadily marching to a throne," and a month later described the "curse of heroism" which, he felt, held Mexico in its grip. He went on to pay his respects to Santa Anna in the following words: "It now appears, that *general* Santa Anna, late one of the loudest bawlers for liberty and now president of the miscalled republic, is in the exercise of power which a constitutional *king* would not venture upon. He has rallied round him an army of priests—a great army of leeches, shouting for the preservation of 'our holy religion' that they may fleece their flocks!—and their miserable dupes, an ignorant people, bellow out, 'down with the heretics!' " [46]

The revolutions of 1835 plunged Niles into the depths of despair. He reiterated his condemnation of the military chieftains and, before laying down his pen, took a final fling at the state religion with, "This is a *beautiful* republic—with an established religion, and government priests." [47]

Niles' strong opposition to the transference of Cuba to Eng-

43 *Register*, XXII, 308, July 13, 1822.
44 *Register*, XXV, 295, January 10, 1824.
45 *Register*, XLIII, 4, September 1, 1832.
46 *Register*, XLVII, 83, October 11, 1834.
47 *Register*, XLVIII, 149, May 2, 1835; 236, June 6, 1835.

land or to any other strong power has been gone into at some length in the preceding chapter. Niles reported an expected revolution in Cuba in 1815, and a year later declared that such an event would be a "grand affair." [48] From 1821 through 1826 there were frequent references in the *Register* to moves toward independence, and Niles emphasized, as has been pointed out in the Anglo-American chapter, the island's strategic position and its importance to the United States in connection with trade. Never did Hezekiah Niles urge, or even favor, Cuba's annexation to the United States, but in next to the last issue, edited by George Beatty, an article was reprinted from the New Orleans *Bulletin* asserting that the "acquisition of Cuba" was " 'Manifest destiny.' " [49]

The relations of the United States and Spain, centering around the Floridas, served as a subject for many an article from 1817 through 1821. Niles had little use for Luis de Onís, Spanish minister to the United States, calling him in 1816 an "arrant fool . . . probably the puppet of a knave." [50] On September 6, 1817, he told of rumors afloat concerning negotiations over the Floridas, and four months later, in an editorial blaming the Florida Indian wars on the British agents there, predicted that one of the most interesting events of the new year would be the possession of the Floridas, "by treaty or by force." [51] The cession of the Floridas occasioned an editorial of one and one-half columns in which he semifacetiously said that General Jackson had acted as a powerful mediator in bringing the long negotiations to a close. He saw that some might object to the determination of the Sabine as the western boundary in Texas, but declared, "Our country is large enough at present!" He was warm in his praise of the settlement of three such questions as the cession of Florida, the settlement of the western boundary, and the adjustment of claims of United States citizens against Spain in one treaty, in summation printing an editorial from the *National Intelligencer*.[52]

During the two-year period of negotiation before Spain rati-

48 *Register*, VIII, 192, May 13, 1815; XI, 207, November 23, 1816.
49 *Register*, LXXVI, 143, September 21, 1849.
50 Niles to Darlington, February 5, 1816, Darlington MSS, Library of Congress.
51 *Register*, XIII, 298, January 3, 1818.
52 *Register*, XVI, 3–4, February 27, 1819.

fied the treaty, the *Register* did not advocate war with Spain over the issue. Niles printed much news and comment through 1819 and 1820, but he did not favor Monroe's suggestion in his December, 1819, message to Congress that the provisions of the treaty be carried into effect and strongly opposed the recommendation of the House foreign-relations committee that the executive be given authorization to occupy the Floridas.[53] He asked whether the United States would risk starting a general European war merely to get hold of the Floridas, "a barren sovereignty," a few months earlier than they would get the area without such precipitate action. He continued: "Again we say, let us wait. We hazard nothing for honor nor interest by a little longer delay, but may risk much by precipitating ourselves into a contest in times like these."[54]

While the treaty was pending, Niles took the opportunity to ridicule the pretensions to Texas of those expansionists in the United States who opposed the treaty on the ground that the country was giving up territory it had obtained by the Louisiana Purchase. He said it would be no more harmful to the nation to give up an entire state to a foreign power than to extend our territorial limits "equal to the wishes of some." He concluded: "Indeed, we have land enough—as great a variety of soil and climate, and as great a diversity of *interests* and *opinions*, too, perhaps, as can be well governed by *general* laws."[55]

In continuing his attack on the expansionists, he employed irony, with a note of warning:

Texas is a rich country—it will produce sugar, cotton, rice, tobacco and bread stuffs, and is therefore very valuable: so is Mexico, New Grenada, Venezuela, Peru, Brazils, the provinces of the Rio de la Plata, and Chili, for these produce silver and gold and diamonds; let us have the whole—nay, let us contend for that newly discovered country in the high southern latitudes where "seals are as tame as kittens." We want more land—we have not room enough—the sphere of the republic is too contracted!—Let us beware of this over-reaching propensity. Our territory is large enough already. Too large, I sometimes fear, for the well being of the republic.[56]

[53] *Register*, XVII, 305–307, January 8, 1820.
[54] *Register*, XVIII, 46–47, March 18, 1820.
[55] *Register*, XVIII, 273–74, June 17, 1820.
[56] *Register*, XIX, 266–67, December 23, 1820.

Rumors reporting the surrender of Florida to the United States were printed before an article described the actual exchange of flags at St. Augustine on July 10, 1821. Subsequent stories told of the founding of the *Florida Gazette* and contained proclamations by Jackson.[57]

Eight and one-half years before the enunciation of the Monroe Doctrine, the *Register* took a stand for strict neutrality in relation to European affairs.[58] Six years before Monroe sent his message to Congress, Niles wrote: "It is not our business to dictate a form of government for European nations—'let them manage their own affairs in their own way;' but it is a solemn duty on us to oppose the introduction of any set of opinions that are hostile to the stability of our own, under which we have prospered beyond example." [59]

Niles' deep-seated hatred of the monarchical form of government, his antipathy toward Great Britain, and his interest in the South American republics, combined with his belief in the fundamental soundness of democracy and his zeal for representative government, caused him to become an early exponent of a policy of isolation from the intrigues and alliances of the Old World.

Commenting in 1817 on a rumored agreement that Russia was to supply Spain with ships but that Turkey, backed by Great Britain, had refused to permit them passage through the Bosphorus, Niles predicted a complete emancipation of Spanish America as the natural consequence of an Anglo-Russian war. Reiterating his sympathy for Mexico and other countries engaged in revolts against Spain, he said that the United States could have destroyed "every vestige of Spanish supremacy on the American continent, . . . if we had not been apprehensive of embroiling ourselves with the *kings* of other countries, united to defend one another against the people. But we trust that this *unholy* alliance may soon be broken. . . ." [60]

The *Register*, during the decade preceding Monroe's pronouncement, printed a surprisingly large amount of foreign

[57] *Register*, XX, 241, June 16, 1821; 321, July 21, 1821; 337, July 28, 1821; 353, 354, August 4, 1821; 404–405, August 25, 1821.
[58] *Register*, VIII, 177, May 13, 1815.
[59] *Register*, XIII, 65–67, September 27, 1817.
[60] *Register*, XIII, 97–99, October 11, 1817.

news. Following the war period, practically all documents of importance and statements of policy made public on the continent and in England sooner or later found their way into the columns of the book-size periodical, accompanied or followed by editorial and interpretative articles. Niles' unceasing campaign for American independence of the Old World did not cause him to shut his eyes to what was going on there. On the contrary, he used European events, including the various actual and proposed alliances, agreements, and actions of the different nations striving for supremacy as examples of entangling alliances for the United States to avoid.

Early in 1818 Niles printed rumors that Spain would give Minorca and the two Californias to Russia in return for ships, and some months later the report that England had asked for Cuba *"as a set-off against the debt of Spain."* [61] By the next year he was convinced that the British were "playing a deep game, helping Ferdinand on one side, and opposing him on the other." This comment followed accounts of British assistance to South America.[62] On September 25, 1819, he wrote that the London *Globe* intimated that the Holy Alliance had resolved to maintain Ferdinand's sovereignty in South America.

The necessity of keeping Cuba in the possession of Spain, or at least preventing its transfer to a strong power was urged early in 1820. No one in the United States with a sane mind would do anything to help Great Britain gain possession of the island, he declared. "We do not wish to have anything to do with Cuba; but as it has pleased Providence to locate this island in such a commanding position, it is impossible that we should be indifferent to its fate." [63]

Clay's Lexington speech pointing to the possible danger to the United States from the Holy Alliance and calling upon a coalition of the two Americas was printed,[64] as was the speech of the Austrian Emperor to the professors of the Lyceum at Laybach spreading the "detestable doctrines of the *holy* alliance," in which the following two sentences were italicized:

[61] *Register*, XIII, 297, January 3, 1818; XIV, 189, May 9, 1818.
[62] *Register*, XVI, 191–92, May 8, 1819.
[63] *Register*, XVII, 306, January 8, 1820.
[64] *Register*, XX, 301, July 7, 1821.

People are occupied elsewhere with new notions that I cannot approve, and I never shall approve.

I do not want learned men; I want only loyal and good subjects, and it is your part to form them.[65]

The *Register* did nothing to arouse its readers against Russia notwithstanding her claims on the northwest coast of North America.

Niles' indifference to expansion or to Russian aggression, or both, led him to remark late in 1821 that even if Russia made good its claim to the fifty-first degree "we *guess* that there will be a region of country large enough left for us." [66] Correspondence between Pierre de Poletica, Russian minister to the United States, and John Quincy Adams concerning Russia's claims to the fifty-first degree was printed without comment.[67]

Events in Europe and their possible effect upon the United States in 1823 turned the attention of the diplomats, statesmen, and editors of the country toward international relations and the course to be followed by this country in that connection.[68] The *Register* was not silent. The French intervention in Spain was condemned as "an unholy conspiracy of kings," and France's "wantonness" in her "illiberal and unjust proceedings against her neighbor," was pointed to with scorn.[69] Rumors that Spain was ready to transfer Cuba to England in return for aid again arose to plague the editor's peace of mind. The reprinting of the "Treaty of Verona" from the London *Morning Chronicle* was followed by editorials expressing the belief that the Holy Alliance would next turn its attention toward the Western Hemisphere.[70] The *Register,* in August and September of 1823, saw in the activities of the European powers a menace to the prized possessions of freedom of speech and of the press and of trial by jury. The following excerpts indicate that Niles' animus against the alliance was equal to his antagonism against his old enemy England:

[65] *Register*, XX, 354, August 4, 1821.
[66] *Register*, XXI, 278–79, December 29, 1821.
[67] *Register*, XXII, 149–53, May 4, 1822.
[68] For an excellent exposition of the situation, see Tatum, *op. cit.*, 251–78, and earlier chapters.
[69] *Register*, XXIV, 17, March 15, 1823; 33, March 22, 1823.
[70] *Register*, XXIV, 347, August 2, 1823.

If the standard of liberty in Spain is trampled under foot by the holy alliance, as we fear it will be, is it unreasonable to apprehend that we may be called upon to defend *our constitution,* to preserve the right of *habeas* corpus, trial by jury and *the freedom of the press,* at once the offspring and the nurse of freemen! Our "pernicious example of successful rebellion" cannot be forgotten, while "legitimacy" survives and prostrates human right; and the opportunity to punish it, if one should occur, will not be neglected. These suggestions, I believe, are entitled to some weight; and, whether we shall with discretion avoid colisions [*sic*] with foreign powers, or repel their assaults on our liberties as we ought, will materially depend on the wisdom and virtue of the executive power of the United States. And, as this is the *people's* affair, let them think seriously on the matter, and resolve, at least, that they will act for themselves.[71]

The affairs of things in Europe, also, is worthy of much reflection. Though separated by a wide ocean from the old world, we are deeply interested in its concerns. A most important crisis is surely at hand. In the perfection of the schemes of the "holy alliance," we must anticipate the extinction of civil and religious liberty, and no one can believe, that, if Europe is forced back to barbarian darkness, we shall be permitted to retain, undisturbed, the light of reason, the freedom of the press and the common rights of man. It is Britain, only, that can decidedly interfere to arrest this terrible march of despotism, and we know that her people would willingly do it: but it is by no means certain that her government, if not really a party to the crusade against personal liberty and national sovereignty in Spain, does not, at least, more encourage than oppose it . . . It is reasonable to believe that we shall have no small difficulties with the powers of Europe, and that our affairs with them will require the greatest circumspection and care—however loath we are to have any sort of relation with them, unless in regard to commercial affairs. We will not interfere with their political institutions; but can it be expected that they will not interfere with our's?—That they will respect, as rights, in our government and laws, what they proclaim to be at variance with the "repose of the world?" It is not to be expected that they will, if the power to act against us shall not be interrupted by events nearer home.[72]

Niles' approval of the Monroe Doctrine has been discussed in the Anglo-American chapter, as has his qualified acquiescence

---

[71] *Register,* XXIV, 369, August 16, 1823.
[72] *Register,* XXV, 2, September 6, 1823.

in joint action of the United States and Great Britain to prevent any incursion of the European powers into South America. Aftermaths of the declaration of United States policy regarding the Western Hemisphere may be found in the *Register* in the printing of the treaty with Russia, news of England's decision to recognize the South American republics, a renewed discussion of the destiny of Cuba, and Niles' distrust of the spread of English influence in South America.[73]

Polk's vigorous restatement of the Doctrine in his first message to Congress on December 2, 1845, brought the editorial hope that the mission to Mexico had arrived at a lasting peace ". . . before the lecture which President POLK has considered it expedient to read to the potentates of Europe upon 'balance of power,'—shall have had time to operate, either for good or for ill." [74]

In another editorial, still optimistically hoping for an adjustment of differences with Mexico, Hughes, then editor, expressed regret that the President's formal notification of the European powers not to interfere in American affairs had been voiced at such a critical juncture in the Mexican negotiations.[75]

The Panama Congress occupied a surprisingly large amount of space in the *Register* throughout 1826. Early in 1825 Niles heartily approved participation of the United States "if for no other purpose than to shew the interest that we take in the progress and success of liberal institutions in the new world. And the time may come, if the *holy alliance* does not perish of its own corrupt principles, when it will be necessary to rally the free nations of this continent in opposition to the despots of the other, with their herds of slaves." [76]

Not until October 22, 1825, did he print Bolívar's circular letter of December 7, 1824, to the American republics, former Spanish colonies, inviting them to send representatives to an assembly at Panama, but from that time on for more than a year the news, correspondence, and debates in the Congress of the

---

[73] *Register*, XXVI, 362, July 31, 1824; XXVII, 323, January 22, 1825; XXVIII, 2, March 5, 1825; 119, April 23, 1825; 334–36, July 23, 1825; XXXII, 131, April 21, 1827; XXXIII, 35, September 15, 1827.

[74] *Register*, LXIX, 209, December 6, 1845.

[75] *Register*, LXIX, 244, December 20, 1845.

[76] *Register*, XXVIII, 131–32, April 30, 1825.

United States about the Congress made up topics which dominated the columns of the thirtieth and thirty-first volumes of
the *Register*. Three days before John Quincy Adams sent his
first message to Congress, Niles, having already printed several
items on the Panama Congress, strongly urged that the nation
send delegates, mentioning the natural interest of the country
in the establishment of republican principles, the identity of
interests of the republics of the New World as against the Old,
and the commercial benefits to be derived from a good understanding as sufficient reason for taking part.[77]

The early issues of 1826 all carried articles on the Congress
and all except five inches of the sixteen pages of the March 25
number, plus an eight-page supplement, and eleven pages of the
April 1 issue were turned over to the executive proceedings of
the Senate, President Adams' message to the House, a report
from Henry Clay, secretary of state, and a list of the twenty-three
papers accompanying Clay's report, all having to do with the
Panama mission. The next three issues contained at least twenty-
five pages, many of them in small type, of messages and documents concerning the mission. Niles argued that Congress had
no right to instruct the mission which was under the executive
branch of the government and that the legislative branch,
through the Senate, would have the opportunity to reject or
ratify any action taken by the commissioners.[78] Throughout the
summer various articles on the Congress, which adjourned on
July 15, were printed and more details were carried in September and October, 1826.

On the eve of the inauguration of Andrew Jackson, Adams
sent to the Senate a copy of the instructions prepared by Clay
for the American commissioners to the Congress. Daniel Webster had moved the resolution, and the debate in the Senate,
Adams' message, and the accompanying documents, filled some
twenty-five pages in three issues in March, 1829.[79] This political
debate, nearly four years after the meeting of the Congress,
ended the *Register*'s record of this first unsuccessful attempt at
co-operation among American republics.

77 *Register*, XXIX, 211–12, December 3, 1825.
78 *Register*, XXX, 153–55, April 29, 1826.
79 *Register*, XXXVI, 42–48, March 14, 1829; 58–64, March 21, 1829; 69–80, March
28, 1829.

Niles' enthusiasm for the struggle of Mexico and the South American colonies against Spanish rule did not extend to approval of separatist movements such as the one for the independence of Texas. In 1819 he warned the young men of the nation against taking part in the "wild scheme" to revolutionize Texas. From that time to next to the last issue published under his editorship in 1836, which condemned taking part in the Texas War as a "direct violation of international law" and criticized "the organization and equipment of troops within our borders," he stood firm against United States intervention, official or unofficial, in what he regarded as Mexico's internal affairs.[80] In 1819 he printed extracts of the Texan Declaration of Independence, signed by James Long, president of the Supreme Council, but called the scheme a bubble, adding, "It is an affair in which we cannot take sides with the 'patriots.' "[81] The last year of Hezekiah Niles' editorship, September, 1835, through August, 1836, the *Register* carried items relating to Texas nearly every week. Niles opposed the organization of military forces in the United States to aid Texas, asserted that the Texas settlers had expatriated themselves and had no claim upon the United States, and resisted the thought of admitting Texas into the Union.[82] From May 7, 1836, when the President's authorization to General Edmund P. Gaines to use troops along the border was printed, through the next four months, pages were given over to newspaper editorials, official correspondence, and news from the scene of action. Niles wrote that events in Texas were not going "as we would have them," and in July the *Register* asserted that Mexico would have strong grounds for complaint against the infraction of the treaty between her and the United States.[83]

Although there was little, if any, editorial comment in the *Register* from September, 1836, to October, 1839, news regarding Texas, diplomatic discussions with Mexico, and activities of the Lone Star Republic was printed. The recognition of Texas, accomplished on the very eve of Andrew Jackson's re-

Latin America 215

tirement from the presidency, went unnoticed in one issue of the *Register*, and only the news of the appointment of Alcée La Branche, of Louisiana, as chargé d'affaires to Texas, was carried in the next.[84] A brief, unsatisfactory item from the Richmond *Enquirer* about the delay in the reception of the Texas ministers by President Martin Van Buren completed the *Register*'s inadequate coverage of the recognition by the United States of the Lone Star Republic.[85]

The *Register*'s coverage of the Texas annexation controversy from early in 1842 through 1845 was unusually complete.[86] Jeremiah Hughes printed documentary material, including Congressional debates, diplomatic correspondence, and speeches, and he also reprinted a large number of editorials from representative newspapers. In an 1842 issue the following papers were quoted: *National Intelligencer*, Washington *Globe*, Galveston *Advertiser*, Galveston *Civilian*, New Orleans *Bee*, New Orleans *Bulletin*, Fayetteville *North Carolinian*, and Macon *Telegraph*. In 1844 one issue contained quotations from the *Morning Courier and New York Enquirer*, Concordia *Intelligencer* of Louisiana, New York *Tribune*, Georgetown *Advocate*, Washington *Madisonian*, *National Intelligencer*, Washington *Globe*, Richmond *Whig*, New York *Evening Post*, and Philadelphia *Public Ledger*.[87]

The growing tension in diplomatic relations with the Mexican government, especially after the Texas annexation treaty, may be followed in diplomatic correspondence printed in the *Register*. Daniel Webster's correspondence with Powhatan Ellis, United States minister to Mexico, about the killing of members of the Santa Fe expeditions; correspondence between Colonel Waddy Thompson, Ellis' successor, and J. M. Bocanegra, Mexican minister of foreign affairs; Bocanegra's correspondence with Benjamin Green, son of Duff Green, who was acting chargé d'affaires in 1844; and a good deal of the correspondence be-

84 *Register*, LII, 17, March 11, 1837.
85 *Register*, LII, 49, March 25, 1837; President Houston's message of May 5, 1837, to the Texas Congress was printed in LII, 237–38, June 10, 1837, and an account of Alcée La Branche's reception in Texas in LIII, 213–14, December 2, 1837.
86 The reader is referred to Volumes LXI–LXIX for details, only some of the high points and the *Register*'s attitude being discussed here.
87 *Register*, LXVI, 116–19, April 20, 1844.

tween John C. Calhoun, secretary of state from April 1, 1844, to March 6, 1845, and Wilson Shannon, United States minister to Mexico from August, 1844, to March, 1845, and between Shannon and M. C. Rejón, Mexican minister of foreign affairs, filled many of the *Register's* columns.[88]

The sectional and political aspects of the controversy over annexation were fully covered in the *Register* between 1842 and 1844. Speeches, addresses, and letters of John Quincy Adams and letters of Andrew Jackson played no small part in the heated discussion which involved the extension of slavery territory, the old question of boundaries of the Louisiana Purchase, and international relations with Mexico and Great Britain particularly.

In the weeks immediately preceding the submission of the Treaty of Annexation to the Senate by President Tyler on April 22, 1844, the *Register* kept its finger on the pulse of editorial opinion in the nation. Quoting the *National Intelligencer* on the progress of negotiations, Hughes, on March 16, 1844, wrote that up until that minute he had believed rumors of negotiations with Texas "to be a perfect humbug." The next week he quoted the New York *Sun,* New York *Evening Post,* and the *Morning Courier and New York Enquirer,* in addition to the *Intelligencer.* In the April 13 issue the Philadelphia *Public Ledger,* New York *Journal of Commerce,* New Orleans *Picayune,* and *Intelligencer* furnished opinions on the treaty, and in the April 20 number the *Madisonian,* the *Morning Courier and New York Enquirer,* Concordia *Intelligencer,* New York *Tribune,* Georgetown *Advocate,* Washington *Globe,* Richmond *Whig,* New York *Journal of Commerce,* New York *Evening Post,* and Philadelphia *Public Ledger* were used to show the opinions of the nation's editors. The Saturday after the President sent the treaty to the Senate, an item told of the secret session and confidential message, said to be the treaty.[89]

[88] *Register,* LXI, 342–43, January 29, 1842; LXII, 2–3, March 5, 1842; LXVI, 332–35, July 20, 1844; 337, July 27, 1844; LXVII, 230–35, 240, December 14, 1844; 241–42, December 21, 1844; 259–66, December 28, 1844; James Morton Callahan, *American Foreign Policy in Mexican Relations* (New York, 1932), 102–45, covers this period.

[89] *Register,* XLVI, 132–33, April 27, 1844; two weeks earlier he had printed a

The following week the *Register* reprinted from the New York *Evening Post* not only the treaty, but Tyler's message, and nearly a page of abstracts of documents accompanying the treaty. Hughes described the indignation of the Senate at the *Evening Post*'s violation of the injunction of secrecy, but added: "As there is no doubt of the authenticity of these papers, we hesitate not to lay the treaty before our readers—and also a synopsis of the accompanying documents." [90]

The next few issues carried a mass of editorial opinion and Congressional speeches. A week after the Senate's rejection of the treaty on June 8, the 35 to 16 vote was analyzed by states, sections, and parties, and Tyler's reference to a "resort to any other expedient," was mentioned.[91]

When Congress reconvened in the fall after the election, a brief notice of the joint resolutions introduced in the Senate by George McDuffie, of South Carolina, and in the House by Charles J. Ingersoll, of Pennsylvania, authorizing the annexation of Texas was printed.[92] From that time through the issue of May 3, 1845, some two months after President Tyler had signed the resolution, the debate on the question occupied more space than any other question in the *Register*.

Through the spring and early summer of 1845 nearly every issue carried extracts from American, Texan, and Mexican newspapers on the probable action to be taken by the Texas Congress in its effect on the three nations. The last issue of the year carried the account of the passage by the American Congress of the bill admitting Texas as the twenty-eighth state of the Union.[93]

Throughout this period the *Register* by no means acted only as a purveyor of news and a reflector of the opinions of other papers. It condemned President Tyler for attempting to usurp

---

rumor story from the *Madisonian* that the treaty had been signed and would soon be submitted to the Senate, LXVI, 107–108, April 13, 1844.

[90] *Register,* LXVI, 149–52, May 4, 1844; one week later nine and one-half pages were devoted to the documents accompanying the treaty, LXVI, 163–73, May 11, 1844.

[91] *Register,* LXVI, 241, 243–44, 250–52, June 15, 1844.

[92] *Register,* LXVII, 240, December 14, 1844.

[93] *Register,* LXIX, 257, December 27, 1845.

the war-making power of the legislative branch by ordering troops into Texas and a naval force into the Gulf of Mexico in 1844.[94] Following the rejection of the treaty by the Senate, Hughes mentioned the extremes to which the "hotspurs" on both sides went, saying that "strict constitutionalists have suddenly been converted into the widest latitudinarians," and those who could swallow Louisiana, Oregon, and the two Floridas, "all at once grow exceedingly squeamish about the constitution having no provision for attaching foreign territory to the union." [95] In June he criticized the "feverish impetuosity" of the Tyler party in pushing the joint resolution through when "cool deliberation" should have been employed, and, commenting on Wilson Shannon's inept handling of affairs in Mexico, added that it would have been better had the United States possessed "a minister . . . during these eventful times, sufficiently a diplomatist to have represented and maintained our interests better than they have been represented by the minister who is now leaving there without having acquitted himself to the satisfaction of his countrymen, or to the credit of the country he went there to serve." [96]

After Texas approved annexation, he said all dispute over the proposition should end, admitting, however, that it was a little too much to expect everyone to settle down at once after such a warm controversy. Adhering to Hezekiah Niles' precept that the majority should rule, Hughes advised the minority to submit with good grace, adding, *"Texas is annexed.* Quibbling about *the way* in which it was done, is of little avail." [97]

The manner in which the *Register* covered the war with Mexico would make an interesting chapter in the history of the periodical. The Mexican War was the first war in which American newspapers co-operated to any extent in the gathering of news.[98]

[94] *Register,* LXVI, 177, May 18, 1844.

[95] *Register,* LXVI, 343-44, July 27, 1844.

[96] *Register,* LXVIII, 225-26, June 14, 1845.

[97] *Register,* LXVIII, 355-56, August 9, 1845.

[98] For accounts of the co-operative coverage see Victor Rosewater, *History of Cooperative News-Gathering in the United States* (New York, 1930), 45; James M. Lee, *op. cit.,* 258-61; the best account of news coverage of the war is in Fayette Copeland, *Kendall of the Picayune: Being His Adventures in New Orleans, on the Texan Santa Fe Expedition, in the Mexican War, and in the Colonization of the Texas Frontier* (Norman, Okla., 1943); a sketchy account is in Thomas Ewing

While the *Register* played no part in this new development of news gathering and distribution, it benefited much from the new methods employed in speeding transmission of intelligence from the war area. The *Sun* of Baltimore and the *Picayune* of New Orleans were leaders. The horse expresses of the *Sun*, combined with existing railroad and telegraph lines, often beat the mail by thirty hours or more, and naturally aided the *Register*, especially if the news was received by the *Sun* near the end of the week when the *Register* went to press.[99]

To one interested in the details of the type of stories printed, the source of war news, the amount of space given to accounts of battles, the progress of the peace negotiators, and the many letters carried from soldiers and officers in the American army, the writer can only suggest that he go direct to the *Register* from May 16, 1846, when the declaration of war was commented upon, to July 19, 1848, when the text of the Treaty of Guadalupe Hidalgo was carried. This period is covered by the seventieth to the seventy-fourth volumes. Nearly every issue of the four volumes preceding the temporary suspension of the periodical from March through June of 1848 contains war material, and not a few are practically turned over to war news and documents. Up to the eve of hostilities, the *Register* advocated a peaceful solution to the Mexican difficulties, saying in November, 1845, that the United States should be willing to pay Mexico for California and the territory in dispute ten times what it would cost to take them by force. It saw no reason why the United States should not make overtures to Mexico and criticized the "intemperate" language used by President Polk in his first message to Congress.[100] The wording of the measure which recognized that by the act of Mexico a state of war existed between the countries displeased Hughes who wrote that war was present without the authority of either the Mexican or the United States Congresses which were supposed to have full

Dabney, *One Hundred Great Years: The Story of the Times-Picayune from Its Founding to 1940* (Baton Rouge, 1944), 65–73.

[99] The *Sun's* coverage is best described by Johnson, Kent, Mencken, and Owens, *op. cit.*, 72–84.

[100] *Register*, LXIX, 161, November 15, 1845; 177, November 22, 1845; 209, December 6, 1845.

authority to make war.[101] He opposed conquest, hoping that the United States would be not only just, but magnanimous toward Mexico, and closed an editorial with "MILLIONS FOR JUSTICE,—FOR CONQUEST NOT A CENT." [102] He was critical of the conduct of the war from Washington, shortly after its declaration reprinting and substantially agreeing with an article from the *Southern Quarterly Review,* extremely critical of William L. Marcy, secretary of war, and of the quartermaster's department.[103] In an impersonal editorial in the January 9, 1847, issue, reviewing the events of the past year in detail, he pointed to Santa Anna's return, "partly from our indiscretion," and asserted that the struggle was assuming a more serious aspect than anticipated by the American executive.

Some notice of the different angles of the *Register*'s coverage of the war may serve to illustrate the variety of material on that subject presented in its columns. Fifteen of the sixteen pages of the May 30, 1846, issue were filled with articles on the geography of the area of the seat of war, on the health and roads of Mexico, an extract from a book by Waddy Thompson, official Mexican army documents, summaries of troops raised by various states, and documents accompanying the President's message of May 11. Letters signed "The Corporal," written for the New Orleans *Bee* from the Army of Occupation, were often used in the *Register*.[104] New Orleans newspapers naturally were the source of a great deal of news. An aeronaut's proposal to bomb from a balloon the fortress of San Juan de Ulloa was reprinted from the Lancaster (Pennsylvania) *Republican*.[105] Successive numbers in April, 1847, carried news of General Zachary Taylor's victory at Buena Vista and the fall of Vera Cruz. The headline in the April 3 issue

GENERAL TAYLOR VICTORIOUS!

THE MEXICAN ARMY, LED ON BY SANTA ANNA,

DEFEATED AT BUENA VISTA WITH GREAT

SLAUGHTER

[101] *Register,* LXX, 161–62, May 16, 1846.
[102] *Register,* LXX, 257, June 27, 1846.
[103] *Register,* LXX, 261–62, 266–68, June 27, 1846.
[104] *Register,* LXX, 341–42, August 1, 1846; LXXI, 55, September 26, 1846.
[105] *Register,* LXXI, 169, November 14, 1846.

was over a lead which in its second paragraph told of the "blood-iest battle of the war" being fought on February 22 and 23. Details of the battle were reprinted from the New Orleans *Delta* of March 23 and 24 and the New Orleans *Picayune* of March 23.[106] The next week's issue carried the headline

BOMBARDMENT, SURRENDER, AND OCCUPATION OF VERA
CRUZ AND THE CASTLE OF SAN JUAN D'ULLOA

over about a column of small type which had been inserted late after the paper was practically made up. The *Sun* supplied the news to the *Register,* and, as related in the *Sunpapers of Baltimore,* telegraphed the news to President Polk, thus giving him his first information of the victory.[107] The *Sun's* ponies had brought the Pensacola *Gazette* of April 3 from the Florida city, that newspaper having received its information from the ship *Princeton,* which had arrived at Pensacola the morning of April 3.

News from the war, in spite of improved means of communi-cation, did not arrive with regularity. Twelve days had elapsed without word when the news of General Taylor's Buena Vista victory was received.[108] No official word was received from Gen-eral Scott from June until October, despite what some of the letter writers reported, the Washington *Union* of October 26 asserted.[109] The *Register* had several times earlier referred to the lack of news from General Scott, and in its issue of November 20, 1847, began the publication of some of his dispatches, call-ing attention to their receipt after a silence of more than five months. A broken press, which delayed publication of the Feb-ruary 19, 1848, number until February 21, enabled Hughes to reprint from the *National Intelligencer* of February 21 the news of the arrival of the treaty of peace in Washington. In the last issue published under his direction, Hughes discussed the sub-mission of the treaty to the Senate by President Polk, on Feb-

[106] *Register,* LXXII, 68–71, April 3, 1847; on 75–79 some of General Zachary Taylor's official correspondence was printed, and on 80 another account from the New Orleans *Picayune,* and the official report of Santa Anna to the Minister of War.
[107] Johnson, Kent, Mencken, Owens, *op. cit.,* 79–81.
[108] *Register,* LXXII, 69, April 3, 1847.
[109] *Register,* LXXIII, 129, October 30, 1847.

ruary 22, and, taking his cue from the Washington *Union*'s "authentic intimations," said there was "little room to doubt the president's approval of the terms." [110] The first issue of the revived *Register,* dated July 5, but undoubtedly published later, carried President Polk's proclamation of the treaty, the ratification of which by the Mexican Congress he had received on July 4. Two weeks later, in the issue dated July 19, 1848, the treaty and the President's message were printed.

A by no means complete but, on the whole, accurate picture of the Mexican War was presented by the *Register*. The custom of waiting for official orders, reports, and correspondence made for accuracy, if not for speed, and the use of rumors and speculations of correspondents and Washington "letter writers" added interest to the coverage. However, the readers were plainly told and could clearly see the difference between the official news and unofficial rumors and thus were not deceived. The letters from men of all ranks in the military forces added interest to the dull official reports, but that this "republican habit" of "speaking, writing, and publishing whatever they please" could be carried too far was the belief of even such an ardent supporter of freedom of speech as the *Register* editor.[111]

The end of the Mexican War and the suspension of the *Register* the next year brought to a close a period of nearly thirty-eight years during which the periodical had followed closely and commented freely on relations between the United States and Latin America. Manifest destiny had no part in its program; none of its editors was an expansionist, and if disappointment replaced hopefulness regarding the affairs of the southern republics, no blame can be attached to the editors, who had the welfare of the nations and of their peoples at heart.

[110] *Register,* LXXIII, 416, February 26, 1848.
[111] *Register,* LXXI, 179–80, November 21, 1846.

Chapter 9

The West

THE intense nationalism of Hezekiah Niles and his idealistic belief in democracy caused him to see in the West the hope of the nation. The sectionalism of New England and of the South aroused his ire. The editor always had been critical of New England. He had little sympathy with—as it appeared to him— its almost complete dependence upon foreign commerce as a means of livelihood. The section's pro-English attitude was a constant irritant to his Anglophobe ideology. With the South he was equally unsympathetic because of its economic dependence upon slavery, an institution which he opposed on economic and moral grounds, although, as will be seen in Chapter 11, he was by no means a rabid abolitionist. A native and lifelong resident of the Middle States, he had the national rather than the sectional viewpoint. The West to him was the open door to opportunity and he exulted editorially in its expanse, fertility, magnificent waterways, products, rapid settlement, and phenomenal growth.[1]

Discussing in the first number of the *Register* Lord John Sheffield's book, *Observations on the Commerce of the American States,* Niles criticized the author's attempt to "derogate the natural advantages" of the nation and pointed out that in the twenty-seven years since the book had been written there had been an "unprecedented increase in wealth and population" west of the Alleghenies, a region in which the English writer had seen but little chance for commerce.[2]

Niles delighted in printing brief items about the growth of the West, with a sentence or sometimes only a caption contrast-

[1] The following are chosen from a twenty-year period as typical of scores of such items printed annually: *Register,* VI, 188, May 21, 1814; 417, August 20, 1814; XII, 416, August 23, 1817; XIV, 280, June 13, 1818; XV, 126, October 17, 1818; XLVII, 53, September 27, 1834.

[2] *Register,* I, 10, September 7, 1811.

ing the past with the present. The following illustrates his method and his obvious pleasure:

[Describing Zanesville, Ohio.]

Scarce seven years have elapsed, since the spot on which the town stands was a wood—there are at this time, between two and three hundred dwelling houses, and about a thousand inhabitants.—[3]

"*The backwoods.*"—An association has been recently formed, to raise $300,000 to build a bridge across the Ohio river.[4]

Lighthouses of stone or brick are to be immediately erected on the shores of Lake Erie; one at Buffalo and one at Presqu'isle.[5]

"*A howling waste and dreary wilderness!*" The exports of New Orleans, for the present year, it is stated, will amount to the value of twenty millions of dollars.[6]

The first number of a *daily* newspaper was issued at Rochester, N. Y. on the 25th ult. Rochester *was not* 12 or 15 years ago.[7]

A daily newspaper of a large size, and called the "Advertiser," is now publishing in the city (late village) of *Buffalo,* New York—a place so remote and unimportant previous to 1812, as hardly to obtain a mark on the map, except as being located at the eastern end of Lake Erie.[8]

During the War of 1812 the editor compiled figures from census reports and from his own records to prove his contention that New England was declining in importance. Written to "expose the folly and delusion of the 'Eastern' faction," the article pointed to the rising importance of the West and, by a series of projections of population trends and Congressional representation, predicted a great increase in power of the West and the South in that body. Niles wrote, "The rapid decrease of the power of the Eastern compared with the Middle or Southern divisions, is too clearly shown in the table as to preclude the necessity of many remarks."

Calling attention to the Republican political complexion of western New York and Ohio, "filled with emigrants from *New-*

3 *Register,* II, 31, March 14, 1812.   4 *Register,* VIII, 48, March 18, 1815.
5 *Register,* X, 334, July 13, 1816.   6 *Register,* XV, 199, November 14, 1818.
7 *Register,* XXXI, 169, November 11, 1826.
8 *Register,* XLVI, 361, July 26, 1834.

England," he asked: "Is it that the 'republicans' are *driven* from the places of their nativity; or, do the sentiments of the people undergo a change with their circumstances? I venture to say that if the native citizens of *Massachusetts,* (residing in *New York* and *Ohio* only) were to vote for a governor of the state, that the 'republican' candidate would have a majority of from 10 to 20,000 votes." [9]

In the foregoing brief excerpt from a six-page article on the importance of the West, Niles raised the question of the effect of environment on emigrants and clearly showed that he recognized the influence that that section was to have on the future political history of the nation.

Niles sympathized with the belligerent spirit of the western "war hawks" and felt that the West furnished an example in the raising of volunteers that the rest of the country might well follow.[10] His democratic philosophy led him to regard the constitutions adopted by the western states, with their extension of suffrage, as models to be copied by the older and more conservative states when revising their restricted suffrage provisions.[11] In fact, although he never penetrated as far as one hundred miles from the seaboard, he was a westerner at heart. His faith in the farmers, laborers, and manufacturers who settled the trans-Appalachian land of promise was often expressed in editorials on economic and political questions as well as those on internal improvements and on the West itself.

He hailed "with delight" the establishment of factories in the West. In 1814 he wrote that if

"Westward the course of empire takes its way," we are not jealous. Where the strength of the population is, there also should be the weight of political influence. The new states of *Kentucky, Ohio, Tennessee* and INDIANA will have a greater representation in the Congress of the United States after the year 1830, than the old states of *Massa-*

---

[9] *Register,* VI, 187, May 21, 1814.

[10] *Register,* III, 45, September 19, 1812; other typical expressions of his sympathy with the West's attitude toward the war may be found in I, 250–51, December 7, 1811; 352, January 11, 1812; II, 207–11, May 30, 1812; 256, June 13, 1812; V, 198–200, November 20, 1813.

[11] *Register,* X, 334–36 (incorrectly paged, should be 234–36), June 8, 1816; 366, July 27, 1816; XI, 146–47, November 2, 1816; XII, 16, March 1, 1817; 79, March 29, 1817; XIX, 115–16, October 21, 1820; XX, 99–101, April 14, 1821; XXXVII, 225, December 5, 1829.

chusetts, *Connecticut, New-Hampshire* and *Rhode Island,* let faction wail as it will. I am glad of it; for I had rather trust my freedom to the *agriculturalist* and *manufacturer* than to the *merchant*—to a *home* rather than to a *foreign* feeling.[12]

The sound of the axe was music in the ears of this editor who obtained vicarious pleasure in the activities of the frontiersmen as reported in the columns of his periodical. In 1819 he wrote that thirty years earlier the heart of Pennsylvania was backwoods and Ohio was just being opened, "a state now containing half a million of freemen having two other *states* further west, and a third ready to start into sovereignty!" He boasted that any of the new states, north or south of the Ohio, would make a kingdom in Europe and each was "preparing beyond any thing that Europe ever witnessed." [13] Ten years later he pointed out with pride that 437 vessels had arrived at the port of Sandusky, Ohio, during the preceding year and that 1,623 wagons were there loaded with goods for the interior.[14]

Readers of the *Register* were constantly supplied with factual articles on geography, geology, and meteorology of the area. Books by Jedidiah Morse and Henry R. Schoolcraft and others and a report by William Davis Robinson, on the Far West, were given mention.[15] River and lake traffic furnished stories on the commerce of the growing section. The boundless opportunities for laborers in the West were listed in the *Register.* Throughout the entire life of the periodical close attention was paid to the infiltration of the West by newspapers.

In every volume the searcher for colorful items on the westward movement is richly rewarded. Space limitations prohibit more than a mere mention of a few typical ones. On March 13, 1813, an "Interesting Biography" [sic] written by Daniel Boone about himself was printed with his memorial to the Kentucky legislature asking aid in his efforts to obtain a grant of ten thousand acres from Congress. In 1818 copper deposits on Lake Superior, a bridge at Pittsburgh, and Transylvania University furnished material for three typical items illustrating the West's

12 *Register,* VI, 207–10, May 28, 1814.
13 *Register,* XVII, 196, November 27, 1819.
14 *Register,* XXXVI, 130, April 25, 1829.
15 *Register,* XIX, 370, February 3, 1821; XXI, 100, October 13, 1821.

resources, activities, and opportunities.[16] Throughout the twenties articles told of the fertility of the soil, the immense numbers of squirrels and pigeons in western New York and Ohio, tavern rates at Chillicothe, Ohio, and of the establishment of a type foundry and printing-press factory at Cincinnati. Twenty years later the *Register* was still carrying articles on the western country.[17]

The steady stream of emigration to the West was watched and recorded in the *Register*'s columns. Western New York newspapers were the source of many of these reports which told of the passage of teams and wagons from the eastern states "to people the fertile forests of New-York, Pennsylvania, and Ohio. . . ."[18] Niles noted on July 20 and July 27, 1816, that foreigners, including "Hardy laborers, ingenious mechanics, intelligent merchants, learned doctors, profound philosophers and gallant soldiers" were seeking in the West the freedom their own lands denied them. The editor welcomed the Irish, English, and Swiss farmers and mechanics saying, "These are the sorts of men that we want." Regretting the necessity which compelled the European "to leave his home in search of freedom and safety," Niles graciously greeted the immigrants:

I greet their arrival, and say to the people of all nations, Come and partake with us of the blessings of independence, and in due time be to us as our own kindred. Come, and help us to dig canals, clear water courses, make roads, build bridges, establish manufactories, and extend commerce, internal and external, by your *labor*, intelligence and capital. Come and open our primeval forests to the rays of the sun, and spread the rich harvest where the wild buffalo ranges. Come, and assist us to prepare by an increased population and strength, to resist any attempt that may be made to "put down our dangerous example of successful rebellion." The flag of the union is large enough for us and you, and we have room enough and to spare. Bring with you a love of liberty, habits of temperance and industry

---

[16] *Register*, XIV, 323, July 4, 1818; 439, August 22, 1818; XV, 132–33, October 24, 1818.

[17] Typical among many are: *Register*, XVIII, 272, June 10, 1820; XIX, 143, October 28, 1820; XX, 111–12, April 14, 1821; XXIII, 134, November 2, 1822; XXXIII, 83, October 6, 1827; LXIV, 241, June 17, 1843; LXV, 27–31, September 9, 1843; 46–47, September 16, 1843; 93–95, October 7, 1843.

[18] *Register*, VIII, 120, April 15, 1815.

—your capital may be useful and convenient; but the others are of more worth to us than the wealth of the Indies.[19]

Commenting on the westward migration because of the "derangement of employment" in the old states, Niles, on November 15, 1834, questioned whether the rapidity of the change was good for either the old or the new states, adding, however, "But it is well, indeed, that the laboring poor and enterprising have a back country to fly to—"

The location of the Harmony Society at Harmony, Indiana, received considerable publicity in the *Register* in the late teens and early twenties. Niles thought that the "invincible perseverance and industry" of the group's members would do much to increase the value of the land and frequently described their agricultural and manufactured products.[20] As a father of twenty children, however, he was unable to understand the rule of abstinence from marital relations imposed upon the members. He mentioned that only one or two children had been born in the colony, and reported that "among many handsome girls and fine young men, an astonishing degree of obedience to supposed orders had been observed." [21]

The five states admitted to the Union in the decade following the War of 1812 filled in the trans-Allegheny region to the Mississippi, with the exception of the Territory of Michigan. The last state to be admitted in the twenties and the first west of the Mississippi was Missouri. These new members of the Union and their neighboring states immediately to the east were the subject of many an enthusiastic article in the *Register*. Niles prepared and printed a series on the resources and improvements of the West in which he took up in some detail the manufactures, trade, natural resources, and population of Ohio, Kentucky and Tennessee, Louisiana and the Territories of Mississippi, Indiana, and Michigan.[22]

Western papers were used extensively as sources of informa-

19 *Register*, X, 373, August 3, 1816.
20 *Register*, IX, 152, October 28, 1815; XIII, 20–21, September 6, 1817; 272, December 20, 1817; XIV, 440, August 22, 1818; XV, 43, September 12, 1818.
21 *Register*, XVI, 431, August 21, 1819; XXIII, 2, September 7, 1822.
22 *Register*, VI, 207–10, May 28, 1814; 249–50, June 11, 1814; 393–95, August 6, 1814.

tion about the section, the St. Louis *Enquirer* supplying many items about the fur trade and the Far West. Niles had newspaper friends and other correspondents in Ohio who kept him well supplied with information about that state. The cities of Columbus, Cincinnati, Athens, Ashtabula, Gallipolis, and Dayton were subjects of articles, as was the state as a whole. Noting that Ohio had forty-two newspapers in 1821, he added, probably with a touch of exaggeration, "Forty-two years ago there were scarcely as many inhabitants of the territory comprised in the state that could read a newspaper." [23] An interesting commentary on the westward movement and the rapid growth of the states in the West was printed in a survey of birthplaces of members of the Ohio General Assembly in 1822. There was not an Ohio-born citizen among the sixty-nine representatives and thirty-three senators, which led Niles to observe ". . . this is not so much to be wondered at, when we recollect that in 1800, only 21 years ago, the whole of the north western territory, composing the present states of Ohio, Indiana, Illinois, and territory of Michigan, contained only 45,365 inhabitants, and of these, except some under ten years of age, very few indeed, were natives of the territory—" [24]

His enthusiasm for Lexington where town lots sold "nearly as high as in Boston, New-York, Philadelphia or Baltimore" was matched only by his detailed interest in the establishment of Indiana as a state. The admission of Illinois brought a series of articles on the twenty-first state. Alabama and Mississippi, Louisiana, Missouri, and the Territory of Michigan were described and their progress reported as living examples of the growth of the West and the expansion of the nation. [25]

The changing policies on the sale of public lands by the United States government to the emigrants from the Atlantic seaboard and from European nations form an important chap-

[23] Register, IV, 314–17, July 17, 1813; VII, 350, January 28, 1815; IX, 35–36, September 16, 1815; X, 334 (incorrectly paged, should be 234), June 8, 1816; 347, July 20, 1816; 399, August 10, 1816; 414, August 17, 1816; XI, 54–55, September 21, 1816; 95, October 5, 1816; 141, October 26, 1816; 321–24, January 11, 1817; XXI, 176, November 10, 1821; XXII, 239, June 8, 1822; XXXI, 105–106, October 14, 1826.

[24] *Register*, XXI, 368, February 2, 1822.

[25] Volumes X through XV contain many such articles, too numerous for individual citation.

ter in the history of the West. The *Register* nowise neglected this troublous question, reporting in detail the news of sales and taking a definite editorial stand on the laws passed and bills proposed. Niles had no more love for the land speculator than for the stockjobber. In 1819 he wrote:

The PUBLIC LANDS have become a most important national concern, and demand an increased care of the representatives of the people, to prevent a waste of this vast fund of *public* wealth. Care should be taken to guard against the sale of any extensive tracts which the current of emigration may not require, whilst every reasonable facility ought to be extended in favor of *actual settlers*—to check *speculations* therein, and forbid *monopoly*. In its general sense, the wealth of individuals constitutes the national wealth—but, if the property of individuals cannot be acted upon to *produce something,* it is of no importance to the nation.[26]

In the period which preceded the agitation for and passage of the law abolishing credit sales, material regarding the public domain printed in the *Register* was almost entirely of informational character. Instructions on how to fill out application blanks for bounty lands under the acts of 1811, 1812, and 1814 were printed in 1815.[27] Other articles describing bounty lands and explaining the procedure to obtain them were carried from time to time.

As discussion over the relative merits of cash and credit policies for land sales grew warm, the *Register* printed arguments on both sides before making its stand known. "Hampden," writing in the *National Intelligencer,* upheld the credit system in a grandiloquent article which declared that no other country or age had produced a land system "so sublime in principle, so perfect in practice, so magnificent in prospect." [28] To this flowery defense, a writer in the *Kentucky Reporter,* quoted in the *Register* from the *Intelligencer,* replied that if the settlers all became debtors of the government in buying the lands they would come to hate and in time wish to overthrow the government which had extended credit to them.[29]

26 *Register,* XV, 423–24, January 30, 1819.
27 *Register,* IX, 36–37, September 16, 1815.
28 *Register,* XVI, 376–77, July 31, 1819.
29 *Register,* XVII, 10–11, September 4, 1819.

Niles bided his time, but in February, 1820, proposed a program, suggesting a curtailment in sales by a policy of opening no land offices in the new territories. Squatters should be guarded against, however, in areas not thrown open. He suggested dividing purchasers into two classes; settlers and nonsettlers, the former to get credit, the latter to pay cash. Sales were to be limited to one section to each purchaser with one-fourth cash down and the remainder in three annual installments. Bona fide residence must be proved at the time of second payment. He felt strongly that the $23,000,000 owed to the government for lands demanded the adoption of new laws.[30]

When the Senate passed the cash measure, he reported on March 11, 1820, his satisfaction with it and felt that it would be advantageous to the national government and to the states. Later in the year, commenting on the inability of those who purchased land at $2.00 per acre to sell, except at a loss, with the government price pegged at $1.25, he gave qualified approval to the bill permitting purchasers to relinquish part of their lands, retaining only the portion paid for. He pointed out, however, that such procedure would result in the settlers keeping the best land and throwing "the refuse land" back on the public.[31] Factual articles on sales, statistical reports on the receipts, and provisions of new laws filled much space during the twenties.

Niles took a definite stand against proposals to change the cash law, writing in the January 24, 1824, issue:

No one has been more anxious for the gradual expansion of the people of the republic than myself, persons interested in the sales of land excepted. But the march west has been more rapid than the public good has justified—weakening the force of the population, embarrassing the government, and inflicting misery on thousands, seduced, as it were, to purchase land without the means of paying for it. Hence it is, that law after law has been passed for the relief of purchasers of the public lands, and that the tables of the members of congress still groan under the weight of resolutions concerning them. The present law may prevent the recurrence of many such things under it; but the difficulties arising out of the old law will not be settled for years to come.

[30] *Register*, XVII, 386–87, February 5, 1820.
[31] *Register*, XIX, 194, November 25, 1820.

Five years later, noting "a simultaneous movement in several of the western states to divest the United States of *all* the public lands, and to acquire them for the use of the states in which they lie," Niles called for a serious consideration of the whole subject, styling the proposal "unreasonable." [32] In the midst of the campaign of 1832 he predicted that Clay's plan for the sale of public lands and the distribution of the proceeds among the states would be accepted after the heat of the campaign had died down.[33] When Jackson vetoed the bill, Niles charged that his action was little short of disgraceful. He condemned the "high self-will" of the Executive and said his refusal to sign the measure was "unparalleled in the history of *constitutional governments.*" [34]

Thirteen numbers of the *Register* in February, March, April, and May, 1841, carried fifty pages of the debate in the Senate on the Pre-emption Act. There was no editorial comment on the debate or on the Act, as signed by President Tyler in September.[35]

Sympathetic with the desires of the settlers for cheap land, Niles nevertheless saw the evils brought about by too rapid a movement westward and urged regulations of land sales. He recognized that the public domain formed an integral and important part of the resources of the nation and opposed its dissipation. Its vast extent pleased his nationalistic pride; and intelligent and nonpolitical administration of it with a view to the benefit of the nation as a whole would have met with his wholehearted approval.

The various vexing problems connected with the relations of the white men and the Indians intermittently occupied the news and editorial attention of the *Register* over a period of thirty years. Niles was deeply sympathetic with the plight of the aborigines, but at the same time he was too realistic in his outlook upon the expanding economic scene to become maudlin over it. As the various proposals to provide a haven for the red men were advanced, Niles punctured the smug complacency

[32] *Register*, XXXV, 313, January 10, 1829.
[33] *Register*, XLIII, 51, September 22, 1832; Clay's speech on 57–64.
[34] *Register*, XLIV, 17, March 9, 1833.
[35] *Register*, LXI, 39–40, September 18, 1841.

of their supporters with the entirely accurate prediction that history would repeat itself with the hapless natives again being forced to pack up and move on to less desirable land.

As was the case with other subjects, much of the material printed about the Indians was in the form of official reports. Informational articles about Indian tribes, population, and trade, and descriptions of the frequent trips made by Governor Lewis Cass of the Territory of Michigan for the purpose of negotiating the cession of lands with the Indians of the Northwest comprised another type of news coverage which might be termed semiofficial. Troubles with Indian tribes were given space in the twenties and thirties, but there was no sensationalism in the handling of the news of this type as there had been during the progress of the War of 1812 concerning the Indian allies of the British. When the final group of Indians left Ohio soil for the West in 1843, their slow trek across the state was reported in articles from the Logan, Urbana, Xenia, and Cincinnati papers.[36]

Using the preceding fifty years as an illustration of what the next half century would bring to the United States, Niles insisted "that if any system is to be adopted to preserve the Indians, it ought to be adopted at once, to make it efficient. A little while, and we shall be treating for lands about the headsprings of the Mississippi, and in a few years we may hear of a national road winding through the passes of the Rocky mountains, the only land carriage between the city of New York and a great city built at the mouth of the Columbia. Seeing what we have seen, there is nothing extravagant in this idea. *The man is living that may travel* the route." [37]

This vision of the continental manifest destiny of the nation did not blind the nationalist editor to the evils of the policy pursued toward the original inhabitants of the country. This policy carried with it "a decree for the deliberate and unnecessary annihilation of the Indian race, the aboriginal possessors of the soil we inhabit," he charged in 1819 in advocating national legislation to alleviate the condition of the tribes. Advocating edu-

---

[36] *Register*, LXIV, 414–15, August 26, 1843.

[37] *Register*, XV, 185–87, November 14, 1818; a second article of some length on the welfare of the Indians may be found in XV, 420–23, January 30, 1819.

cation and schools rather than religion and churches as a means of bettering the lot of the Indians, the next year he suggested making farmers of the present generation and Christians of the next. Civilize first, Christianize next, was his text.[38]

As the inexorable march of the white men forced the Indians farther and farther West, Niles suggested in 1826 that no new territories or states be established "without special reference to the lands given to them [Indians] in exchange for those which they have relinquished." [39]

While Niles had but slight interest in the Far West and distinctly was not of the expansionist school, the *Register* carried many news items on the expeditions into that area and on the activities of the traders, especially in the Santa Fe country. In the first decade of its existence the periodical contained articles on the Missouri Company, the Pacific Fur Company, and the comings and goings of Manuel Lisa, famed fur trader operating out of St. Louis.[40] When the St. Louis *Enquirer,* from which much of the *Register*'s western news was obtained, urged incorporation by Congress of a company to carry on the fur trade on the Mississippi, Missouri, and Columbia, to meet the competition of the rumored consolidation of the Hudson's Bay and North West companies of the English, Niles opposed it strongly on constitutional grounds. He had no objection, however, to the formation of private companies and gave encouragement to the trade by printing items about the rich returns from investments in such enterprises.[41]

The expedition receiving the most space in the *Register,* which furnished its readers with more than a dozen abridged accounts from the St. Louis *Enquirer,* was the one under the command of Major Stephen H. Long which went up the Missouri in 1819–1820. Earlier expeditions had been noted,

[38] *Register,* XVI, 405–409, August 14, 1819; XVIII, 154–55, April 29, 1820; 257–58, June 10, 1820; XIX, 281–82, December 30, 1820.

[39] *Register,* XXX, 185, May 13, 1826.

[40] *Register,* I, 61, September 28, 1811; IV, 264, June 19, 1813; 265–67, June 26, 1813; XIII, 32, September 6, 1817; XIV, 389–90, August 1, 1818; XIX, 64, September 23, 1820, this last item being the death notice of Manuel Lisa.

[41] *Register,* XII, 348, July 26, 1817; XV, 182, November 7, 1818; XVI, 409, August 14, 1819; XVIII, 328, July 1, 1820; XXIII, 53, September 28, 1822; 164, November 16, 1822.

but an attempt was made to give fairly complete coverage to this military and scientific exploring expedition.[42] On October 5, 1822, extracts of an article in the *National Gazette* on the expedition were printed, and the following year one and one-half columns were devoted to a review of a book on the journey, compiled by Dr. Edwin James from the notes of Long T. Say and other members of the expedition. A second expedition under Long's direction to the Northwest, which covered more than four thousand miles in less than six months, was described in 1823.[43]

As has been shown in the Latin-American and Anglo-American chapters, the editor of the *Register* had little sympathy with the territory grabbers who wanted to claim the continent from the North Pole to the equator and cast longing eyes on the islands of the Caribbean. The territorial ambitions of the St. Louis *Enquirer,* which in 1821 sought the election of a President who would "re-purchase" that part of Louisiana to the Rio del Norte, caused Niles to write: "Texas, no doubt, is a fine country—so is Mexico, New Grenada, Venezuela—Peru— Guian, Brazil, the provinces of Rio de la Plata and Chili: nay, New South Iceland is a fine place for catching seals and getting cargoes of congealed water—we might supply the Chinese with that cooling article of commerce, WHEN the 'trade of Asia,' for the supply of the people of the United States, shall pass up the Columbia, across the Rocky mountains, and down the Missouri, as has been anticipated in the 'St Louis Enquirer.' " [44]

The Santa Fe traders furnished many news items in the twenties, and again in the forties.[45] Most of them were factual ones about the goods traded or were descriptive of the Southwest.

Little attention was paid to California by the *Register* under

[42] *Register*, XV, 111, October 10, 1818; XVI, 320, July 3, 1819; 368, July 24, 1819; 377–78, July 31, 1819; XVII, 44, September 18, 1819; 73–74, October 2, 1819; 96, October 9, 1819; 160, November 6, 1819; 288, December 25, 1819; 328–31, January 15, 1820; XVIII, 96, April 1, 1820.

[43] *Register*, XXIII, 353–54, February 8, 1823; XXV, 136–37, November 1, 1823.

[44] *Register*, XX, 289, July 7, 1821.

[45] *Register*, XXIII, 177, November 23, 1822; XXV, 230, December 13, 1823; XXVIII, 299–300, July 9, 1825; XXIX, 100, October 15, 1825; 263, December 24, 1825; LXI, 209, December 4, 1841; LXII, 192, May 21, 1842; LXIV, 323, July 22, 1843; LXXIV, 224, October 4, 1848.

the editorship of Niles. His interest in the West did not extend beyond the Mississippi basin except for occasional references to the country beyond the Rocky Mountains. In 1821 a report made by William Davis Robinson to John H. Eaton on the western coast, suggesting the use of naval vessels and army officers in surveying and exploring that area, was printed and with it the report of Commodore David Porter to President Madison on October 31, 1815, suggesting a voyage of discovery along the coast.[46] By the forties, interest in California was aroused, but the *Register* retained its equilibrium. A rumor that the province would be ceded to the United States by Mexico to satisfy the claims against that nation was printed on December 17, 1842. An article was reprinted on November 29, 1845, from a New York newspaper advocating the desirability of obtaining California and quoting a former United States consul on the advantages of building a railroad to San Francisco. The emigration to Oregon and expeditions of John C. Frémont in 1843–1844, 1846, and 1848 were described.[47] The gold rush in California, occurring in the last year of the *Register*'s life, received inadequate coverage. On October 18, 1848, the St. Louis *Republican* was quoted, charging the stories of gold "came from interested land-holders, who expect to profit by the increased immigration." Early the following year extracts of letters from Thomas O. Larkin, former consul, and Commander Thomas A. Catesby Jones, describing the gold madness, were printed, as was an editorial from the New York *Evening Post* which saw nothing but ill effects as certain to come from the discovery. Brief news items told of the hordes leaving for the Eldorado of the West.[48]

Published during the period in which the American frontier moved from the Ohio country well into the prairies west of the Mississippi and then suddenly leaped the plains and the mountains to locate in the California gold regions, the *Register* recorded the nation's expansion from year to year. Editorial en-

[46] *Register*, XX, 21–25, March 10, 1821.

[47] *Register*, LXVII, 19, September 14, 1844; 338–39, February 1, 1845; LXVIII, 129, May 3, 1845; 203, May 31, 1845; LXX, 161, May 16, 1846; LXXI, 173–74, November 14, 1846; LXXIV, 244–45, October 18, 1848; 257, October 25, 1848.

[48] *Register*, LXXV, 69–70, January 31, 1849; 88–89, February 7, 1849; 288, May 2, 1849.

thusiasm for the West as exemplifying the finest and best in American life was tempered by timely warnings against ruthless disregard for the rights of the Indians and thoughtless dissipation of that part of the nation's wealth represented in the public domain. All in all a sane picture of the West and of the forces which opened and developed that section in the first half of the nineteenth century may be obtained from the columns of the *Register*.

Chapter 10

Roads, Rivers, Canals, and Railroads

T H E thirty-eight-year life span of the *Register* coincided with
an amazing development in the nation's means of transportation. The periodical was launched upon its editorial career the
same year that the first steamboat was launched in the West.[1]
During its life, roads were built into the western country, rivers
were improved, canals dug, and railroads, just beginning to be
talked about in 1811, had 6,421.75 miles of track in operation
by 1849,[2] the year of the periodical's suspension. With internal
improvements an integral part of the American System, it is not
surprising to find in the *Register*'s columns a complete contemporary picture of the rapid development in the means of
communication and transportation.

Economist and editor, Hezekiah Niles recognized early the
necessity of developing a system of transportation by which the
sections of the country would be more closely linked together.
As the settled area expanded from the Alleghenies to the Mississippi and westward, he campaigned constantly for improved sys-
tems of conveyance, so that the products of the fertile soil
and the newly established factories could find a ready market.

Roads, rivers, canals, and railroads, the subject of countless
news items and editorials, will be discussed in that order in this
chapter.· On the first page of the first number of the *Register,*
Niles announced that he planned to print Albert Gallatin's report on roads and canals made on April 4, 1808, but it was seven

[1] *Register*, XLI, 240, November 26, 1831; see Balthaser Henry Meyer and Caroline E. MacGill (comps.), *History of Transportation in the United States before
1860* (Washington, 1917), 102, and John H. B. Latrobe, *The First Steamboat Voyage on the Western Waters* (Baltimore, 1871).

[2] *Register*, LXXV, 156, March 7, 1849; Meyer and MacGill, *op. cit.,* 572, quote
a table from the *Register,* commenting that the figures are "apparently not quite
accurate."

years before the report appeared in the *Register*'s columns.[3]
In the meantime, hundreds of pages had been devoted to accounts of and comments on the progress of internal improvements which, in this septennium, were chiefly the building of roads, the deepening and straightening of rivers, and the myriad plans for canals in every section of the republic.

As a comment to a reprinted article on roads under construction Niles on October 22, 1825, wrote:

The whole presents a most interesting and cheering view of the attention paid by the government of the United States to the great work of internal improvements—and a delightful *linking* of the various parts of our extensive country together, to *consolidate* the good wishes and feelings of the whole people, and yet not interfering with the "rights of the states." Without the aid of a paternal government, many of the surveys could not have been well accomplished; and local jealousies would have prevented the ascertainment of facts important to the nation, that we may profit by all the natural advantages which a kind Providence hath bestowed upon us.

Written when the administration was friendly toward a comprehensive federal system of internal improvements, the editorial voiced Niles' philosophy on the question. Objections of preceding and following administrations to the constitutionality of federal aid in such projects brought forth strong editorial defenses of that essential part of the American System. However, they were written in a restrained manner and entered into a discussion of the points of issue with an absence of the vituperation characteristic of that period in American journalism.

There is something very melancholy in the idea that no great *national* work of internal improvement can be effected by the broad patronage of the government of the United States. . . .
On the whole, then, I conclude—that if it is constitutional to establish a national bank and found a national university, and unconstitutional to make roads and dig canals, that it would be much better for the people to recal [*sic*] the power delegated for the first and second and grant it for the third, than to let the matter rest as it now is. The latter would assist honest industry in its struggle to arrive at independence—the others seem particularly designed to make the

---

[3] *Register*, XV, 10–24, August 29 and September 5, 1818; 44–58, September 12 and September 19, 1818.

rich richer and the poor poorer; the immediate advantages of them being secured to the wealthy. Riches are apt enough to grow into luxury, and luxury into despotism, without such aids.[4]

Five years later, when President Monroe refused to approve the Cumberland Road Bill, Niles characteristically granted space not only to the veto message, but also to the long additional message in which the Executive detailed "his views of the powers and rights of the general government as to roads and canals and other internal improvements," which, it is probably unnecessary to interpolate, were directly opposed to those held by the editor.[5]

The veto of the Maysville Road Bill by President Jackson signalized defeat, during Hezekiah Niles' lifetime, of the American System's broad interpretation of internal improvements. His first editorial expressed the opinion that the President had vetoed the measure on the ground of expediency rather than of constitutionality and regretted that the power had been put to such use. The following week, however, he had come to the conclusion that the President, in spite of favorable votes on seven different bills for internal improvements while a Senator in the early twenties, had "adopted a 'strict construction of the constitution,'" attitude toward them. "There is no cause for violence in these things. The president is within the exercise of the power which has been placed in his hands by the constitution and the people," wrote the editor. But he did take the opportunity to point out that in Pennsylvania, Ohio, and Kentucky, at least, the President, when a candidate, had been called a "decided friend of internal improvements" by his supporters.[6] Jackson's second annual message to Congress brought this comment on the issue from the *Register:* "It appears that the question as to internal improvements is settled—so far as it depends on President Jackson."[7]

[4] *Register,* XII, 25–26, March 8, 1817, contains the veto message of President Madison; XII, 67–69, March 29, 1817, the editorial.

[5] *Register,* XXII, 161, 171, May 11, 1822; 362–78, August 3 and August 10, 1822; 391–400, August 17, 1822.

[6] *Register,* XXXVIII, 271–75, June 5, 1830, contained the veto message; editorial comment on 269, June 5, 1830, and 285, June 12, 1830.

[7] *Register,* XXXIX, 249, December 11, 1830; message on 253–62, December 11, 1830.

Niles praised the states for going ahead with internal improvement projects, followed the westward course of the National Road, and printed Congressional debates and committee reports on roads and canals throughout the score of years that the question was before the public. Construction of military roads and the building of bridges furnished many items. Interspersed with the news items on the spread of internal improvements were editorial remarks indicative of the editor's intense interest. Internal improvements fostered the spirit of nationalism in addition to saving money for industry by speeding transportation, according to Niles' expressed beliefs.[8] After Jackson's stand in opposition to federal expenditures for public improvements had been taken, Niles suggested a plan by which the national government, under certain conditions, would appropriate one fifth of the estimated cost of roads or canals, the management of which was to remain with the respective states or corporations constructing them. He could see no reasonable objection to the plan which, he pointed out, would result in an annual expenditure of $10,000,000 for public works, costing the national government only $2,000,000.[9]

The development in the means and speed of travel by road may be easily traced by reading brief items in the department entitled "A Chronicle" in the *Register*. In 1816 it was noted that wagons carrying 3,500 pounds had reached Pittsburgh from Philadelphia in thirteen days. The next year a plan to cut this time to seven days by traveling day and night was mentioned. In 1818 a line of packets and wagons had been established between New York and Detroit, the cost not exceeding $4.50 per hundredweight. That same year a post chaise trip could be made from New York to Philadelphia in "a little more than eleven hours," and the traveler could go on to Baltimore with less than twenty-four hours on the road, although thirty-six hours of elapsed time were taken in order that passengers could have a full night's rest at Philadelphia. In 1819 the time between New York and Philadelphia was reduced to eight hours and thirty-five minutes, "at the rate of $11\frac{1}{2}$ miles per hour!" With the building of good roads, persons with sporting in-

[8] *Register*, XXX, 201, May 20, 1826; XLV, 3–4, August 31, 1833.
[9] *Register*, XL, 434, August 20, 1831.

stincts tried to see how fast they could drive or how far they could go in a specified time. One article described a trip from Utica to Albany and return, two hundred miles, made in seventeen hours and twenty-eight minutes. Another party drove eighty miles in six hours, twenty-six and one-half minutes. The ingenuity of the American manufacturers in making products to meet certain cónditions pleased Niles, always a patron of domestic industry, and in 1834 he advised immigrants not to waste money by bringing wagons with them because the American "Conestoga wagon" had not its equal anywhere in the world.

Space granted to river transportation was given over to the improvement of the streams and to the application of steam power to river craft, especially on the Mississippi and its tributaries. The steady growth of river traffic on the Ohio and Mississippi was the subject of many a news and editorial item. On July 11, 1818, for instance, he reported that a passenger on a steamboat ascending the Mississippi and Ohio had counted 643 flatboats met on their way down the rivers. Recorded also was the arrival at Kaskaskia, Illinois, on August 10, 1818, of the *Franklin* from New Orleans, with a cargo worth $8,500. The voyage up had been made in eighteen days' running time by this first steamboat to reach Kaskaskia.[10]

Activities of the several states to survey and improve their own watercourses were encouraged in the *Register*. Niles never gave up his belief that Congress had the power to appropriate money for internal improvements. On November 3, 1821, when a Kentucky newspaper reported the arrival of army engineer-corps officers to survey the Ohio and Mississippi, Niles wrote that Monroe must have changed his opinion, asserting that if there were no "power to *improve*, it is ridiculous to suppose that money can be appropriated to *survey, with a view to improvement.*"

Not only the inland steamboat traffic but the building of the boats at the various river towns supplied news which the *Register* printed. The departure of the *Vesuvius* from Pittsburgh on April 22, 1814, was described, with a later mention of her "astonishing passage" to New Orleans in 227 hours' running time. The voyage was an event of importance to the whole country,

10 *Register*, XV, 64, September 19, 1818.

Niles wrote.[11] A friend of free enterprise, Niles opposed monopolies granted by states to navigate certain waters. The court case of Robert R. Livingston and Robert Fulton, possessors of the exclusive right to navigate the Mississippi by steam from New Orleans to the Red River, was followed through the state and into the federal courts. Before it reached the United States Supreme Court, the issue had been decided by Chief Justice Marshall's famous decision in Gibbon *vs*. Ogden, carried in full in the *Register*.[12]

Appreciative items told of the building of steamboats at Pittsburgh, Louisville, and other river cities, often with some detail as to their construction. Passenger fares, developments in the speed and efficiency of the steamboats, statistics on the number of steamboats on the western waters, and literally hundreds of brief items recorded the advances made in river transportation. In watching and recording transportation progress in the West, Niles did not fail to include notice of the building and operation of steamboats on the Great Lakes. The arrival of boats, launching of new vessels, and the establishment of new ports all received mention. Nor did Niles neglect to report the progress of steam as it affected navigation on eastern rivers, the coastwise trade, and transatlantic voyages. On the tenth anniversary of Robert Fulton's first successful voyage on the Hudson, it was remarked that no one had been injured in the decade that steamboats had been running on that river.[13]

On November 12, 1825, the *Register* printed figures that forty-three steamboats were operating from the port of New York. In the thirties and forties items began to appear on the speed of transatlantic steamships. In 1838 the *Great Western* made the trip from Bristol to New York in fourteen days and the *Sirius* reached Falmouth from New York in eighteen days and returned to the latter city from Cork in seventeen. From *Hunt's Merchants' Magazine* in 1839 the *Register* abstracted statistics on the seventeen trips made by the *Great Western* which had averaged thirteen and three-quarters days from New

11 *Register*, VI, 197–98, May 21, 1814; 320, July 9, 1814.

12 *Register*, X, 231–32, June 1, 1816; 320, July 6, 1816; XIV, 321, June 27, 1818; XXVI, 54–62, March 27, 1824.

13 *Register*, XII, 336, July 19, 1817.

York to Bristol. The shortest voyage had been made in twelve and one-half days. On the westward passage the average time was sixteen and one-half days. The arrival of the *Great Britain,* the "iron Leviathan," at New York in August, 1845, after a fourteen-day, twenty-hour passage from Liverpool, occasioned a column of description in the *Register.*[14]

The application of steam to land and water transportation had interested Niles from the start. To Volume III of the *Register,* he appended an "Addenda" [sic] written by Oliver Evans to support his claim that he was the earliest to attempt to apply steam to moving objects, such as boats or carriages. The article carried a notice from Niles in fairness to his readers that he had been reimbursed for printing it.[15] Many stories on steam engines, safety devices, the power of steam, and the development of different types of engines were printed; some of these were original, others were reprinted from American and English newspapers and magazines. The demonstration by the United States frigate *Princeton* of the superiority of the underwater propeller over the paddle wheels and sails of the *Great Western* was described in 1843, an indication that the *Register* recorded the various improvements in transportation machinery and equipment.[16]

At the same time that the *Register* was noting the improvement of the natural waterways of the nation, it was reporting for its contemporary readers and recording for the future the wave of enthusiasm for canal building which swept across every section of the country. Hundreds of these projects, many of which never got beyond the project stage, were outlined in the *Register.* Items concerning canals and canal building were printed in probably every volume, but they were especially numerous during the twenties when canal construction was at its peak and before attention was turned to the railroad as a means of transportation.

In the September 10, 1825, number of the *Register* two columns were devoted to the following seven separate items on

---

[14] *Register,* LIV, 257, June 23, 1838; LVI, 416, August 24, 1839; LXVIII, 369, August 16, 1845.

[15] *Register,* III, Addenda [sic].

[16] *Register,* LXV, 134, October 28, 1843.

canals: ground-breaking ceremonies for the Hudson and Delaware Canal; Erie Canal tolls for the year estimated at $500,000; ground-breaking ceremonies for the Miami Canal from Cincinnati to Dayton; Delaware and Raritan Canal routes proposed; the starting of work on the Blackstone Canal in Connecticut; a report that government aid had been asked in surveying the Champlain and Connecticut Canal, and a story that 500 men were working on the Delaware and Passaic Canal.

On July 1, 1826, the *Register* printed this estimate: "CANALS. It is reported that, from an actual examination of the subject, no less than one hundred and two canals are made, making and projected in the United States."

The Erie Canal, as might naturally be expected, received more space than any other canal project. Having printed an informational article on twenty-one canals in France, the *Register* turned its attention to "The Grand Canal" which was to connect Lake Erie and the Hudson River.[17] Various interests favored the utilization of rivers and lakes in a proposed waterway either to Lake Erie or Lake Ontario.

In 1816 Niles' stamp of editorial approval was put on the canal in the following effusive editorial comment: "The most sublime and magnificent object of its kind that ever presented itself to an enlightened statesman, is that of uniting our great inland seas with the Atlantic, by means of a grand canal from Lake *Erie* to the waters of the Hudson."

This enthusiastic outburst was accompanied by the report of the canal commissioners, made to the New York legislature on March 8, 1816, recommending immediate start of the work. Debate on the measure and on substitute bills was printed, as was the act as passed on April 17, 1816.[18] The ceremonies "commencing the excavation" at Utica on July 4, 1817, were recorded.[19] Niles' policy on internal improvements, voiced that fall in an editorial on the canal, clearly showed his nationalism: "It is true economy to encourage it—not as productive only of national wealth, but as one of the strongest links that can possibly be contrived to keep us together as a band of brothers, in

17 *Register*, I, 98, October 12, 1811; II, 46–47, March 21, 1812.
18 *Register*, X, 100–102, April 13, 1816; 128, April 20, 1816; 198–99, May 18, 1816.
19 *Register*, XII, 340, July 26, 1817.

love and unity; as a whole, dependent on its parts for prosperity. . . . I do not care a straw by whom, or by what honest means these improvements are effected—my only wish is that they may be effected, as rapidly as the increase of population and true political economy may require." [20]

Items the next two years were chiefly concerned with the progress of the work, statistics, and information about construction, tolls, and locks. For instance, on October 10, 1818, it was reported that 2,967 men and 1,516 horses and oxen were employed in 1818.

The opening of the first section of the Erie Canal, from Rome to Utica, with its attendant ceremonies, was described the next year.[21] From that time until the final completion of the inland waterway, each successive step in construction progress was noted in the *Register*. The opening of navigation to within eleven miles of Rochester, the need for more laborers, the announced opening of navigation from Schenectady to Rochester, all were reported prior to the completion of the eastern portion of the canal. More than half of the October 18, 1823, number was turned over to the description of the Albany celebration of October 8 when the first boats passed through the canal into the waters of the Hudson. Before the work was finally completed, Niles predicted that as soon as the West reached its growth, the canal would pour into the state treasury and the lap of New York City "an amount of business, wealth and population, that it would look like madness to estimate now." [22] In June, 1825, he reported that the waters of Lake Erie "commenced feeding in the western extremity of the Erie canal"; when work was completed and water admitted into the canal at Black Rock on October 26, that was noted, as was the arrival of the first boat from Lake Erie at New York City on November 4. Over this same period the income from tolls on completed sections, the low cost of canal transportation, and the type and quantity of merchandise transported were subjects of news articles. De Witt Clinton, canal commissioner and later New

[20] *Register*, XIII, 116–17, October 18, 1817.
[21] *Register*, XVII, 160, November 6, 1819.
[22] *Register*, XXVII, 5–6, September 4, 1824.

York governor, supplied facts and figures for informational articles.[23]

Miscellaneous items in the late twenties told of the increase of business. The arrival of 3,321 boats at Albany during 1829 and the receipt of 634,726 gallons of whisky at Troy were used as examples of the importance of the waterway.[24] Articles through the thirties were concerned chiefly with the amount of freight carried, the excellent condition of the stock in the canal, and annual reports of the canal commissioners.[25] The *Register's* coverage of the progress of the Erie Canal has been related in some detail because of the importance of that work and its influence on canal building in the nation. That Niles fully recognized these factors was demonstrated by his editorial treatment of the subject.

The canal projects of Pennsylvania and the Middle Atlantic states of New Jersey, Delaware, and Maryland included the Union, Chesapeake and Delaware, Susquehannah, Delaware and Hudson, Delaware and Raritan, and the Pennsylvania canals. The Union Canal, seventy-seven miles long, connected the Susquehannah, at Middletown, to the Schuylkill, near Reading. At both termini it connected with other canals, by which—with the rivers—it was planned to make a continuous watercourse from Philadelphia to Pittsburgh. The connection of Chesapeake and Delaware bays had long been considered. Although laws were passed by Delaware and Pennsylvania in 1801, work had to be suspended in 1803 because of the failure of many to pay their subscriptions. With the revival of the company in 1822, subscriptions were made by the states of Pennsylvania, Maryland, and Delaware, by the United States government, and by many individuals. The start in the work of excavation in 1824

23 Among scores of articles the following are typical: *Register*, XVII, 456, February 26, 1820; XVIII, 326, July 1, 1820; XX, 304, July 7, 1821; XXI, 160, November 3, 1821; XXII, 275–76, June 29, 1822; XXIII, 64, September 26, 1822; XXV, 199, November 29, 1823; XXVIII, 259, June 25, 1825; XXIX, 129, October 29, 1825; 173–74, November 12, 1825; 397–98, February 11, 1826.

24 *Register*, XXXIV, 282, June 28, 1828; XXXV, 431–32, February 21, 1829; XXXVII, 340, January 16, 1830.

25 *Register*, XXXVIII, 365, July 17, 1830; XLIV, 292–93, June 29, 1833; XLV, 49, 59–60, September 21, 1833; XLVIII, 211–12, May 23, 1835; LV, 391, February 16, 1839.

occasioned a page of description.[26] The next few years saw occasional reports on the progress of the work, the completion of which was referred to in the 1830 annual report of the directors.[27]

Chief mention of the Susquehannah Canal, agitation for which continued for years before its completion in 1840, had to do with the activities of Baltimoreans in 1823. Niles defended his home city against the charges of avariciousness brought by the *National Intelligencer* because of Baltimore's preference for the Susquehannah over the Potomac Canal and reported a mass meeting which voted 100 to 1 for the Susquehannah.[28]

The Delaware and Hudson Canal, authorized by acts of the New York and Pennsylvania legislatures, was built by private capital. Philip Hone was president of the company. Groundbreaking ceremonies over which he presided were described in the *Register* on August 6, 1825. This canal, which opened "the rich coal regions of Pennsylvania to New York," was completed from the Delaware to the Hudson in 1827, and to the Lackawaxen in 1828, at which time President Hone reported the railroad from the end of the canal to the coal mines "in a state of forwardness. . . ." By 1829 coal was being transported on its waters.[29]

Niles' interest in the West naturally caused him to watch the development of artificial water-communication routes in that section. His discussions of the possibility of inland water communication from New York to New Orleans led him to follow with keen attention the various proposals to link the Great Lakes and the Mississippi. The proposal to connect Lake Michigan and the Illinois River was mentioned intermittently from 1818 to 1835. The network of canals in Ohio to connect Lake Erie with the Ohio River, and the Ohio Canal with the Little Beaver in order to connect with the Pennsylvania Canal system occasioned scores of news and editorial articles during the twenties

[26] *Register*, XXVI, 180, May 15, 1824.

[27] *Register*, XXXVIII, 361–62, July 10, 1830; the twelfth annual report was printed in *Register*, XL, 333–34, July 9, 1831.

[28] *Register*, XXV, 145, November 8, 1823; 241, December 20, 1823; 257, December 27, 1823.

[29] *Register*, XXXI, 228, December 9, 1826; XXXII, 323, July 14, 1827; XXXV, 433, February 21, 1829; XXXVII, 130–31, October 24, 1829.

and early thirties. A summary of the various proposed routes was printed in 1825—a year which witnessed the starting of the Ohio Canal. De Witt Clinton made a trip to Ohio on July 4; he spoke at the ground-breaking exercises at Licking Summit. One thousand laborers were employed on this project and four hundred on the Miami Canal that season.[30] Difficulties encountered, including the construction of forty-four locks between Portage Summit and Lake Erie, and a note on the employment of two thousand laborers on the canal's northern division furnished material for an item reprinted from the Cleveland *Herald* in 1826.[31] An item from the Chillicothe *Scioto Gazette* in 1832 said that the canal was completed from Lake Erie to Portsmouth, on the Ohio, with the exception of one lock, and commented on the "astonishing moral" spectacle of the state completing the work virtually unaided within seven years.[32]

Noteworthy was the interest taken by the *Register* in a Florida ship canal, construction of which was started more than a century after Niles argued for such a waterway. In 1825 he wrote: "FLORIDA. Ever since the cession of this country, we have thought that the time was not far distant when the peninsula of Florida would be converted into an island, by means of a canal, large enough for the passage of heavy ships, whereby the tedious and dangerous navigation round the cape would be avoided; and, from all that we had learned on the subject, the cost of effecting it would hardly be worth a moment's consideration, compared with the advantages to be gained, provided it can be accomplished with any thing like a reasonable disbursement." [33] Later articles emphasized the safety to navigation and the shortening of the distance to New Orleans by one thousand miles if the waterway could be constructed.[34]

Early-nineteenth-century plans for a canal across the Isthmus of Panama or Nicaragua uniting the Atlantic and Pacific oceans

30 *Register*, XXVIII, 79–80, April 2, 1825; 195–96, May 28, 1825; 322–23, July 23, 1825; XXIX, 16, September 3, 1825.

31 *Register*, XXX, 380–81, July 29, 1826.

32 *Register*, XLIII, 117, October 20, 1832.

33 *Register*, XXVIII, 117, April 23, 1825.

34 *Register*, XXIX, 88, October 8, 1825; 293, 294, January 7, 1826; XXXII, 241, June 9, 1827.

were printed and commented upon in the *Register*. By 1825 the project was being debated in the House of Commons, and the relative merits of the two routes were discussed on both sides of the Atlantic.[35] Formal sanction of the Republic of Guatemala granted to a New York company—The Atlantic and Pacific Ocean Company—was reported in 1826. Niles favored a canal but strongly opposed the incorporation of a company by Congress to build it. This comment followed a report on a canal to be built across Nicaragua by "The Central American and United States Atlantic and Pacific Junction Canal Company." [36] This project seems to have dropped out of the news, or from the *Register*'s columns, at least, until in the forties when a number of reprinted articles were carried on the desirability of an isthmian canal.[37]

Niles' long friendship for Oliver Evans, already mentioned, early acquainted him with that engineer's theories about the application of steam power to moving vehicles which led many of his hearers to call him insane. Niles at least gave the man a chance to present his ideas to the public by distributing the "Addenda" [*sic*] to the third volume of the *Register* comprised of an article by the inventor and by printing his open letter to Congress in 1816.[38] In the former statement of his beliefs Evans said it was too much to expect one generation to step from bad roads to steam carriages. Having failed to interest New Yorkers and Pennsylvanians in a railway from Philadelphia to New York, he pessimistically wrote that the present generation might adopt canals, the next railways with horses, and the third steam carriages. He prophesied: "I do verily believe that the time will come when carriages propelled by steam will be *in general use,* as well for the transportation of passengers as goods, travelling at the rate of 15 miles an hour, or 300 miles per day." [39]

Niles often referred to a statement he had heard Evans make shortly after 1790 that "the *man* was then living who would see the Ohio and Mississippi covered with steamboats, and

[35] *Register*, XXVIII, 152–53, May 7, 1825.

[36] *Register*, XXX, 447, August 26, 1826; XXXI, 2–3, September 2, 1826; 72–73, September 30, 1826.

[37] *Register*, LXIV, 302–303, July 8, 1843; LXV, 57–61, September 23, 1843; LXVI, 103, April 13, 1844.

[38] *Register*, X, 213–14, May 25, 1816.   [39] *Register*, III, Addenda [*sic*].

that the *child* was then born who would travel from Philadelphia to Boston in one day, by steam boats and steam wagons." [40] His national pride is reflected in his claim in 1828 that Evans had proposed a plan in 1783 to apply steam to land carriages. And further, that in 1804 he had propelled a scow on wheels by steam a mile and a half to water where he had navigated it down the Schuylkill to the Delaware and up the Delaware to Philadelphia under steam power. Niles' editorial statement was in answer to English claims made on behalf of Sir Goldsworthy Gurney's steam coach and one invented by James Nasmyth.[41]

Keeping his readers abreast of the developments of the application of steam power to locomotives and to carriages which used the turnpikes in England, Niles merely printed the items as interesting news, without editorial comment.

Through the twenties scores of articles were printed about English railroads. Abstracted from magazines and books, reprinted from Liverpool, Leeds, and London newspapers, the accounts described the use of steam locomotives and horse power and discussed the relative merits of the two types of power. The Stockton and Darlington Railway, owned chiefly by the Society of Friends, and the Liverpool and Manchester Railway were two English roads, the construction and operation of which were closely followed by the *Register*.

Niles took his time in making his decision on the relative merits of canals and railroads. In the dispute between the Baltimore and Ohio Railroad and the Chesapeake and Ohio Canal over the former's right to purchase a right of way, Niles called the canal company's action in obtaining an injunction, later denied, "unjust," adding: "There is room enough for these two great projects—admitting the practicability of both—and we

---

40 An early reference to this statement may be found in *Register*, XXII, 179, May 18, 1822; Niles reiterated this again and again in editorials on steamboats and railroads; see *Register*, XXX, 185, May 13, 1826; XXXV, 19, September 6, 1828; XLIV, 193–94, May 25, 1833.

41 *Register*, XXXV, 72, September 27, 1828; James Rumsey is now credited by many with having been the pioneer in steam navigation; in 1783–1784 and later he too was carrying on experiments on the Potomac and elsewhere with "steamboats" as well as with steamboats; see *e.g.* Ella May Turner, *James Rumsey Pioneer in Steam Navigation* (Scottdale, Pa., 1930).

know not how to esteem one as a friend of his country who shall embarrass the progress of either." [42]

In 1828, according to figures reprinted from the *Yeoman's Gazette*, ten canals, totaling 747 miles, were completed; eleven were started, which would add 1,644 miles to that total; seven were planned. Only two railroads had been completed, the Quincy, three miles in length, and the Mauch Chunk, twelve miles long. An eight-mile Schuylkill West Branch railroad had been started and those planned included Boston to Providence, 42 miles; Boston to the Hudson near Albany, 187 miles; Albany to Schenectady, 16 miles; and a number of others. [43]

Early in 1829 the *Register* reported that the republic was coming more and more to believe that railroads would supersede canals, but was noncommittal itself. [44]

By August, 1830, Niles' mind was made up and in an editorial entitled "Rail Roads and Canals" he showed the line of reasoning he had followed in making the decision. He estimated that a railroad journey to Pittsburgh or Wheeling over a railroad 350 miles in length would take not more than twenty-three hours, at the moderate speed of fifteen miles an hour. A canal over the same route not only would require four hundred locks, which would take sixty-six hours to pass through, but could not be traveled much faster than six miles an hour. Having stated his case, he concluded: "Thus, while heavy and coarse and cheap goods may pass on the canal, passengers and all sorts of goods seeking a prompt market, will be transported on the railroad—the saving of time, only, exceeding the difference in the cost of carriage, if any there shall be." [45] Not a bad prediction as to the uses to which the two types of transportation would be put. In the December 31, 1831, issue, Niles wrote: "The time has passed when questions as to the relative utility of rail roads and canals might be discussed—at least, we believe so, and are content with the election that we have made."

Three weeks earlier he had carried an item that the "great New York canal" had been closed by ice before the first of

[42] *Register*, XXXIV, 250, June 14, 1828; 282, June 28, 1828.
[43] *Register*, XXXIV, 412–13, August 23, 1828.
[44] *Register*, XXXV, 299, January 3, 1829.
[45] *Register*, XXXVIII, 416, August 7, 1830.

December, adding, "but our rail road is expected to remain open the whole season!" [46]

The fact that Niles was convinced of the superiority of rail over water transportation in no way altered his handling of news of canal projects. Space forbids mention here, but all through the thirties articles on the building of canals and railroads may be found impartially reported in the *Register*. Railroads, steamboats, and canals so speeded the mails and the transportation of other goods that Baltimore 'in 1833 got the New York morning papers and the Philadelphia evening papers on the day of publication, he reported. The boom in canal and railroad building brought a warning from the economist-editor that he hoped the people would not "run wild" over such projects.[47] In the spring of 1835 he collected "scraps" about canals and railroads from Baltimore, Philadelphia, New York, Norfolk, Cleveland, Charleston, New Orleans, Washington, Wilmington, and Richmond newspapers. These he condensed and printed in three pages of small type, calling attention in an editorial to "the gigantic works that are contemplated or in operation." [48]

An absorbing story of the development of railroads in the United States could be written from material available in the *Register* for the last twenty-five years of its existence. Every phase of the expansion of rail transportation at home and abroad was recorded. Informational and editorial articles from United States and English newspapers and magazines were abstracted. Niles' pithy editorial comments introduced or followed many of these items. The nature of this study, however, makes necessary the compression of the story of railroads into a few pages in the larger subject of internal improvements. Niles' complete conversion to a belief in rail transportation in 1830 came at the end of a five-year period over which rail experiments in England and in the United States at Quincy, Massachusetts, and Mauch Chunk, Pennsylvania, were reported upon. Skeptical but open-minded was his attitude on March 26, 1825, when he wrote:

[46] *Register*, XLI, 266, December 10, 1831.
[47] *Register*, XLIV, 222, June 1, 1833.
[48] *Register*, XLVIII, 113, April 18, 1835; 129, 132–35, April 25, 1835.

The British people appear to have run wild with projects to invest their surplus capital. Any bubble is grasped at that affords a prospect of income. The great prevailing notion is, that railroads, travelled by wagons, driven or dragged by steam power, is a cheaper and more expeditious mode of transporting commodities than by the way of canals, and it is probable that the experiment will be extensively tried during the present year. . . . From what we see stated on the subject, it appears very probable that certain rail roads might be made which would be as productive as most of the canals—if the facts stated about *"resistance." "velocity." &c.* are true. . . .

We intend to give some articles on this matter to show what is going on. . . .

A week after the Mauch Chunk railway was opened in 1827, the *Register* printed a description of its operation from the Pottsville *Miner's Journal*. The road, which carried coal from the mines to Mauch Chunk on the Lehigh Canal, was nine miles long and operated most of the way by gravity.[49] The next month an item from the Boston *Traveller* briefly described the operation of the Quincy railroad the "first work of the kind in the union," which attracted so much attention from those "stopping to survey the enterprise" that a lunch stand had been set up. Two horses easily drew four carriages, carrying fifty tons; much of the freight transported was stone for Bunker Hill Monument.[50]

Plans for railroads from Boston to the Hudson, Boston to Providence, and a grand project for a railway from New York to Missouri by Colonel De Witt Clinton were reported upon in the next few years. The experiment of using the wind as motive power for a sail car on the Charleston road was described in an item from the Charleston *Southern Patriot*.[51] The enthusiasm engendered in Niles' mind by the unmistakable practicability of railroads did not cause him to forget his economic beliefs; in 1828 he opposed a bill authorizing the importation of railroad iron and machinery duty free.[52]

Having been convinced that railroads were practical and

[49] *Register*, XXXII, 196–97, May 19, 1827; additional details in XXXII, 344, July 21, 1827, and XXXV, 42–43, September 13, 1828.
[50] *Register*, XXXII, 227, June 2, 1827.
[51] *Register*, XXXVIII, 107, April 3, 1830.
[52] *Register*, XXXIV, 105, April 12, 1828; 154, May 3, 1828.

that steam would become the motive power on them, Niles, in the last six years of his editorship, wrote many editorials propagandizing for this new system of transportation. Not only the railroads themselves, but such technical matters as descriptions of various types of steam locomotives, improvements made in the coaches, the use of steam for carriages on the highways, and the need for safety precautions formed the subject matter of articles which added much to the informational background of his readers. At first somewhat skeptical of the practical use to which the steam locomotives could be put, Niles was soon won over and in 1830 wrote that the "experiments made with Mr. Cooper's 'steam car' on the Baltimore and Ohio rail road, would seem to leave no doubt on the subject." [53]

American-built locomotives were welcomed by this ardent advocate of domestic industry. Among these were engines built at York, Pennsylvania, by "Messrs. Davis and Gartner"; one invented by an army officer in use on the Germantown railroad and another manufactured by the Locks and Canal Manufacturing Company at Lowell, Massachusetts.[54] Improved "railwagons" designed by Dr. William Howard, Baltimore civil engineer, and Ross Winans, of New Jersey, and tests of the latter car in Baltimore and in England were described in detail.[55] Niles was one of two men who, with a five-hundred-pound weight, took part in a demonstration of the Winans car in Baltimore.

In the thirties, after the novelty of riding on the first railroads had worn off, Niles embraced the opportunity to suggest to the management that a little attention "to seeming trifles that add much to the *comfort* of the travellers, and which, without interfering with the urgency of the journies on business, induce persons to make pleasurable excursions," might not be amiss. As a rider, he had suffered the jolting to which early passengers were subjected, and in 1833, after a trip between Bordertown and Amboy, he wrote: "We hope that the pro-

[53] *Register*, XXXIX, 90–91, October 2, 1830.
[54] *Register*, XXXIX, 458, February 26, 1831; XLII, 386, July 28, 1832; XLIV, 267, June 22, 1833; LVI, 403–404, August 24, 1839.
[55] *Register*, XXXV, 212, November 29, 1828; 299, January 3, 1829; 432–33, February 21, 1829; XXXVI, 333–34, July 18, 1829; XXXVII, 2, August 29, 1829.

prietors of the rail road may find out, that persons who travel on this route, are not exactly 'live lumber'—and that they will 'regulate things' at the stopping houses." [56]

To attempt to describe the contents of or even list the news stories about railroads which appeared in the *Register* during the thirties is impossible in this volume. However, some of the significant editorials must be mentioned or quoted in part to give a picture of the *Register*'s attitude, and some of the news highlights touched upon to illustrate the extent of the periodical's coverage of the new method of transportation.[57]

Apparently written in reply to canal partisans, an editorial, printed on March 26, 1831, summed up the railroad's advantages in the following words:

It is now established, we think, that rail ways will supersede canals. They can be made for less money, and any where. They are not affected by floods, or droughts, or frosts. They engender no diseases. The travel on them will be about four times as rapid, steam being used as the moving power; and we see that the Majestic engine, on the Liverpool and Manchester way, moved 142 tons, 32 miles, (the distance between the places), in one day—travelling 180 miles, at the cost of 5 dollars for fuel, oil and superintendence on the engine—that is, 50 tons were moved one mile at the cost of one cent.

An eight-page essay on railroads was printed in the April 25, 1831, number. English and American roads, Oliver Evans' claims to the honor of being the first to suggest steam locomotion, and numerous other phases of the subject were considered. Niles made the claim for himself that he had been "perhaps, among the first who had pronounced an opinion, that transportations on rail roads would probably cost less than on canals —*time being altogether disregarded.*"

When William Huskisson, English statesman, was run over and killed by a locomotive while on his way to the dedication of the Liverpool and Manchester Railroad, in 1830, the *Register* gave over two pages to a description of the accident and of the dedicatory ceremonies.[58] Often as many as nine or ten articles

[56] *Register*, XLIV, 338, July 20, 1833; XLV, 67–68, September 28, 1833.
[57] Persons particularly interested in details of the *Register*'s news and editorial articles are referred to Volumes XXVIII–LXXV, with especial attention to XXXVIII–L.
[58] *Register*, XXXIX, 177–79, November 6, 1830.

about as many different railroads were gathered into a sort of railroad department. Jeremiah Hughes, third editor of the *Register,* established such a department in which a variety of items were printed.[59]

As was the case with the other types of news, much of that about railroads was merely reprinted from other newspapers after the retirement of Hezekiah Niles. Valuable statistical articles found their way from other papers into the *Register's* columns. In 1839 results of a survey by Franz Anton Ritter von Gerstner, European engineer and author, were reprinted from the Boston *Daily Advertiser.* It was estimated in this article that 3,000 miles of railroads were completed in the United States and 425 locomotives were in use.[60] Eighteen months later the *United States Gazette* reported 3,319 miles of track in the country, constructed at a cost of $86,000,000. By 1845 track mileage had grown to 4,752, according to figures compiled by the Cincinnati *Chronicle.*[61]

Asa Whitney's project to build a railroad from Lake Michigan to the Pacific in the forties was described by him in a letter written from Prairie du Chien, June 30, 1845, and reprinted from the *Morning Courier and New York Enquirer.*[62] In 1848–1849 some space was given to the project to build a railroad across the Isthmus of Panama.[63]

The railroad in which Hezekiah Niles was most interested and about which the *Register* printed more news and editorials than all others combined was, as might be expected, the Baltimore and Ohio. This great pioneer undertaking had the warm support of the editor from the time it was incorporated on

<hr/>

[59] Typical of such groupings are: *Register,* XLIV, 98–99, April 13, 1833; XLVII, 196, November 29, 1834; LI, 96, October 8, 1836; LXIII, 264, December 24, 1842; LXIX, 103–109, October 18, 1845; 169–70, November 15, 1845; 204–205, November 29, 1845.

[60] *Register,* LVI, 360–61, August 3, 1839; cf. Franz Anton Ritter von Gerstner, *Die innern Communicationen der Vereinigten Staaten von Nordamerika* (Wien, 1842–1843).

[61] *Register,* LX, 32, March 13, 1841; LXVIII, 168–70, May 17, 1845; readers interested in contemporary statistics on railroad mileage are referred to *Register,* LIX, 16, September 5, 1840; 64, September 26, 1840; LXXIII, 114, October 23, 1847; LXXV, 156, March 7, 1849.

[62] *Register,* LXVIII, 312, July 19, 1845.

[63] *Register,* LXXIV, 385, December 20, 1848; LXXV, 113, February 21, 1849.

February 28, 1827, to the time of his retirement when he requested in his will that his stock in the road be the "last resorted to" to settle claims against his estate.[64] The periodical continued its interest in the railroad after his retirement and death.

Selections from Niles' editorial comment illustrate his enthusiasm: "BALTIMORE AND THE WEST. Though room cannot be just now afforded to go into particulars, which may, however, be given hereafter for public information, it is with no ordinary feelings we announce the fact—that a plan for making *a rail road from the city of Baltimore to some point on the Ohio river,* has been considered and adopted by certain of our most intelligent, public spirited and wealthy citizens, and a bill to incorporate a company for this purpose has passed the legislature of Maryland, with very small opposition, indeed—"

He declared that "the length of a rail-way" could have no effect upon the principle of the application of steam power to land vehicles. The following prediction, in the light of present-day railroad accommodations, is of peculiar interest: "Some may feel disposed to smile at the prediction, but we have no doubt the time will soon come, when a person may pass from the city of Baltimore to some point on the Ohio river, with the same sort of certainty, ease and convenience, that he may make a voyage from Baltimore to Norfolk, in a steam boat—that little travelling palaces will be prepared, in which persons may eat, drink, sit, stand or walk, and sleep, *just as they do in steam boats.*" In the same article, he predicted that the shares to be offered to the public on the following Thursday would be taken at once "as fast as the names can be written down." [65]

In the period which elapsed between the incorporation and the ground-breaking exercises, the *Register* reported the engineering activities, including surveys and estimates; inspections by officials of the Mauch Chunk and Quincy roads; meetings of Ohio citizens, seeking extension of the road west of the Ohio; speculation in B. & O. stock; and the Maryland legislature's subscription of five thousand shares of stock.

The ceremonies held on July 4, 1828, in connection with

[64] Certified Copy, Last Will and Testament of Hezekiah Niles.
[65] *Register,* XXXII, 33, 34, March 17, 1827.

the laying of the first stone of the railroad by Charles Carroll of Carrollton, only surviving signer of the Declaration of Independence, occupied nearly ten pages of one number of the *Register*. Because the Fourth fell on Friday, the *Register*'s press day, only a brief mention appeared in the July 5 number, but it reflected Niles' enthusiasm:

The most splendid civic procession, perhaps, ever exhibited in America, took place in this city, yesterday, the 4th of July, on the occasion of laying the first or corner stone of the Baltimore and Ohio Rail road, by Charles Carroll, of Carrollton, the most interesting individual now living in the United States. Between fifty and sixty different associations appeared with their banners, cars and various insignia, all furnished in the most beautiful and appropriate manner, of which a full account will be given hereafter. The concourse of spectators, citizens and strangers, was exceedingly great, and a glorious tribute was paid to one arm of the triumphant AMERICAN SYSTEM —internal improvement, in displaying the progress of the other, domestic manufactures, all the principal trades being represented and in *full operation,* on their several stages drawn by horses.

In the July 12 number appeared the "full account" of the parade. Reprinted from the Baltimore *American,* it described in detail each of the half-hundred divisions in the procession and the elaborate floats on which craftsmen of almost every conceivable branch of manual occupation demonstrated their skill in their particular fields.[66]

As work progressed on the thirteen-mile section to Ellicott's mills, the *Register,* through 1828, 1829, and 1830, kept pace with the construction, including the tracklaying, building of bridges and culverts, and making of cuts.

Miscellaneous articles on the "noble spirit" of eleven of Baltimore's capitalists who took 5,722 shares in the road, the election of directors, a trial ride over a mile and one half of completed track, and the ease and rapidity with which snow was cleared from the tracks serve to illustrate the variety given to the periodical's coverage of the affairs of the road. Experiments with a sail car and excursions for Congressmen who visited the railroad, occasioned an item which concluded: ". . . and they also saw one horse draw *four* carriages, laden with about

[66] *Register,* XXXIV, 316–25, July 12, 1828.

one *hundred and fifty persons,* the whole thought to weigh *fifteen* tons, at the rate of six miles an hour. The display of this cargo, at the viaduct, had a fine effect." [67]

The official opening of traffic on the first section of the road on May 22, 1830, naturally was the occasion of several editorials. A week before the event, the *Register* announced it as follows:

THE BALTIMORE AND OHIO RAIL ROAD will be travelled in wagons, 13 miles, to Ellicott's upper mills, in a day or two, at the rate of at least ten miles an hour. Tens of thousands will embrace the opportunity of seeing the noblest work yet attempted in the United States, of travelling 26 miles in 2½ hours, without danger or fatigue, of enjoying the fresh air, and passing through one of the most romantic and beautiful countries that we have—every minute presenting something new to be admired by strangers on the road.

The wagons will start at different hours in the day—and soon, perhaps, hourly. Each wagon (drawn by one horse), will carry from 25 to 30 persons, with entire convenience. The 13 miles will be divided into two stages, for a change of horses, which may be effected in about half a minute, from the excellency of the gearings. The fare will be moderate. These wagons are hung on low springs, and it hardly seems possible that any accident can happen to injure the passengers, unless of their own extreme carelessness. The carriages, we suppose, cannot be upset, and a powerful lever, operating against the wheels, will immediately check the speed of a horse should any attempt to go forward faster than is desired.[68]

This excellent piece of propaganda for the railroad was followed two weeks later by a description of the ceremonies held in connection with the opening of traffic. Niles was one of the invited guests among whom were "the members of the legislature and other officers of the state of Maryland, and mayor and city councils, the editorial corps, and some distinguished strangers and other," including "the venerated and venerable *Charles Carroll of Carrollton.*" The editor described the trip from the city to Ellicott's mills, after which two of the four cars containing the notables returned. Niles and twenty-seven others, including Mr. Carroll, were among those returning. At Elk Ridge, Niles got off the railroad car and "took the stage and proceeded to Washington, being the first person, who so used this road as on a journey for business not connected with its immediate concerns." [69]

Niles never let a note of doubt appear in his news and editorial articles in support of the extension of the railroad. When Congress in 1830 refused to appropriate money for the road, he wrote: "We would rather 'pawn our clothes,' to eke out a payment on the little stock that we have in the Baltimore and Ohio rail road, than ask congressional aid again—." [70] To the last of his editorial career he sincerely felt that "The natural seaport of the west is Baltimore," and he believed that the railroad when completed would bring to that city greatly increased commerce in the products of the West. The railroad "*must* go on" was the keynote of his campaign to get additional funds from the Maryland legislature, which failed in 1835, but won a $3,000,000 appropriation in 1836. [71]

Plans, construction, and opening to traffic of the Washington branch of the road were the subject of many news items and editorials from 1828 to 1835. When the branch was formally opened on August 25, 1835, Niles was among the eight hundred persons who witnessed the ceremonies. He wrote about one column of description, the opening paragraph of which bears quoting: "We had the pleasure, (and truly it was a great pleasure), to make one of a party of about *eight hundred* that attended on Tuesday last, the 25th inst. to witness the ceremony of formally opening the Baltimore and Washington rail road. . . . The procession consisted of seventeen cars, loaded with about fifty happy persons each, seated entirely at their ease— which were drawn by four locomotive engines, the *George Washington, John Adams, Thomas Jefferson,* and *James Madison. . . .*" [72]

Destined to disappointment and defeat in his fight for the principles of his American System, Hezekiah Niles at least had

[69] *Register*, XXXVIII, 253–54, May 29, 1830.
[70] *Register*, XXXVIII, 317–19, June 26, 1830.
[71] *Register*, L, 101, April 9, 1836.
[72] *Register*, XLVIII, 449, August 29, 1835; news and editorial mention of the progress of plans for and construction of this branch may be found in *Register*, XXXIV, 155, May 3, 1828; XXXIX, 201, November 20, 1830; 298–99, December 25, 1830; XL, 1, March 5, 1831; 57–58, March 26, 1831; XLVIII, 361, July 25, 1835.

the satisfaction of seeing this one project of internal improvement for opening up a speedier means of communication to the West well on its way to successful completion in his lifetime.

While Niles' prophetic sense did not enable him to visualize air transportation, it is worthy of note that balloon ascensions received not a little space in the *Register*. Under the head "AEROSTATION," an announcement of "an actual experiment on the practicability of propelling balloons through the air, and of giving them a direction at pleasure" was printed on March 31, 1827. Through the thirties a number of ascensions were made at and near Baltimore. The log of one such flight was printed on October 19, 1833. The next year Niles reported flights on two occasions in the following words:

A young Baltimore mechanic named *James* Mills, made a beautiful ascent from Federal Hill on Wednesday evening last. It is thought to have been a more splendid one than either of Mr. *Durant's*—but we are rather "used" to such things. The balloon, and all the preparations for the voyage, were made by Mr. Mills himself. He ascended a little before 5 o'clock, and landed at the Bodkin—16 miles, in 70 minutes after his balloon was let-go, without accident or injury.[73]

Baltimore must soon lose all pretensions to novelty in our cities, so numerous are candidates for fame—in rising.[74]

In next to the last volume of the *Register* appeared an item on "Aerial Navigation," with a quotation from which this chapter on that periodical's treatment of land, water, rail, and air transportation will be brought to a close. In the description of a model flying machine exhibited in New York, by means of which it was asserted one might go from that city to California in five days, was the following: "The float or buoyant part, is made of strong cloth, coated with vulcanized Indian rubber, supported internally by a series of longitudinal rods, and inflated with hydrogen gas. From this float is suspended, at some distance below, a saloon for passengers. . . . The inventor, having carefully estimated the atmospheric resistance, is confident

[73] *Register*, XLVI, 85, April 5, 1834.
[74] *Register*, XLVI, 397-98, August 9, 1834.

of propelling these aerials at the rate of 100 miles per hour. Should he succeed according to his anticipation, the invention will produce a greater revolution in mercantile facilities than the original introduction of steam power." [75]

[75] *Register*, LXXV, 159, March 7, 1849.

Chapter 11

Slavery and the Negro

TRUE to his Quaker background, Hezekiah Niles opposed the institution of slavery. But his clear perception of the dangers involved in sudden and wholesale emancipation and his innate respect for the rights of property kept him from joining or approving the acts of the later abolitionists who favored emancipation at any cost. Some years before he established the *Register*, he had been a member of the Delaware Abolition Society, but apparently did not continue his membership after going to Baltimore.[1]

Editorials on the evils of slavery and the slave trade and news on the national and international aspects of legislative measures and diplomatic negotiations resulting from attempts to solve the problems were carried in the *Register* throughout its lifetime. It was, however, no crusader of the *Liberator* or *Emancipator* type. Niles' sane attitude came from recognizing on the one hand the evils of the institution, and on the other the conditions under which it had come to exist and the rights of slaveowners. He was condemned by the abolitionists, but his lifelong habit of judiciously examining both sides of controversial questions was too strongly ingrained to permit him to close his eyes to the facts and the arguments advanced by the South.

Before turning to an examination of the *Register*'s expressed attitude toward the trade in negro slaves, Niles' comments on slavery itself made in a twelve-page open letter to William Campbell, printed December 21, 1816, will be quoted in part. Niles wrote that the million or more slaves constituted a "great drawback" to the effective population of the country, but admitted that "these unfortunate beings" contributed immensely to the national wealth by their labor. He went on: "I never reflect on

[1] Wilmington *Mirror of the Times and General Advertizer*, January 19, 1803.

the condition of this people without extreme pain—but *negro* slavery is more easily reasoned against than removed, however sincerely and honestly desired. There is no man, . . . that feels more earnest for the emancipation of the blacks than I do—I hold none in slavery; I never will hold any;—but their *color* is, I apprehend, an eternal barrier to their admission into society. . . ."

The slave trade furnished items for the *Register* over a period of thirty years. In fact, while editing the *Apollo,* Niles had published an article condemning the trade, both African and among the states.[2] In an informational and historical article on the trade, printed in the *Register* on November 21, 1812, Niles concluded: "The introduction of slaves into the United States, was forbidden by law on the first day of January, 1810 [*sic*]— the earliest period that such a provision could be *constitutionally* made. The present trade is chiefly carried on in *Spanish* and *Swedish* bottoms."

Many of his one-paragraph news items contained strong propaganda against the trade. The conditions on the slave ships, including the almost incredible crowding of the negroes, the spread of ophthalmia which blinded many, the alleged high death rate on the voyages, and the throwing of shackled slaves into the ocean to avoid capture with them aboard as related in news items in the *Register* must have assisted in arousing sentiment against the brutal traffic.[3]

Niles' antagonism toward Great Britain made it difficult for him to give that nation credit for its fight against the traffic in negroes. He compared the barbarity of impressment with that of the "abominable trade to *Africa* for slaves—." Asserting that twelve slave ships had entered the harbor of Bahia, Brazil, in one month in 1816, he charged that the British treaties with Brazil and the declaration of the Congress at Vienna had accomplished nothing. He wished the British success in the war which they were carrying on against the slave traders off the coast of Africa, but qualified his approval with the reported

---

[2] The *Apollo* (Baltimore, 1805), I, 131–32, June 8, 1805.

[3] *Register*, XX, 48, March 17, 1821; 63, March 24, 1821; 117–18, April 21, 1821; XXI, 287, December 29, 1821; XXIX, 419, February 25, 1826; XXXIII, 119, October 20, 1827; XLI, 436, February 11, 1832, are typical of many similar items.

rumor—which he hoped was unjust—that they sometimes virtually transferred the slaves captured to their own use.[4]

In 1818 he was giving Great Britain a little more credit for her vigorous action on the water against the vessels engaged in the trade and on the land in negotiating treaties for abolishing the trade. Whatever her motives, the world should be grateful for the zeal with which she had prosecuted the business for some years past, he wrote. Commenting on Castlereagh's announcement to the Commons that the Netherlands had joined Spain and Portugal in establishing the right of search in order to end the slave trade, Niles said it was to England's "immortal honor" to have pushed the undertaking. Reports of debates in the Commons on the slave trade were printed in 1820 and 1821.[5] The next two years, the *Register* reverted to a more critical tone when discussing English activities along this line. "It is not in the character of that government to spare human life or lessen human misery—," wrote Niles in discussing an article reprinted from the *National Intelligencer,* which impugned England's motives in her campaign against the slave trade. Praising the capture of two slave ships by English cruisers, he added that he could not approve the motive back of it.[6]

His inherent hatred and suspicion of England is revealed in a comment on a speech by William Wilberforce in the Commons on July 25, 1822: "All this is as nothing. The British have 120 millions of slaves in Asia alone. White, brown, or black—all is the same to them, if profit is made by the proceeding. Some in parliament, no doubt, hated slavery because it was slavery; but I believe that the whole secret of the British interference to prevent the *African* slave trade, was a regard for the *price* of *sugar* and the support of the West India colonies, *well-stocked* with this miserable class." [7]

The economist in Niles was too strong to permit him to ac-

4 *Register,* III, 62, September 26, 1812; X, 412, August 17, 1816; 427, August 24, 1816; for a complete picture of the abolition of the Brazilian trade, see Lawrence F. Hill, *Diplomatic Relations between the United States and Brazil* (Durham, N. C., 1932), V, "The Abolition of the African Slave Trade to Brazil."

5 *Register,* XIV, 136, April 18, 1818; 166, May 2, 1818; XIX, 139–40, October 28, 1820; XX, 357–58, August 4, 1821; XXI, 23–28, September 8, 1821.

6 *Register,* XXI, 82–83, October 6, 1821; 163, November 10, 1821.

7 *Register,* XXIII, 53–54, September 28, 1822.

cept an altruistic explanation as the only one for Great Britain's crusade. In the March 24, 1823, issue, in a two-page editorial, "Pretence and Reality," Niles discussed the "pompous accounts of the zeal of British statesmen and of the efforts of their naval officers to suppress the slave trade, and also . . . of their desire to abolish slavery. . . ." He admitted that probably some of the leading men in England were as anxious to abolish the slave trade and slavery as were the "mass of people in the United States," but he said he believed the real contést was over the West Indian sugar planters who did not want the duty lowered on East Indian sugar. The British government, he charged, on the one hand was sending out ships and making treaties to abolish the slave trade, and on the other was depriving itself "of a revenue of a million of pounds sterling, that slavery may be kept up in the West Indian colonies, at the cost of the free people of the East Indian colonies!" Continuing, he added: "In such a state of things, who can believe that the British government is sincere in its professions of hatred to slavery? It is impossible that it should be so—else they should not maintain such an odious and oppressive distinction as exists in favor of the holders of slaves."

When 29,664 Manchester and 9,400 Leeds residents signed petitions for the abolition of the slave trade, Niles wrote: "The people had much better petition parliament to equalize the duties on East and West India sugars. This would do more to abolish the slave trade, than all other laws that Britain can make on the subject, supported by the whole power of her arms." [8]

Descriptions of meetings and reports of the African Institution in London, addresses of the English Society of Friends against the trade, reports of the capture of twelve slave-trading vessels by a British sloop, and English diplomatic correspondence, including the procès-verbal signed at Verona, were printed, indicating the scope of the *Register*'s coverage of the movement in England. [9]

[8] *Register*, XXIV, 294, July 12, 1823.

[9] *Register*, XXII, 325–27, July 20, 1822; XXIII, 12–14, September 7, 1822; XXIV, 52, March 29, 1823; 285–88, July 5, 1823; XXXIII, 9–10, September 1, 1827; XXXIV, 386–87, August 9, 1828; see Frank J. Klingberg, *The Anti-Slavery Movement in England: A Study in English Humanitarianism* (*Yale Historical Publications, Miscellany*, XVII) (New Haven, 1926).

The negotiation of a convention with England in 1824 by which the mutual right of search of vessels suspected of being engaged in the slave trade was affirmed brought a flood of diplomatic correspondence. Printed also were Senate proceedings on the treaty that the Senate ratified with reservations which Great Britain would not accept.[10]

Niles had no sympathy for Americans engaged in the slave trade. He condemned the use of American ships, American capital, and American "wretches" who commanded and manned vessels of other nations. Discussing capital punishment, which in general he opposed, he asserted that the "murders" by the slave traders must be halted.

I apprehend that there is an immense difference between those who hold slaves, and such as introduce them from Africa.* The first is an evil not of our own making, and which the wisest heads and best hearts have not as yet discovered any practicable plan to relieve us of —but the other is a voluntary affair, without the shadow of an excuse to palliate it, and as sincerely deprecated in one part of the union as the other. And it is believed, that far the greater part, perhaps nine-tenths of the supposed American vessels engaged in this traffic, except those presumed to be owned in Baltimore, belong to the non-slaveholding states!

* I make this remark because I have seen some observations on the subject which I consider as exceedingly ungenerous and unjust— calculated to do harm rather than to answer any good purpose to the cause of emancipation.[11]

Niles was even more vigorous in his condemnation of the domestic slave traffic. In 1817, writing on "Trade in Negroes," he asserted: "If there is any thing that ought to be supremely hated,—it is the present infamous traffic that is carried on in several of the middle states, and especially in *Maryland,* in negroes, for the *Georgia* and *Louisiana* markets. I blush for the honor of the art of printing when I see advertisements pub-

10 *Register,* XXV, 77–78, October 4, 1823; XXVI, 150, May 6, 1824; 209–10, May 29, 1824; 226–39, June 5 and June 12, 1824; 346–62, July 24 and July 31, 1824; XXVII, 245–50, December 18, 1824; cf. Hugh G. Soulsby, "The Right of Search and the Slave Trade in Anglo-American Relations 1814–1862," (The Johns Hopkins University *Studies in Historical and Political Science*) (Baltimore, 1933), LI, No. 2.

11 *Register,* X, 334, July 13, 1816; XV, 268–69, December 12, 1818; XVI, 439, August 28, 1819; XVIII, 241, June 3, 1820; 278–79, June 17, 1820.

lished in the newspapers, openly avowing for the trade, and soliciting business, with the indifference of dealers in horses." [12] When Baltimore newspapers in 1821 excluded advertisements of "cash for negroes," Niles took the opportunity to condemn all slave traders, domestic and foreign. He wrote that the increase of slaves in certain states, compared with that of the white population, should lead to the adoption of legislation against the domestic trade. "I could name a county in which the white population is only 703, and that of the slaves 7,214. The sun shines and it is day—we may as well expect day without a rising of the sun, as to suppose that such an alarming state of things can always remain undisturbed. It is against every rule and principle of nature. History teaches us this, and like causes will produce like effects until time shall be no more." [13]

Projects for colonizing free negroes were sympathetically reported in the *Register* over a period of more than thirty years. Annual meetings of the American Colonization Society were reported in detail.[14] Memorials to Congress leading up to the incorporation of the Society, appeals to the public for funds to carry on the colonization program, reports on the Liberian settlement, the formation of auxiliary organizations, Thomas Jefferson's approval of such a project, and the opposition of

12 *Register*, XII, 323, July 19, 1812; the *Register*, of course, carried no advertisements of any kind; in the light of this criticism of advertisements, it is interesting to note that the Baltimore *Evening Post*, edited and partly owned by Niles from 1805 to 1811, carried advertisements of sales of slaves and rewards for fugitive slaves; cf. Baltimore *Evening Post*, January 2 and January 3, 1811; as Niles' interest always lay in the editorial side of his publications, it is entirely possible that these advertisements were accepted by a clerk or other employee; on the other hand, Niles, as publisher of a daily newspaper in Baltimore, where such advertisements were printed in other newspapers, may have seen no objection to printing them. The *Post* had no strong editorial characteristics; from reading it, one gathers the impression that Niles used it as a commercial venture to aid in repaying his debts and gave no great attention to its news and editorial content; his job printing and his book and stationery store undoubtedly took much of his time during the period before he established the *Register*.

13 *Register*, XX, 323-24, July 21, 1821.

14 *Register*, XIII, 378, January 31, 1818; XVII, 371-72, January 29, 1820; XXIX, 329-30, January 21, 1826; XXXVI, 85, April 4, 1829; LIII, 264-66, December 23, 1837; LV, 264-65, December 22, 1838; LXI, 355-56, February 5, 1842; LXX, 2-3, March 7, 1846; LXXIII, 344-46, January 29, 1848, carry accounts of the first, third, ninth, twelfth, twenty-first, twenty-second, twenty-fifth, twenty-ninth, and thirty-first annual meetings.

some free negroes to the African plan—all were given space.[15]
The high death rate among the early colonists who settled on
Sherbro Island, off the coast of Sierra Leone, West Africa, was
factually reported.[16] The later and more successful attempt in
the area which was to become Liberia was followed in some
detail in the *Register* during the early twenties and, in fact,
throughout the life of the periodical. Letters from government
agents and colonization society officers accompanying the mi-
grants and ship captains furnished much of the information
from the colony. In 1827 Niles wrote that news from the colony
reported "health, peace and prosperity"; he praised the plans
for educating the colonists. Four years later he reprinted an
article from the *African Repository,* official publication of the
colonization society, which told of the colony's trade, including
$88,911.25 of exports.[17] The founding in 1847 of the Republic
of Liberia evoked the following introduction, an illustration, it
may be noted, of the difference in the styles of Niles and of
Jeremiah Hughes, then editor:

With heart felt joy, of gratitude to heaven for the blessings, which
have already accompanied the effort to establish a free and enlightened people upon the coast of Africa, and a home for the emancipated sons of Africa, that are here in fact neither freemen nor slaves,
and for the further blessings which we firmly believe to be in store
for both the colored and the white races of men from this benevolent
enterprise, do we hail the advent of a NEW REPUBLIC—a republic of
Africans, in Africa, as a new era in the Christian as well as the political world, full of hope and promise.
On the 26th day of July, 1847, the colonies of Liberia, by the action

15 *Register*, XI, 260, December 14, 1816; 275, December 21, 1816; 296, December
28, 1816; 355–56, January 25, 1817; XII, 103–104, April 12, 1817; 122, April 19,
1817; 348, July 26, 1817; XVI, 165–66, May 1, 1819; 233–34, May 29, 1819; XVII,
201–202, November 27, 1819; XX, 106–107, April 14, 1821; XXIII, 39–40, September 21, 1822; 138–39, November 2, 1822; XXXIII, 38–40, September 15, 1827;
XXXV, 209, November 29, 1828; XLV, 122–23, October 19, 1833; LX, 227–28, June
12, 1841.
16 *Register*, XIII, 200–203, November 22, 1817; XVIII, 240, May 27, 1820; 432,
August 12, 1820; XIX, 97, October 14, 1820; 169, November 11, 1820; 296, December 30, 1820; 328, January 13, 1821.
17 *Register*, XXXII, 129, April 21, 1827; 261, June 16, 1827; XLI, 251–52, December 3, 1831.

of their inhabitants, assumed a form of sovereignty under the title of the republic of Liberia. . . .[18]

Niles felt that the basic problem in connection with slavery was the rapid increase of the negro race in the United States. Because the colonization project did not offer a solution to this problem, he never approved it editorially, although he granted it space in his columns. His practical view of the project may be obtained from the following excerpts from an editorial printed on October 4, 1817:

I entirely dislike the cynical spirit that finds fault without offering a substitute for the thing condemned. Yet, while I profess myself without any hope of success in the colonization project I freely acknowledge that I have nothing better to offer. . . .

If, at so much cost and trouble, we find 15,000 annually *willing* to go to a strange land, and effect their transportation, what is the consequence?—in the meantime we shall have had 55 or 60,000 such persons born amongst us, and no sensible effect will be to be discerned. . . .

After which, in the same editorial, he turned to the larger question of slavery itself, saying: "No question that ever presented itself to my mind, was so much hedged by difficulties. I have thought much upon it, for I have believed that 'God is just;' but never yet was able to fix upon any thing even agreeable to my own mind, regarding, alike, the rights and safety of the two parties concerned in the affair. To effect this, would be to me a greater glory than to have won the victory of Waterloo:— but it has *bothered* wiser heads than mine."

In support of his contention as to the impracticability of the colonization scheme, he printed an estimate from the Philadelphia *United States Gazette* that the annual cost of transporting 15,000 colonists would be $4,797,500 which would total $163,115,000 by the time 500,000 had been moved. In the meantime, the negro population in the country would have doubled.

Characteristically, Niles gave four pages to an article from

[18] *Register*, LXXIII, 221–22, December 4, 1847.

a Delaware friend of colonization, although certain that the "benevolent writer" was mistaken in his statements. The next week, the editor took about the same amount of space to reply to the article. Again, he regretted his inability to think of a plan to solve the problem; however, on the last page of his four-page editorial he made three suggestions:

1. To encourage, by all proper means, the emancipation of slaves.

2. To make arrangements with the non-slave-holding states for receiving the freed negroes, and to *compel them* by "acts of violence," if necessary to reside in those states. . . .

3. Zealously to promote their employment in such healthy, and otherwise proper branches of business, that we know serve as *checks to population.*

Concerning the second point, Niles stated his belief, often reiterated, that the free blacks in slave states were "the worst part of the population." He also had the naïve belief that by scattering the negroes among the whites "a gradual change of *complexion* would be effected, from natural causes . . . a simple *association* . . . with white people." [19] The editor did not suggest intermingling of the races; in fact he stated specifically in a later article that negro families isolated in white communities would turn white over a period of years, "without sexual intercourse with the whites." [20]

He looked with more favor upon the plan to send the blacks to Haiti. He printed many items about the proposal and declared the cost would be much less than the African plan which he suggested dropping. But he still saw difficulties in accomplishing much in the way of reducing the increase of the negroes. He graphically illustrated his point by saying that if means could be found to provide ships carrying 200 negroes every day, only 73,000 would be sent abroad in a year, during which time the increase in the negroes on the mainland would total not less than one third of that amount.[21]

[19] *Register*, XIII, 164–67, November 8, 1817; 177–81, November 15, 1817.
[20] *Register*, XVI, 343, July 17, 1819.
[21] *Register*, XXVI, 282–84, July 3, 1824; 327–28, July 17, 1824; one interested in the Haitian project will find it mentioned in *Register*, XV, 117–18, October 17, 1818; XIX, 415, February 17, 1821; XXVI, 287–89, July 3, 1824; 373–74, August 7, 1824; XXVII, 29–31, September 11, 1824; 289, January 8, 1825; XXVIII, 253–64, June 25, 1825.

Through the twenties, Niles often discussed the African project, which he approved as a humane, if impractical, one. As an experiment for providing a haven for emancipated slaves and in offering them an opportunity to benefit themselves, Niles watched it with interest, but he had no illusion about its efficiency in reducing the negro population in the states, which he felt, after all, was, or should be, its main purpose. Colonization might accomplish some good if "young females" were exported, he wrote on July 17, 1824. This suggestion was reverted to again and again during the decade by Niles who saw in it a means of checking the rapid increase of the negroes. In support of his plan he pointed to the export of cargoes of young women from England to her colonies "to check population at home and increase it" in the colonies.

Having examined the *Register's* editorial attitude toward the slave trade and the colonization projects, a brief consideration of editorials on slavery in the period preceding the adoption of the Missouri Compromise is in order. In 1817 Niles remarked: "This business of negro slavery is much easier deprecated than removed, even if all were consenting to it." [22] In the last number of the fifteenth volume he noted that one of the "leading topics" to be discussed in the sixteenth was slavery and the negro. "No one supposes, or if so, turns with horror from the idea, that this description of persons, must *forever* remain as they are," he wrote. He felt that the condition of the slaves might be ameliorated to a considerable extent if the owners could be convinced that kind treatment could bring mutual benefits.[23] Throughout the spring and summer of 1819 Niles published a series of eight articles on "Mitigation of Slavery," in which he laid before the public his ideas on the evil which he said most people agreed ought not to exist. He opposed a general emancipation, saying that while it was wrong to hold slaves, "it would be almost as wrong, generally speaking, to grant them their freedom." He offered a five-point program, which he discussed in detail in subsequent articles. Briefly he stated: First, that slavery must, at some future day, be abolished in the United States; second, that it would be wise to educate the slaves and encourage them

22 *Register*, XI, 399–400, February 8, 1817.
23 *Register*, XV, 477, February 20, 1819.

to acquire property; third, to arrive at some means of "checking the propagation of the *slave-species*"; fourth, emancipation in the South should not be supported unless some means were devised to separate the free and slave negroes; fifth, that the free states should encourage the free negroes who wish to live therein and to "adopt some measures to lessen the prejudices and antipathies of the whites" toward them.[24]

In the first of the articles he argued that it was inconsistent for the United States to be known as the land of freedom, when more than one seventh of its population was held in slavery. The next three articles under the head of education of the negro discussed what today would be called welfare work or social betterment. Niles was not interested in giving the slave instruction in language, literature, and the arts. He advocated giving him some qualified freedom, treating him with kindness, possibly paying him a small wage, and giving him time off to cultivate his own piece of land.[25]

Niles' plan to check the increase of the negroes was, to say the least, impractical and did not take into consideration human nature. Briefly, it was an adaptation of his plan suggested two years earlier when he discussed colonization; that is, to transfer young negro girls. He apparently believed that if twelve thousand or fifteen thousand girls were taken from their southern environment and scattered among white families in free states a great check would be imposed upon the propagation of the species. To the objection that no right existed to remove the girls, he answered that the end justified the means; to those who cited the danger to which white women in the South might be exposed, he asserted that the process would be so gradual that the "male slaves would naturally acquire habits of restraint. . . ."[26] Whether miscegenation was less of a problem in the early nineteenth century than it was to become later, or whether Niles, for once, permitted theory to blind him to facts, it is not within the scope of this work to speculate. He opposed moving groups of negroes into free states. On August 14, 1819, he was not ready

24 *Register*, XVI, 177, May 8, 1819.
25 *Register*, XVI, 193–95, May 15, 1819; 211–13, May 22, 1819; 274–77, June 19, 1819; 292–94, June 26, 1819.
26 *Register*, XVI, 342–44, July 17, 1819.

to express an opinion on the introduction of slavery beyond the Mississippi, "frankly confessing that we have not yet made up a decided opinion on it."

In the final article of the series, Niles took up the fourth and fifth points concerning his opposition to emancipation in the South and his suggestion that the free states welcome the negroes. He asserted that the presence of free negroes with slaves was bad for both and dangerous to the whites, a fact evident to anyone who had lived in slave areas. The removal of negro girls to the North where they would be bound out to "respectable families" again was advocated. He argued against simple liberation, without a thought to the future of the freed negro who in many cases was injured by the emancipation, according to Niles' views. In closing he stated:

. . . but if we have said one word that any person can construe into a desire to maintain the *system*, we shall always regret it. Nothing could have been further from our intention. . . .

We agree also, that slavery must *some day* end, and generally look to its accomplishment by acts of violence. Is it not seriously demanded of us to guard against that period—and in obedience to all that is honorable, all that is just, all that is humane, to endeavor to do away with the *causes* that must and will inevitable [*sic*] produce scenes of havoc and desolation to our people, such as the locusts of Asia inflict on the herbage, as though the country had been burned with fire.[27]

As was the case in all controversial questions, the Missouri Compromise debate in Congress was reported faithfully and fully, with a careful selection of what Niles believed the strongest speeches on each side. Abridged debates, important speeches in full, and committee reports filled many of the *Register*'s pages.[28] Niles' ever-careful attention to impartiality and his

---

[27] *Register*, XVI, 419–20, August 21, 1819.

[28] Space forbids listing more than a few; the reader is referred to Volumes XVII–XVIII; early debate may be found in *Register*, XVI, Supplement, 161–79; abridged debates in XVII, 404–15, February 5 and February 12, 1820; 430–35, February 19, 1820; XVIII, 17–24, March 4, 1820; Senator William Pinkney's speech against restriction on admission and Representative John Sergeant's favoring a constitutional restriction against slavery were printed in XVIII, 349–57, July 15, 1820, and 367–84, July 22, 1820; other speeches in XVIII, 403–12, August 5, 1820; 436–40, August 19, 1820; 453–59, August 26, 1820.

feeling of editorial responsibility are evident in the following excerpt:

> We have now inserted all that we design to give place to, of the speeches in congress, on the Missouri question. It has cost much time and attention to make the selection which we have—the purpose was, to avoid a repetition of the same arguments and present a *full view* of the subject, on both sides of the question. How far we have succeeded in this, our readers will determine. Considering Messrs. Clay or Lowndes as the most powerful of those opposed to restriction, we wished to have published the speech of one of them, but that of neither of those gentlemen has yet been given to the public.[29]

Typical of its nation-wide coverage of matters of moment, the *Register* printed news articles on meetings held in Missouri, Delaware, New Jersey, New York, Pennsylvania, Massachusetts, and Maryland whether opposing or upholding a constitutional restriction on the admission of Missouri to the Union. Resolutions of the legislatures of Pennsylvania, New Jersey, Delaware, New York, and Ohio, opposed to the extension of slavery, and of Maryland, Virginia, and Kentucky, opposed to any restriction on Missouri's admission as a state, were printed.[30] That the news coverage was eminently fair is evident to the student who follows the question through the pages.

Editorially, Niles had arrived at a decision some time between his acknowledged indecision in August and November 27, when he wrote that "The decision . . . as to the prohibition of slavery in the projected state of Missouri, for a condition on which it will be received into the union, . . . is pregnant with more important consequences than any other, perhaps, that can be submitted to the national legislature—inasmuch as the principle thereby to be established is to spread an *acknowledged evil* over a large part of our country, and operate upon posterity for ages and ages."

Niles felt that the "plain history of the facts" of the Ordinance of 1787 and the reasons given why slavery was permitted in the

29 *Register*, XVIII, 449, August 26, 1820.

30 *Register*, XVII, 71, October 2, 1819; 151–55, November 6, 1819; 177, 189, November 20, 1819; 199–201, November 27, 1819; 241–42, December 11, 1819; 296–97, 304, January 1, 1820; 334, January 15, 1820; 342–44, January 22, 1820; 399–400, February 5, 1820; 416–17, February 12, 1820.

new states in the South were *"conclusive . . .* as to the right of congress to forbid slavery in the Missouri country." Declaring the issue was one of expediency, rather than the determination of a right of Congress, he concluded: "—and we hope that it will appear to be the interest of *all* parties to forbid the extension of an acknowledged evil, the effect of which must be to render it perpetual." [31]

More than a month before the adoption of the Compromise, he predicted that the Senate would vote for admission without restriction, that the House would refuse to concur, and that a compromise would thereby result in which a line would be "drawn beyond which slavery shall not extend." He added that he was "severely opposed" to the drawing of such a line because of the interests and parties that would be established, "But, as the principle of compromise was adopted at the formation of the constitution, perhaps we may resort to it again with equal success." [32] The Senate vote, bearing out his forecast, was printed. He disliked the Senate's action in linking the admission of Maine with that of Missouri in the same measure. The principles involved and the merits of the two questions were wholly different, he felt. As the debate grew warmer, Niles' nationalism won over his repugnance to the bill providing for joint admission of the two proposed states. Writing that he would not, at the time, argue on the propriety of a compromise, he showed his love for the nation in the following sentences: "But I am personally disposed to give up much, even of what I believe to be right in itself, to prevent the worst of all wrongs. The harmony and union of the states is [*sic*] a matter of the first consideration— the former may be much disturbed, but I will not believe that the people can be so moved by a few *Hotspurs* as to destroy the latter, on account of this concern—yet it is a disgusting fact that a separation is talked of by some on either side, and even in congress!!!" [33]

In the last available space on the last page of the first number of the eighteenth volume a brief paragraph told of the passage

---

[31] *Register*, XVII, 209, December 4, 1819.

[32] *Register*, XVII, 362–65, January 29, 1820.

[33] *Register*, XVII, 385, February 5, 1820; 425, February 19, 1820; 442–44, February 26, 1820.

on March 2 of the Missouri Compromise. Niles informed his readers of the separation of the Missouri and Maine measures and forecast the passage of the latter. The first item in the succeeding number told of the signing of the two bills by the President. In a two-page editorial on "The Slave Question," in the same number, Niles discussed the importance of the issue, asserting that it was more serious than any other question submitted to Congress since the formation of the country. He took some credit for the amicable adjustment of the controversy, writing:

> I was among the first, I believe, who espoused, and the only editor that I know of who openly advocated, a compromise, and recommended a recurrence of that spirit of conciliation which prevailed when our constitution was adopted.—Not because, that I myself had any doubt as to the power of congress to impose the contemplated restriction on Missouri, but for the reason that, in this extreme case, I would waive the full exertion of such power, rather than jeopardize the harmony and perpetuity of the system of government under which we live. . . . Not that I would make a bargain with iniquity, . . . but a choice of evils being presented, it seemed wise to accept the least of them, as congress finally agreed to do.[34]

This editorial, written some days after the passage of the bill, evidently expressed the sober second judgment of the editor. His immediate reaction to the law, penned in a hasty letter to his friend, Congressman Darlington of Pennsylvania, was unfavorable. "Though friendly to compromise, I am not satisfied with the decision on the Missouri question— I would not have voted for it, let happen what might. Too much has been conceded & the dirty conduct of the senate has succeeded."

Some two weeks earlier he had written Dr. Darlington explaining his reasons for favoring a compromise. He said, "I reverence, my friend, the principles on which you oppose a compromise with sin—yet I am myself almost willing to sacrifice something even in this way to harmony." In this letter, he wrote that if "neither restriction nor compromise" prevailed, he favored setting up an administration opposed to the "erection of any new territory—in that region—let it forever remain a waste and a wilderness." [35]

Unfortunately, the passage of the Compromise did not settle the vexatious question which dragged on for more than a year, and which was reported on in detail in the *Register*'s columns through 1820 and 1821.

Through the early months of 1821 Niles followed events in Washington and in Missouri. Clay's second compromise was commented on and the joint resolution setting up conditions for the admission of Missouri printed. Niles wrote to Dr. Darlington that nothing would tempt him to admit Missouri "with the *impudent* provisions in her constitution. . . ." [36] Niles' appraisal of the motives of those on both sides was expressed in an editorial, reaffirming his nationalism:

. . . a great majority on one side was guided by principles of humanity and justice, and on the other, by considerations of personal security; both honestly believing that the constitution was on their side. . . .

We have had enough of sectional matters. . . .

The south has gained as much as it ought to ask for, and the east most immediately profits by the commerce of the south—the middle and the west are gathering a rightful sense of what belongs to them, and why should not all be well? . . . Let us cultivate good fellowship, cherish a love of the union, and esteem as we ought, the blessings that flow from our republican institutions. [37]

The troublesome question as finally decided by the passage of the act by the Missouri legislature was covered factually by the *Register*. Governor Alexander McNair's message, President John Quincy Adams' letter of transmittal accompanying the joint resolution, the act of the legislature, and the proclamation by the President of August 10, 1821, declaring the admission of Missouri complete, furnished a documentary closing chapter to the controversy, of the importance of which Niles was acutely aware. [38] The Missouri question has been examined

[35] Niles to Darlington, February 18, 1820, and March 4, 1820, Darlington MSS, Library of Congress.

[36] *Id.* to *id.*, February 20, 1821, Darlington MSS, Library of Congress.

[37] *Register*, XX, 83–84, April 7, 1821.

[38] *Register*, XX, 240, June 9, 1821; 300–301, July 7, 1821; 323, July 21, 1821; 388–89, August 18, 1821.

in so much detail here, not only to reveal Niles' attitude on the entire slavery question, but to demonstrate the keenness of his understanding of the sectional aspects of the controversy, and to illustrate his frequently expressed love for the nation as a whole.

Abolition of slavery in the British colonial possessions received considerable attention throughout 1833 and 1834 in the *Register*. Many of the news and editorial items discussing the progress of the measure through Parliament and its operation in the West Indies, particularly, were, as might be expected, colored by Niles' anti-English feeling. He wrote on July 20, 1833, in commenting on the two million signers of abolition petitions in England: "The question has become a *national* feeling—and such feelings, in seeking their own gratification, pay little respect to consequences; and things which may be right in themselves, are oftentimes brought about in a wrongful manner."

This opinion of English abolitionists could as well have been applied to their American brethren by Niles who disliked slavery, but to whom the acts of the abolitionists were even more distasteful. While one may find news and editorials about abolitionist activities in every volume of the *Register* from 1820 on, it is in the forty-eighth and forty-ninth volumes (1835) that most of this material is concentrated. Factual coverage was unbiased and comprehensive.

The serious study which Niles had given the problem for years and his ability to see and understand both sides of the question made him impatient of the growing spirit for the abolition of slavery and the emancipation of the slaves without consideration of the consequences.

When Harrison Gray Otis, of Boston, upon the *Liberator*'s request, stated his stand on slavery which was that the general government had no right to "interfere with the plantation states in the management of their own slaves," Niles printed the letter and said that it expressed "nearly the universal opinion . . . of persons . . . opposed to slavery." In 1834, acknowledging that he could devise no solution to the slave problem, he suggested that the British experiment in the West Indies be studied before any steps were taken.[39]

[39] *Register*, XLV, 33, 42–43, September 14, 1833; XLVII, 4–5, September 6, 1834.

Niles' earlier remarks on the abolitionists were fair. Mentioning the publication at Mount Pleasant, Ohio, of the *Philanthropist* and the *Genius of Universal Emancipation,* he referred in an editorial on October 20, 1821, to Elisha Bates and Benjamin Lundy, the editors, as "excellent men, influenced by the most benevolent and praiseworthy considerations." But freedom without equality or at least opportunity was not enough, Niles declared, reiterating his stand that the *"free blacks are decidedly the worst part of the population of Baltimore. . . ."*

On May 13, 1826, he wrote: "There is not a man in the United States, I presume, whose opinion is worth respecting, that wishes a sudden and forced liberation of the slaves—and surely, none but a mad enthusiast would disturb the provisions of the constitution, and cast into hazard the lives of his fellow citizens of the south."

These editorial opinions were expressed five years apart—in 1821 and in 1826. In the next five years the abolitionists greatly expanded their operations of which Niles became increasingly impatient. He felt that theirs was a mistaken and misdirected zeal. Authors of inflammatory literature distributed among the slaves should be "blasted by the contempt and scorn of every honest man," he wrote in 1831. The circulation of the *Liberator* among the blacks "for the seeming purpose of provoking insurrection and massacre" brought instant and decided condemnation. "A sudden emancipation, either by *force,* or through *principle,* would be a calamity that *must* desolate the south, *and cause a terrific destruction of both masters and slaves!* No one of a sane mind, we suppose, can entertain such a project, unless reckless of misery and blood." [40]

The *Liberator's* editor, William Lloyd Garrison, took issue with Niles, who replied:

I shall not argue the right of my opinion with the *madness* of a man who is doing all possible injury to the cause of emancipation, which he affects to support; and increases the difficulties that stand in the way of rendering *efficient* service to people of color, bond or free. It is a great misfortune, that persons so impotent to do good may have a mighty power to do evil. I was the friend of black men

[40] *Register,* XLI, 35, September 17, 1831; 66, September 24, 1831.

before Mr. Garrison was born—and, if my life is a little lengthened, expect to be so after his *fever* shall have left him.[41]

When the *Emancipator* made its appearance in New York, favoring "entire and immediate emancipation of all slaves, even by the *physical force of the enslaved*," Niles expressed his opposition, adding, "We doubt whether immediate emancipation, and prompt extermination, would not practically mean the same thing, in the United States." [42] In the fall of 1833 he deplored activities of "many desperate politicians in the south" and "a few wild or wicked fanatics in the north" in connection with slavery. He said that there could be no objection in the South to a discussion of slavery as it affected representation in Congress, but

. . . that there is not the shadow of a disposition in the people of the non-slave holding states (a few solitary fanatics excepted) to interfere with the constitutional rights of the south, as to the preservation of its property in slaves, or in any wise disturb the public tranquility on account of the negroes, bond or free. Not less than nine hundred and ninetynine in a thousand agree, and will support their agreement, that the abolition of slavery rests with the *states* in which slaves are held—and there is no idea of a constitutional power entertained, or of any other power to be exerted, to interfere with the relations between masters and slaves—unless in the consent and with the approbation of the former, much as the large majority are opposed to slavery, much as that majority would do to relieve our country of slaves.[43]

In the December 28, 1833, number he condemned the methods of Garrison and other abolitionists and asserted that their actions made the slaves more miserable by arousing the owners to new acts of oppression. His stand on the constitutional question involved was reiterated: "There is no constitutional right in the government of the United States to interfere in *property* in slaves. The *states* are not *colonies;* and, in this matter, must be allowed to act for themselves—and be the sole judges of their own concerns."

Niles in 1834 suggested—and apparently carried out his own suggestion—that the press ignore the activities of the abolition-

41 *Register*, XLI, 145–46, October 22, 1831.
42 *Register*, XLIV, 82, April 6, 1833.　43 *Register*, XLV, 97, October 12, 1833.

Slavery and the Negro 283

ists. Their "indiscreet proceedings" obtained "frequent and uncalled for notices," he wrote, citing as an example the Reverend Samuel H. Cox, of New York City, who had preached a sermon to prove that Jesus Christ was a colored man. By "colored" the Reverend Mr. Cox meant an Asiatic or a Mongolian, but Niles said the minister should have realized that the term was generally used in the United States in reference to the negro race.[44] When he ran across an item in another paper, copied from the *Liberator,* which he no longer read, that a white man wanted to marry a negro woman because he was "convinced that our brethren and sisters are entitled to all the rights and privileges which are claimed by the whites," Niles remarked: "We wish that the gentleman may soon get a wife—in *all* respects answering his wishes, and that we may have the honor of announcing his marriage. Persons so chivalrous ought not to be thwarted in their desires." [45]

The increasing number of abolition meetings in the North and meetings of those opposed in both the North and the South may be traced through the *Register's* columns. Eight and one-half pages of the October 3, 1835, number were given over to selections from a "peck" of clippings which Niles had "carefully overhauled" in order to present a *"full* view" of the subject. Twenty-nine newspapers from sixteen cities in eleven northern and southern states were quoted, in addition to a number of items which did not state their source. On the first page of this issue, Niles summed up the slavery situation, which he felt had been aggravated by the actions of the abolitionists. Because it epitomized his editorial attitude and because it was his last editorial expression of any length on the subject before his retirement, it will be examined in some detail. Niles remarked that the new *"arrayment of parties"* caused uneasiness in the minds of true friends of the country. The antiabolition meetings in the North were mentioned as illustrating the fact that the North was by no means united in favor of abolition. The South's demands that the North prohibit discussion of the slave question were, inferentially, at least, criticized. Having noticed activities in both sections, he went on:

44 *Register,* XLVI, 301, June 28, 1834.
45 *Register,* XLVI, 346-47, July 19, 1834.

In this case we now stand—and heaven only knows what will result from the excitements which the wicked agents of abolition have caused. They appear to gather strength every moment—and ultraism on the one side is perpetually begetting it on the other—the whole being nurtured by a wild party spirit. . . .

A forced emancipation is out of the question—it would render the condition of the slaves much worse than it is—*infinitely worse*. Why not imitate the example of the Friends, or Quakers, who, bearing by precept and *example*, believe they accomplish their duty in the performance of kind offices to the people of color—without violence.

But it is a sickening subject—and we refer our readers to the large collection of extracts that we have made for their use. It will require the best talents by the country to quiet the *feelings* which they disclose. The only man, perhaps, that may attempt it, is HENRY CLAY. But will that abused MAN make the attempt? *Will the people support him, in it?*

Unsympathetic as he was personally and editorially to the abolitionists, Niles' editorial code was adhered to in printing news of their meetings and organizations. He exercised his editorial judgment, as has been mentioned, in discarding items of proceedings held, as he thought, mainly to obtain publicity. But letters from Lewis Tappan; the address of the American Anti-Slavery Society on September 3, 1835, signed by Arthur Tappan and others; a description of the convention of the New York Anti-Slavery Society; and a condemnation by a New York newspaper of the reported $50,000 price on the head of Arthur Tappan, "notorious abolitionist," in Louisiana, serve to illustrate the extent of the periodical's impersonal attitude in its handling of the news.[46]

Niles' accident while attending a New York convention in October, 1835, prevented him from doing much writing thereafter. Hence the accounts of the seizure of Garrison in the *Liberator* office and the mob's futile search for George Thompson, English abolitionist, were reprinted from Boston and New York papers with no editorial comment.[47] On August 6, 1836, the rescue of two runaway slaves from a courtroom in Boston by a mob of abolitionists was termed one of the "most flagrant

[46] *Register*, XLIX, 20–21, 28–29, September 12, 1835; 162–63, November 7, 1835; 172, November 14, 1835.
[47] *Register*, XLIX, 145–50, October 31, 1835.

outrages" which had ever disgraced the courts. The action exhibited "a most revolting degree of fanatacism" and was certain to alarm the South, the *Register* stated.

One more angle of abolitionist activities remains to be mentioned before the *Register*'s handling of slavery in the period following the retirement of Hezekiah Niles is examined briefly. That has to do with the sending of incendiary literature through the mails to negroes in the South by northern abolitionists. Here the editor faced a real problem. Throughout his life he had fought for freedom of the press and of speech. Censorship he abhorred. Yet, he sincerely believed that the circulation of the *Liberator, Emancipator,* and other magazines and pamphlets of their type encouraged the negroes to insurrection and endangered the peace and safety of the South and of the whole nation. Furthermore, Amos Kendall, the postmaster general of the Jackson administration to which Niles was personally opposed, unofficially suggested disregard of the law to the Charleston, South Carolina, postmaster. Here was an occasion of government interference with press freedom; a perfect editorial target. Notwithstanding his unwavering defense of the press, Niles gave at least implied approval to Kendall's extralegal suggestion, qualified by a mild condemnation, in the only expression of opinion printed in the *Register.* It must have been a hard decision for the editor to arrive at. He weighed the evils of a slave insurrection, which he felt would result from continued distribution of the literature, against the right to express and circulate freely opinions or propaganda and apparently decided that the end justified the means.[48]

After Hezekiah Niles' retirement in 1836 the *Register* covered the antislavery agitation, as it did other contemporary events, almost entirely by reprinting news and editorials from representative newspapers. Thus, the periodical mirrored the scene without taking an active part in shaping or commenting on the events so pictured. However, there were times when this policy was departed from. Mob action on either side was deprecated. When Cincinnatians wrecked the office where James G. Birney was printing the *Philanthropist,* the *Register* pointed out that

[48] *Register*, XLVIII, 402–405, August 8, 1835; 410, August 15, 1835; 446–48, August 22, 1835; Kendall's letter is on 448, August 22, 1835.

such acts of violence only aroused sympathy for the abolitionists
—"and the tears of sympathy blind the eyes of truth." [49] The
Alton, Illinois, riots which resulted in the death of the Reverend
E. P. Lovejoy, former editor of the Alton *Observer*, abolitionist
organ, on November 7, 1837, were, however, reported without
comment.[50] The long controversy in the House over that body's
refusal to consider antislavery petitions may be followed factually in the *Register*. John Quincy Adams' eight-year battle to
obtain repeal of the rule is reported in the fifty-first to the sixty-
seventh volumes (1837 through 1844).

Activities and speeches of Garrison, Wendell Phillips, and
Lewis and Arthur Tappan may be followed by reading the reports of the annual meetings of the American Anti-Slavery Society. Infiltration of the abolitionists into American politics and
the formation of the Liberty party occasioned expression of
editorial opinion by Jeremiah Hughes in the forties. He looked
with disfavor upon the use of the word "liberty" by those chiefly
interested in abolition. After the 1844 election, in which votes
polled for abolition candidates in New York probably decided
the election against Clay, Hughes remarked concerning members of the new party, "They confidently believe, that at least,
it will be in their power to name one of the leading candidates
for the next presidency." [51] Through 1846, 1847, and 1848 the
Register reported the bitter struggle in Congress over the Wilmot Proviso and the act authorizing free-soil government in
Oregon.

The *Register* ceased to exist before the Compromise of 1850
was adopted. But the rumblings which preceded the outbreak
of that struggle were heard in the last year of the periodical's
life. The newspaper dispute over President-elect Zachary Taylor's statement on abolitionists was summarized. The Natchez
Courier was quoted as reporting that General Taylor's remark
had to do with the "right of property" in slaves in the slave states

[49] *Register*, L, 393, 397–98, August 13, 1836.

[50] *Register*, LIII, 192, November 18, 1837; 196–97, November 25, 1837; the acquittal of all parties charged with rioting, arson, and murder in connection with
the riots, was reported in LIV, 6, March 3, 1838.

[51] *Register*, LXV, 47, September 16, 1843; LXVII, 247, December 21, 1844; Cincinnati and Boston conventions of 1845 are mentioned in *Register*, LXVIII, 395–97,
August 23, 1845.

and that he had said that "if the *Northern fanatics* attempted
to interfere with *that,* he was in favor of drawing the sword and
throwing away the scabbard." To which the New Orleans *Bulletin* was quoted as saying that such a defense of the right of
property "would be unanimously responded to by the entire
South." [52] The conventions of the southern members of Congress were reported in some detail early in 1849. Henry Clay's
letter of February 17, 1849, favoring a gradual emancipation of
slaves carried on in connection with a colonization program was
given space.[53]

Because it was not carried away by the impractical and reckless idealism of the abolitionists and yet was by no means a proslavery organ, the *Register,* especially under the editorship of
Hezekiah Niles, was attacked by extremists on both sides. Its
very neutrality in reporting the news and its judicious editorial
discussions of the legal, social, moral, and religious aspects of the
slavery question immeasurably increase its value to the student
interested in obtaining a "full view" of the controversy during
the years in which it was published.

[52] *Register,* LXXV, 25, January 10, 1849.
[53] *Register,* LXXV, 84–88, February 7, 1849; 100–104, February 14, 1849; 161,
March 14, 1849; 185–87, March 21, 1849.

Chapter 12

The *Register* and the Historian

"To the future HISTORIAN we commit the record, and await the judgment with full confidence," wrote the third editor of the *Register* in his valedictory editorial.[1]

Historians, economists, political scientists, biographers, journalists, and others interested in reconstructing an accurate picture of the United States for the first half of the nineteenth century have justified the faith that the founder-editor and his successors had in the usefulness of the news magazine to future generations.

The conviction of Hezekiah Niles that he was editing and publishing a work which would be of increasing value as the years went by has been gone into in detail in Chapter 2; one more typical expression of his faith, written in 1833, will be printed here. "We believe this work is the most copious record of miscellaneous public papers in the world, presented cotemporaneously, and in book-form, for preservation and reference."[2]

Hughes, printing a letter from a Baltimore citizen in 1840 praising Niles' zeal in collecting and recording facts about General William Henry Harrison, wrote that his predecessor had done only justice to the General and that other volumes "whenever examined with equal industry, in search of information relative to other prominent men of this country, who have acted within the period of its publication, *their* doings and sayings will be found no less faithfully *'registered'* in its pages, as though they too had been especially in the view of the editor. —It is a trait that essentially belongs to the character of the work, and contributes greatly to its intrinsic value."[3] The next

1 *Register*, LXXIV, 1, July 5, 1848.
2 *Register*, XLV, 241, December 14, 1833.
3 *Register*, LIX, 257, December 26, 1840.

year the editor wrote: "It is not necessary at this day to say one word in commendation of the character of the REGISTER, as a historical record; for it is so closely identified with the progress of the nation, that no man, who desires to attain correct information in relation to 'men and things,' can do so, satisfactorily, without a reference to its pages. Those who possess entire copies of the work are, indeed, rich in its possession, and there is not a volume that is not daily increasing in value." [4]

No other publication remotely approaches the *Register* in value as a source of Americana of the period in which it was published. Frank Luther Mott, whose three-volume work on the history of American magazines won the Pulitzer prize in history in 1938, styles the *Register* the "chief reliance of the historiographer for the first half of the nineteenth century. . . ." [5] To achieve such recognition the *Register* has had to stand the test of time and to undergo successfully careful examination by a procession of scholars who have delved into its pages for information on almost every subject pertaining to the American scene from 1811 to 1849.

To one who has carefully studied all seventy-six volumes, and not only those for a particular year or a limited period, the *Register* rather naturally divides itself into two distinct editorial epochs. The first extends from 1811 to 1833; the second from 1833 to 1849. While there are some few exceptions to and deviations from the rule, it may be said generally that throughout the first period the *Register* was constantly and actively engaged in attempting to mold and influence public opinion; during the second period its primary purpose was to report and reflect opinions as expressed by others.

The *Register* of both periods is of great value to the historian. But he should realize, as many have not, that the *Register* of 1832, engaged in a fight to save the American System, represented an entirely different editorial philosophy than the *Register* of 1844, reporting the political maneuverings leading up to the nomination and election of James K. Polk to the presidency.

From the publication of its first issue, the *Register* was an avowed supporter of domestic industry. Before the twenties,

4 *Register*, LXI, 1, September 4, 1841.
5 Mott, *A History of American Magazines 1741–1850*, 268.

it had come to advocate a protective tariff in order that this industry might prosper. In the decade between 1820 and 1830 the *Register* was recognized as the leading periodical in the fight for the tariff. From 1824 to 1833 it campaigned ceaselessly for the American System, which included internal improvements along with adequate tariff protection for domestic industry. Thus, for more than twenty years the *Register* had a definite editorial program, a goal which it constantly kept before the eyes of its readers. It was an out-and-out propaganda organ and many of its articles are reminiscent of those of the early pamphleteers. In fact, many of Hezekiah Niles' essays on the need for a protective tariff, which were distributed by the thousands of copies, were, as has been noted, first printed in the columns of the *Register*. Niles' expressed beliefs on slavery, on the republics of Latin America, and on Great Britain have each been discussed in sufficient detail in preceding chapters to make more than a mere mention here unnecessary to prove that the *Register* from 1811 to 1833 was filled with editorial opinions, vigorously expressed. At the same time it maintained an impartiality, rare in its day, by printing both sides of every controversial question.

The triumph of Jacksonian Democracy at the polls in 1832 marked the turning point in the *Register*'s editorial policy. The electorate's approval of President Jackson's vetoes of internal improvement and bank legislation, followed by the passage of the Compromise Tariff of 1833, killed, for the time being, the American System. Niles had nothing left to fight for. Obeying his own precepts as to majority rule, he completely changed the editorial policy of the *Register* almost overnight. From a crusading editorial organ, filled with propaganda for protection, the *Register* became a periodical the contents of which were composed almost entirely of articles reprinted or abridged from other publications. Varying shades of press and public opinion were recorded, but with few notable exceptions, after 1833 one does not find in the *Register* original editorials on controversial measures. However, one does find, and this is of peculiar interest and value to the historian, a well-chosen selection of editorial excerpts from the nation's newspapers which in a small compass presents a surprisingly accurate résumé of

American press opinion. William Ogden Niles and Jeremiah Hughes, especially, in their tenure of the editorial chair extending from 1836 to 1848, efficiently sampled public opinion as voiced by the newspapers on public questions of the day.

No historical source should be used unless it is subjected to the fundamental tests known to every scholar. Newspapers certainly should be held to the same standards as are other sources and material printed in them should be carefully checked, critically examined, and accepted only after being exposed to an intelligent skepticism based upon a thorough knowledge of the circumstances surrounding the event or the issue described in print.

The reliability of the *Register* as a source of nineteenth-century information is enhanced by two significant factors, the first of which is the esteem in which the periodical was held by its contemporaries in the newspaper and magazine field. This recognition was universal and it came from editors who disagreed violently with Hezekiah Niles and the *Register* on economic and political questions as well as from friends. The editor of the Charleston *Southern Patriot* in 1817 wrote that the *Register*, ". . . for the variety and usefulness of its statistical, agricultural and political facts, will serve hereafter as a book of reference for the historian. . . ." [6] Other editors who differed with Niles paid tribute to him and to his publication. A writer in the *Aurora*, taking issue with an editorial in the *Register*, prefaced his attack with the following encomium: "That paper is a very valuable one, from the diligence and care with which the passing events and documents of every public kind, are preserved in it. Mr. Niles has presented at different times many discussions on political economy and statistics, and the opinion has prevailed, that on these subjects he was a good authority to be referred to, and his personal character has sanctioned this opinion." [7]

The editor of the Albany *Register*, reprinting a *Register* editorial, referred to the "bold and independent editor of that invaluable journal." [8] The *German Correspondent*, a magazine

[6] *Register*, XI, 397, February 8, 1817.
[7] *Register*, XIII, 329, January 17, 1818.
[8] *Register*, XVII, 18, September 11, 1819.

published in New York, quoted the *Weimarische Zeitung* on the value of the *Register*.[9] In 1821 the *National Intelligencer* welcomed "so important an ally . . . as the popular and intelligent editor of the Weekly Register," in the fight for government aid for roads.[10] The New York *Evening Star* in 1835 called the *Register* ". . . decidedly the best and most authentic history of the United States extant from 1811 to this moment. Its style is remarkably pure and sententious—its statistics accurate and complete, and its political opinions undisfigured by misrepresentation, personal invective, or narrow-minded prejudice." [11]

In 1837, shortly after Hezekiah Niles' retirement, the New York *American* printed and the *National Intelligencer* reprinted expressing its "entire concurrence," a tribute, quoted here in part: "It may seem somewhat like supererogation to say ought at this time of day in praise of a periodical so well known as the *Weekly Register;* but having at the moment experienced its value, we may as well acknowledge it. The last number happening before us, when we were desirous of looking back at two or three public documents, to find which in the file of a daily paper would have required both time and research—we turned to it, and there lighted on them ready to our hand. . . ." [12]

When William Ogden Niles moved the publication office of the *Register* to Washington, D. C., in 1837 and changed the name of the periodical to *Niles' National Register,* the press of the nation generally carried the announcement of the change and commented on it editorially. Some twenty-nine excerpts from these congratulatory editorials were printed in a circulation circular of which only a few will be further condensed and quoted here. The Charleston *Mercury,* an editorial antagonist of long standing, wrote, ". . . it has no partizan character—" and mentioned the "uniform judgment, and good sense" which had governed the editor of the *Register*. Another,

9 *Register*, XIX, 371, February 3, 1821.

10 *Register*, XXI, 178, November 17, 1821.

11 *Register*, XLVIII, 161, May 9, 1835.

12 *Register*, LI, 353, February 4, 1837.

but somewhat more friendly opponent, the Richmond *Enquirer,* said, "It is the best general collection of historical facts and references, that is published in the United States with a table of contents." The *National Intelligencer* declared that the *Register* was "already almost the only authority that can easily be referred to, and entirely relied upon, for an important portion of our country's history." The St. Louis *Republican* wrote that "no periodical in the union, probably not in the civilized world, . . . has won itself so lasting and so enviable a reputation. . . ." The Buffalo *Journal* mentioned the *Register*'s high reputation, adding that important details of United States history for the past twenty-six years could "in vain be looked for in any other publication. . . ." The Pittsburgh *Gazette,* first newspaper published west of the Alleghenies, then past the half-century mark, asserted that the *Register* had "obtained a most enviable reputation with men of all parties." [13]

Mathew Carey in the preface to *The Olive Branch,* published in 1814, wrote: "It would be unjust were I not to acknowledge the numerous and weighty obligations I owe to the Weekly Register, edited by H. Niles, the best periodical work ever published in America, from which I have drawn a large proportion of the facts and documents which I have employed." [14]

James Wilson, grandfather of the twenty-eighth President of the United States, editor of the *Western Herald* of Steubenville, Ohio, emphasized the value of the *Register* in making economics understandable to the common man when he wrote:

A man might read Adam Smith's wealth of nations till doomsday, before he could get half as much light on the subject of the *economy of nations,* as Mr. Niles has furnished within the last two years. . . . A mental labor, like Mr. Niles', is worthy, every way worthy, of its due reward. He possesses a mind of great compass, and embraces at a *glance,* the *means,* and *aggregate* of a nation's wealth. He views the minutiae and the fragments of man's industry scattered over the various climate and soil of every state. He combines the substance

13 This circular was found inserted between pp. 40–41 of *Register,* LV, in the bound copy in the Library of the University of California at Los Angeles.

14 Mathew Carey, *The Olive Branch: or Faults on Both Sides, Federal and Democratic. A Serious Appeal on the Necessity of Mutual Forgiveness & Harmony, to Save Our Common Country from Ruin* (Philadelphia, 1814), 25.

and the industry of all, and presents to the nation a view of its whole mass of wealth.[15]

When William Cobbett grossly attacked Niles in 1817, friends in Wilmington, Delaware, requested the editor of the *Delaware Watchman* to publish an article containing an expression of their esteem as to his character and achievements, which they hoped other editors would reprint.[16] That same fall the editor of the Richmond *Compiler* showed the respect in which Niles was generally held when he suggested that the *Register*'s editor draw up "canons for the management of the press" in the United States.[17]

Editors were not the only contemporaries who recognized the value of the *Register*. At least five Presidents of the United States expressed opinions regarding the magazine. John Adams, writing from Braintree, Massachuetts, in 1817, paid this tribute: "I have motives of private honour and public duty for wishing to preserve these papers in print. Your repository is the best; and if you will insert them, you may." [18]

Thomas Jefferson, writing from Monticello on February 11, 1815, to William H. Crawford, then United States minister to France, after mentioning the *Historical Register of the United States,* added "Niles' Weekly Register is also an excellent repository of facts and documents, and has the advantage of coming out weekly. . . ." [19] Jefferson's testimonial letter of August 22, 1817, in reply to Niles' request, has already been referred to and quoted in part.

James Madison, wanting to preserve for posterity a statement regarding Virginia's attitude on relinquishing the navigation of the Mississippi in 1780–1781, wrote in 1822: "In the hope that this explanation may find its way to the notice of some future historian of our revolutionary transactions, I request for it a place, if one can be afforded in your REGISTER; where it may

15 *Register,* XII, 402, August 23, 1817.
16 *Register,* XIII, 162–63, November 8, 1817.
17 *Register,* XIII, 210, November 29, 1817.
18 *Register,* XII, 289, July 5, 1817.
19 Thomas Jefferson, *The Writings of Thomas Jefferson* (Washington, 1905), XIV, 243.

more readily offer itself to his researches, than in publications of more transient or miscellaneous contents." [20]

John Quincy Adams subscribed to the *Register* over a long period of years and his many allusions to the periodical in his diary indicate that he regularly read it and had frequent conferences with its editor.[21]

Andrew Jackson in the early twenties wrote a friend that Niles was "an independent, virtuous Editor, and who I believe will support no man for office, and particularly, the Presidential, unless he believes them [*sic*] honest and virtuous. . . ." [22]

When Martin Van Buren was engaged in writing his autobiography in the fifties, he wrote Thomas Hart Benton asking for a letter. The Missouri Senator, who had lost all his papers in a fire, referred the former President to the *Register* for April, 1844, where the letter had appeared. Benton's memory or chronology was faulty, for he went on to call Niles "a great rascal" who "filled the Register with every thing the Whigs said and did to hurt us. . . ." Niles, of course, had been dead for five years at the time to which Benton was referring. Critical as he was of the *Register*, Benton closed his letter to Van Buren: "You had better get access to his Register for the time you will write of." [23]

Satisfied subscribers were another group which praised the accuracy and utility of the *Register*. Letters from readers praised the *Register*'s "lofty tone of national dignity, free from the vulgar bickerings of party," its "strict and steady devotion to the principles of republicanism," and its aid in spreading a "truly American, and less of a foreign feeling," among the people. A Revolutionary soldier wrote in 1817 that he believed that Niles, through the *Register*, had "done more for America than a thousand of the best bayonets that ever were in it." An en-

<hr/>

20 Letter from Madison to Niles, January 8, 1822, printed in *Register*, XXI, 347, January 26, 1822.

21 Adams, *Memoirs*, VI, 46, 532; VII, 337; VIII, 330, 417, 444–45; IX, 386; X, 51.

22 Andrew Jackson to Dr. James C. Bronaugh, May 29, 1822, in Bassett, *Correspondence*, III, 163; that Jackson was a subscriber to the *Register* as late as 1825 is indicated in an item for its postage in *Correspondence*, III, 284.

23 Thomas H. Benton to Martin Van Buren, September 1, 1855, Van Buren MSS, Library of Congress.

thusiastic subscriber wrote that the *Register*'s "extent and variety" of information had caused it to supersede with him "all the other periodical publications of this country." Another asserted that the *Register* "certainly surpasses any other similar journal, with which I am acquainted." Still another thanked Niles for his labor in selecting, arranging, and preserving "such a mass of useful matter in a perspicuous and permanent form." Other readers called the *Register* "the most respectable repository in the nation" and the "most extensively useful" periodical work in the United States. Subscribers wrote that they paid their subscriptions with pleasure. Attorneys informed the editor that they used the *Register* "in their *professional* character" as much as any other book in their libraries, and that the *Register* was frequently "partially admitted as evidence in the proof of facts" in court. The periodical, as well as its editor, was often toasted at dinners. Governor William Plumer of New Hampshire wrote in 1816: "I consider the REGISTER as the most important and useful periodical work ever published in the United States. . . . I think none of them [other periodicals] contain such a variety of well digested facts, and so much useful information on such a variety of facts."

Charles S. Todd, ordering a complete file of the *Register* for himself and for Governor Isaac Shelby of Kentucky, wrote: ". . . every true American should feel a national pride, in the character of your paper; for it contains more useful matter, as well as more acceptable political information than any periodical work in the country." [24]

A Havana resident, writing in the Baltimore *American* in 1823, said that he had lent a volume of the *Register* to "an agent of the Mexican government, to translate from it our state constitutions" which were to be used as models for the federative republic to be set up in Mexico.[25] In 1833 the author of a city directory for Baltimore, which included a description of the city and its industries, referred to the "extensively circulating" *Register* as being "first in utility" among the weeklies.[26]

Readers prized the accuracy for which the *Register* was noted

---

[24] *Register*, XI, 195, November 23, 1816.
[25] *Register*, XXV, 213, December 6, 1823.
[26] Varle, *op. cit.*, 79–80.

and co-operated with its editor by sending in corrections to errors picked up from other papers. A Louisiana subscriber, correcting misstatements about a flood, the account of which the *Register* had reprinted from a newspaper, wrote, "everyone who reads your paper must be convinced that you are a lover of truth." [27]

Public officials looked upon the *Register* as a repository for speeches and documents. In 1826 Congressman George Cary of Georgia wrote to Peter Force, then editor of the *National Journal*, requesting a correction in a speech printed in the *Journal*. Saying that it might seem unimportant, he added that he had noticed that his remarks had been "transferred from your Journal to Niles' Register, a permanent record of political events and opinions." Therefore, he felt that he owed it to himself to have a correct report printed. If Mr. Niles would not insert the correction, "I shall have failed of realizing the principal object which I had in view, in troubling you." It is hardly necessary to add that Niles printed the correction.[28]

Mention has been made of the purchase of sets of the *Register* by the Senate and the House for their members. The latter body in 1826 started to subscribe for four copies, changed to six, and then to ten, at the request of many members. Colonel Thomas Newton of Virginia said in offering the measure to order the sets: "The character of the Register is so well known and properly appreciated, that nothing I can say in commendation of it can raise it higher in the public estimation. It is a work useful to every man; it comprises much various information, and is a faithful record of the occurrences of these eventful times. To the statesman it serves as a *memoria technia;* it saves him much labor, and rewards his researches with the information he seeks.[29]

Philip Hone, New York financier, philanthropist, and famous diarist, noted the death of Hezekiah Niles in his diary in the following words: "April 5—Died on Tuesday last, at Wilmington, Delaware, Hezekiah Niles, the conductor of 'Niles' Register' (the best statistical publication and record of national events in this country) and the father of the 'American System.' His

27 *Register*, XXV, 50, September 27, 1823.
28 *Register*, XXX, 249, June 10, 1826.
29 *Register*, XXX, 152, April 22, 1826.

name stood high on the *tariff* of private worth and public service." [30]

The public in general showed its appreciation of the value of the *Register* by subscribing to it in greater numbers during much of its career than to any other periodical published in the United States. Throughout its life it maintained a circulation approached by few of its contemporaries, many of which printed only a few hundred copies.[31]

The sum total of this testimony, representative of much more for which there is not space, indicates the confidence which newspaper editors, public officials, and the general public had in the *Register* during its lifetime. Without a doubt this contemporary prestige raises its value as a source.

The second factor which proves the reliability of the *Register* as a source for the period is the widespread use made of it by American historians, economists, political scientists, and biographers of national figures of that era. An editor, commenting on the periodical at the time of Niles' death, wrote, "The *Register* had a character and circulation in every part of the civilized world:—was read in the palaces of kings, in the haunts of commerce, and in the cabin of the pioneer; it is referred to as an authority in the courts of justice and in legislative assemblies; and at this day constitutes the best and truest foundation extant of the history of our country, for the period over which it extends." [32]

One has only to examine the works of historians of the United States covering the period in which the *Register* was published to confirm the accuracy of the evaluation of the periodical made by this editorial writer.

Citations to the periodical are numerous in almost every history or biography which makes use of contemporary periodicals. In some works the citations to the *Register* far outnumber

[30] Philip Hone, *The Diary of Philip Hone 1828–1851*, edited by Bayard Tuckerman (New York, 1889), I, 351.

[31] See Mott, *A History of American Magazines 1741–1850*, 199–200; 513–16. *Godey's Lady's Book* (Philadelphia, 1830–1898), with a circulation of 40,000 in 1849 was an exception.

[32] *Register*, LVI, 81, April 6, 1839; this same editorial was reprinted in the *Daily National Intelligencer* on April 6, 1839.

those to any other single source.[33] Modern historians have expressed their opinions as to its value in prefaces, in the body of their works, and in essays on authorities, in addition to the recognition expressed in citing the *Register* as the source of many of their statements. Edward Channing wrote: "For many years Hezekiah Niles's 'Weekly Register,' published at Baltimore, Mathew Carey's 'American Museum' and Dennie's 'Portfolio,' both published at Philadelphia, occupied the first place among American magazines and deservedly. . . ."[34]

John Bach McMaster, who used newspapers and periodicals extensively, turned to the *Register* as a reliable source. Allan Nevins, journalist and historian, lists the *Register* as one of three distinguished newspapers of the early part of the nineteenth century, the other two being the New York *Evening Post* and the *National Intelligencer*. He also praises the "excellent journalistic and even literary quality" of Hezekiah Niles' editorials.[35] Albert J. Beveridge, in his monumental work, *The Life of John Marshall*, wrote of the *Register*, from which he quoted Niles' attacks on the decision of the Chief Justice in McCulloch *vs.* Maryland: "This periodical had now become the most widely read and influential publication in the country; it had subscribers from Portland to New Orleans, from Savannah to Fort Dearborn. Niles had won the confidence of his far-flung constituency by his honesty, courage, and ability. He was the prototype of Horace Greeley, and the *Register* had much the same hold on its readers that the *Tribune* came to have thirty years later." The biographer added: "Copious quotations from the *Register* have been here made because it had the strongest influence on American public opinion of any publication of its time. Niles's *Register* was, emphatically, the mentor of the country editor."[36]

[33] Cf. George Pierce Garrison, *Westward Extension 1841–1850* (Volume XVII, The American Nation Series (New York, 1906), 27–312; also Glyndon G. Van Deusen, *The Life of Henry Clay* (Boston, 1937), 122–375.

[34] Channing, *op. cit.*, V, 284.

[35] Allan Nevins, *American Press Opinion: Washington to Coolidge: A Documentary Record of Editorial Leadership and Criticism: 1785–1927* (Boston, 1928), iv, 9.

[36] Albert J. Beveridge, *The Life of John Marshall*, 4 vols. (Boston, 1916–1919), IV, 309, 312; quoted by permission of Houghton Mifflin Company.

The monographs in *The American Nation* Series covering the thirty-eight-year period during which the *Register* was published contain many citations to that periodical. Each of the five authors in the "Critical Essay on Authorities," with which each volume was closed, specifically mentioned and praised the *Register*. Kendric Charles Babcock wrote: "Next to the great collections of government documents, and almost in a class by itself, stands unquestionably Hezekiah Niles (editor), *Niles' Weekly Register* (later *National Register*) (76 vols., 1811–1849). It is a broad-minded, judicious summary of the news of the country and of the world, with comment, contributions, clippings from contemporary journals, and reprints of many public documents; it constitutes a remarkable storehouse of varied and valuable material for the historian, to be used steadily and always with profit." [37]

Frederick Jackson Turner, whose writings contain many references to the *Register*, wrote that "Easily first in importance among the periodicals on the period from 1819 to 1829 is *Niles' Weekly Register*, . . . which abounds in material, political, social, and economic; although Niles was a strong protectionist, he was also fair-minded and conscientious in collecting information." [38]

William MacDonald listed the *Register* as the "most valuable single work" among the many newspapers and periodicals of the Jacksonian period.[39] Albert Bushnell Hart, somewhat anti-slavery in his approach to the slavery problem, wrote in 1906 that the *Register* was on "the whole impartial, though rather inclined to proslavery. . . ." [40] That Niles was less biased than Hart would probably be the verdict of a disinterested jury. George Pierce Garrison, who undoubtedly made more use of the *Register* in his volume of the series than any of the other four under discussion here, wrote that the *Register*, among

[37] Kendric Charles Babcock, *Rise of American Nationality* (Volume XIII, *The American Nation* Series) (New York, 1906), 315; permission, Harper & Brothers.

[38] Frederick Jackson Turner, *Rise of the New West 1819–1829* (Volume XIV, *The American Nation* Series) (New York, c1906), 341; permission, Harper & Brothers.

[39] William MacDonald, *op. cit.*, 322; permission, Harper & Brothers.

[40] Albert Bushnell Hart, *Slavery and Abolition 1831–1841* (Volume XVI, *The American Nation* Series) (New York, c1906), 332; permission, Harper & Brothers.

contemporary periodicals, was of "greatest value" for the period.[41]

It is not the purpose of this final chapter to cite a long series of statements of American historians as to the value of the *Register* as a contemporary source, but a few such citations serve to bear out the conclusions reached by the author. Edward Stanwood, in his *American Tariff Controversies in the Nineteenth Century*, wrote that the *Register* and Mathew Carey's pamphlets had much more power than the New York *Evening Post* and the *National Intelligencer*.[42] In discussing the propaganda campaign which preceded the passage of the Tariff of 1828, Stanwood, in praising Niles' fairness, indirectly indicated the value of the *Register* to the historian seeking truth.

He was the most magnanimous of disputants, incapable of garbling the language of his opponents in the smallest degree or of suppressing any part of their arguments, severe only when his own words were perverted or when his position was misrepresented. In selecting speeches to illustrate debates, he invariably chose for insertion in the "Register" the strongest on each side, and made it a point to give an equal number of them, or at least an equal amount of space, to friends and opponents. His guileless frankness, his conspicuous fairness, his absence of any motive save a profound belief that the causes he advocated were for the general welfare, secured for him the respect of all men and added immensely to the weight of his opinions on public questions. Since he was a close and intelligent student of politics, an expert in statistics, and a writer of clear and strong English,— although he was commonly diffuse,—his influence in moulding the thought of his readers was great. His constituency was the best-informed part of the community in every part of the country.[43]

A New York newspaper editor, author of the most voluminous history of American journalism, wrote in the early seventies that the *Register* was the "most valuable newspaper in its day, as we all find it to be in our researches for historical facts. . . ." [44]

[41] Garrison, *op. cit.*, 337–38; permission, Harper & Brothers.

[42] Edward Stanwood, *American Tariff Controversies in the Nineteenth Century*, 2 vols. (Boston, c1903), I, 249.

[43] Stanwood, *ibid.*, 246–47.

[44] Frederic Hudson, *Journalism in the United States from 1690 to 1872* (New York, 1873), 307.

A twentieth-century historian of journalism in the United States styled it the "most important newspaper of the era." [45]

Another link in the chain of evidence showing that the *Register* has unique standing as a source is the fact that compilers of official document collections have used the *Register*'s copies of such documentary material when originals could not be located. James D. Richardson reprinted six of President Madison's proclamations and one by President Monroe from the *Register* in his *Messages and Papers of the Presidents*.[46] John Spencer Bassett, editor of Jackson's correspondence, obtained from the *Register* several letters not to be found in the Jackson manuscripts. He referred a number of times to the correspondence between members of the cabinet, following the wholesale resignations in 1831, to be found in the *Register*. In one instance, at least, Bassett mentioned a letter which had been "improved textually" before being printed in the *Register*. In the introductions to five of the six volumes Bassett listed at least ninety-five of Jackson's letters, not included in his work, which had been printed in the *Register*.[47] The fact that the *Register* reprinted treaties, messages of the Presidents, state constitutions, and correspondence between public officials immeasurably increases its usefulness to the student.

Messages of the Presidents, treaties, diplomatic correspondence, proceedings of Congress, and other official material checked by the author against such printed sources as Richardson, Hunter Miller, and William R. Manning, and the *Statutes at Large* and various reports of the Congressional debates have been found to be uniformly accurate. Niles and his successors in the chair obtained official copies and typographical errors were reduced to a minimum. It is noteworthy that while errors in news items reprinted or condensed from other newspapers frequently were called to the attention of the *Register*'s editor by readers, few mistakes apparently were made in printing documents.

---

[45] James Melvin Lee, *op. cit.*, 151.

[46] James D. Richardson (comp.), *A Compilation of the Messages and Papers of the Presidents 1789–1897*, 10 vols. (Washington, 1901), I, 512, 514, 532, 543, 545–46, 560; II, 11.

[47] Bassett, *Correspondence*, II, xxvii–xxx, 136–38, 171; III, xxix–xxxiv; IV, xvii–xxii, 136, 140–41, 162–63, 301, 302, 343, 350; V, xix–xxiv, 110, 446; VI, xix–xxi, 143–46, this last being a letter to Lewis F. Linn, written from the Hermitage on March 12, 1842, and printed in *Register*, LXII, 212–13, June 4, 1842.

The *Register* reflected every facet of American life because in its columns are found not only the news stories and editorials of its own editors but also, more often than not, news and editorial comment from newspapers in all parts of the rapidly growing nation. From the War of 1812 through the Era of Good Feelings, into the turbulent days of Jacksonian Democracy, and down through the Mexican War almost to the mid-century mark, the *Register* carried representative comment from the daily and weekly press. The slavery controversy, the steady movement westward, the development of new means of transportation, the fight for and against a protective tariff, and the ever-changing pattern of party politics, as has been demonstrated in previous chapters, all may be followed in the pages of the *Register;* pages which are given over to a surprisingly complete and accurate sampling of editorial opinion. The scrupulous fairness observed in selecting material for reprinting in the *Register* makes this material valuable to the student of today seeking an approximation of truth of the events of that day.

Newspapers have always been the most ephemeral of publications and many periodicals are of little value a few years after publication. The press, in trying to record the length and breadth of human happenings, seldom goes beneath the surface. Superficiality in its treatment of affairs lessens its value to the future; hence its ephemerality. Speed, the enemy of accuracy and of profundity, was and is necessary in the production of a daily newspaper. The *Register,* published weekly, had an advantage over its daily contemporaries in that the editor had time to give subjects second thought; to reflect before expressing his opinion.

All of the *Register*'s editors constantly kept the future reader in mind, whether writing editorials or selecting them from other sources. A discerning student of newspapers has written that while the press in general does a great service for the future, "of this it is unconscious." She added, "In the hundreds of newspaper mottoes examined, but a single one has been noted that looks beyond the present. A hundred years ago *Niles' Register* proclaimed its aim to be 'The Past—the Present—for the Future.' . . ." [48] The fidelity to this motto by those charged with

[48] Lucy Maynard Salmon, *The Newspaper and Authority* (New York, 1923), 456; permission, Oxford University Press.

the responsibility of editing the *Register* is what has made the *Register* so valuable to historians and others. The same student quoted above, in another work discussing the three mottoes of the *Register*, wrote: "It does not seem possible to find a statement of the functions of a journal that more perfectly expresses the idea of the historian on this point than does the motto finally selected for *Niles' Register*." [49]

Without detracting from the editorial labor and keen judgment which combined to produce the periodical, there is no question but that the format—its convenient book size—greatly increased its value and availability to latter-day students. Printed on small-size pages and purchased bound by many subscribers, the *Register* was treated as a book of reference rather than as a newspaper or a periodical and found a permanent place on the shelves of many public and private libraries. The very bulk of newspapers prevents their collection and retention by few save the office of publication and the largest libraries. The same thing is true to a lesser extent of many magazines. But, Hezekiah Niles, by determining upon an octavo size and in reducing bulk by eliminating advertisements, greatly enhanced the chances of the *Register* for a longer life on the nation's shelves. Many libraries today have more or less complete sets of seventy-three volumes, which cover the period to the temporary suspension of publication in 1848. Not a few have seventy-five volumes. The three numbers of Volume LXXVI, published after another suspension in 1849, are rarer, but they are available. [50]

To the twentieth-century reader, accustomed to highly calendered paper, many illustrations, and a typographical make-up designed to heighten the pleasure of reading, the closely packed pages of the *Register* printed in small type present a forbidding aspect. The ordeal for the casual reader is not at all lessened by the documents filling page after page of many numbers, by the lengthy articles arguing the benefits of a protective tariff, by the diffuse editorials—often running to six or eight pages—on a

[49] Lucy Maynard Salmon, *The Newspaper and the Historian* (New York, 1923), 44; see also 462; permission, Oxford University Press.

[50] Winifred Gregory (ed.), *American Newspapers 1821–1936 A Union List of Files Available in the United States and Canada* (New York, 1937), 1021.

variety of subjects, or by the numbers given over completely to abridged accounts of Congressional debates. It was a meaty fare that the *Register* offered its readers. But, because the periodical was substantial and solid, it has stood the test of time. To the student interested in the American scene from 1811 to 1849, the *Register* offers a rich field for investigation. And the reading is not all dull, by any means. The dry wit and the quiet humor of Hezekiah Niles enliven many an otherwise dull page. His splenetic notices of England and the English are apt to appear anywhere, adding to the interest, if not to the value of the work. Jeremiah Hughes employed irony, sometimes slightly heavy, in his editorials in the forties. However, there is much less spice to be found in the *Register*'s columns in the second period when it served chiefly as a mirror of the contemporary scene, with fewer asides by its editors.

As it must to all men and to most magazines, death was to come to the *Register*. Probable reasons for the suspension of publication have been implied, if not directly stated, in earlier chapters. Had an experienced editor with an intelligent grasp of contemporary conditions succeeded Jeremiah Hughes without a break in continuous publication, the periodical might have been saved. A period of suspension is always disastrous to any publication and few survive its effects. Two such periods within two years, coupled with the ineffectual efforts of an inexperienced editor, were too much for the *Register*. And so it died after thirty-eight years of notable service. At that, it outlived all but two magazines, both of them of a religious nature, which were being published when it was founded.[51] Of 149 magazines founded between 1741 and 1811, only these two religious periodicals had as long a life as did the *Register*. And of 398 established during its career only 54 lasted longer than thirty-eight years.[52] Its long life in a period when many maga-

---

[51] This statement is based upon a compilation made from the chronological list of magazines in Mott, *A History of American Magazines 1741–1850*, 785–809. The two magazines were the *American Baptist Magazine,* published from 1802 to 1909 under various names, and the *Herald of Gospel Liberty,* founded in 1808 and still published after a number of changes of name and location and several mergers.

[52] This statement also is based upon Mott's list which, he states, contains only such periodicals as "have seemed important enough in some respect for treatment (or at least enumeration) in the text." Mott states that the list might be indefinitely

zines failed to last even one year has been styled an "extraordinary achievement" by one historian of American magazines.[53]

Another factor which undoubtedly brought about a diminution in the *Register*'s circulation list and thereby hastened its demise was the great growth in numbers of daily and weekly newspapers in the United States. Daily newspapers increased from 26 to 254 during the *Register*'s lifetime. The increase in all publications, including dailies, weeklies, and periodicals, was even more marked. Three hundred seventy-one newspapers were printed in the country in 1810. By 1840, 1,404 publications were listed. And in 1850, a year after the *Register* ceased publication, 2,526 dailies, weeklies, monthlies, and quarterlies were being printed.[54]

The *Register* thus faced serious competition from newspapers and periodicals, both of which had sprung up in increasing numbers as the nation expanded westward and cities were founded in the trans-Allegheny region. The invention of the telegraph and its adoption as a means of transmitting news, and the increasing use of the railroad as a means of expediting the mails gave an advantage to the daily press and to the weeklies in all sections of the growing nation. On the other hand, the miscellaneous contents of the horde of magazines which issued from the country's presses undoubtedly offered attractions to readers with which the staid columns of the *Register* with its dull documents and sober news summaries could not hope to compete. An editor with Hezekiah Niles' vision and ability might have been able to cope with the changing conditions, but none appeared when Hughes felt that he must relinquish the editorial chair. So the *Register* was destined to pass into that numerous company of magazines which have suspended pub-

---

extended by the use of Winifred Gregory's *Union List of Serials in Libraries of the United States and Canada* (New York, 1927), which makes the *Register*'s record of publication all the more remarkable.

[53] Algernon Tassin, *The Magazine in America* (New York, 1916), 180.

[54] These figures were arrived at from information from a variety of sources, chief of which are Clarence S. Brigham, "Bibliography of American Newspapers, 1690–1820," published serially in *Proceedings of the American Antiquarian Society*, New Series (Worcester, Mass., 1891—), XXIII—XXX (1913–1920); XXXII (1922); XXXIV—XXXV (1924–1925); XXXVII (1927); Alfred M. Lee, *op. cit.*, 711–19; *Compendium . . . of the . . . Seventh Census*, 154–59.

lication. But unlike the majority of its companions, its passing did not mean oblivion.

The penetrating editorial judgment, the accuracy in reprinting documents from official sources and in making abstracts of and choosing quotations from newspaper editorials and news articles, coupled with the responsibility assumed by the editors in presenting a "full view" of controversial subjects, combined to produce a periodical, which, without exaggeration, can be called the most important contemporary source for its period available to the student today. The *Register* fully met the wish of its first motto by becoming and remaining "an honest chronicler" throughout its career. It faithfully chronicled "The Past —the Present—for the Future" and therein lies its value to the student of today and tomorrow and of the yet-distant future.

Critical Essay on Authorities

Manuscript Sources

The William Darlington Papers in the Library of Congress contain ninety-four letters written by Hezekiah Niles between December 31, 1814, and September 23, 1834, more correspondence than has been located in any other single place. A few miscellaneous letters of Niles are in the Hezekiah Niles Papers in the Library of Congress. Letters to and from Niles also in the Library of Congress may be found in the following collections: Henry Clay Papers, Joseph Gales, Jr., and William Winston Seaton Papers, Andrew Jackson Papers, Thomas Jefferson Papers, and James Madison Papers. Mrs. Charles F. Bachman of Decatur, Illinois, daughter of Henry Clay Niles, furnished a picture of her grandfather and permitted use of manuscript material in her possession. Mrs. Hannah Niles Freeland Miller, Elizabeth, New Jersey, a descendant of another branch of the Niles family; Miss Reba N. Perkins, Indiana, Pennsylvania, a great-granddaughter; and Miss Laura Niles, Philadelphia, a granddaughter of Hezekiah Niles, were helpful in answering inquiries.

Contemporary Newspapers and Periodicals

The columns of the *Register,* under its three different titles, are the source of most of the contemporary material. In writing the history of the periodical every page of every issue of the seventy-six volumes has been read. The *Register,* in incomplete or broken sets, is in many libraries in the United States, as a check of Winifred Gregory's *Union List of Serials in Libraries of the United States and Canada* (New York, 1937) will show. Not a few libraries have seventy-three volumes. The number having seventy-five is fewer. Seventy-three volumes of the *Register* were used in the Ohio State University Library and in the Los Angeles Public Library. Sixty-two volumes are in the Library of the University of California at Los Angeles. Volumes LXXIV and LXXV were examined in the Henry E. Huntington Library, San Marino, California. The three numbers of Volume LXXVI used by the author are in the Library of Congress. For a history of the periodical itself and indeed for a contemporary history of the period, the *Register*'s pages are invaluable. The wealth of material reflecting the contemporary scene is inexhaustible.

Many other daily and weekly publications of the period are useful, in some instances to check the accuracy of the *Register*'s quotations and in others to obtain more nearly complete quotations of editorials or news stories. Newspapers and magazines used in the Library of Congress include: The *Apollo or Delaware Weekly Magazine* (Wilmington, 1805), short-lived magazine venture of Niles; Baltimore *American and Commercial Daily Advertizer;* Baltimore *Evening Post,* edited and published by Niles from 1805 to 1811; Baltimore *Republican; Claypoole's American Daily Advertiser* of Philadelphia; *Daily Evening Transcript* of Boston; *Delaware Gazette* of Wilmington; *Delaware State Journal* of Wilmington; the *Globe* of Washington; *National Intelligencer* of Washington, daily and weekly editions; *Poulson's American Daily Advertiser* of Philadelphia; *Mirror of the Times and General Advertizer* of Wilmington; Richmond *Enquirer,* Springfield *Republican* of Massachusetts; and the Baltimore *Sun.*

In the Library of the University of California at Los Angeles use was made of *Cobbett's Weekly Political Register* of London, the *Edinburgh Review or Critical Journal,* the London *Quarterly Review,* and the London *Times.* The Library of the Ohio State Archaeological and Historical Society on the campus of the Ohio State University is the source of files of the *North American Review, Ohio State Journal* of Columbus, and other Ohio newspapers briefly used.

Printed Sources and Contemporary Works

Following are the most important of the memoirs, diaries, collections of correspondence, and compilations of papers utilized: John Quincy Adams, *Memoirs of John Quincy Adams, comprising Portions of his Diary from 1795 to 1848,* edited by Charles Francis Adams, 12 vols. (Philadelphia, 1874–1877) contains references to Niles and to the *Register.* A number of letters of Andrew Jackson, taken from the files of the *Register,* may be found in John Spencer Bassett (ed.), *Correspondence of Andrew Jackson,* 7 vols. (Washington, 1926–1935). Of use because of his common interest with Niles in the tariff and because of frequent references to Niles and of Niles to him is Mathew Carey, *The Olive Branch: or Faults on Both Sides, Federal and Democratic. A Serious Appeal on the Necessity of Mutual Forgiveness & Harmony, to Save Our Common Country from Ruin* (Philadelphia, 1814). Henry Clay, *The Works of Henry Clay, Comprising His Life, Correspondence and Speeches,* edited by

Calvin Colton, 10 vols. (New York, 1904); Philip Hone, *The Diary of Philip Hone, 1828–1851*, edited by Bayard Tuckerman, 2 vols. (New York, 1889); and Thomas Jefferson, *The Writings of Thomas Jefferson*, 20 vols. (Washington, 1905) furnish valuable sidelights on men and issues. James D. Richardson, *A Compilation of the Messages and Papers of the Presidents 1789–1897*, 10 vols. (Washington, 1901) in addition to being a valuable source to check documents lists a number of documents obtained from the *Register*. John C. Fitzpatrick (ed.), *The Autobiography of Martin Van Buren* (American Historical Association *Annual Report*, 1918, II) (Washington, 1920) contains much of value for the thirties.

Because of Niles' hatred for England and the English which found expression in the majority of the 1,300 issues of the *Register* edited by him, a number of contemporary publications of English travelers, a target for many of his editorial attacks, are here listed. Among the more significant, not a few of which undoubtedly merited scathing criticism, are: Thomas Ashe, *Travels in America, Performed in 1806, for the Purpose of Exploring the Rivers Alleghany, Monongahela, Ohio, and Mississippi, and Ascertaining the Produce and Condition of their Banks and Vicinity* (London, 1808); Morris Birkbeck, *Notes on a Journey in America, from the Coast of Virginia to the Territory of Illinois* (2d ed.; London, 1818); George Combe, *Notes on the United States of North America during a Phrenological Visit in 1838–9–40*, 2 vols. (Philadelphia, 1841); Henry Bradshaw Fearon, *Sketches of America* (3d ed.; London, 1819); Thomas Colley Grattan, *Civilized America*, 2 vols. (2d ed.; London, 1839); Basil Hall, *Travels in North America in the Years 1827 and 1828*, 3 vols. (Edinburgh, 1829); Lieut. Francis Hall, *Travels in Canada, and the United States, in 1816 and 1817* (2d ed.; London, 1819); [Thomas Hamilton], *Men and Manners in America*, 2 vols. (London, 1834); [Thomas Horton James], Rubio, *Rambles in the United States and Canada during the Year 1845 with a Short Account of Oregon* (London, 1846); Charles William Jonson, *The Stranger in America* (London, 1807); Charles Joseph Latrobe, *The Rambler in North America: MDCCCXXXII–MDCCCXXXIII*, 2 vols. (London, 1835); Captain R. G. A. Levinge, *Echoes from the Backwoods, or Sketches of Transatlantic Life*, 2 vols. in 1 (2d ed.; London, 1847); Charles Lyell, *Travels in North America; with Geological Observations on the United States, Canada, and Nova Scotia*, 2 vols. (London, 1845), and by the same author, *A Second Visit to the United States of North America*, 2 vols. (New York and London, 1849); Captain [Frederick] Marryat, *A Diary in America, with Remarks on Its Institutions,*

2 vols. (Philadelphia, 1839); Harriet Martineau, *Retrospect of Western Travel*, 2 vols. (New York, 1838); John Melish, *Travels in the United States of America, in the Years 1806 & 1807, and 1809, 1810 & 1811* . . . , 2 vols. (Philadelphia, 1812); Charles Augustus Murray, *Travels in North America during the Years 1834, 1835 & 1836* . . . , 2 vols. (London, 1839); John Ferdinand Dalziel Smyth, *A Tour in the United States of America* . . . , 2 vols. (London, 1784); James Stuart, *Three Years in North America*, 2 vols. (London, 1833); Mrs. [Frances] Trollope, *Domestic Manners of the Americans*, 2 vols. (4th ed.; London, 1832); Godfrey T. Vigne, *Six Months in America* (Philadelphia, 1833); Isaac Weld, *Travels Through the States of North America and the Province of Upper & Lower Canada, in the Years 1795, 1796 and 1797* . . . (London, n.d.); and C. H. Wilson, *The Wanderer in America, or Truth at Home* . . . (Thirsk, England, 1823).

Useful in following debates on issues which the *Register* reported and in its first two decades editorialized upon are *Annals of the Congress of the United States, 1789–1825*, 42 vols. (Washington, 1834–1856); *Congressional Globe, 1834–1873*, 46 vols. (Washington, 1834–1873); *Register of Debates in Congress 1825–1837*, 14 vols. (Washington, 1825–1837).

Volumes written or edited by Hezekiah Niles fall into two classifications: first, those reprinted from the columns of the *Register* and the *Evening Post*, and second, compilations of speeches, proceedings, etc., from a variety of sources. Among them are: H. Niles, *Agriculture of the United States, or An Essay concerning Internal Improvement & Domestic Manufactures, Shewing Their Inseperable [sic] Connection with the Business and Interests of Agriculture, In the establishment of a home-market for bread-stuffs and meats, wool, cotton, flax, hemp, &c. as well as the Supplies that they furnish in aid of the foreign commerce of the United States* (no place, 1827?); H. Niles (ed.), *Centennial Offering Republication of the Principles and Acts of the Revolution in America. Dedicated to the Young Men of the United States, fifty-four years ago by the late Hezekiah Niles, Editor of the "Weekly Register,"* with a foreword by Samuel V. Niles (New York, 1876); H. Niles, *Journal of the Proceedings of the Friends of Domestic Industry, in General Convention met at the City of New York, October 26, 1831* (Baltimore, 1831); H. Niles, *Politics for the Working Men. An Essay on Labor and Subsistence; Addressed to the Free Productive People of the U. States* (Baltimore?, 1831?); H. Niles (ed.), *Principles and Acts of the Revolution in America: Or, An Attempt to Collect and Preserve Some of the Speeches, Orations,*

*& Proceedings, with Sketches and Remarks on Men and Things, and
Other Fugitive or Neglected Pieces, Belonging to the Revolutionary
Period in the United States: Which, Happily, Terminated in the
Establishment of Their Liberties: with A View to Represent the
Feelings That Prevailed in the "Times That Tried Men's Souls," to
Excite a Love of Freedom, and Lead the People to Vigilance, as the
Condition on Which It Is Granted. Dedicated to the Young Men
of the United States* (Baltimore, 1822); [H. Niles, alias Jerry Didler],
*Things As They Are; or, Federalism turned inside out!! Being a Col-
lection of Extracts from Federal Papers, &c. and Remarks upon
Them, Originally written for, and published in the Evening Post*
(Baltimore, 1809?).

Also of use are *American State Papers,* edited by Walter Lowrie
et al., 38 vols. (Washington, 1833–1861); *Annual Register or a View
of the History, Politics and Literature for the Year* . . . (London,
1758—); *British and Foreign State Papers* (London, 1841—); *Compendium of the Enumeration of the Inhabitants and Statistics of the
United States as Obtained at the Department of State, from the Returns of the Sixth Census* . . . (Washington, 1841); J. D. B. De Bow
(comp.), *The Seventh Census of the United States: 1850* . . . (Washington, 1853) and *Statistical View of the United States* . . . *Being
a Compendium of the Seventh Census* . . . (Washington, 1854), also
compiled by De Bow; Theodore Dwight, *History of the Hartford
Convention with a Review of the Policy of the United States Gov-
ernment, which Led to the War of 1812* (Boston, 1833); Franz Anton
Ritter von Gerstner, *Die innern Communicationen der Vereinigten
Staaten von Nordamerika,* 2 vols. (Wien, 1842–1843); William R.
Manning (ed.), *Diplomatic Correspondence of the United States
Inter-American Affairs 1831–1860,* 11 vols. (Washington, 1932—)
and the three volumes of *Diplomatic Correspondence of the United
States concerning the Independence of the Latin American Nations*
(New York, 1925), also edited by Manning; Hunter Miller (ed.),
*Treaties and Other International Acts of the United States of Amer-
ica* (Washington, 1931—); William Ogden Niles (comp.), *The Tippe-
canoe Text-Book Compiled from Niles' Register and Other Authen-
tic Records* (Baltimore, 1840); Charles Varle, *A Complete View of
Baltimore* . . . (Baltimore, 1833); and Henry Wheaton (ed.), *Re-
ports of Cases Argued and Adjudged in the Supreme Court of the
United States,* 12 vols. (Philadelphia and New York, 1816–1827).

Histories of Journalism, Histories of Individual Newspapers and Biographies of Early Nineteenth-Century American Newspapermen

The best history of American journalism is Frank Luther Mott's *American Journalism A History of Newspapers in the United States through 250 Years, 1690 to 1940* (New York, 1941). His two sections on the Party Press, Chaps. IX through XIX, are of especial interest for the period in which the *Register* was published. The same author's *A History of American Magazines 1741–1850* (New York, 1930), the first volume of his three-volume Pulitzer-prize-winning history, is the most detailed and the most valuable study of magazines for the period. His brief, but nonetheless significant, *Jefferson and the Press* (Baton Rouge, 1943) clarifies the third President's views on and relations with early American newspapers. Alfred McClung Lee's *The Daily Newspaper in America The Evolution of a Social Instrument* (New York, 1937) is sociological in approach and while less satisfactory than Mott's volume provides interesting interpretation. For background Isaiah Thomas' two-volume *The History of Printing in America. With a Biography of Printers, and an Account of Newspapers. To Which is prefixed a concise view of the Discovery and Progress of the Art in Other Parts of the World* (Worcester, Mass., 1810) is invaluable in spite of inaccuracies. The second edition of this work, published under the supervision of the American Antiquarian Society in Albany in 1874, is also useful.

Frederic Hudson, *Journalism in the United States from 1690 to 1872* (New York, 1873) is the earliest and most voluminous history of American journalism. Written by a newspaperman it suffers from the lack of application of the historical method. It is, however, of great value to the person who uses it with care. Unfortunately, some later historians of American journalism have accepted Hudson's statements as facts, thereby tending to perpetuate his many errors. Willard Grosvenor Bleyer, *Main Currents in the History of American Journalism* (Boston, c1927) was the most nearly accurate history until publication of Mott's work. Less satisfactory is James Melvin Lee's *History of American Journalism* (Boston, 1917, rev. ed., 1923). Much less comprehensive is George Henry Payne, *History of Journalism in the United States* (New York, 1920).

Essential to the historian interested in American newspapers is Clarence S. Brigham's "Bibliography of American Newspapers 1690–1820," *Proceedings* of the American Antiquarian Society, XXIII–XXX (1913–1920), XXXI (1922), XXXIV–XXXV (1924–1925),

XXXVII (1927) (Worcester, Mass., 1891—). Planned to be published in book form, the bibliography not only tells in what libraries issues may be found, but lists dates of founding, changes in names, and other pertinent information. From 1821 into the twentieth century the source of bibliographical information on American newspapers is Winifred Gregory, *American Newspapers 1821–1936 A Union List of Files Available in the United States and Canada* (New York, 1937), which should be used with her earlier mentioned *Union List of Serials in Libraries of the United States and Canada* because the line between newspapers and magazines is often next to indistinguishable. Bernard Fäy, *Notes on the American Press at the End of the Eighteenth Century* (New York, 1927) gives good background. Douglas C. McMurtrie, *A History of Printing in the United States The Story of the Introduction of the Press and of its History and Influence during the Pioneer Period in each State of the Union*, Volume II, *Middle & South Atlantic States* (New York, 1936) contains much of value. Allan Nevins, *American Press Opinion; Washington to Coolidge: A Documentary Record of Editorial Leadership and Criticism: 1785–1927* (Boston, 1928) is a collection of outstanding editorial comments on national affairs with an excellent introduction for each of four periods. *The Newspaper and Authority* (New York, 1923) and *The Newspaper and the Historian* (New York, 1923), both by Lucy Maynard Salmon, contain cogent comments on the place of newspapers in the social scene. Algernon Tassin, *The Magazine in America* (New York, 1916), while less valuable than Mott because of numerous errors, is worth examination.

The beginnings of modern methods of news gathering, transmission, and distribution are described in Victor Rosewater, *History of Cooperative News-Gathering in the United States* (New York, 1930). The authorized story of the Associated Press is Oliver Gramling's *AP The Story of News* (New York, c1940). More detailed information on early methods of gathering and speeding news from its source to point of publication is found in Fayette Copeland, *Kendall of the Picayune . . .* (Norman, Okla., 1943). This volume is chiefly valuable here for its description of the coverage of the Mexican War by George W. Kendall, one of America's most famous early war correspondents. Less reliable, but of some interest, is Thomas Ewing Dabney, *One Hundred Great Years: The Story of the Times-Picayune from Its Founding to 1940* (Baton Rouge, 1944). Interesting passages on Mexican War news and on newspapering in general are also found in *1837–1937, The Sunpapers of Baltimore* (New York, 1937) by Gerald W. Johnson, Frank R. Kent, Henry L. Mencken, and

Hamilton Owens, all of the *Sun*'s staff. The first dozen years of the *Sun*'s life coincided with the declining years of the *Register*. The history of a contemporary newspaper, now near the sesquicentennial mark, Allan Nevins' *The Evening Post: A Century of Journalism* (New York, 1922) throws additional light on the journalism of the first half of the nineteenth century. Nevins has a high opinion of the *Register* which he ranks with the *Post* in importance. Frank M. O'Brien, *The Story of The Sun, New York, 1833–1918* (New York, 1918), describes the phenomenal success of the daily penny paper of which the *Sun* is the shining example. These three volumes are the best histories of individual American newspapers thus far produced.

Biographies of early American editors are not numerous and generally are not too satisfactory. In many instances the brief biographical sketches in the *Dictionary of American Biography*, 21 vols. (New York, 1928–1937) are the chief sources of factual material on editors. Richard Gabriel Stone, *Hezekiah Niles As an Economist* (Baltimore, 1933), also published in the Johns Hopkins University *Studies in Historical and Political Science*, LI, No. 5 (Baltimore, 1933), is the only published life of Niles. Four of the five chapters of this work are devoted to economic aspects of Niles' activities. The chapter "Life of Niles" describes his editorial career. Charles Henry Ambler, *Thomas Ritchie: A Study in Virginia Politics* (Richmond, Va., 1913), while stressing the political side of the editor's life is fairly adequate in its treatment of Ritchie's editorial activities. Marjorie Bowen [pseud.], *Peter Porcupine: A Study of William Cobbett, 1762–1835* (London, 1936) is the best study of the stormy English editor with whom Hezekiah Niles first co-operated, later battled. Biographies of the editors of the *National Intelligencer* are lacking. Allen Culling Clark, *Joseph Gales, Junior, Editor and Mayor* (Washington, 1920) leaves much to be desired. Joseph Seaton, *William Winston Seaton of the "National Intelligencer." A Biographical Sketch. With Passing Notices of his Associates and Friends* (Boston, 1871) is also unsatisfactory but should not be overlooked. Oran Andrew Seaton (ed.), *The Seaton Family, with Genealogy and Biographies* (Topeka, Kan., 1906) contains some useful facts. Francis Phelps Weisenburger, "A Life of Charles Hammond," *Ohio Archaeological and Historical Quarterly*, XLIII, No. 4 (October, 1934), 340–427, gives some attention to Hammond's scurrilous attacks on Rachael Jackson. Erik McKinley Eriksson, "President Jackson's Propaganda Agencies," *Pacific Historical Review*, VI, No. 1 (March, 1937), 47–57, discusses contemporary publicists. James Parton, *The Life of Horace Greeley, Editor of the New York Tribune* (New York, 1855) is the standard contemporary biography of Greeley. William E. Smith, *The Francis Preston Blair Family in Politics,* 2 vols. (New York, 1933) contains much valuable material on the first editor of the *Globe* and member, of the "kitchen cabinet." For material on other newspapermen of the Jacksonian era turn to William Stickney (ed.), *Autobiography of Amos Kendall* (Boston and New York, 1872); Thomas Hart Benton, *Thirty Years' View* . . . 2 vols. (New York, 1854), and Ben: Perley Poore, *Perley's Reminiscences of Sixty Years in the National Metropolis* (Philadelphia, 1886).

Histories and Monographs

For general background over the period of the *Register*'s life (1811–1849) the following can be consulted with profit: Henry Adams, *History of the United States of America during the Administrations of Jefferson and Madison,* 9 vols. (New York, 1889–1891); James Truslow Adams, *New England in the Republic* (Boston, 1926); Kendric Charles Babcock, *Rise of American Nationality 1811–1819* (Volume XIII of *The American Nation,* edited by Albert Bushnell Hart, New York, 1904–1918) (New York, 1906); Edward Channing, *A History of the United States,* 6 vols. (New York, 1905–1925); George Pierce Garrison, *Westward Extension 1841–1850* (Volume XVII of *The American Nation*) (New York, 1906); John Bach McMaster, *A History of the People of the United States, From the Revolution to the Civil War,* 8 vols. (New York, 1888–1914); Arthur Meier Schlesinger, *New Viewpoints in American History* (New York, 1922); James Schouler, *History of the United States of America under the Constitution,* 7 vols. (New York, c1880–1913); Alexis de Tocqueville, *Democracy in America,* 2 vols. (New York, 1898). Of great value for background is Vernon Louis Parrington, *Main Currents in American Thought,* 3 vols. in 1 (New York, c1927 and 1930).

Local histories, while containing many inaccuracies, are useful because they contain material not found elsewhere. Facts about Niles' birth and early life are found in J. S. Futhey and Gilbert Cope, *History of Chester County, Pennsylvania* (Philadelphia, 1881). Anna T. Lincoln, *Wilmington Delaware Three Centuries under Four Flags 1609–1937* (Rutland, Vt., c1937) supplies facts concerning Niles' residence in that city. Brief facts about Niles are found in George W. McCreary, *Ancient and Honorable Mechanical Company of Baltimore* . . . (Baltimore, 1901). Biographical sketches, not entirely accurate but of value, are in Col. J. Thomas Scharf, *The Chronicles of Baltimore* . . . (Philadelphia, 1874), *History of Baltimore City and*

County . . . (Philadelphia, 1881), and *History of Delaware,* 2 vols. (Philadelphia, 1888). Niles' activities in the Masonic lodge are recorded in Edward T. Schultz, *History of Freemasonry in Maryland* . . . , 3 vols. (Baltimore, 1885). Charles Burr Ogden, *The Quaker Ogdens in America* . . . (Philadelphia, 1898) contains facts about Niles' second wife. The biography of a fellow townsman, John E. Semmes, *John H. B. Latrobe and His Times, 1803–1891* (Baltimore, c1917), supplies facts on Niles' civic activities. The recollections of a young man hired to compile an index for early volumes of the *Register*—John Neal, *Wandering Recollections of a Somewhat Busy Life. An Autobiography* (Boston, 1869)—furnish additional details about Niles.

For background on Niles' fight for high tariffs and against the Bank of the United States, Stone's *Hezekiah Niles As an Economist,* mentioned earlier, is valuable. Ralph C. H. Catterall, *The Second Bank of the United States* (Chicago, 1903) gives necessary background as does Albert J. Beveridge, *The Life of John Marshall,* 4 vols. (Boston, 1916–1919), the latter with especial attention to Niles' opposition and influence. Davis Rich Dewey, *Financial History of the United States* (8th ed.; New York, 1922) gives factual background as does Harold U. Faulkner, *American Economic History* (rev. ed.; New York, 1931). Edward Stanwood, *American Tariff Controversies in the Nineteenth Century,* 2 vols. (Boston, c1903) discusses Niles' hard but unsuccessful battle for protection. Carl Brent Swisher, *Roger B. Taney* (New York, 1935) is of interest because of Taney's decision on removal of deposits.

The objective reporting of party politics in the *Register,* unique in American journalism of that era, makes the political figures and battles of that day of interest. Biographies of Andrew Jackson of use are John Spencer Bassett, *The Life of Andrew Jackson* (new ed.; New York, 1925) and two volumes by Marquis James, *Andrew Jackson: The Border Captain* (New York, c1933) and *Andrew Jackson: Portrait of a President* (Indianapolis, c1937). For Henry Clay, the Colton edition of *The Works of Henry Clay,* mentioned earlier, is useful as is Carl Schurz, *Life of Henry Clay* (Volumes XIX, XX of *American Statesmen*) (Boston, c1899). Newer interpretations may be found in Glyndon G. Van Deusen, *The Life of Henry Clay* (Boston, 1937). Claude G. Bowers, *The Party Battles of the Jackson Period* (Boston, 1922) describes the partisan bitterness often mentioned in the *Register.* Emergence of the new party is detailed in E. Malcolm Carroll, *Origins of the Whig Party* (Durham, N. C., 1925). Abortive attempts of labor to become a political force are described in John R. Commons (ed.), *History of Labour in the United States*, 2 vols. (New York, 1921). Carl Russell Fish, *The Rise of the Common Man, 1830–1850* (Volume VI, *History of American Life*) (New York, 1929) and William MacDonald, *Jacksonian Democracy 1829–1837* (Volume XV, of *The American Nation*) (New York, 1906) furnish necessary background. Party history and political developments may be traced in Frank R. Kent, *The Democratic Party, A History* (New York, c1928); William O. Lynch, *Fifty Years of Party Warfare (1789–1837)* (Indianapolis, 1931); M. Ostrogorski, *Democracy and the Organization of Political Parties*, 2 vols (New York, 1908); Edgar E. Robinson, *The Evolution of American Political Parties: A Sketch of Party Development* (New York, c1924); Edward McChesney Sait, *American Parties and Elections* (New York, c1927); Edward Stanwood, *A History of the Presidency from 1788 to 1897*, 2 vols. (rev. ed.; Boston, 1928), and James Albert Woodburn, *American Politics . . .* (New York, 1924). Niles' successful fight to drive out the Congressional caucus as a method of choosing candidates is outlined in detail in M. Ostrogorski, "The Rise and Fall of the Nominating Caucus, Legislative and Congressional," *American Historical Review* (New York, 1895—) V (December, 1899), 253–83. For the varied factors entering into the 1832 election, Samuel Rhea Gammon, Jr., *The Presidential Campaign of 1832* (The Johns Hopkins University *Studies in Historical and Political Science*, XL, No. 1) (Baltimore, 1922), and Charles McCarthy, *The Antimasonic Party: A Study of Political Antimasonry in the United States, 1827–1840* (American Historical Association *Annual Report*, 1902, I, 365–574) (Washington, 1903) are valuable.

An unbiased appraisal of the works of early English travelers, attacked so strongly by Hezekiah Niles, is available in Allan Nevins (ed.), *American Social History As Recorded by British Travelers* (New York, c1923). Diplomatic negotiations with England and with Latin-American nations may be followed in Samuel Flagg Bemis, *A Diplomatic History of the United States* (New York, c1936) and in the volumes edited by the same author, *The American Secretaries of State and Their Diplomacy*, 9 vols. (New York, 1927–1929). John Holloday Latané, *A History of American Foreign Policy* (New York, 1927) and Joseph Byrne Lockey, *Pan-Americanism: Its Beginnings* (New York, 1920) are also useful. Edward Howland Tatum, Jr., *The United States and Europe 1815–1823: A Study in the Background of the Monroe Doctrine* (Berkeley, Calif., 1936) presents new and interesting theories on the doctrine. Standard authority on the Monroe Doctrine is Dexter Perkins, whose *The Monroe Doctrine 1823–1826*

(Harvard Historical Studies, XXIX) (Cambridge, Mass., 1927) and *The Monroe Doctrine 1826–1867* (Albert Shaw Lectures on Diplomatic History, XVII) (Baltimore, 1933) are invaluable. Also useful in connection with Niles' mixed feelings concerning Anglo-American co-operation in Latin America are J. Fred Rippy, *Rivalry of the United States and Great Britain over Latin America (1808–1830)* (Albert Shaw Lectures on Diplomatic History, XIII) (Baltimore, 1929) and William Spence Robertson, *Hispanic-American Relations with the United States* (New York, 1923). Best work on the Mexican War is Justin H. Smith, *The War with Mexico*, 2 vols. (New York, 1919). Mexican diplomatic relations may be followed in James Morton Callahan, *American Foreign Policy in Mexican Relations* (New York, 1932); Jesse E. Reeves, *American Diplomacy under Tyler and Polk* (Albert Shaw Lectures on Diplomatic History, III) (Baltimore, 1907); and William R. Manning, *Early Diplomatic Relations between the United States and Mexico* (Albert Shaw Lectures on Diplomatic History, VIII) (Baltimore, 1916).

Niles' enthusiasm for the West was expressed in editorial comments in thousands of items in the *Register*. His belief that this new section of the country would play a most significant role in the future of the nation makes the works of Frederick Jackson Turner of especial interest. Among them are: *Rise of the New West 1819–1829* (Volume XIV of *The American Nation*) (New York, 1906); *The Frontier in American History* (New York, 1921); *The Significance of Sections in American History* with an introduction by Max Farrand (New York, c1932); and *The United States 1830–1850: The Nation and Its Sections* (New York, c1935). Useful in this connection are Everett E. Edwards (comp.), *The Early Writings of Frederick Jackson Turner with a List of All His Works* with an introduction by Fulmer Mood (Madison, Wis., 1938) and *Essays in American History Dedicated to Frederick Jackson Turner* (New York, 1910). Other phases of the West of Niles' time may profitably be followed in Dixon Ryan Fox (ed.), *Sources of Culture in the Middle West Backgrounds versus Frontier* (New York, c1934); Julius W. Pratt, *Expansionists of 1812* (New York, 1925); Albert K. Weinberg, *Manifest Destiny: A Study of National Expansionism in American History* (Baltimore, 1935); and Cardinal Goodwin, *The Trans-Mississippi West (1803–1853)* (New York, 1922). On the land question, Benjamin Horace Hibbard, *A History of the Public Land Policies* (New York, 1924) gives background.

Closely connected with the opening of the West was the development of transportation, which can be followed in detail in the *Regis-*

ter. The following are useful: Charles Henry Ambler, *A History of Transportation in the Ohio Valley* . . . (Glendale, Calif., 1932); Hiram Martin Chittenden, *History of Early Steamboat Navigation on the Missouri River* . . . , 2 vols. (New York, 1903); Seymour Dunbar, *A History of Travel in America,* 4 vols. (Indianapolis, 1915); John H. B. Latrobe, *The First Steamboat Voyage on the Western Waters* (Baltimore, 1871); Ella May Turner, *James Rumsey, Pioneer in Steam Navigation* (Scottdale, Pa., 1930). Standard work is Balthaser Henry Meyer and Caroline E. MacGill (comps.), *History of Transportation in the United States before 1860* (Washington, 1917).

Works used in connection with the *Register'*s reporting of the slave-trade industry and slavery in general include Albert Bushnell Hart, *Slavery and Abolition 1831–1841* (Volume XVI of *The American Nation*) (New York, c1906); Frank J. Klingberg, *The Anti-Slavery Movement in England: A Study in English Humanitarianism* (Yale Historical Publications, Miscellany XVII) (New Haven, 1926); Hugh G. Soulsby, *The Right of Search and the Slave Trade in Anglo-American Relations 1814–1862* (The Johns Hopkins University Studies in Historical and Political Science, LI, No. 2) (Baltimore, 1933). A scholarly monograph in which phases of the abolition of the slave trade are discussed is Lawrence F. Hill, *Diplomatic Relations between the United States and Brazil* (Durham, N. C., 1932).

Index

Abolitionists, decide 1844 election, 158; opposed by H. Niles, 280-84

Accounts receivable, 14

"A Chronicle," department in *Register*, 77, 96, 241

Adams, James, Jr., Niles' partner, 20

Adams, John, subscribes to *Register*, 8; discourages idea of book on Revolution, 53; death notices, 88; on *Register*, 294

Adams, John Quincy, 59, 60, 87, 129, 130, 133, 138, 141, 210, 213, 216, 279; obituary notice, 5, 89; farewell to Lafayette, 84; inaugural, 86; message praised, 91; signs Tariff of Abominations, 112; bill on tariff, 115; review of news stories on, 135-36; fight to repeal rule against antislavery petitions, 286; references in diary to *Register*, 295

Adams-Onís correspondence, 92

Advertising, 72; accepted in last three issues, 16

"Aerostation," 262

African Institution, 267

African Repository and Colonial Journal, 270; advertised, 16

Agriculture in the United States, pamphlet by H. Niles, 52, 54

Air transportation, article on, 262-63

Alabama letters of Henry Clay, 156-57

Albany *Advertiser*, 186

Albany *Argus*, 186; opposes *Register* in caucus fight, 128

Albany *Journal and Mercantile Advertiser*, edited by William Ogden Niles, 24

Albany, N.Y., 242, 252; canal boats' arrival, 247; celebrates opening of Erie Canal, 246

Albany *Register*, on H. Niles, 291

Allegania, opposed as name for U.S., 95

Allen, William, on Oregon boundary, 192

Alton *Observer*, 286

Alton riots, 286

Ambrister, Captain Robert Cherry, execution defended, 135

Americana, *Register* as source of, 289

American Anti-Slavery Society, 284, 286

American Colonization Society, 269

American Institute, subject of editorial, 118

American Museum, 299

American Nation Series, *The*, 300

American Notes, reviewed, 175

American Sentinel (Philadelphia), opposes *Register* in caucus fight, 128

American slave trade, condemned, 268

American Society of Newspaper Editors, code of ethics, 61

American System, 112, 146, 239, 240, 261, 289, 290, 297; H. Niles' support of, 54-55; campaign for, 75; essays on, 77; Jefferson on, 113; Alexander Hamilton on, 113; defended in 1829, p. 114

American Tariff Controversies in the Nineteenth Century, 301

American Tourist and Merchants' and Travellers' Guide, advertised, 16

Analectic, 92

Anderson, Richard Clough, minister to Colombia, 197

Anglo-American sea rivalry, 179-81

Anglophobe attitude, 164

Anonymous letters, attitude toward, 42, 63

Anti-British bias, in news items, 185

Antimasonic activities, fairness toward, 57

Antimasonic conventions covered, 146

Antimasonic National Convention of 1838, p. 151

Antimasonic party, 143

Apollo or Delaware Weekly Magazine, founded by H. Niles, 21; on domestic manufactures, 108; slavery article, 265

Arbuthnot, Alexander, execution defended, 135

Arce, Don Manuel José, 196
Arkansas Gazette, 102
"Army Register," printed, 99
Aroostook War, 187
Arrearages in subscription payments, 13-14
Ashe, Thomas, 170
Ashtabula, Ohio, 229
Assistant burgess, H. Niles serves as, 21
Athenaeum, quoted, 173
Athens, Ohio, 229
Atlantic and Pacific Ocean Company, 250
Atrocity stories, 166-68
Aurora (Philadelphia), H. Niles writes for, 20; bought by James Wilson, 49; source of South American news, 200; on H. Niles and *Register,* 291

Babcock, Kendric Charles, on *Register,* 300
Bahia, 265
Balloon ascensions, 262
Baltimore, described, 80
Baltimore *American,* 68, 102-103, 186, 259, 296; as source of news, 83; on Zachary Taylor, 161; on Oregon boundary, 190; source of South American news, 200
Baltimore *Chronicle,* on H. Niles, 64
Baltimore City Council, H. Niles serves on, 57
Baltimore Coffee House, books furnish foreign news, 104
Baltimore *Daily Evening Gazette,* edited by William Ogden Niles, 68
Baltimore *Evening Post,* bought by H. Niles and partner, 22; description, 22; scant attention to manufactures, 108
Baltimore & Ohio Railroad, 257-61
Baltimore *Patriot and Commercial Gazette,* prints H. Niles' obituary, 64; opinion on Thomas Ritchie quoted, 71
Baltimore *Republican,* 151; prints H. Niles' obituary, 64; as source of news, 147
Baltimore *Sun,* 221; notes H. Niles' death, 64; praises Zachary Taylor's independence, 159; uses horse expresses for Mexican War news, 219
Baltimore Typographical Society, H. Niles a member, 57
Bancroft, George, 89
Bank bill of 1816, constitutionality questioned, 118

Barbour, James, 88
Barnburners, 1848 convention, 162
Barron, James, duel with Stephen Decatur, 30
Bassett, John Spencer, 302
Bates, Elisha, 281
Battle of Ayacucho, 199
Battle of New Orleans, news of, 81, 82
Beatty, George, editor of *Register,* 3; as editor, 72-74; moves *Register* to Philadelphia, 72; sells advertising, 72; lacks editorial experience, 73-74; address quoted, 73
Bell's Weekly Messenger (London), 102; on Monroe message, 184
Bennett, James Gordon, 95
Benton, Thomas Hart, 58, 150, 153, 159, 162; on H. Niles, 295
Beveridge, Albert J., on *Register,* 299
Big news stories, 81-85
Birney, James G., 151, 156, 285
Black Dwarf, 176
Black Rock, 246
Blackstone Canal, 245
Blair, Francis Preston, 40; impugns editorial integrity of Gales and Seaton, 49; H. Niles battles editorially, 50; sells *Globe,* 71
Bocanegra, J. M., 215
Bogotá *Constitucional,* 200
Bolívar, Simón, 199; H. Niles expresses doubts about, 200; comments on, 202; calls Panama Congress, 212
Bolivia, 202
Bombing proposal reprinted, 220
Bonsal, Vincent, partner of H. Niles, 20
Boone, Daniel, 226
Boston, 251, 252, 254
Boston *Courier,* source of South American news, 200
Boston *Daily Advertiser,* 257; source of South American news, 200
Boston *Daily Courier,* prints H. Niles' obituary, 64
Boston *Daily Evening Transcript,* prints H. Niles' obituary, 64
Boston *Patriot,* quoted, 166, 168, 181
Boston *Traveller,* 254
Bound volumes of *Register* bought by subscribers, 11
Brackenridge, Henry M., letters supply news, 201
Branch, John, 142
Brattleboro *Vermont Reporter,* story from, 94-95
Brazil, 198-99

Index

Gales and Seaton, re-elected printers to Congress, 61

Gallatin, Albert, 132; report on roads and canals, 238-39

Gallipolis, Ohio, 229

Galveston *Advertiser*, 215

Galveston *Civilian*, 215

Gambling on elections condemned, 156

Gardner, Julia, marries President Tyler, 81

Garrison, George Pierce, on *Register*, 300-301

Garrison, William Lloyd, 281, 282, 284, 286

Gatesby Jones, Commander Thomas A., 236

Gazeta (Buenos Aires), 200

Genius of Universal Emancipation, 281

George IV, coronation, 178

Georgetown *Advocate*, 215, 216

Georgia Journal (Milledgeville), on H. Niles, 61-62

German Correspondent, 291

Gilmer, Thomas W., 81

Globe and Traveller (London), on Monroe message, 184

Government aid to internal improvements, 239-41

Government fur companies opposed, 234

Government news, 89-93

Governor's Council, H. Niles refuses to run for, 58

Governors' messages, 93

Granger, Gideon, postmaster general, rules on postage for *Register*, 10

Great Britain, 244

Great Western, 243, 244; 1844 crossing, 106

Greeley, Horace, 299

Green, Benjamin, 125

Green, Duff, 39, 215; H. Niles' opinion of, 50

Guatemala, grants canal rights, 250

Gurney, Sir Goldsworthy, 251

Haiti, as site for Negro colonization, 272

Hall, Captain Basil, 174

Hallam, Henry, 174

Hamilton, Alexander, 99; on American System, 113

Hammond, Charles, editor of Cincinnati *Gazette*, 138

"Hampden," on public lands, 230

Hannegan, Edward A., on Oregon boundary, 192

Harmony Society, 228

Harrison, William Henry, death notice, 4; campaign biography, 68; death reported, 83; inaugural, 87; presidential candidate, 150; nominated by Ohio Whigs, 151; nominated by Antimasonic convention, 151; chosen by Whigs, 151

Hart, Albert Bushnell, on *Register*, 300

Hartford Convention, 34; H. Niles' opposition to, 7

Harvey, Sir John, 187

Hayne, Robert Y., 88; opposes American System, 115

Heiss, John P., buys *Globe* with Thomas Ritchie, 71

Henry Clay, editor rebuked, 145

Herald (London), on McLeod trial, 188

Hibernia, crossing in 1844, p. 106

Historical Register of the United States, 294

Holden's Dollar Magazine, advertised, 16

Holy Alliance, 183, 184, 209, 210, 211, 212

Hone, Philip, heads canal company, 248; on H. Niles and *Register*, 297-98

Hood, Thomas, 174

Horn's U.S. Railroad Gazette, advertised, 16

Houston, Sam, 89

Howard, Dr. William, 255

Hubbard, Governor Henry, 86

Hubles, Paul T. E., 89

Hudson and Delaware Canal, 245

Hudson *Gazette*, 102

Hudson River, 243, 246

Hudson's Bay Company, 234

Hughes, Jeremiah, 151, 216, 305, 306; editor of *Register*, 3, 68-72; makes up missing issues, 11; issues prospectuses, 13; editorial background, 68; friend of temperance, 70; headline techniques, 70-71; writes valedictory editorial, 72; dies, 72; nine-point program for *Register*, 77; on Robert Owen, 96; uses contemporary newspapers, 103; favors reciprocity, 117; prints monthly political summaries, 153-54; on Democratic policy in 1844, p. 154; abstracts pre-election claims in 1844, pp. 157-58; prints probable result of 1844 election, 158; analyzes causes for Clay's 1844 defeat, 158; praises Zachary Taylor's letters, 158; prints Oregon articles, 189; favors peaceful settlement of Oregon dispute, 190-92; friendly toward England, 193; hopes for Mexican peace, 212; coverage of Texas annexation, 215-18; criticizes method of declaring war with Mexico, 219-20; establishes railroad department, 257; writes on Liberia, 270-71; on Liberty party, 286; valedictory editorial, 288; on *Register's* coverage of nation's leaders, 288; cites *Register's* value as reference, 288-89; samples public opinion, 291

Hunt, Leigh, 174

Hunt's Merchant's Magazine, 243

Huskisson, William, death of, 256

Illinois River, 248

Immigrants, H. Niles welcomes, 227-28

Impartiality of H. Niles in editorial selections, 38, 40

Impressment, 165-66; omitted in Treaty of Ghent, 169

Inaugurations, presidential, covered, 86-87

Independence of H. Niles, 38

Index to *Register*, 101

Indian problems, 232-34

Indices, inadequacy, 100; for each volume, 101

Industrial revolution, H. Niles on, 112

Influence of West, 224-25

Ingersoll, Charles J., 217

Ingersoll, Joseph R., name forged to letter to Zachary Taylor, 160

Ingham, Samuel D., 142, 143

Instruction of members of Congress, commented on, 127

Integrity of H. Niles, 39

Internal improvements, editorials on, 239

International copyright law, Charles Dickens seeks passage, 174-75

Irving, Washington, 175; novels reviewed, 33

Ithaca *Journal*, starts story on James K. Polk's slaves, 157

Iturbide, Augustín de, 204-205

Jackson, Andrew, 60, 123, 129, 130, 132, 138, 144, 213, 214, 216, 241, 290; *Register* subscriber, 8; opinion asked on *Register*, 12; nullification proclamation praised, 41-42; H. Niles writes to on 1824 candidacy, 59; re-election ends H. Niles' political activities, 60; receives threatening letters, 63; attempts on life, 80; reports on Battle

of New Orleans, 82; inaugurations, 86; farewell address, 87; death notice, 89; 1830 message summarized, 91; effect of re-election on tariff seen by H. Niles, 116; *Register* criticizes stand on U.S. Bank, 120; veto of U.S. Bank Bill, 121; removes deposits from U.S. Bank, 122; as presidential candidate, 133; election as senator approved, 134; news space to his activities, 135; correspondence on House election, 137; H. Niles recounts conversation with, 137; *Register* editorial on election, 139-40; first message discussed, 141; use of veto condemned, 141-42; veto of U.S. Bank criticized, 141-42; *Register's* attitude in 1832 campaign, 145; use of veto criticized, 149; attacks on reported, 149; honorary LL.D., defended, 149-50; farewell message, 150; supports James K. Polk, 157; in Floridas, 206; public-lands veto condemned, 232; vetoes Maysville Road Bill, 240; on H. Niles, 295

Jamaica newspapers as news sources, 103

James, Dr. Edwin, 235

Jay, John, 99

Jefferis, James, 17

Jefferson, Thomas, subscribes to *Register*, 8; H. Niles solicits opinion on *Register*, 12; urged by H. Niles to compile schoolbooks, 33; eulogies of, 88; approves Liberian project, 269; on *Register*, 294

Johnson, Benjamin, H. Niles apprenticed to, 19

Johnson, Richard M., 68-69, 150, 153

Kaskaskia, Ill., 242

Kendall, Amos, 285; leads fight to remove deposits, 122

Kentucky Reporter, 230

Kingston *Chronicle*, 186-87

Kremer, George, card reprinted from *National Intelligencer*, 136; letters and addresses, 137

La Branche, Alcée, 215

Lackawaxen, 248

Lafayette, Marquis de, subscriber to *Register*, 8; tour of U.S., 84-85; H. Niles' tribute to, 85; death notice, 89

Laguira, 195

Lancaster *Republican*, 220

Lancastrian system, in editorials, 30

La Prensa Argentina (Buenos Aires), 200

suggested for president, 62; toasted, 62-63; two cities named for, 63; signs will with left hand, 63; valedictory editorial quoted, 63; returns to Wilmington, 64; dies, 64; life history promised, 65; on Battle of New Orleans, 82-83; lapses into plain language, 85; policy on government news, 90-91; nonpartisan news policy, 91; predicts population, 99-100; obtains foreign news from letters, 104-105; fights for tariff, 107, 109, 111-12; Henry Clay's desertion a blow to, 116-17; urges observance of Compromise Tariff of 1833, p. 117; changes position on U.S. Bank, 118; suggests states tax U.S. Bank, 119; criticizes Chief Justice Marshall's decision on U.S. Bank, 119-20; changes attitude on U.S. Bank, 120-21; denies favors received from U.S. Bank, 122; on vote on removal of deposits, 122-23; on rejection of Roger B. Taney as secretary of the treasury, 123; political affiliations, 125; belief in two-party system, 127; fights Congressional caucus to choose presidential candidates, 128-32; impartiality in 1824 election despite personal feelings, 134; goes to Washington to cover House election, 136; regrets bitterness of 1828 election campaign, 139; editorial on Jackson's election, 139-40; denies tie-up with Antimasonic party, 144; delegate to National Republican convention, 147; editorial on 1832 election, 148-49; hatred of England, 164; mother threatened by British soldiers, 164; editorial policy on War of 1812, pp. 168-69; comments on English travelers, 170, 176; hatred for royalty, 177-78; fears British interest in Cuba, 182-83; comments on Monroe's message in 1823, p. 183; editorial on English recognition of South American republics, 184-85; disinterest in Oregon, 189; urges recognition of South American republics, 196; on Bolívar, 200; loses faith in South American democracy, 202-203; on Mexican independence, 204; opposes Mexican empire, 204-205; denounces Santa Anna, 205; favors isolation, 208; urges U.S. participation in Panama Congress, 213; opposes intervention in Texas, 214; on influence of West, 224-25; welcomes

immigrants, 227-28; on public-land sales, 231; visualizes westward growth, 233; editorial on Maysville veto, 240; on Florida ship canal, 249; editorial on railroads and canals, 252; writes on B. & O. Railroad, 257-61; on slavery, 264-85; on Missouri Compromise, 273-79; criticizes William Lloyd Garrison, 281-82; on future value of *Register*, 288; tariff essays, 290; tributes to, 291-92

Niles, Hezekiah, father of editor, 18; killed by signpost, 19

Niles, Hezekiah, grandson of editor, dies, 68

Niles, Hezekiah, great-grandfather of editor, 18

Niles, Mary Way, mother of editor, 18; death, 23

Niles' National Register, 1; see *Register*

Niles, Sally Ann Warner, Niles' second wife, 24

Niles, Samuel, brother of editor, 19; dies, 20

Niles, Samuel, son of editor, dies, 23

Niles, Samuel V., grandson of editor, reprints book on Revolution, 54

Niles, Tobias, grandfather of editor, 18

Niles' Weekly Register, 1; see *Register*

Niles, William Ogden, 65, 151, 187, 193, 291, 292; associated with father, 2; editor of *Register*, 3, 66-68; statement on circulation, 7; makes up missing issues, 11; moves office to Washington, 13; on delinquent subscription payments, 14; trained by father, 23-24; edits Albany *Journal and Mercantile Advertiser*, 24; partner of father, 1827-1830, p. 24; purchases Frederick *Herald*, 24; editorial abilities, 66; interest in politics, 66; bitterness toward father's widow, 67; writes valedictory editorial, 67; seeks editorial post, 67-68; edits Baltimore *Daily Evening Gazette*, 68; compiles campaign biography of William Henry Harrison, 68; death of, 68; gives space in *Register* to Congressional debates, 77; use of contemporary newspapers, 103

Noah, Mordecai M., H. Niles' dislike for, 49-50

Non-Intercourse Law, 108

Nonpartisan news handling, 91

Norfolk *Herald*, 101; praises H. Niles, 61; reports Ingham removal, 142

North West Company, 234

Warrentown *Jeffersonian*, 187
Washington, George, mentioned by H. Niles, 19
Washington *Globe*, 49, 63, 64, 66, 67, 87, 102, 115, 143, 151, 215, 216; sale of, 71; source of news, 81, 83; upholds Jackson and Van Buren, 142; Jackson's statement reprinted from, 145; quoted on Harrison's election, 152
Washington letter writers, 192
Washington *Union*, 221, 222; replaces *Globe*, 71; 1848 election editorial quoted, 163; on Oregon boundary, 190, 191
Webster, Daniel, 152, 215; in bank fight, 123; presidential candidate, 150; nominated for Antimasonic Vice President, 151; 1848 campaign speeches, 162; on Panama Congress, 213
Webster, Noah, 88
Weekly expenditures of *Register*, 14
Weekly Register, 1; see *Register*
Weimarische Zeitung, 292
Western Herald (Steubenville), 49, 102, 293
Wheeling, W. Va., 252
Whig gains and losses listed, 158
Whig National Convention of 1844, p. 154
White House, burning of, 167
White, Hugh L., presidential candidate, 150

Whitney, Asa, 257
Wilberforce, 266
William IV, 178-79
Williams, John, address printed, 196
Willmer & Smith's European Times, on *Times* and Oregon boundary, 190
Will of H. Niles, 63
Wilmington, Del., 108, 294; Niles' parents flee from, 17; H. Niles returns to, 64
Wilmot Proviso, 286
Wilson, James, 44; friendship with H. Niles, 49; praises H. Niles' economic writings, 293-94
Winans, Ross, 255
Wirt, William, 88; Antimasonic candidate, 146
Wooler, Thomas Jonathan, 176
Working Men's party, 143-44; organization praised, 145-46
World Almanac, *Register* served as, 99
Wright, Silas, refuses vice-presidential nomination by telegraph, 97-98, 155

Xenia, Ohio, 233

Yeoman's Gazette, 252
York, Pa., 255
Young Whigs Convention of 1844, p. 154

Zanesville, Ohio, 224
Zanesville *Messenger*, 102